Author's Message:

NOBUYUKI ANZAI PRESENTS 安西信行

Thank you so much for your continued support all this time. This is farewell. Goodbye!

MÄR
Vol. 15
Story and Art by Nobuyuki Anzai

English Adaptation/Gerard Jones
Translation/Kaori Inoue
Touch-up Art & Lettering/James Gaubatz
Design/Izumi Evers
Editor/Andy Nakatani

Editor in Chief, Books/Alvin Lu
Editor in Chief, Magazines/Marc Weidenbaum
VP of Publishing Licensing/Rika Inouye
VP of Sales/Gonzalo Ferreyra
Sr. VP of Marketing/Liza Coppola
Publisher/Hyoe Narita

Printed in the U.S.A.

Published by VIZ Media, LLC
P.O. Box 77010
San Francisco, CA 94107

10 9 8 7 6 5 4 3 2
First printing, September 2007
Second printing, November 2007

www.viz.com
store.viz.com

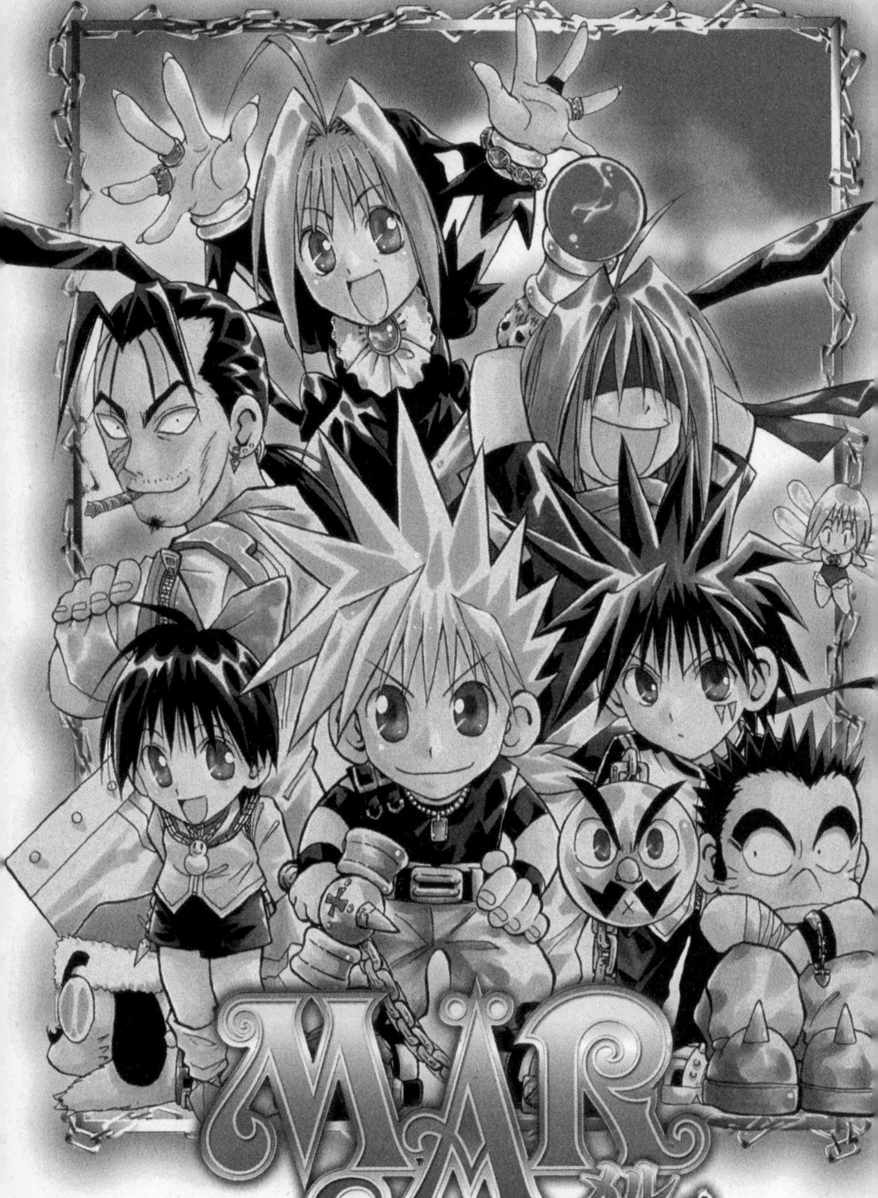
MÄR
メル
MÄRCHEN AWAKENS ROMANCE

Vol. 15

Nobuyuki Anzai

Characters

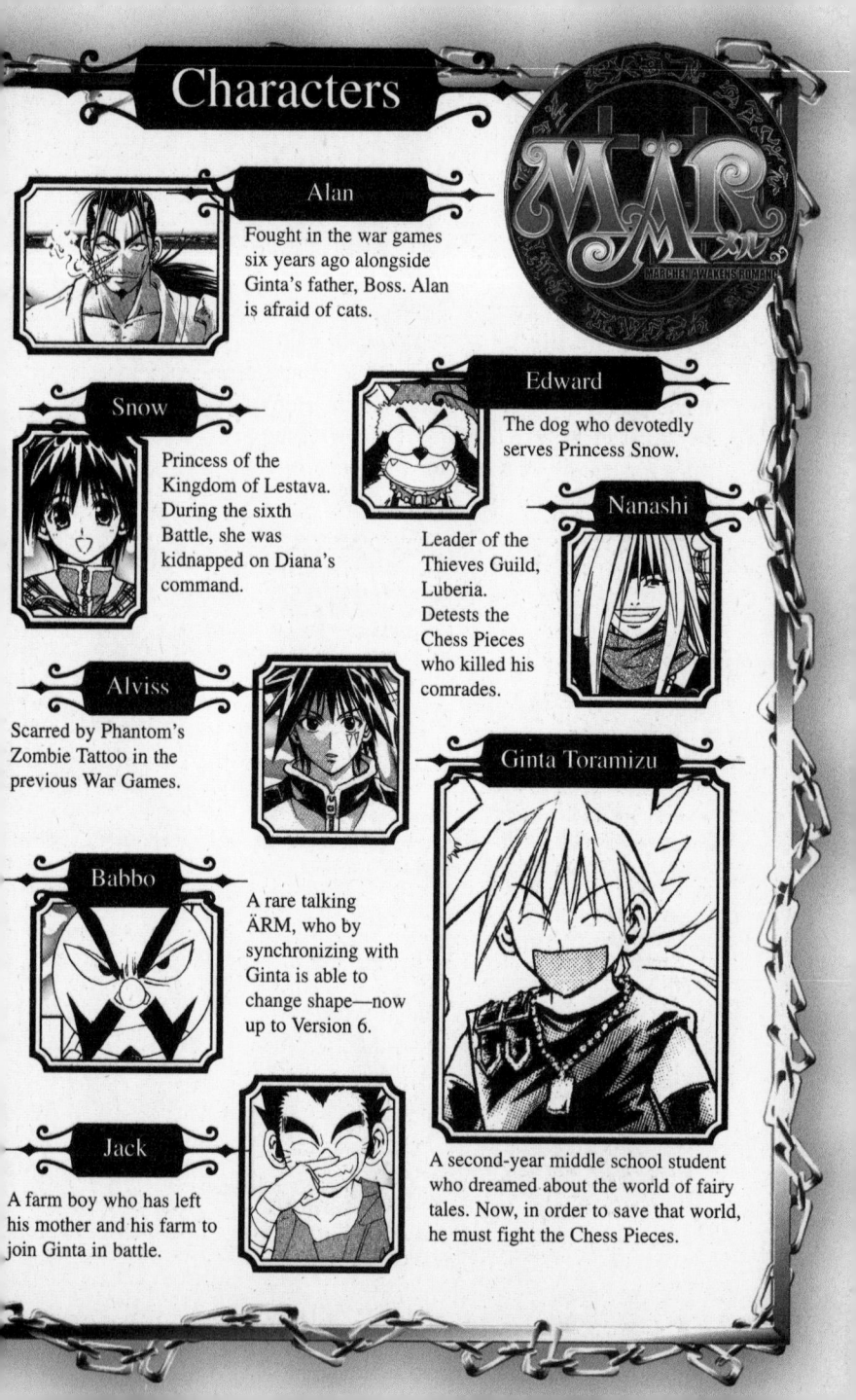

Alan

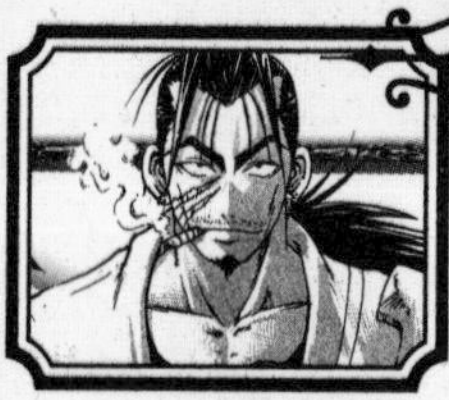

Fought in the war games six years ago alongside Ginta's father, Boss. Alan is afraid of cats.

Snow

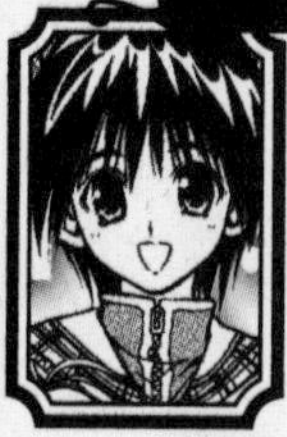

Princess of the Kingdom of Lestava. During the sixth Battle, she was kidnapped on Diana's command.

Edward

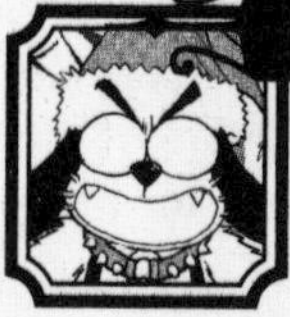

The dog who devotedly serves Princess Snow.

Nanashi

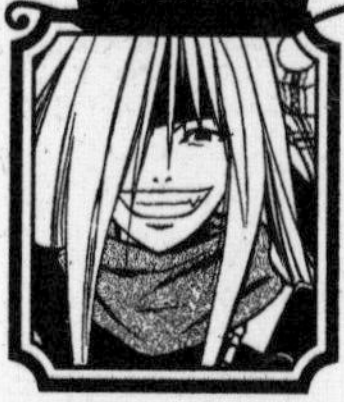

Leader of the Thieves Guild, Luberia. Detests the Chess Pieces who killed his comrades.

Alviss

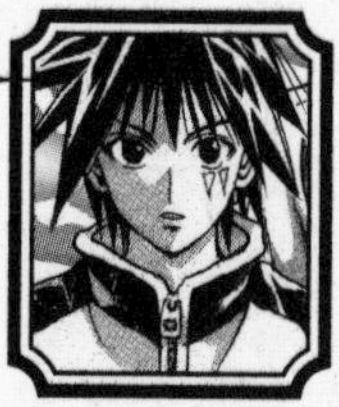

Scarred by Phantom's Zombie Tattoo in the previous War Games.

Ginta Toramizu

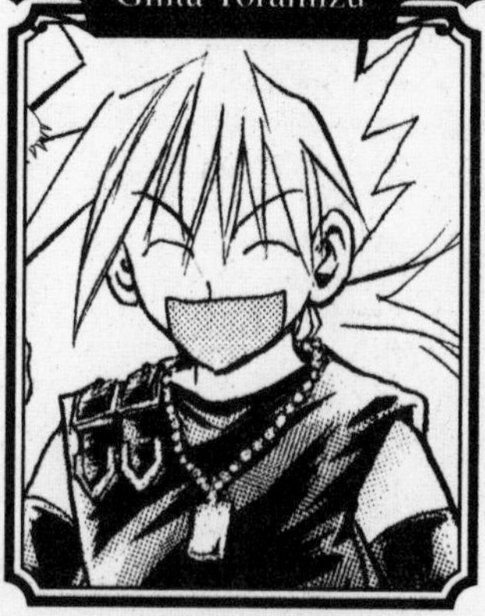

A second-year middle school student who dreamed about the world of fairy tales. Now, in order to save that world, he must fight the Chess Pieces.

Babbo

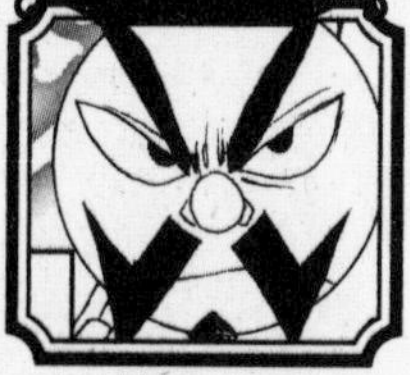

A rare talking ÄRM, who by synchronizing with Ginta is able to change shape—now up to Version 6.

Jack

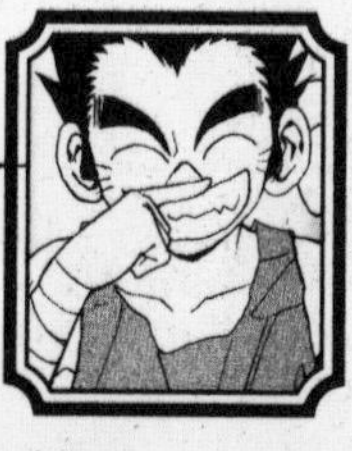

A farm boy who has left his mother and his farm to join Ginta in battle.

Previous Volume

Ginta jumps through a "door" that suddenly appears in his classroom, and finds himself in the magical world of his dreams. Now, at the "request" of the Chess Pieces, the War Games have begun—and Ginta and his eight friends, calling themselves Team Mär, must battle the Chess warriors. It's been a long and difficult campaign, but Ginta triumphs over Phantom in the final deciding match, and Team Mär stands victorious over the Chess Pieces! Before they can celebrate, they must first storm Lestava Castle to rescue Snow from the clutches of the Queen. Emanating from the center of the castle is a sublime level of magical power.

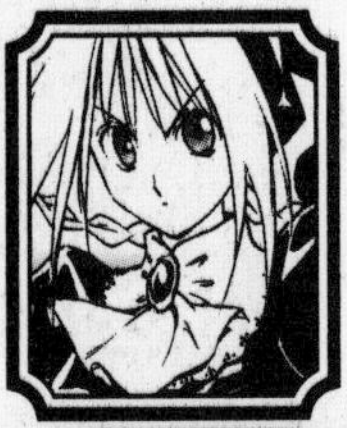

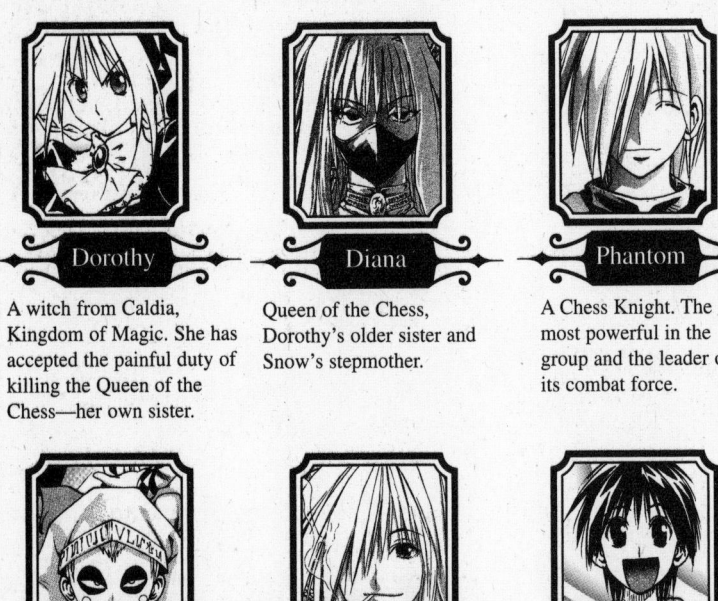

Dorothy

A witch from Caldia, Kingdom of Magic. She has accepted the painful duty of killing the Queen of the Chess—her own sister.

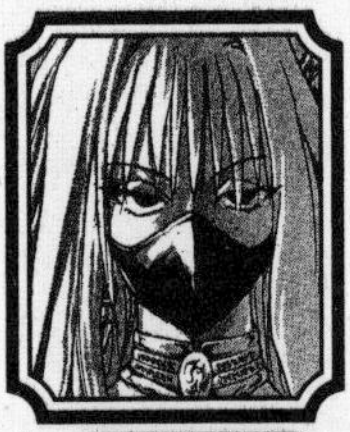

Diana

Queen of the Chess, Dorothy's older sister and Snow's stepmother.

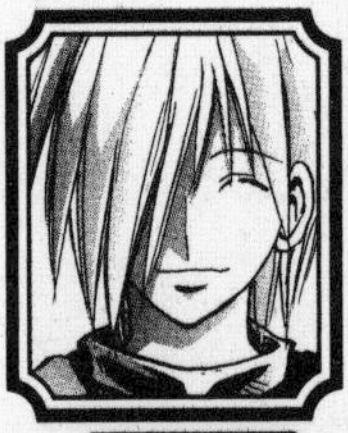

Phantom

A Chess Knight. The most powerful in the group and the leader of its combat force.

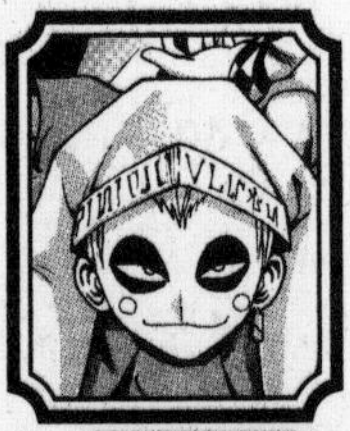

Magical Ro

A Chess Knight who used to be Snow's babysitter.

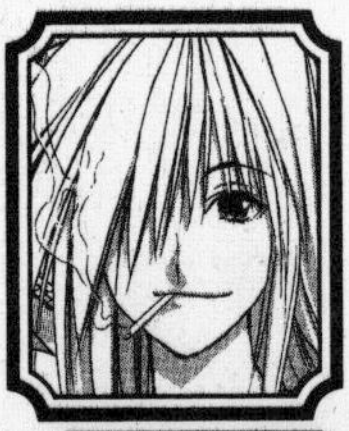

Ginta's Mom

A fairy-tale writer who awaits the return of her husband and son.

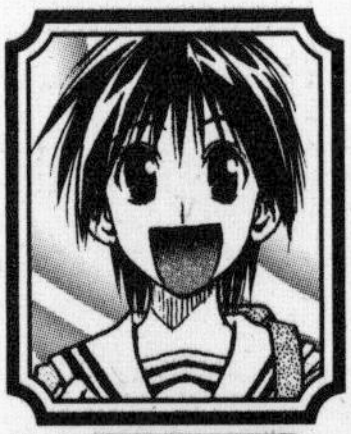

Koyuki

Ginta's classmate who shares a connection to Princess Snow.

CONTENTS

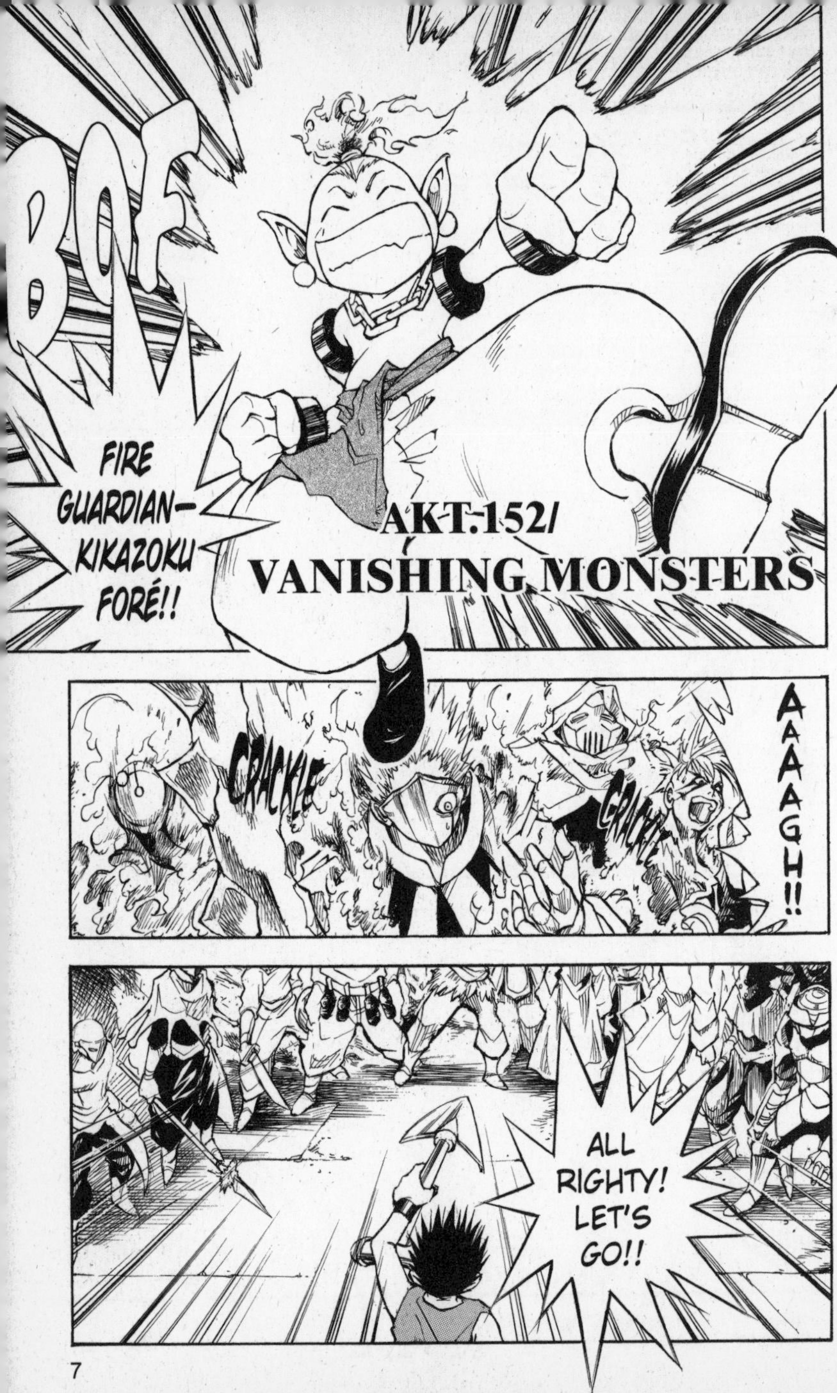
BOF
FIRE GUARDIAN— KIKAZOKU FORÉ!!
AKT.152/ VANISHING MONSTERS
AAAAGH!!
CRACKLE
CRACKLE
ALL RIGHTY! LET'S GO!!

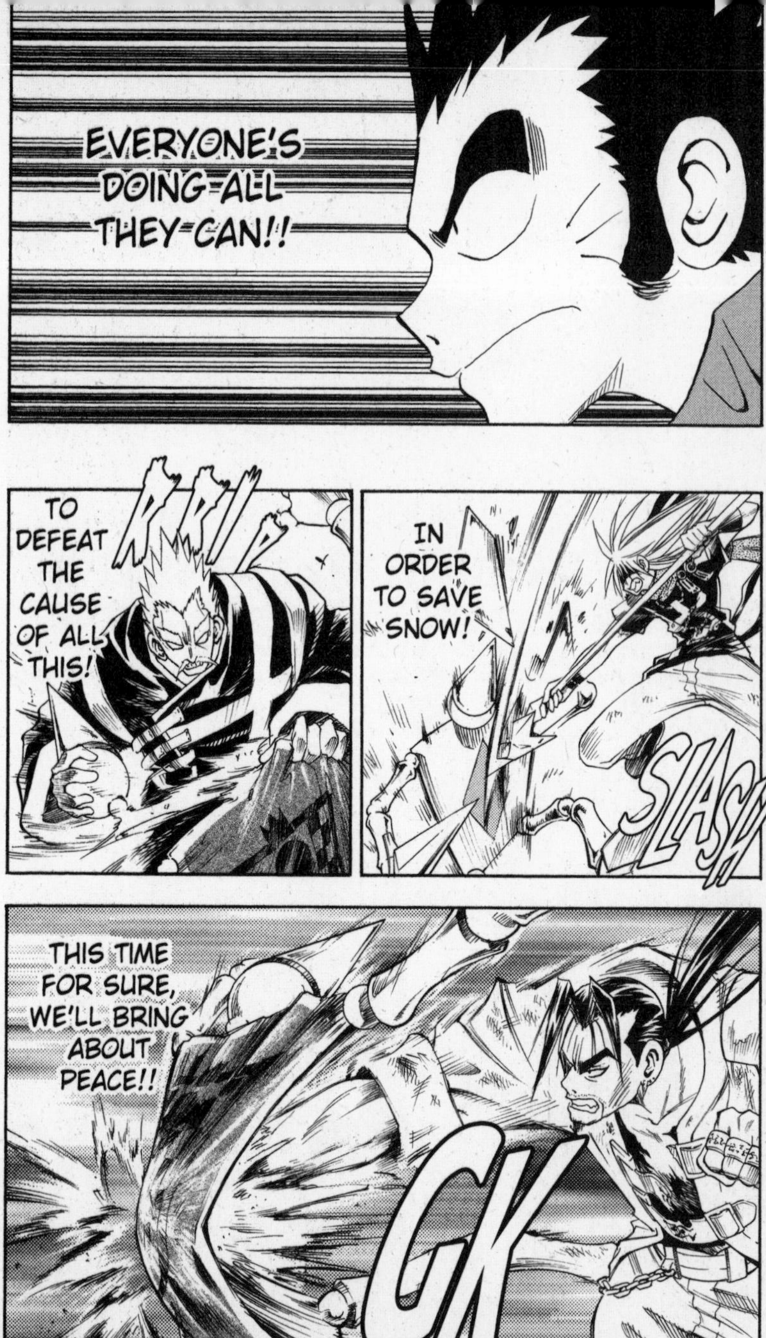
EVERYONE'S DOING ALL THEY CAN!!
IN ORDER TO SAVE SNOW!
SLASH
TO DEFEAT THE CAUSE OF ALL THIS!
THIS TIME FOR SURE, WE'LL BRING ABOUT PEACE!!
GK

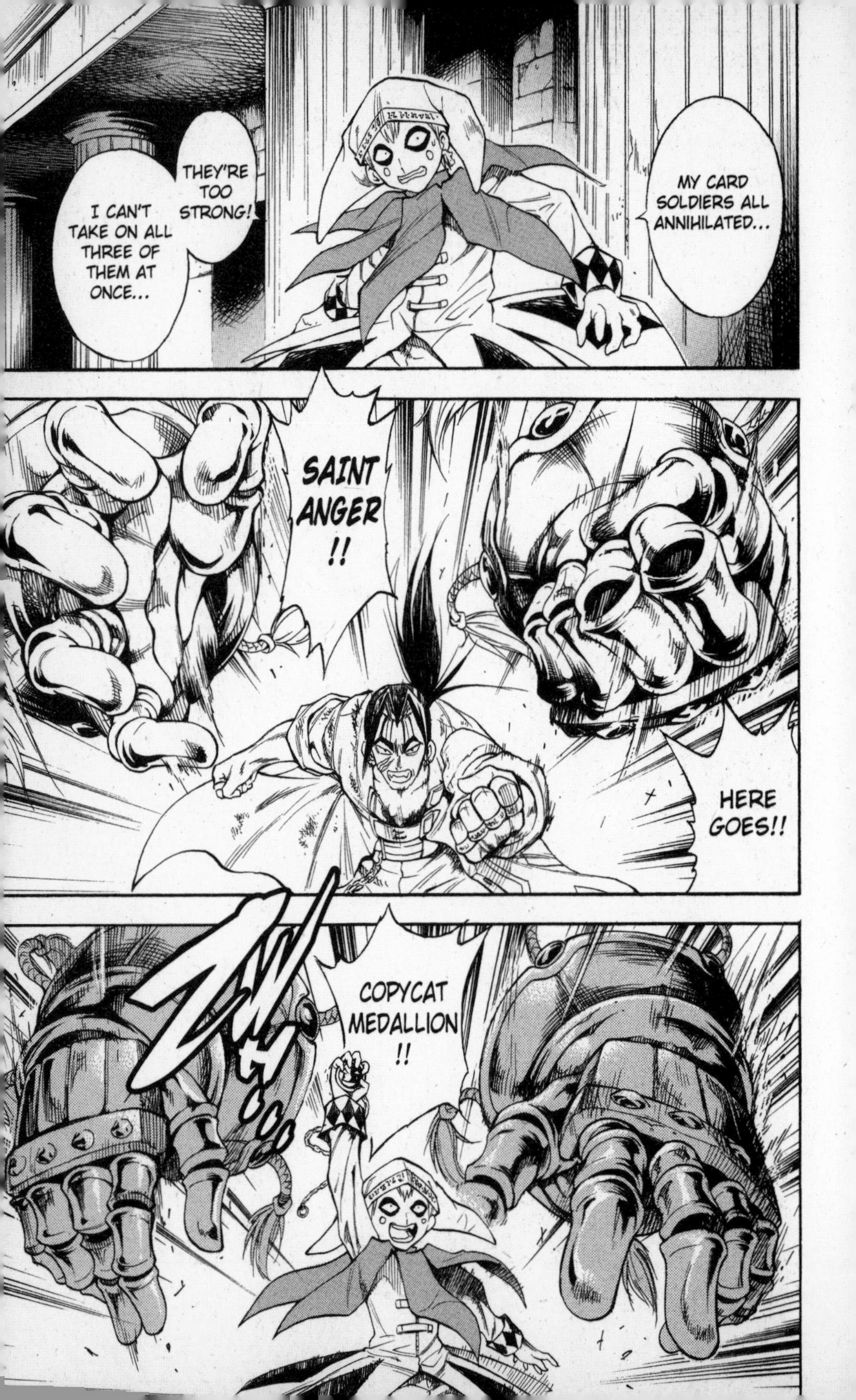
MY CARD SOLDIERS ALL ANNIHILATED...
THEY'RE TOO STRONG!
I CAN'T TAKE ON ALL THREE OF THEM AT ONCE...
HERE GOES!!
SAINT ANGER !!
COPYCAT MEDALLION !!

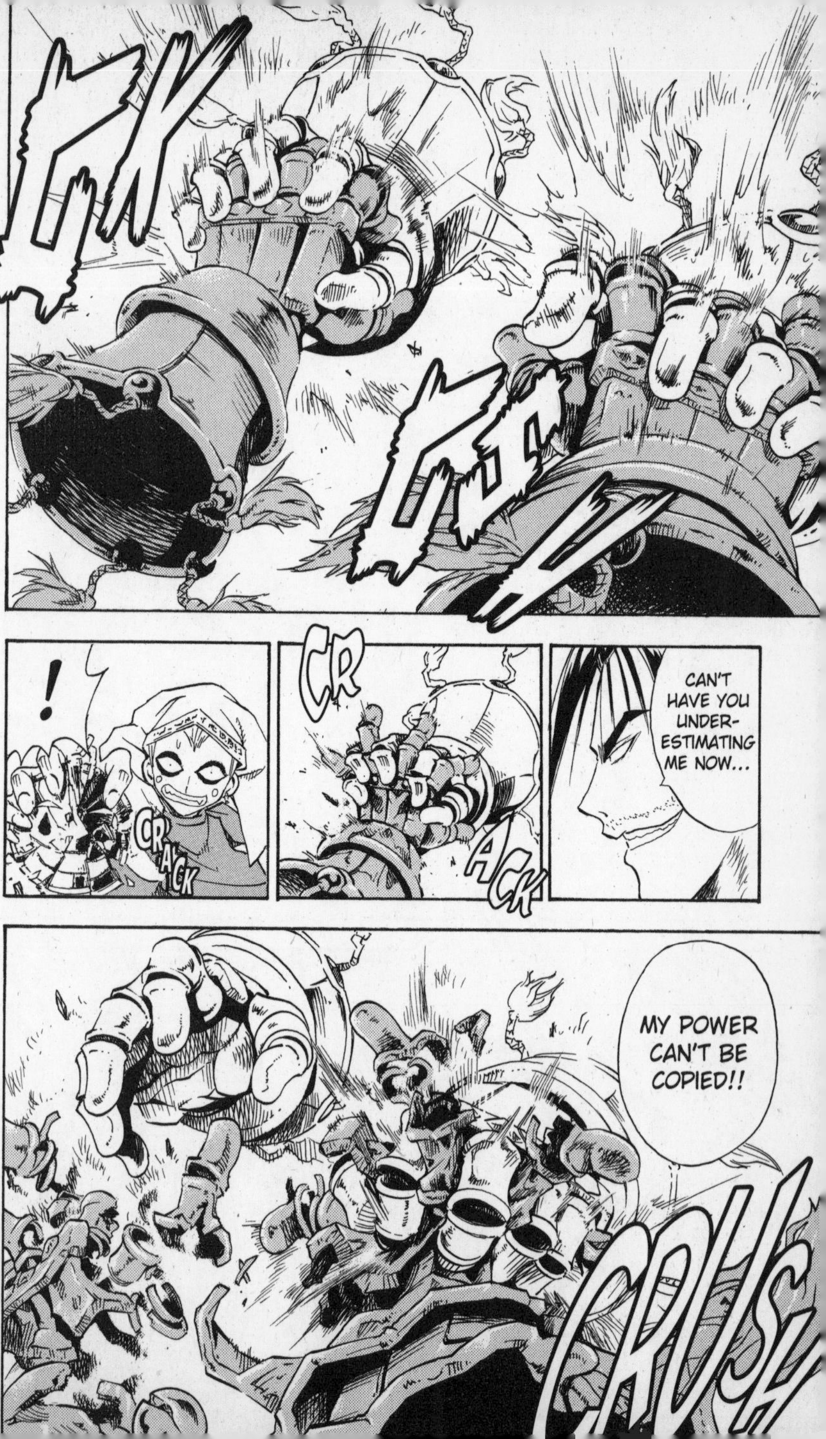
CAN'T HAVE YOU UNDER-ESTIMATING ME NOW...
CR
ACK
!
CRACK
MY POWER CAN'T BE COPIED!!
CRUSH

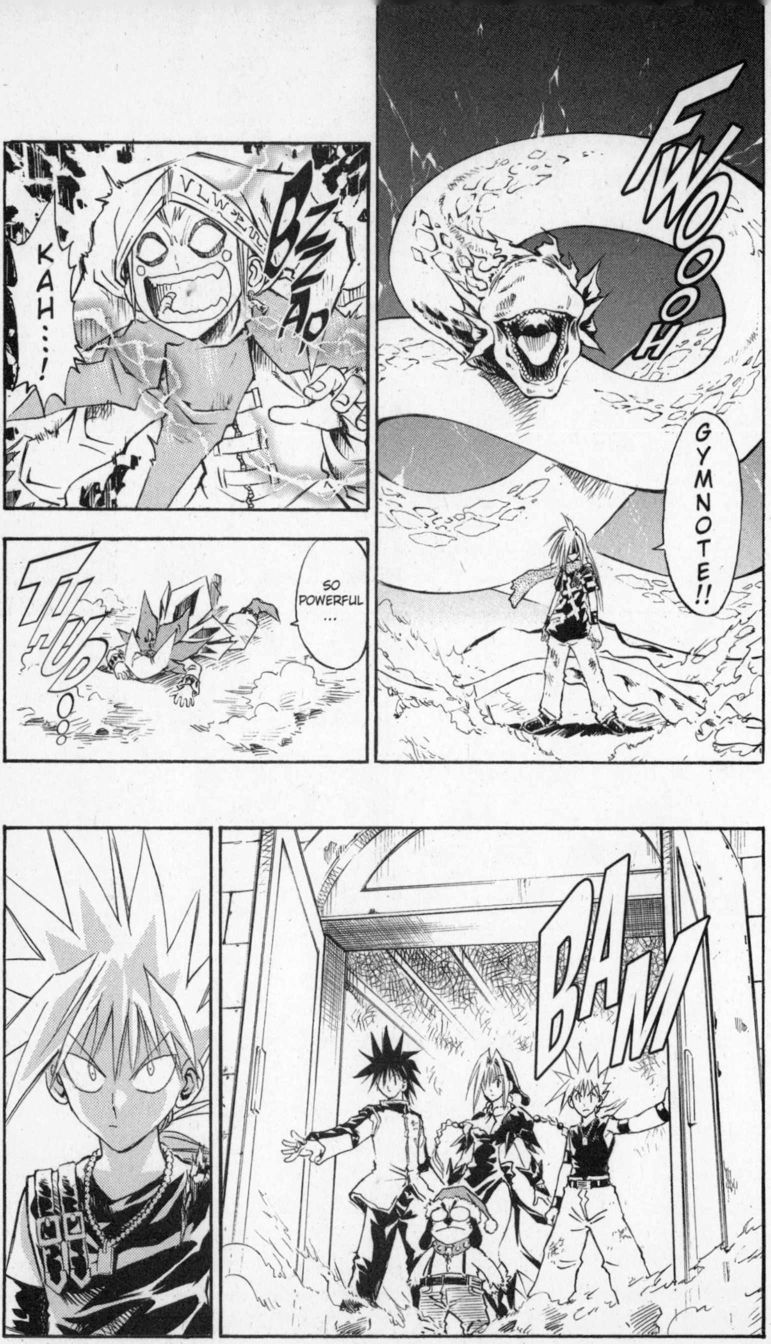
FWOOOOH
GYMNOTE!!
KAH...!
BZZZAP
THUD...
SO POWERFUL ...
BAM

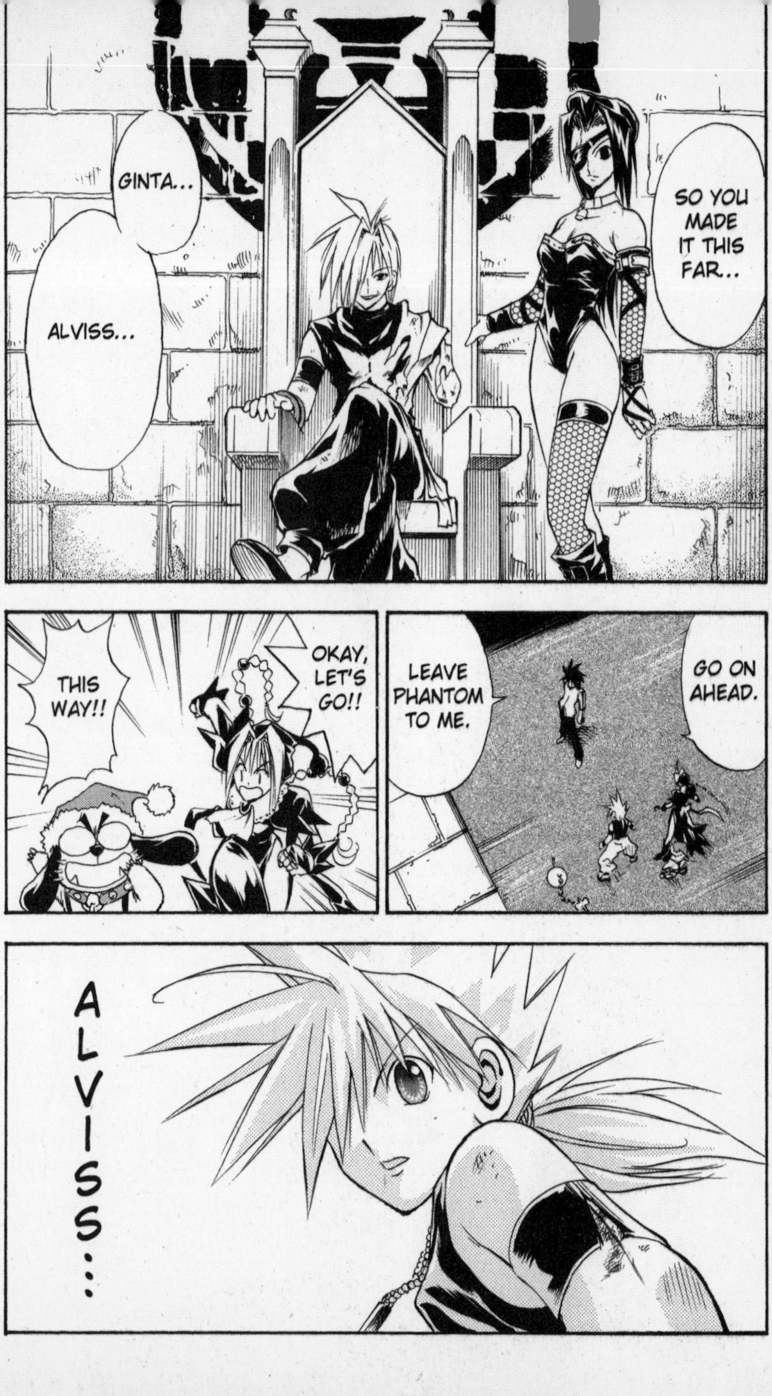
SO YOU MADE IT THIS FAR...
GINTA...
ALVISS...
GO ON AHEAD.
LEAVE PHANTOM TO ME.
OKAY, LET'S GO!!
THIS WAY!!
ALVISS...

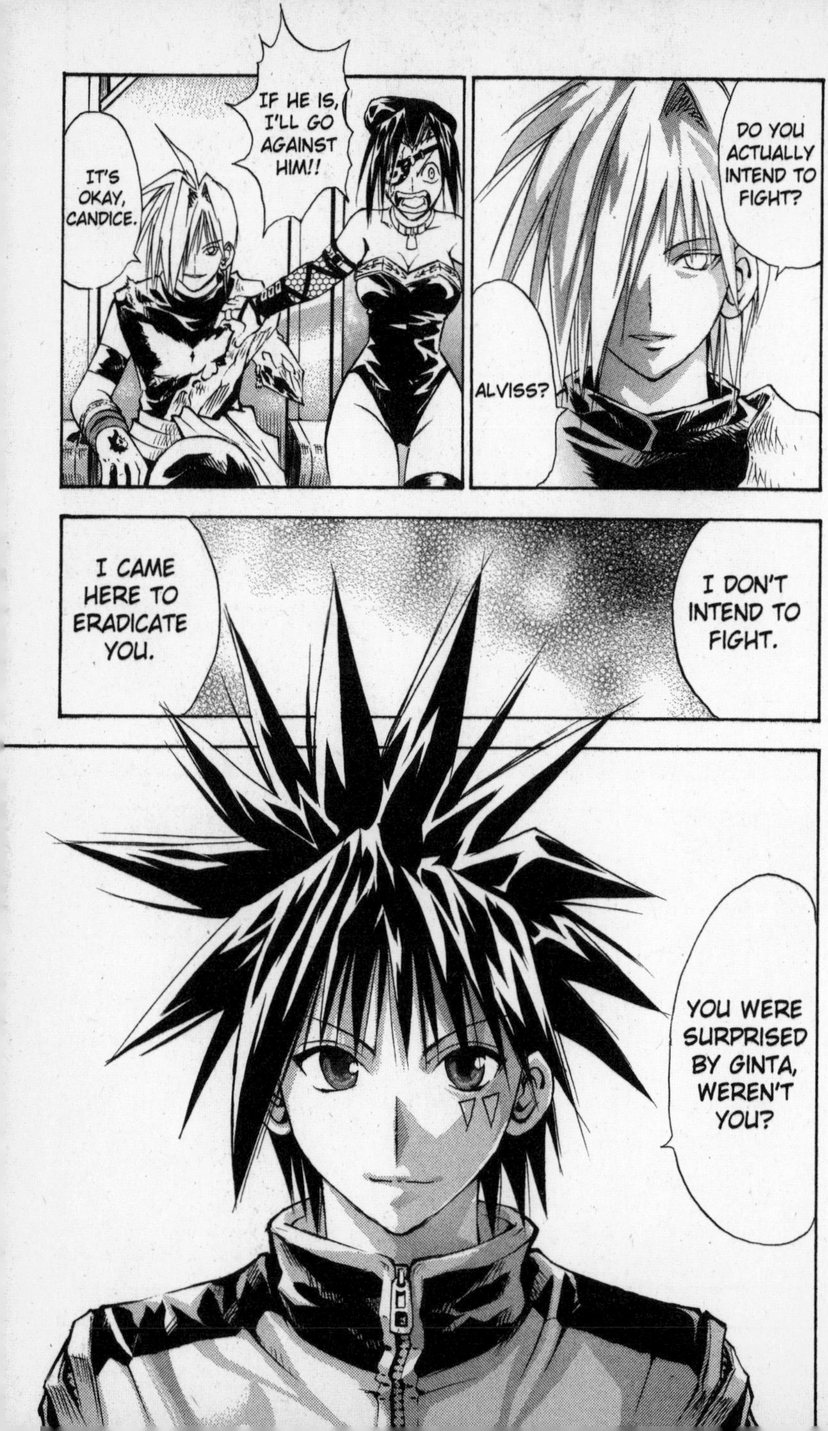
DO YOU ACTUALLY INTEND TO FIGHT?
ALVISS?
IF HE IS, I'LL GO AGAINST HIM!!
IT'S OKAY, CANDICE.
I DON'T INTEND TO FIGHT.
I CAME HERE TO ERADICATE YOU.
YOU WERE SURPRISED BY GINTA, WEREN'T YOU?

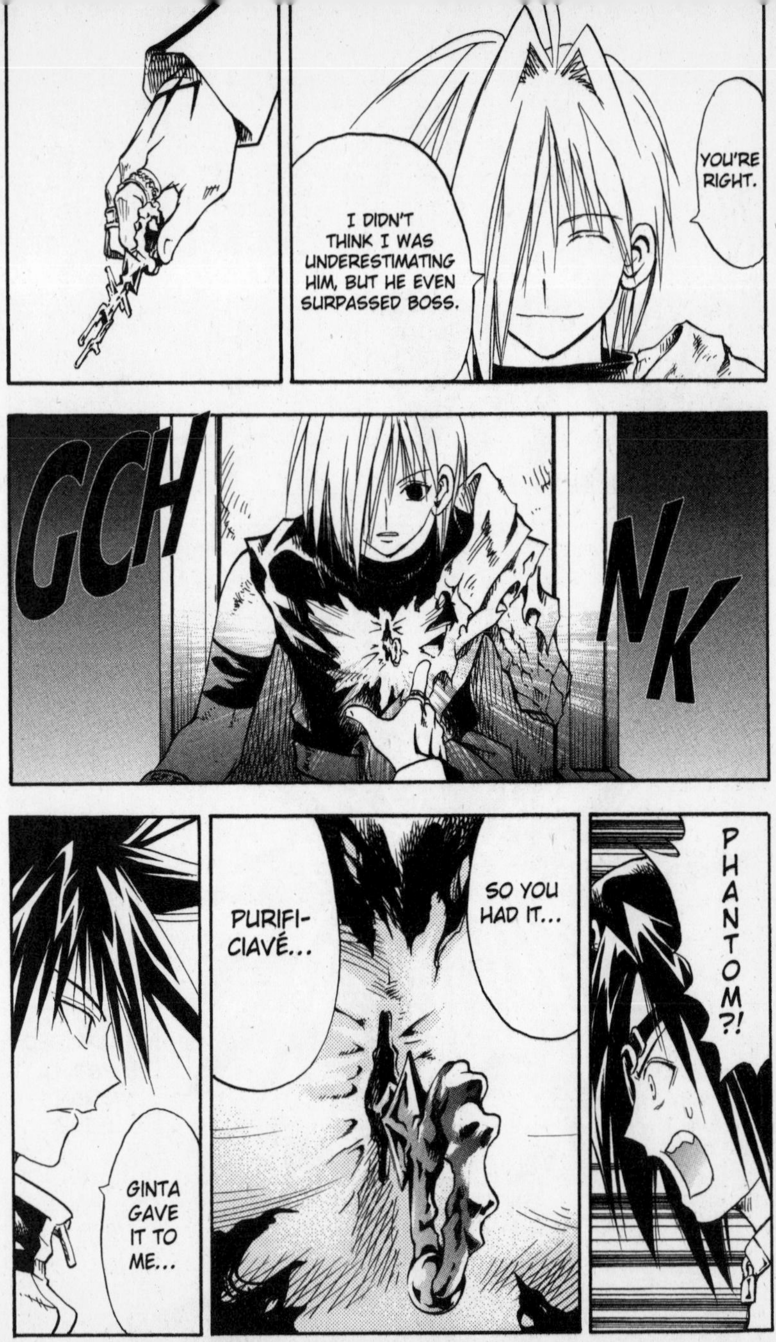
YOU'RE RIGHT.
I DIDN'T THINK I WAS UNDERESTIMATING HIM, BUT HE EVEN SURPASSED BOSS.
GCH
NK
PHANTOM?!
SO YOU HAD IT...
PURIFI-CIAVÉ...
GINTA GAVE IT TO ME...

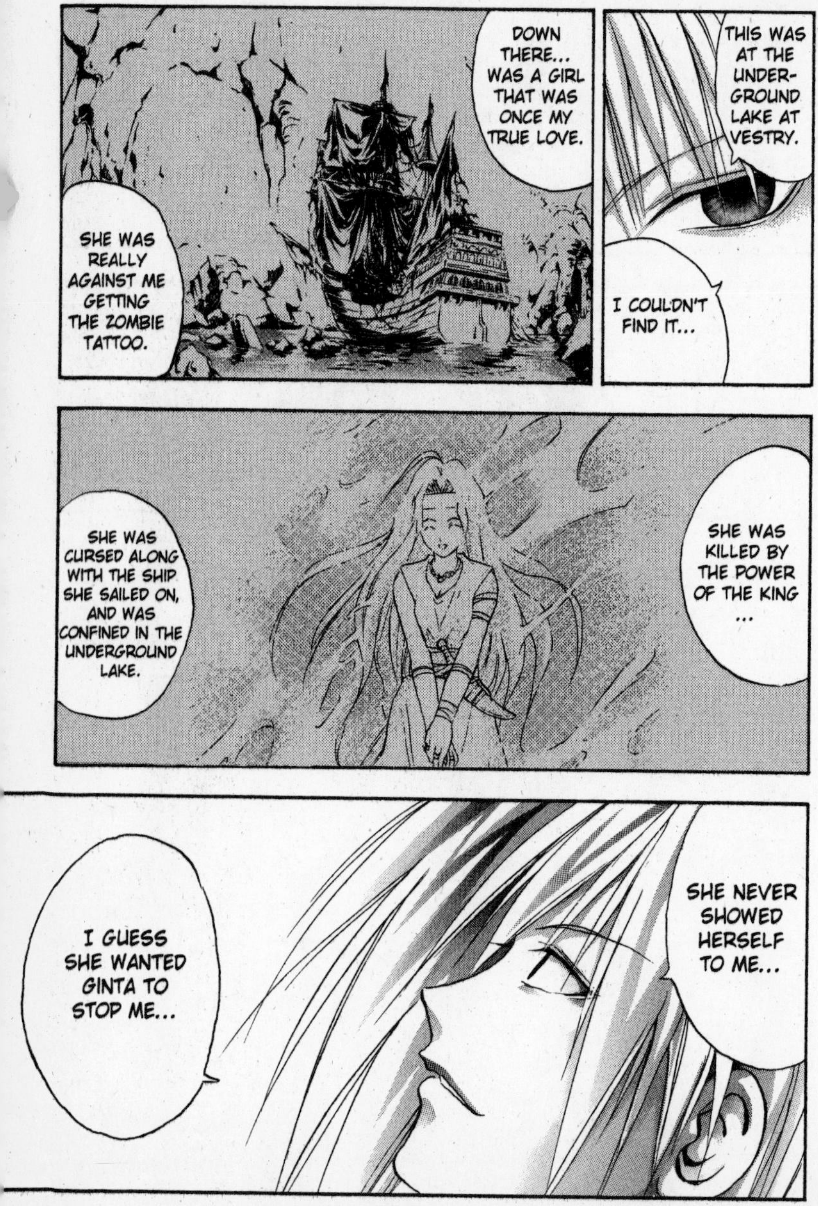
THIS WAS AT THE UNDER-GROUND LAKE AT VESTRY.
I COULDN'T FIND IT...
DOWN THERE... WAS A GIRL THAT WAS ONCE MY TRUE LOVE.
SHE WAS REALLY AGAINST ME GETTING THE ZOMBIE TATTOO.
SHE WAS KILLED BY THE POWER OF THE KING ...
SHE WAS CURSED ALONG WITH THE SHIP SHE SAILED ON, AND WAS CONFINED IN THE UNDERGROUND LAKE.
SHE NEVER SHOWED HERSELF TO ME...
I GUESS SHE WANTED GINTA TO STOP ME...

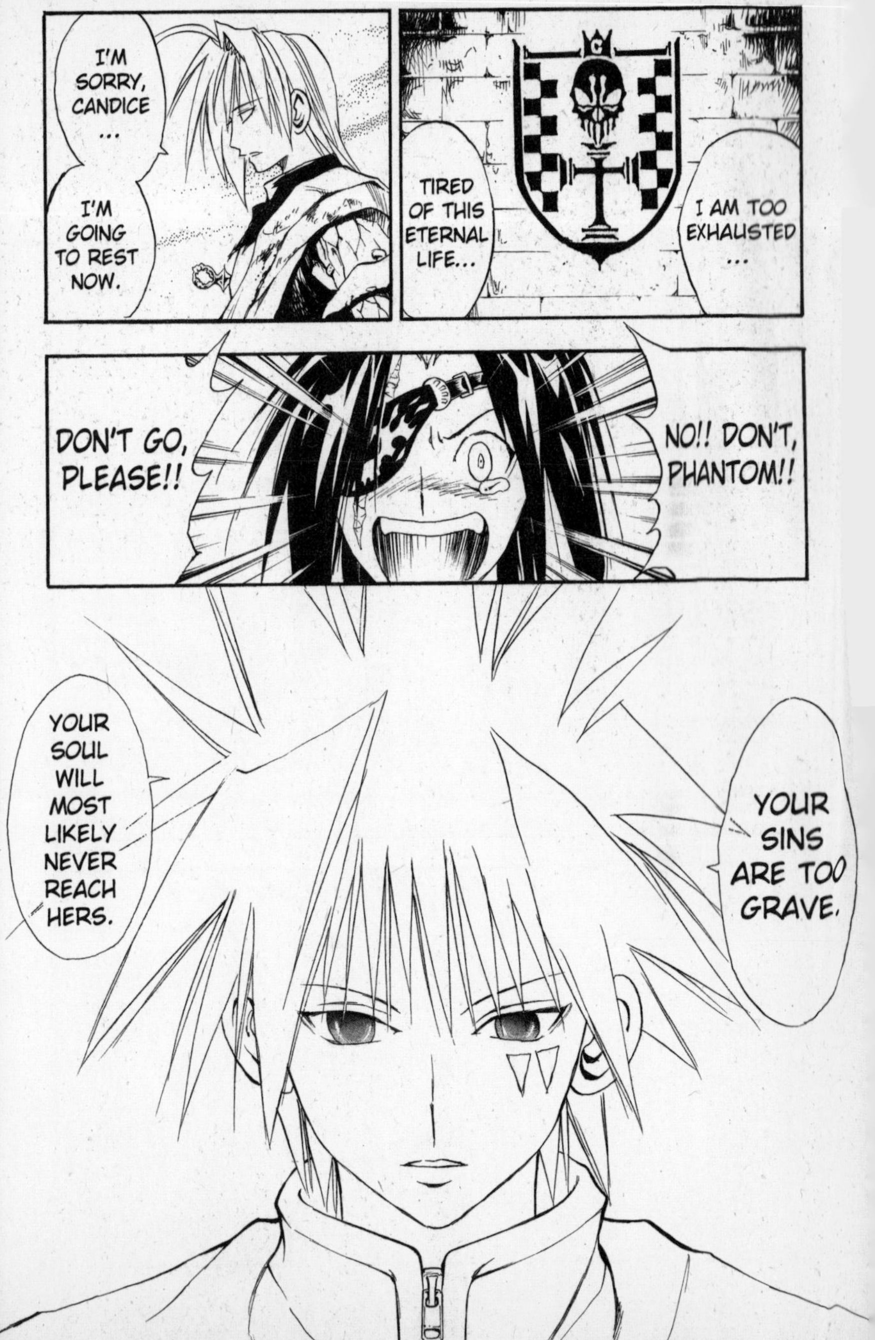
I AM TOO EXHAUSTED ...
TIRED OF THIS ETERNAL LIFE...
I'M SORRY, CANDICE ...
I'M GOING TO REST NOW.
NO!! DON'T, PHANTOM!!
DON'T GO, PLEASE!!
YOUR SINS ARE TOO GRAVE.
YOUR SOUL WILL MOST LIKELY NEVER REACH HERS.

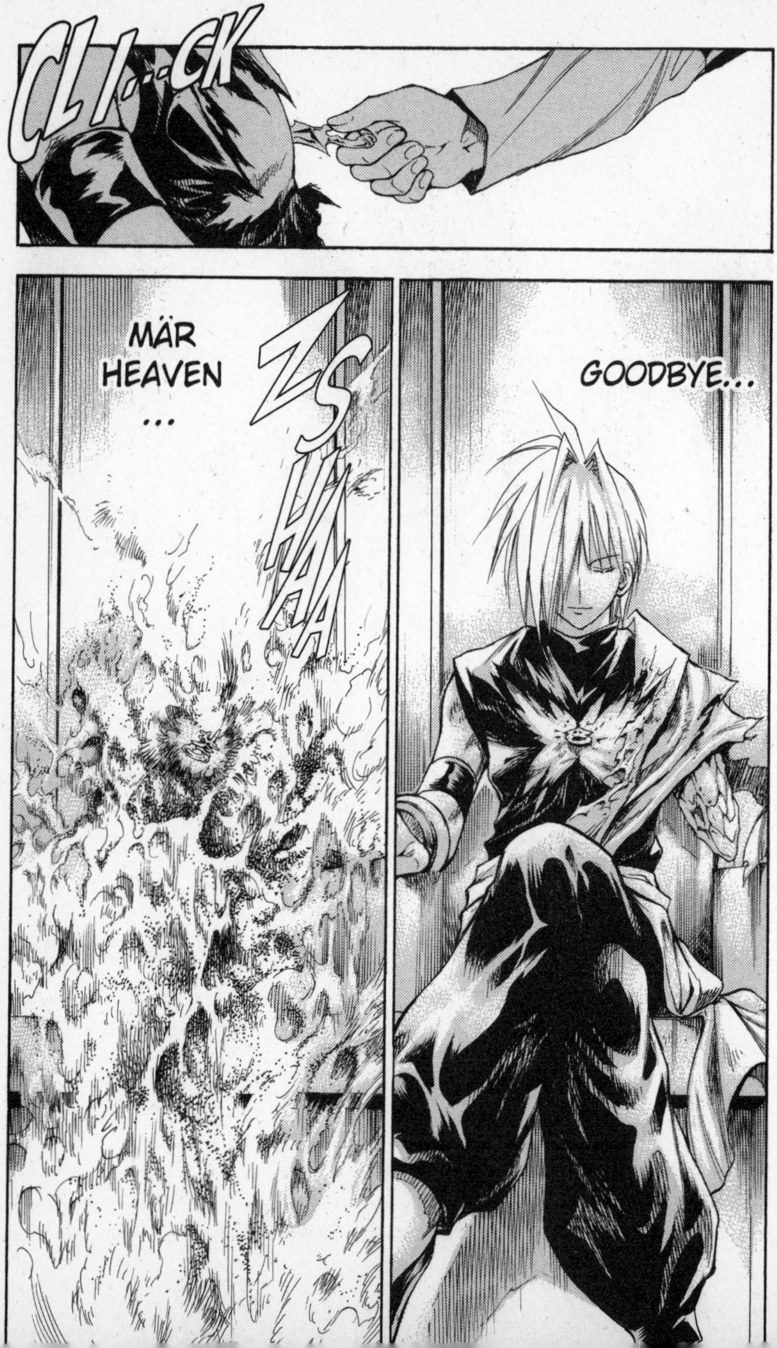
CLI..CK
GOODBYE...
MÄR HEAVEN ...
ZSHAAA

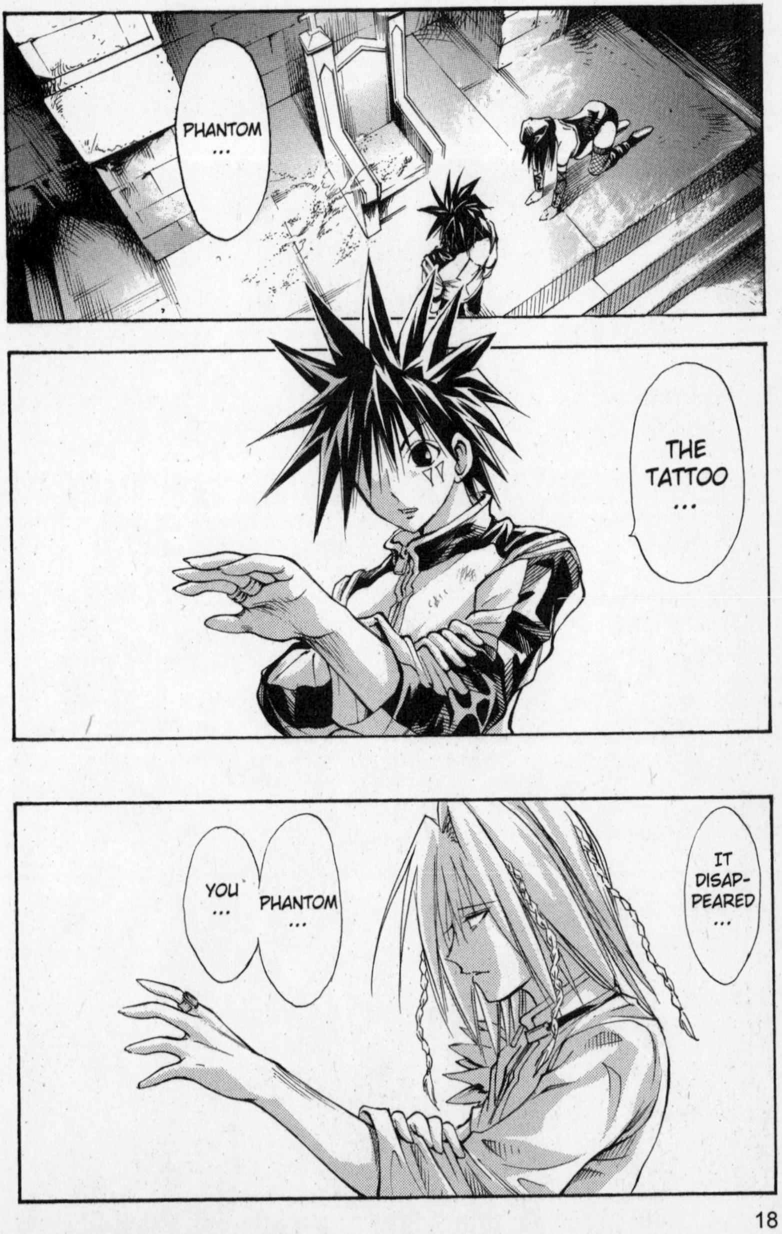
PHANTOM ...
THE TATTOO ...
IT DISAP-PEARED ...
PHANTOM ...
YOU ...

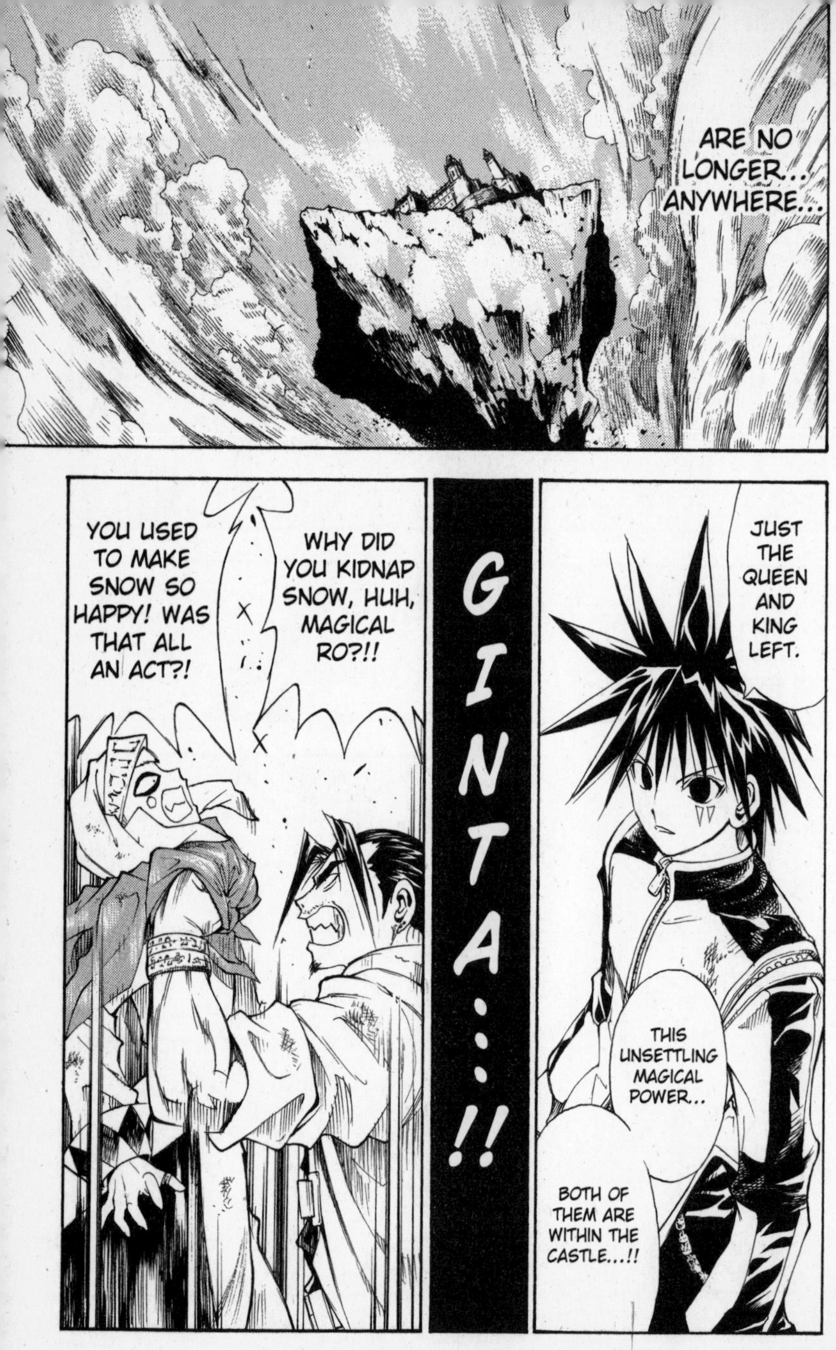
ARE NO LONGER... ANYWHERE...
JUST THE QUEEN AND KING LEFT.
THIS UNSETTLING MAGICAL POWER...
BOTH OF THEM ARE WITHIN THE CASTLE...!!
GINTA...!!
WHY DID YOU KIDNAP SNOW, HUH, MAGICAL RO?!!
YOU USED TO MAKE SNOW SO HAPPY! WAS THAT ALL AN ACT?!

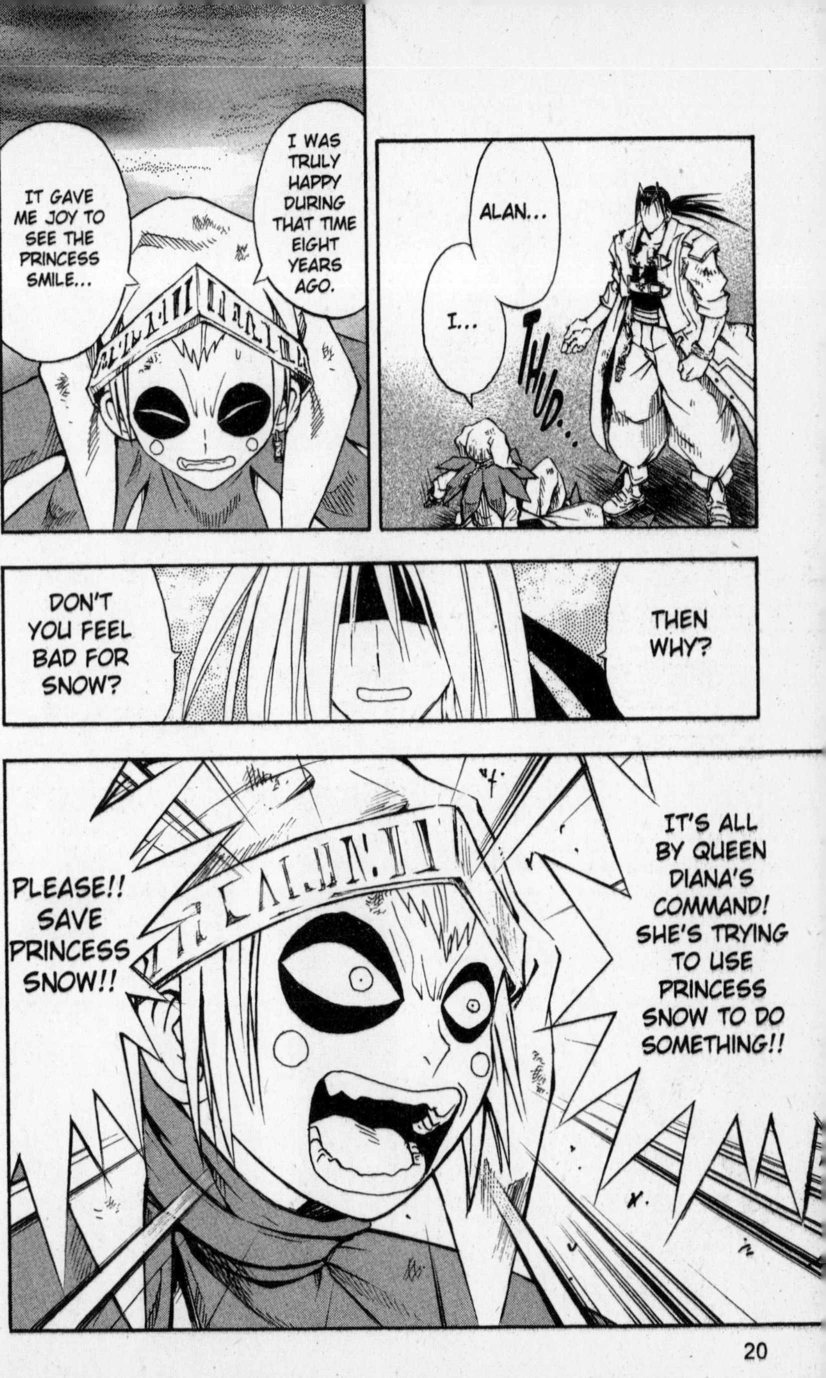
ALAN...
I...
THUD...
I WAS TRULY HAPPY DURING THAT TIME EIGHT YEARS AGO.
IT GAVE ME JOY TO SEE THE PRINCESS SMILE...
THEN WHY?
DON'T YOU FEEL BAD FOR SNOW?
IT'S ALL BY QUEEN DIANA'S COMMAND! SHE'S TRYING TO USE PRINCESS SNOW TO DO SOMETHING!!
PLEASE!! SAVE PRINCESS SNOW!!

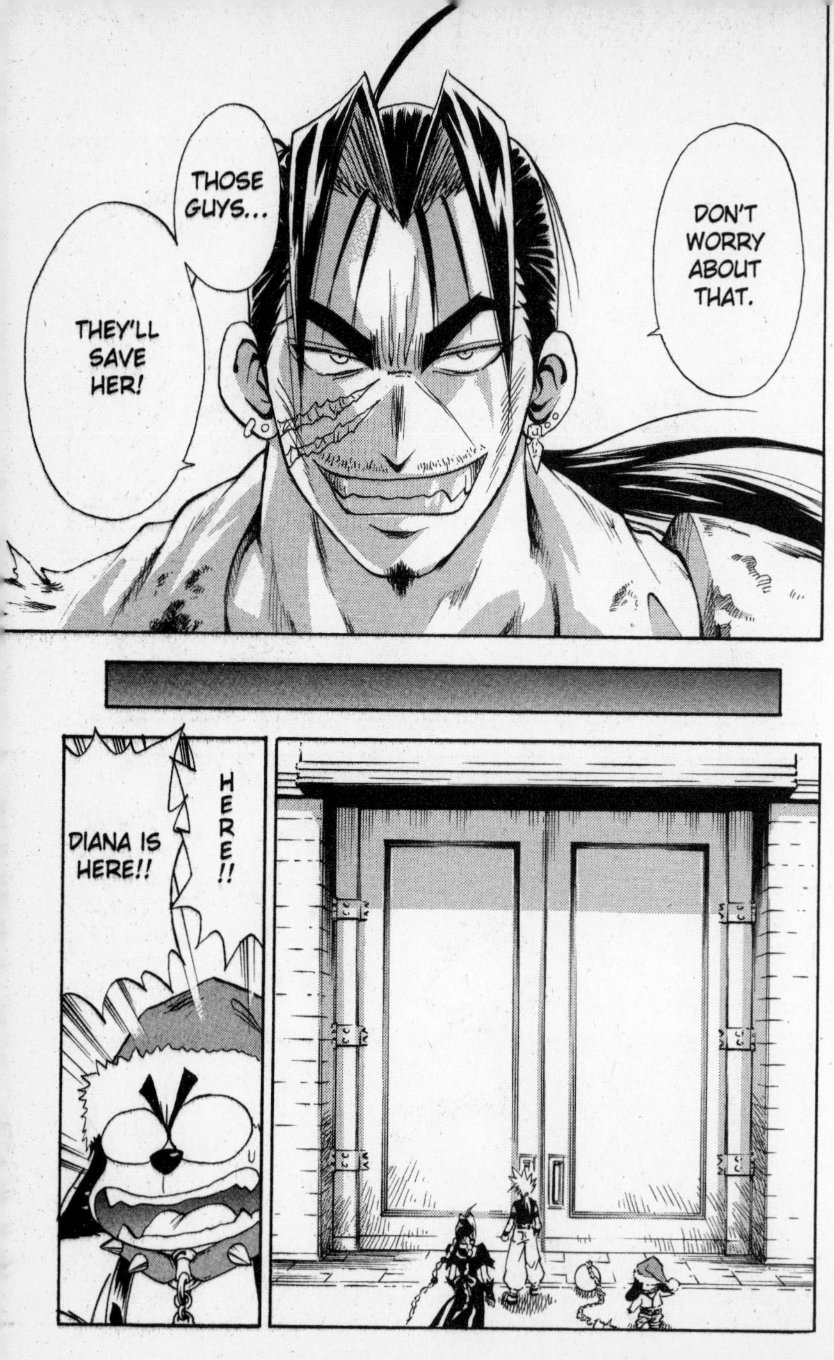
DON'T WORRY ABOUT THAT.
THOSE GUYS...
THEY'LL SAVE HER!
HERE!!
DIANA IS HERE!!

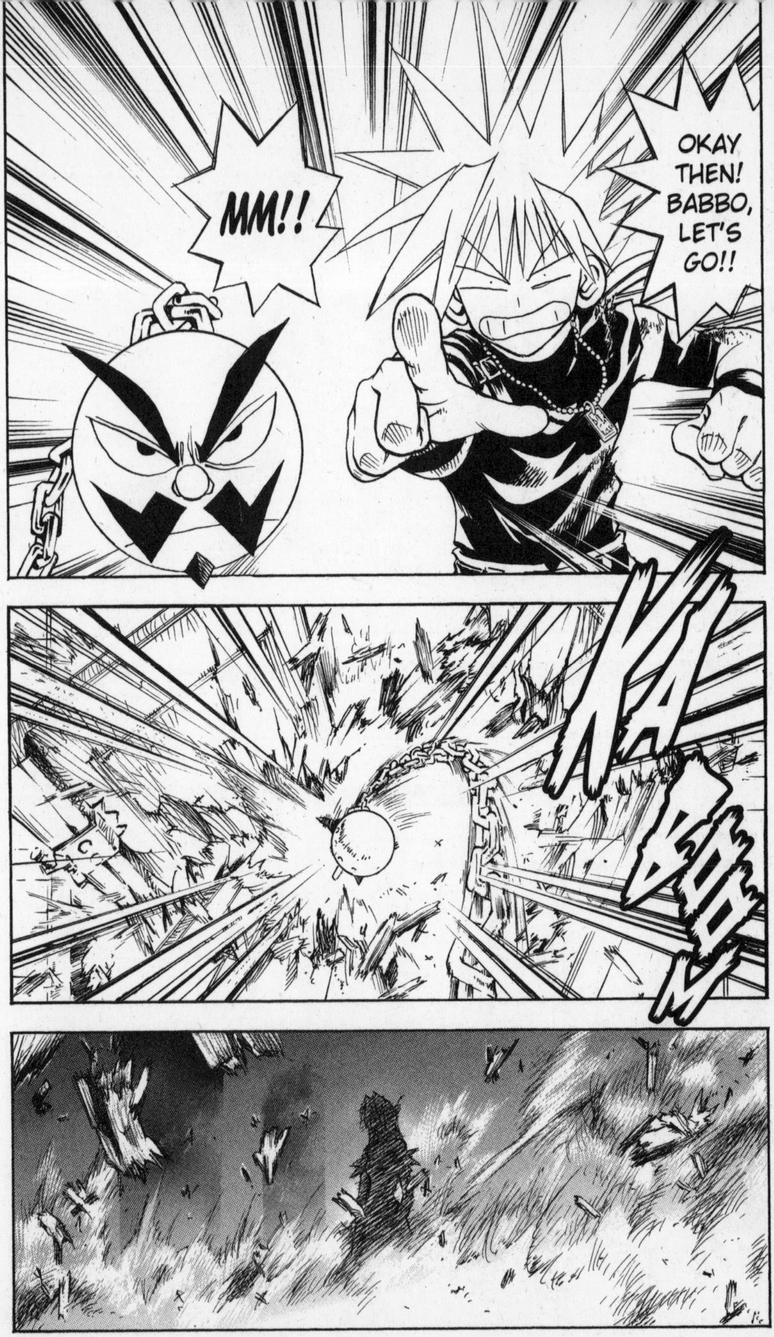
OKAY THEN! BABBO, LET'S GO!!
MM!!
KA BOOM

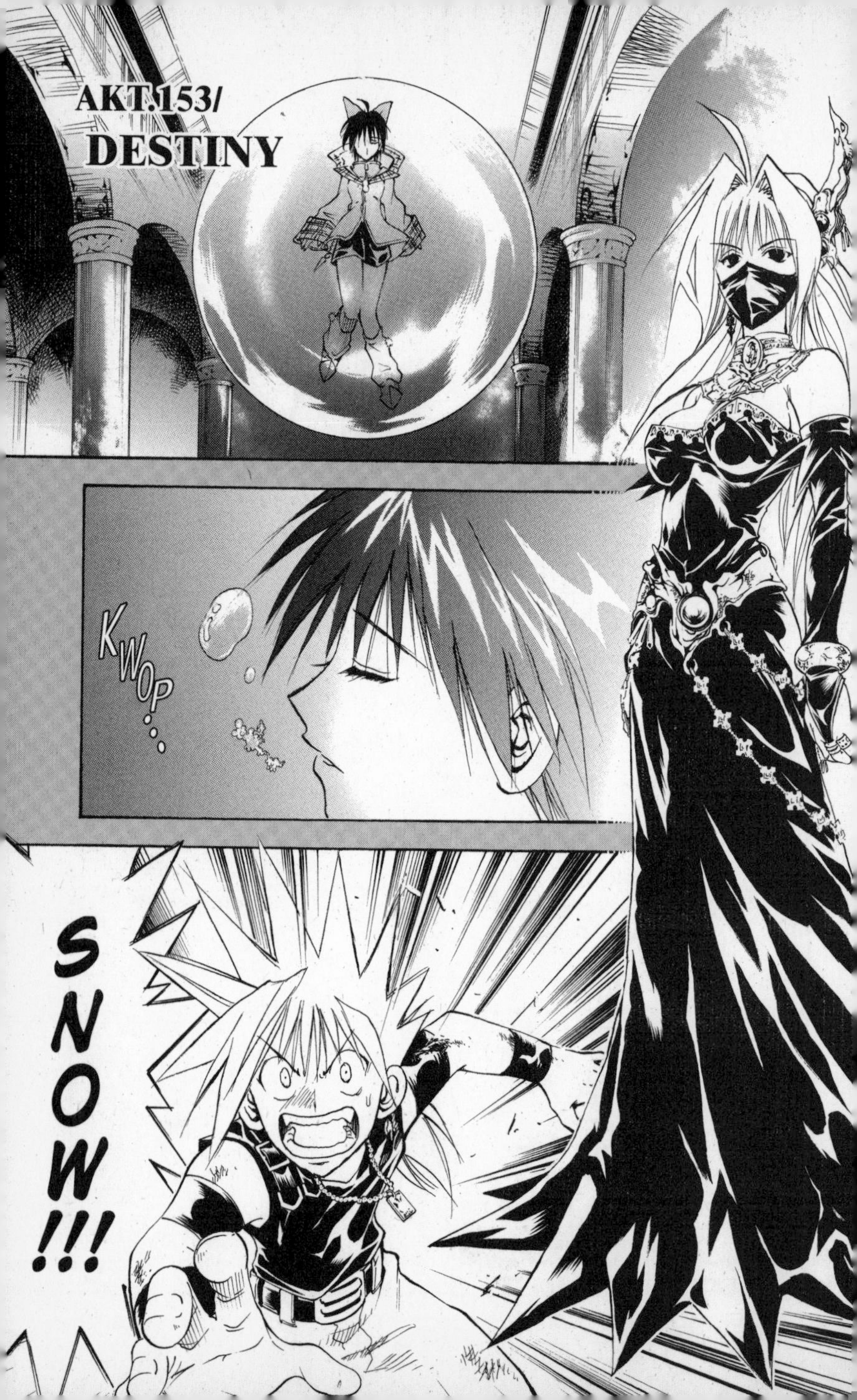
AKT.153/
DESTINY
KWOP...
SNOW!!!

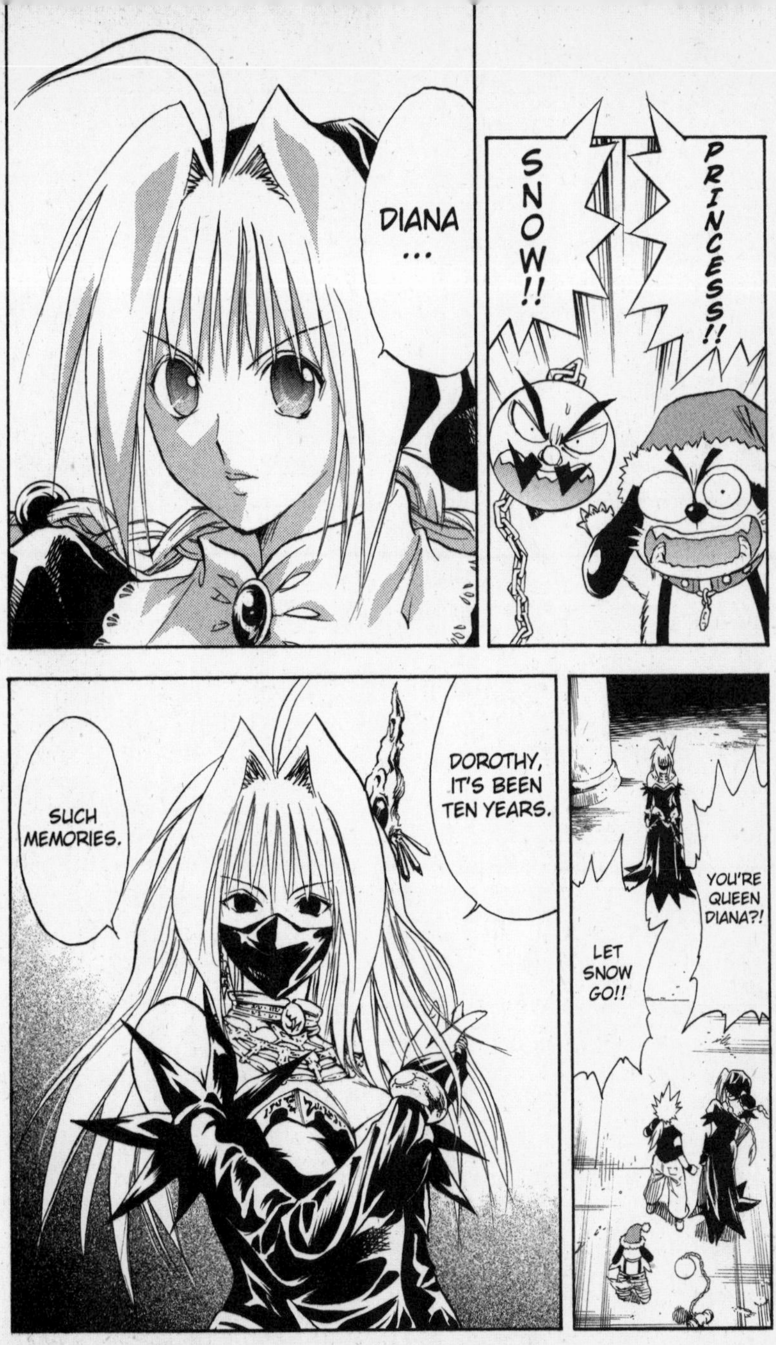
PRINCESS!!
SNOW!!
DIANA ...
YOU'RE QUEEN DIANA?!
LET SNOW GO!!
DOROTHY, IT'S BEEN TEN YEARS.
SUCH MEMORIES.

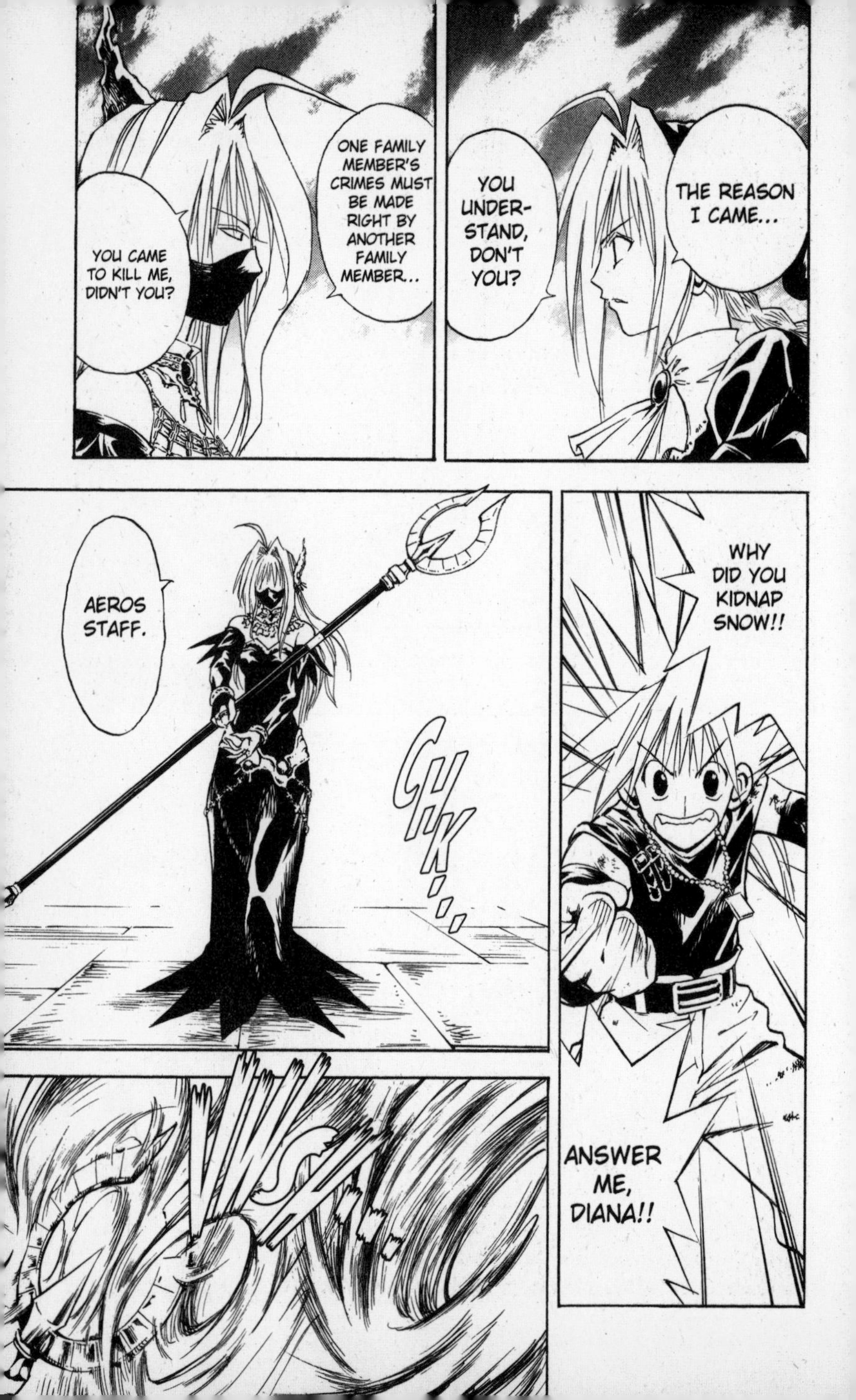
THE REASON I CAME...
YOU UNDER-STAND, DON'T YOU?
ONE FAMILY MEMBER'S CRIMES MUST BE MADE RIGHT BY ANOTHER FAMILY MEMBER...
YOU CAME TO KILL ME, DIDN'T YOU?
WHY DID YOU KIDNAP SNOW!!
ANSWER ME, DIANA!!
AEROS STAFF.
CHK...

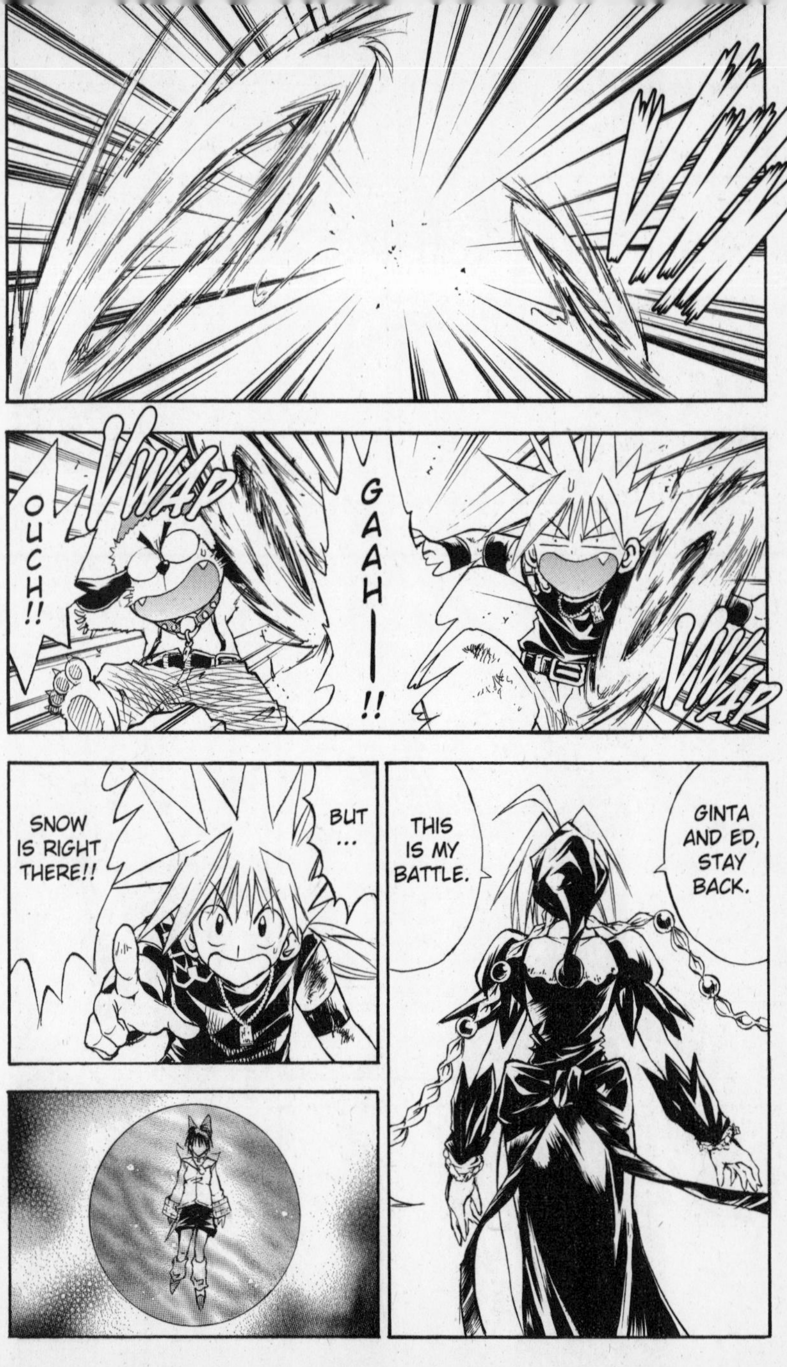
VWAP
GAAH—!!
VWAP
OUCH!!
GINTA AND ED, STAY BACK.
THIS IS MY BATTLE.
BUT ...
SNOW IS RIGHT THERE!!

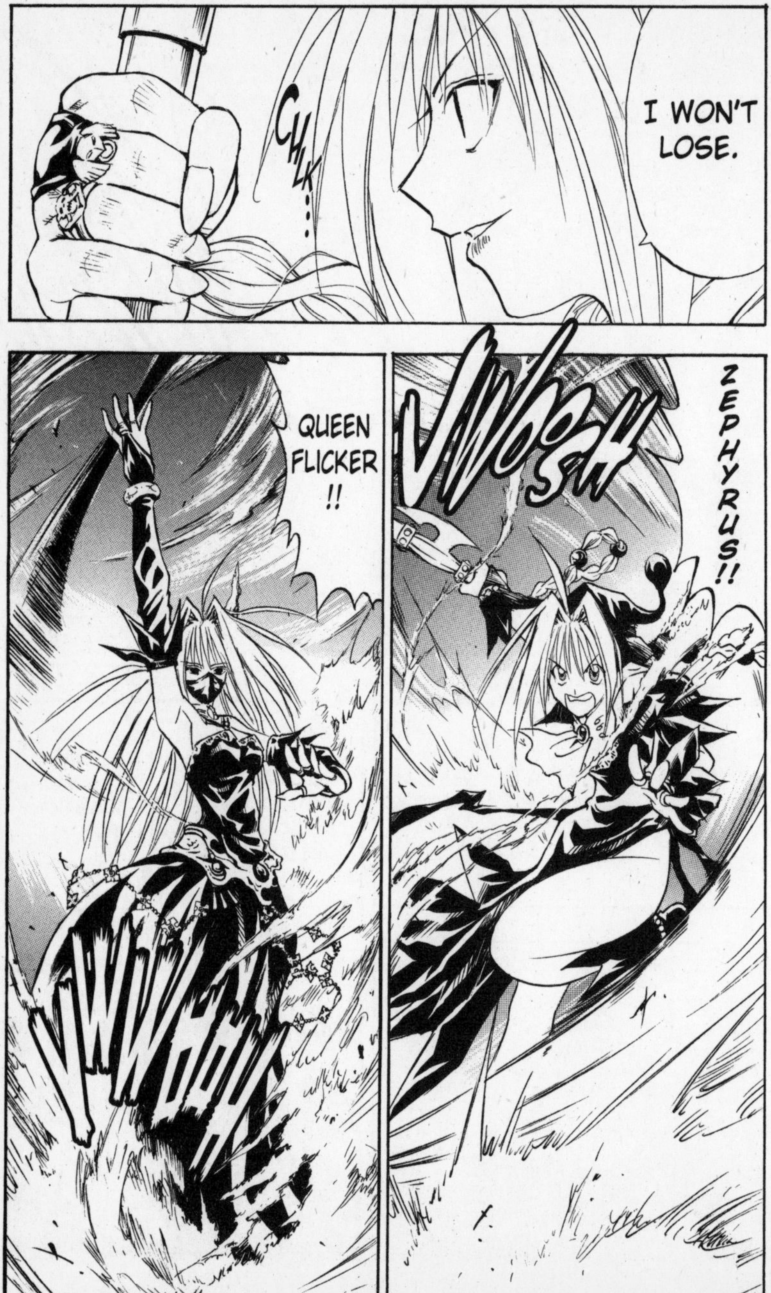
I WON'T LOSE.
CHLK...
ZEPHYRUS!!
WOSH
QUEEN FLICKER !!

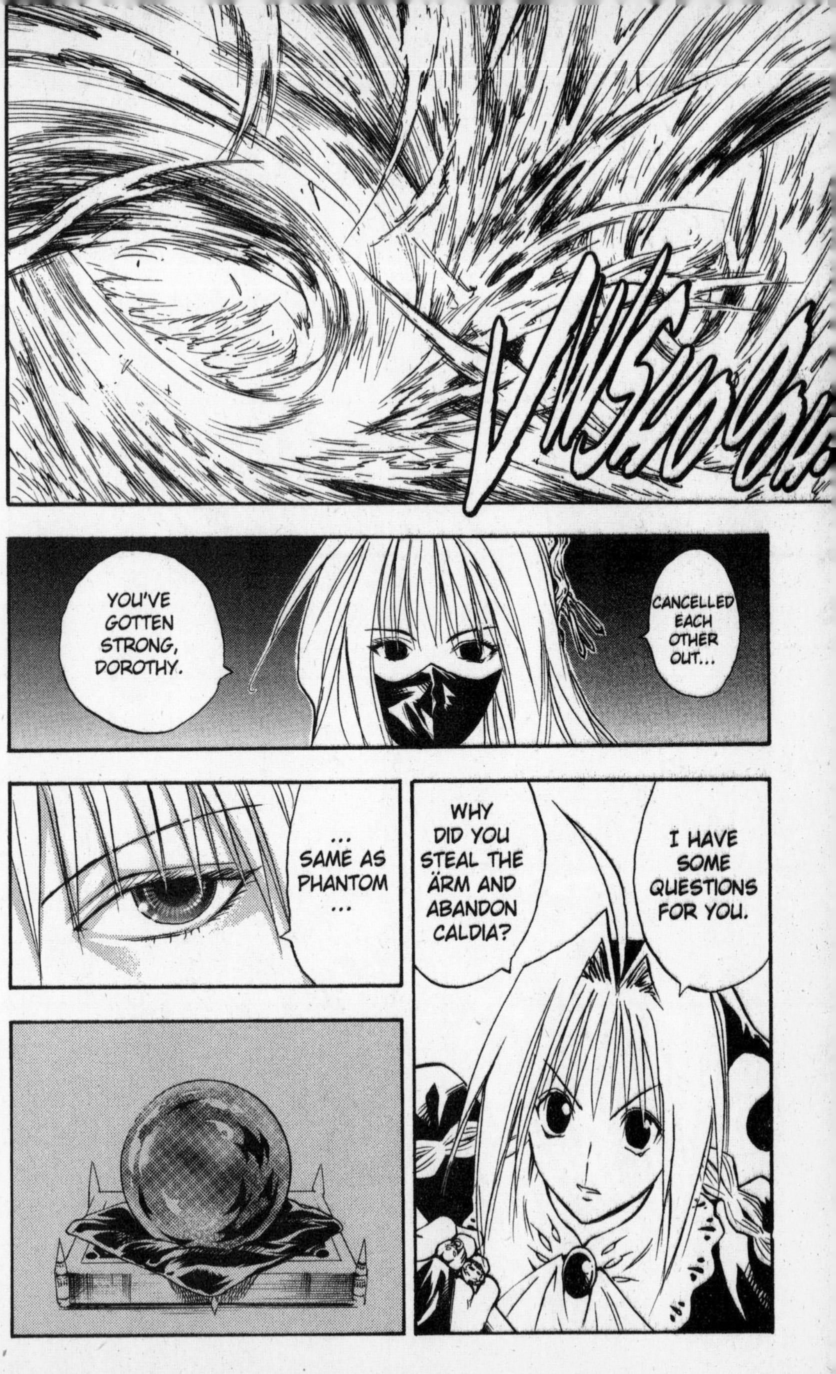
CANCELLED EACH OTHER OUT...
YOU'VE GOTTEN STRONG, DOROTHY.
I HAVE SOME QUESTIONS FOR YOU.
WHY DID YOU STEAL THE ÄRM AND ABANDON CALDIA?
... SAME AS PHANTOM ...

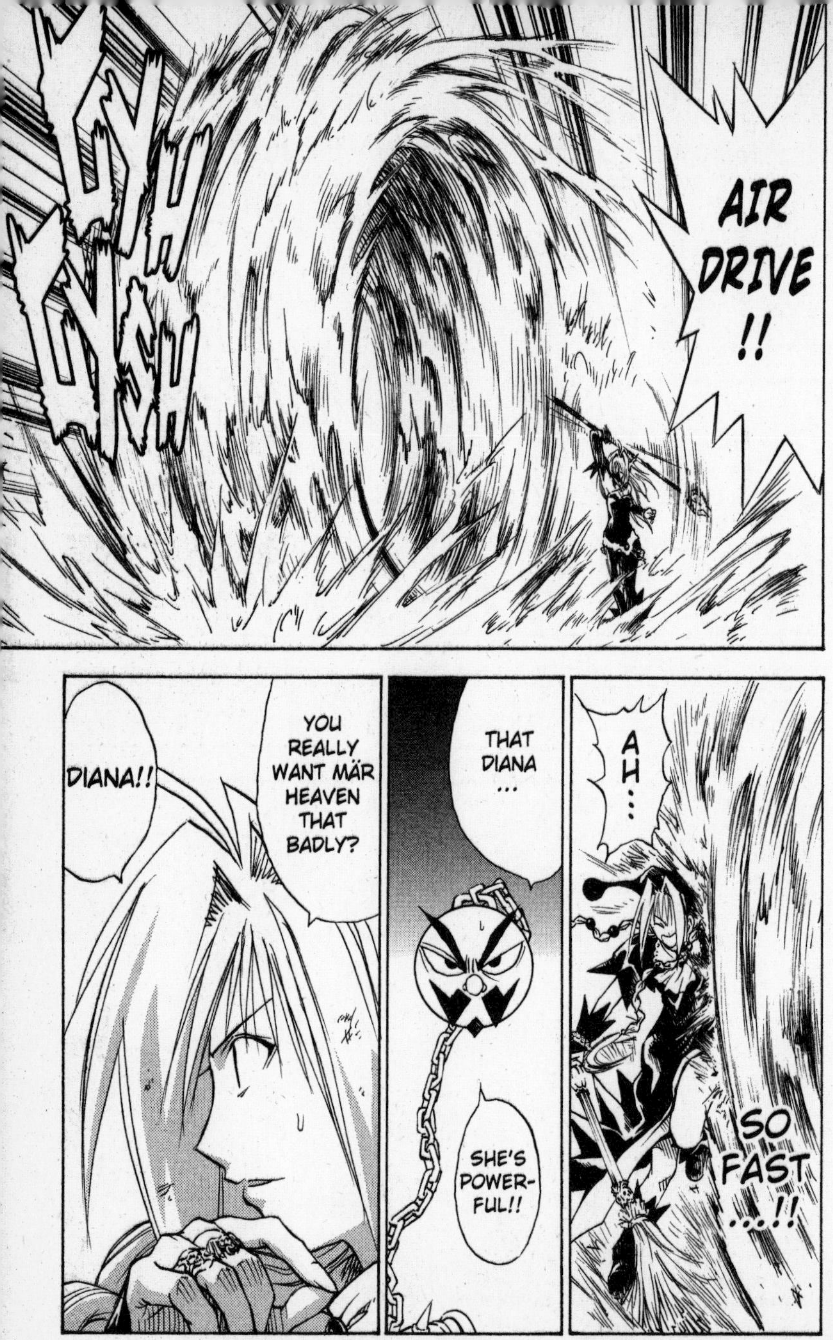
AIR DRIVE!!
GYSH GYSH
AH...
SO FAST...!!
THAT DIANA...
SHE'S POWER-FUL!!
YOU REALLY WANT MÄR HEAVEN THAT BADLY?
DIANA!!

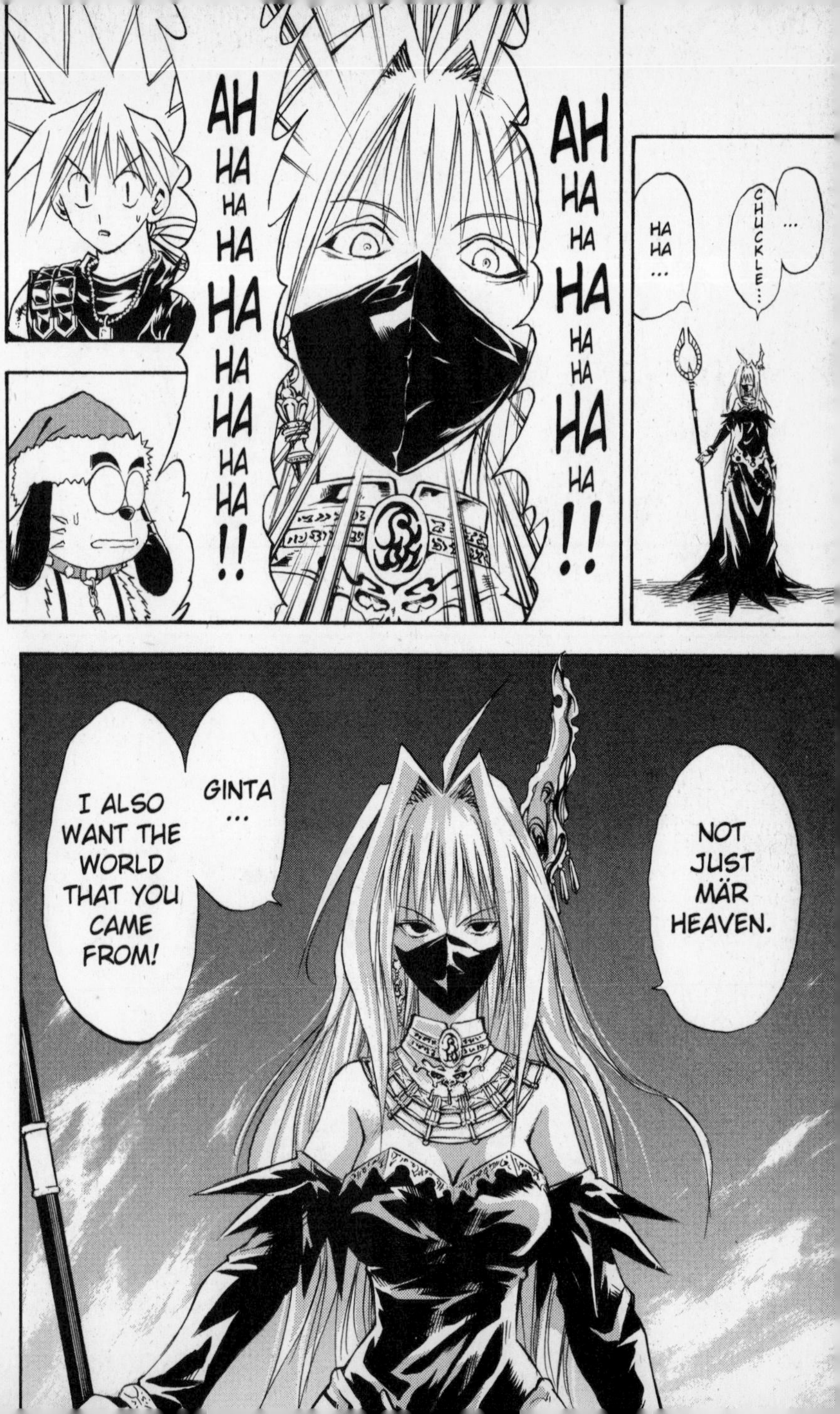
CHUCKLE...
...
HA HA...
AH HA HA HA HA HA HA HA HA!!
AH HA HA HA HA HA HA HA HA HA!!
NOT JUST MÄR HEAVEN.
GINTA...
I ALSO WANT THE WORLD THAT YOU CAME FROM!

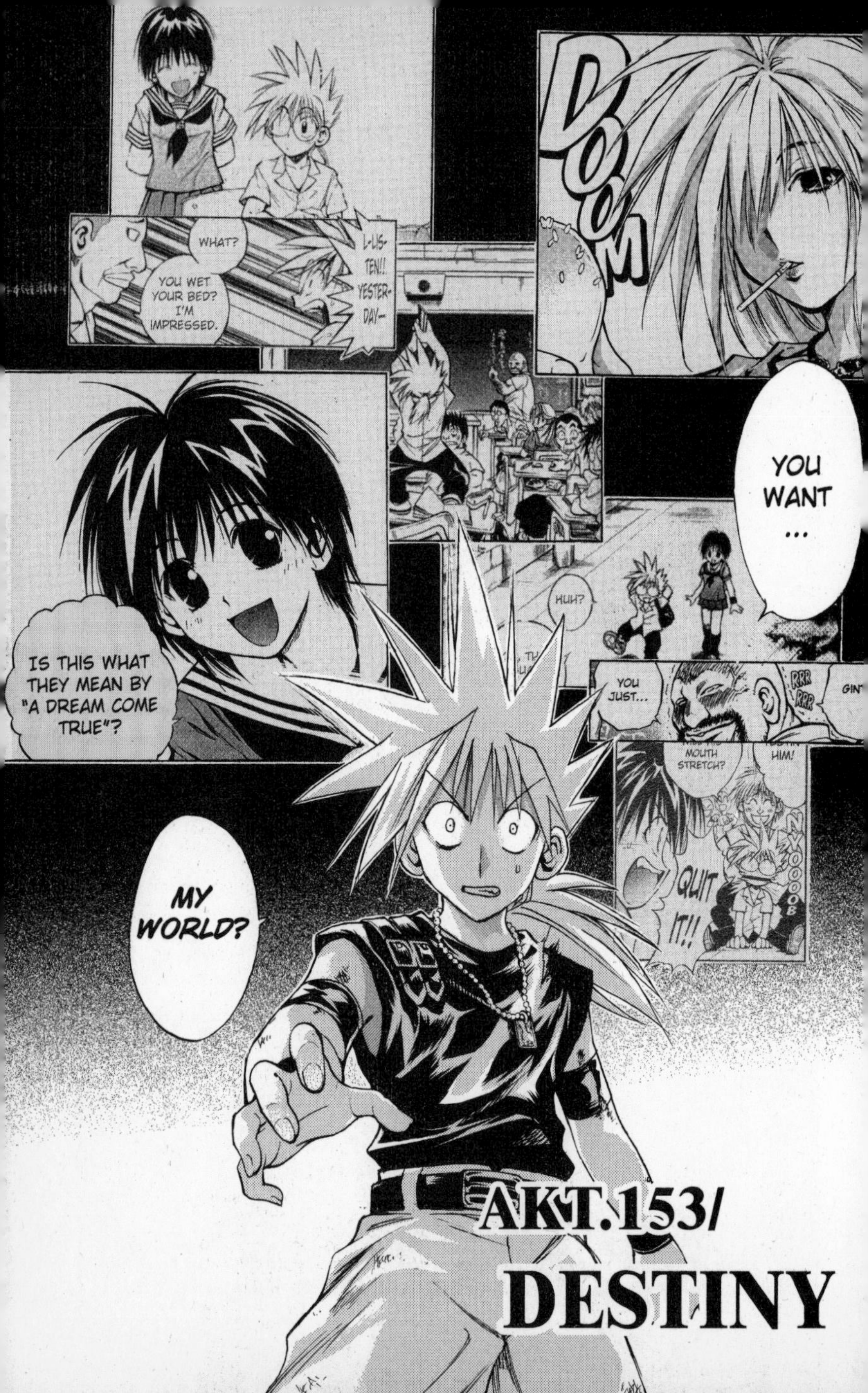
DOOM
L-LISTEN!! YESTERDAY—
WHAT?
YOU WET YOUR BED? I'M IMPRESSED.
YOU WANT ...
RRR RRR
YOU JUST...
HIM!
MOUTH STRETCH?
NYOOOOB
QUIT IT!!
HUH?
IS THIS WHAT THEY MEAN BY "A DREAM COME TRUE"?
MY WORLD?
AKT.153/
DESTINY

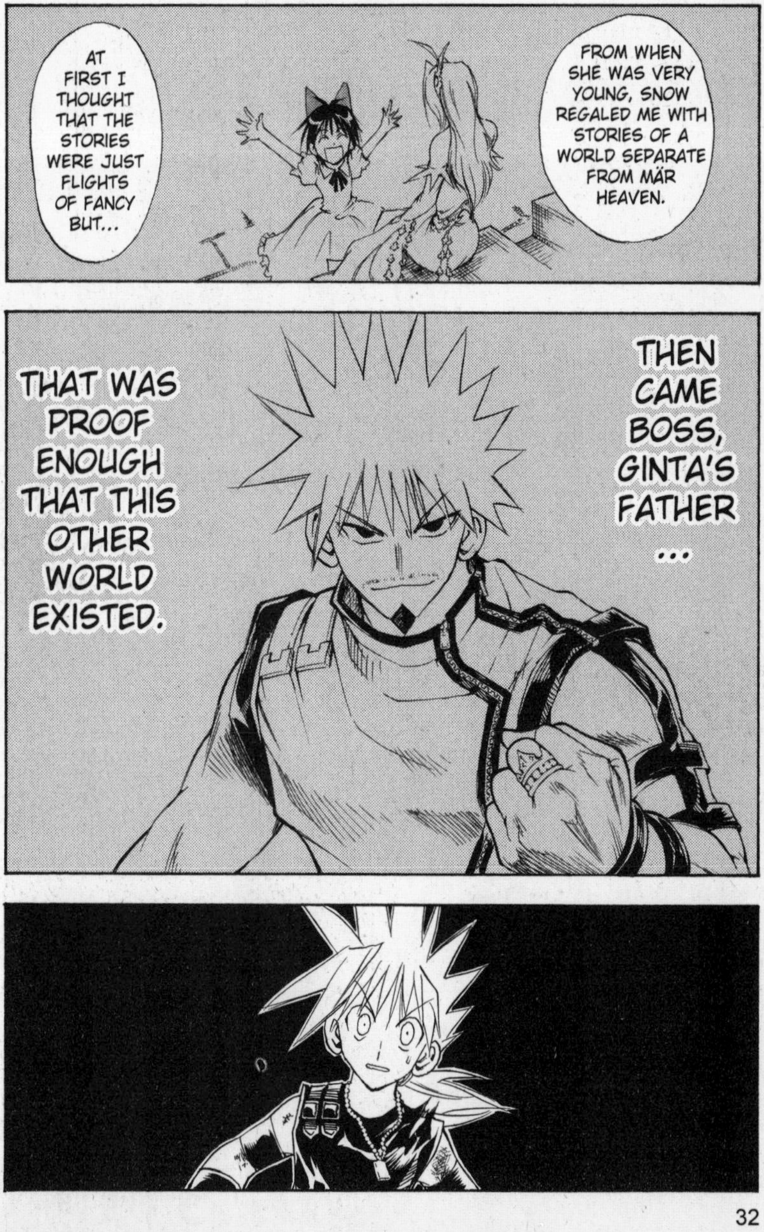
FROM WHEN SHE WAS VERY YOUNG, SNOW REGALED ME WITH STORIES OF A WORLD SEPARATE FROM MÄR HEAVEN.
AT FIRST I THOUGHT THAT THE STORIES WERE JUST FLIGHTS OF FANCY BUT...
THEN CAME BOSS, GINTA'S FATHER ...
THAT WAS PROOF ENOUGH THAT THIS OTHER WORLD EXISTED.

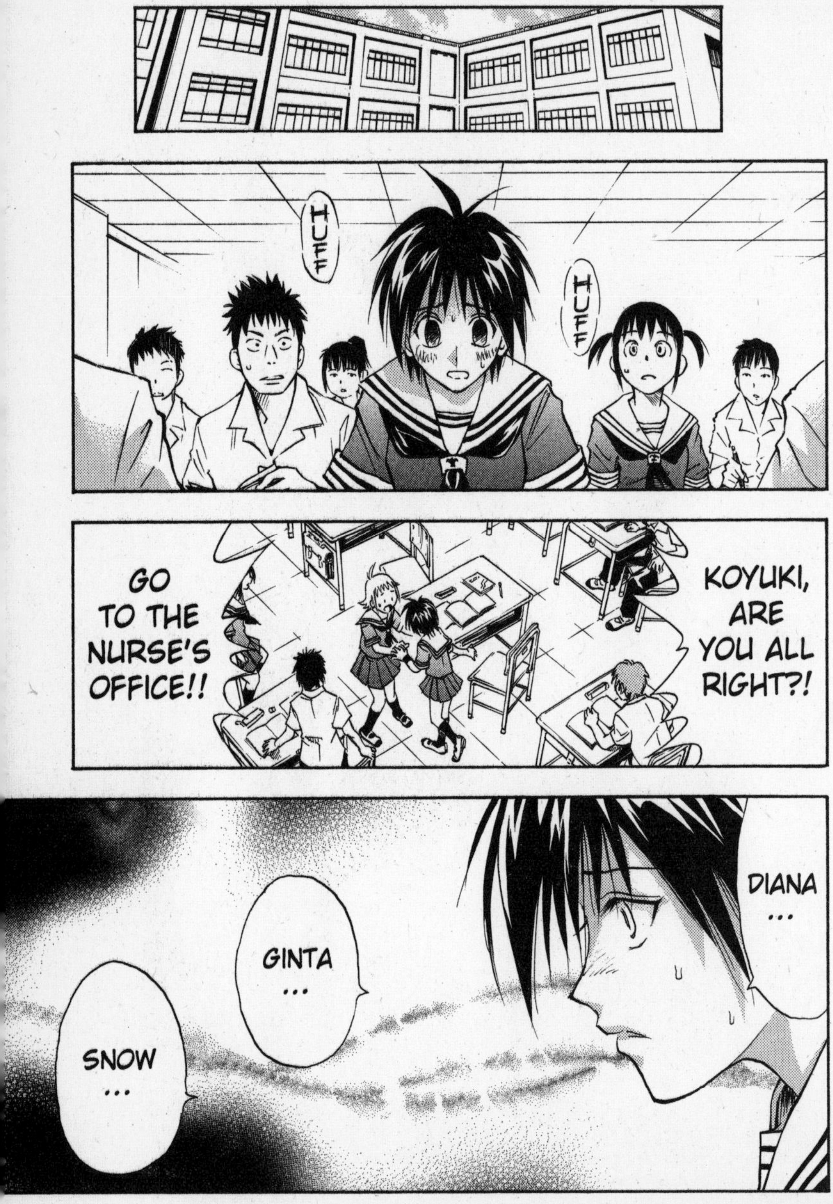
HUFF
HUFF
KOYUKI, ARE YOU ALL RIGHT?!
GO TO THE NURSE'S OFFICE!!
DIANA ...
GINTA ...
SNOW ...

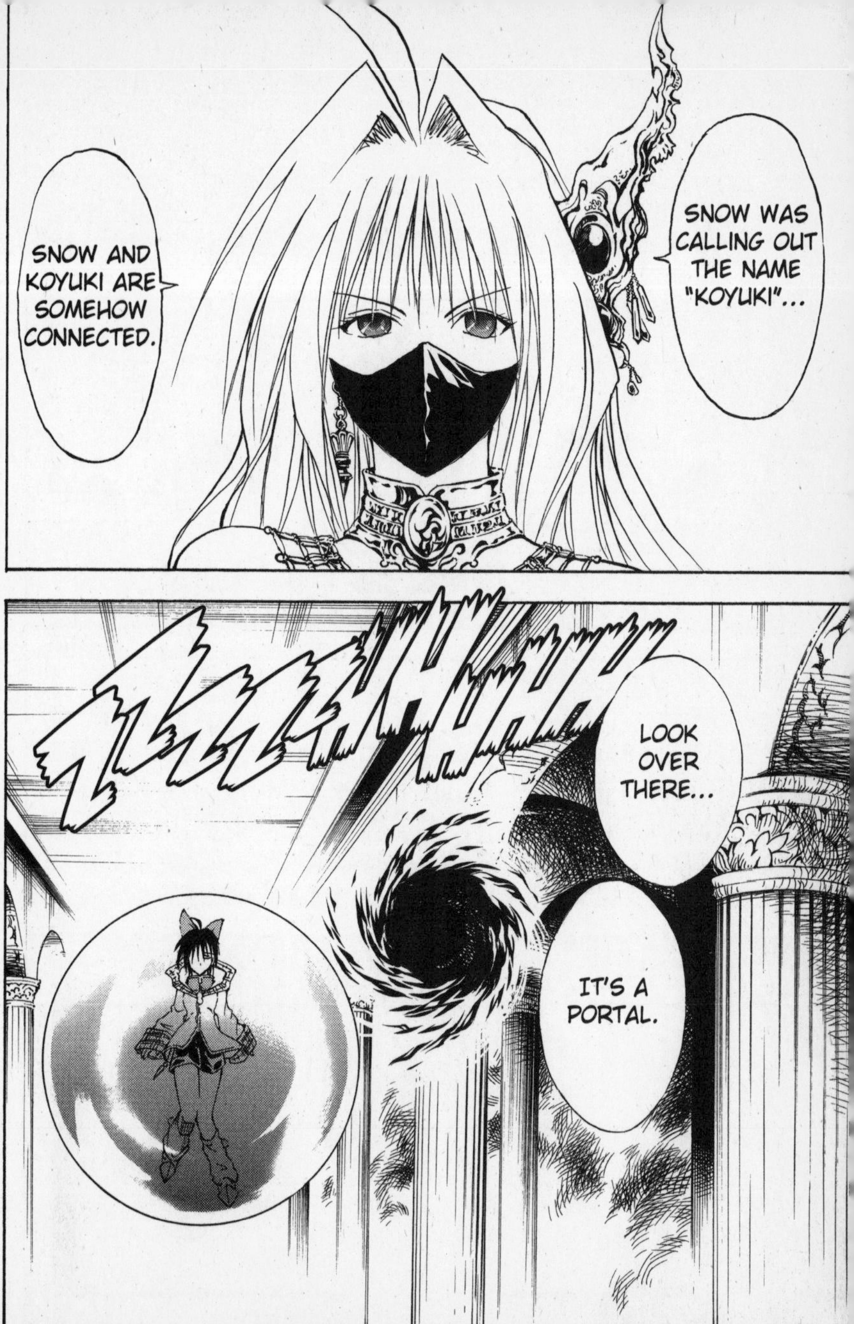
SNOW WAS CALLING OUT THE NAME "KOYUKI"...
SNOW AND KOYUKI ARE SOMEHOW CONNECTED.
ZZZWHHHH
LOOK OVER THERE...
IT'S A PORTAL.

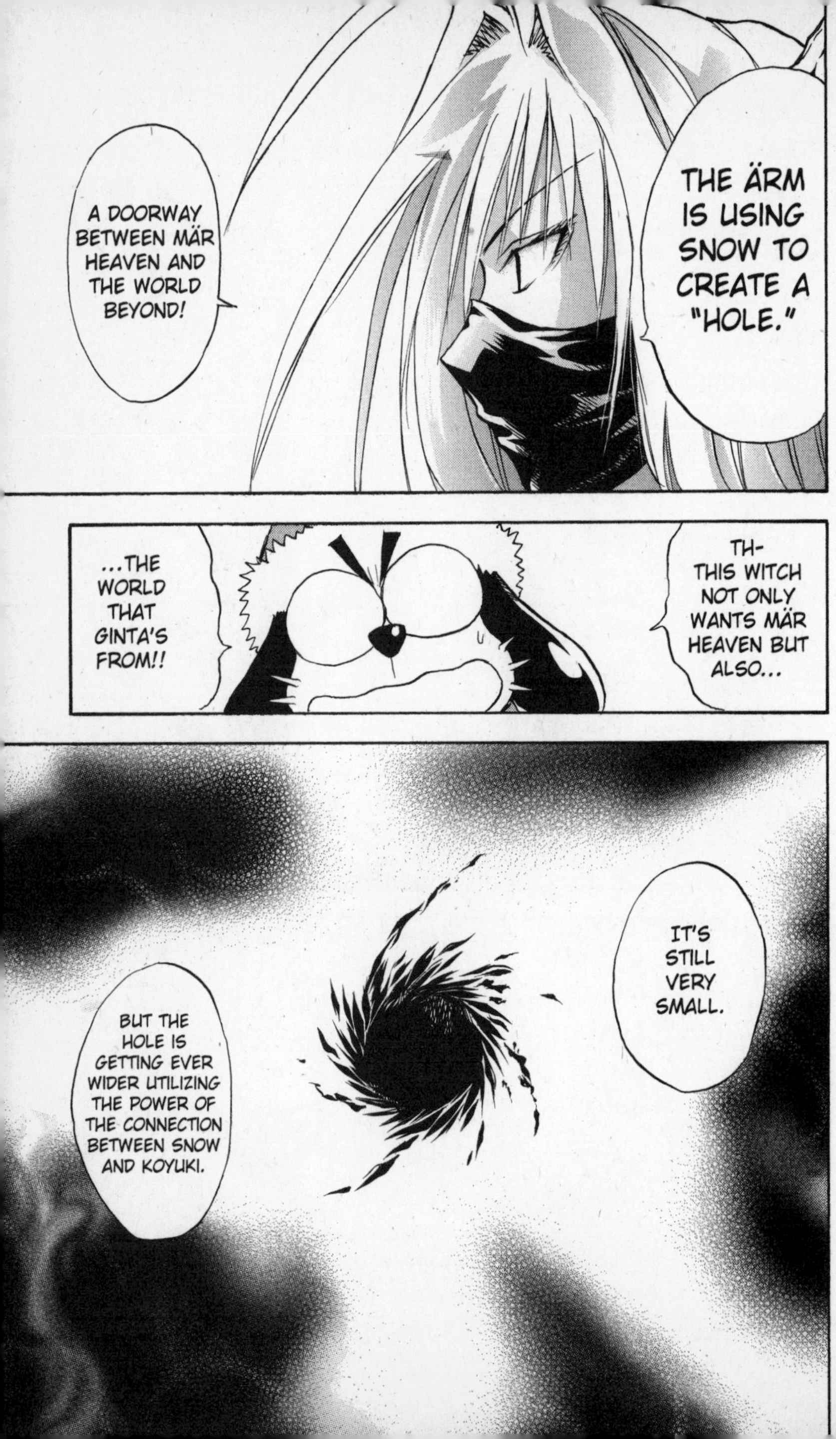
THE ÄRM IS USING SNOW TO CREATE A "HOLE."
A DOORWAY BETWEEN MÄR HEAVEN AND THE WORLD BEYOND!
TH- THIS WITCH NOT ONLY WANTS MÄR HEAVEN BUT ALSO...
...THE WORLD THAT GINTA'S FROM!!
IT'S STILL VERY SMALL.
BUT THE HOLE IS GETTING EVER WIDER UTILIZING THE POWER OF THE CONNECTION BETWEEN SNOW AND KOYUKI.

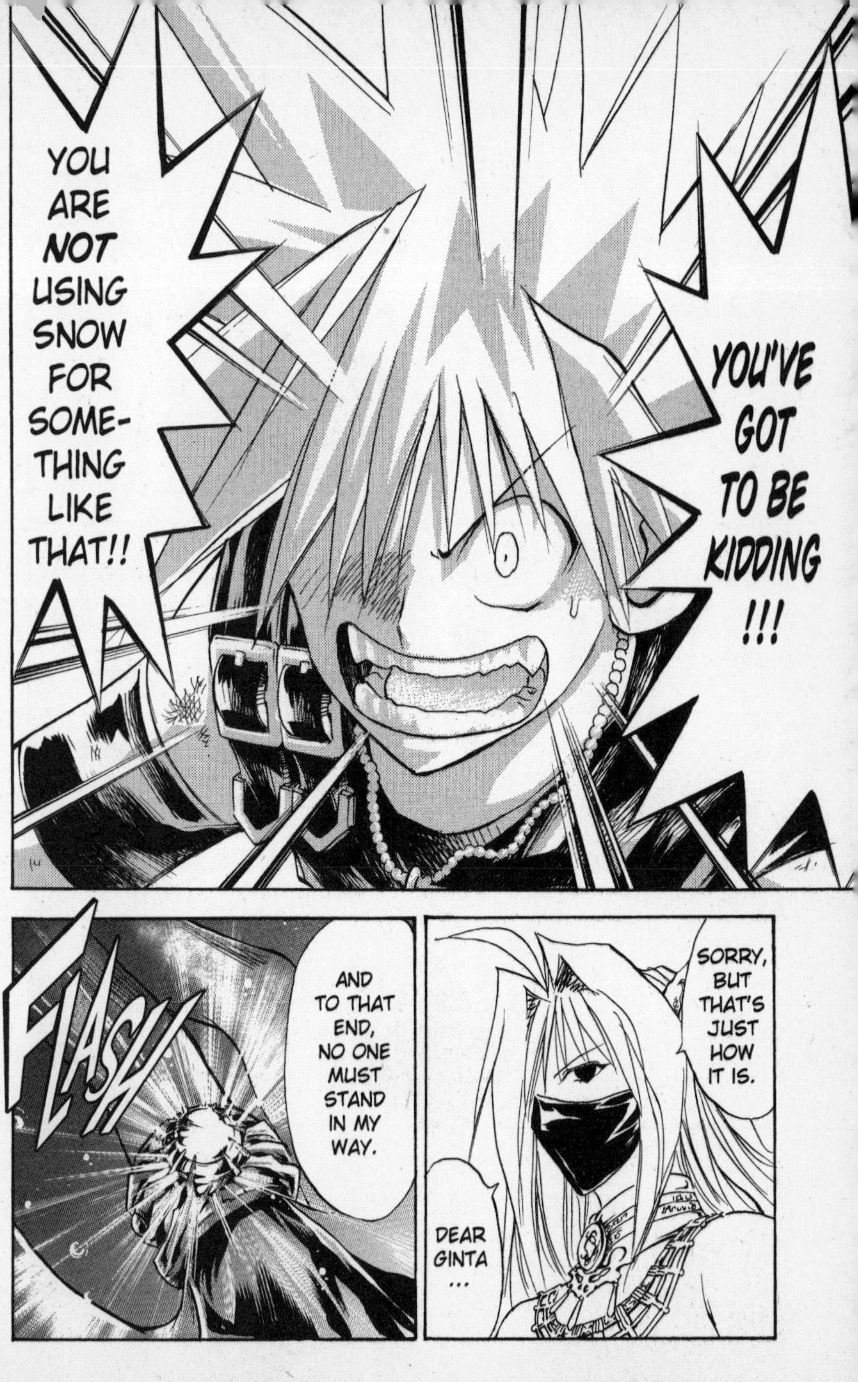
YOU'VE GOT TO BE KIDDING!!!
YOU ARE NOT USING SNOW FOR SOME-THING LIKE THAT!!
SORRY, BUT THAT'S JUST HOW IT IS.
DEAR GINTA...
AND TO THAT END, NO ONE MUST STAND IN MY WAY.
FLASH

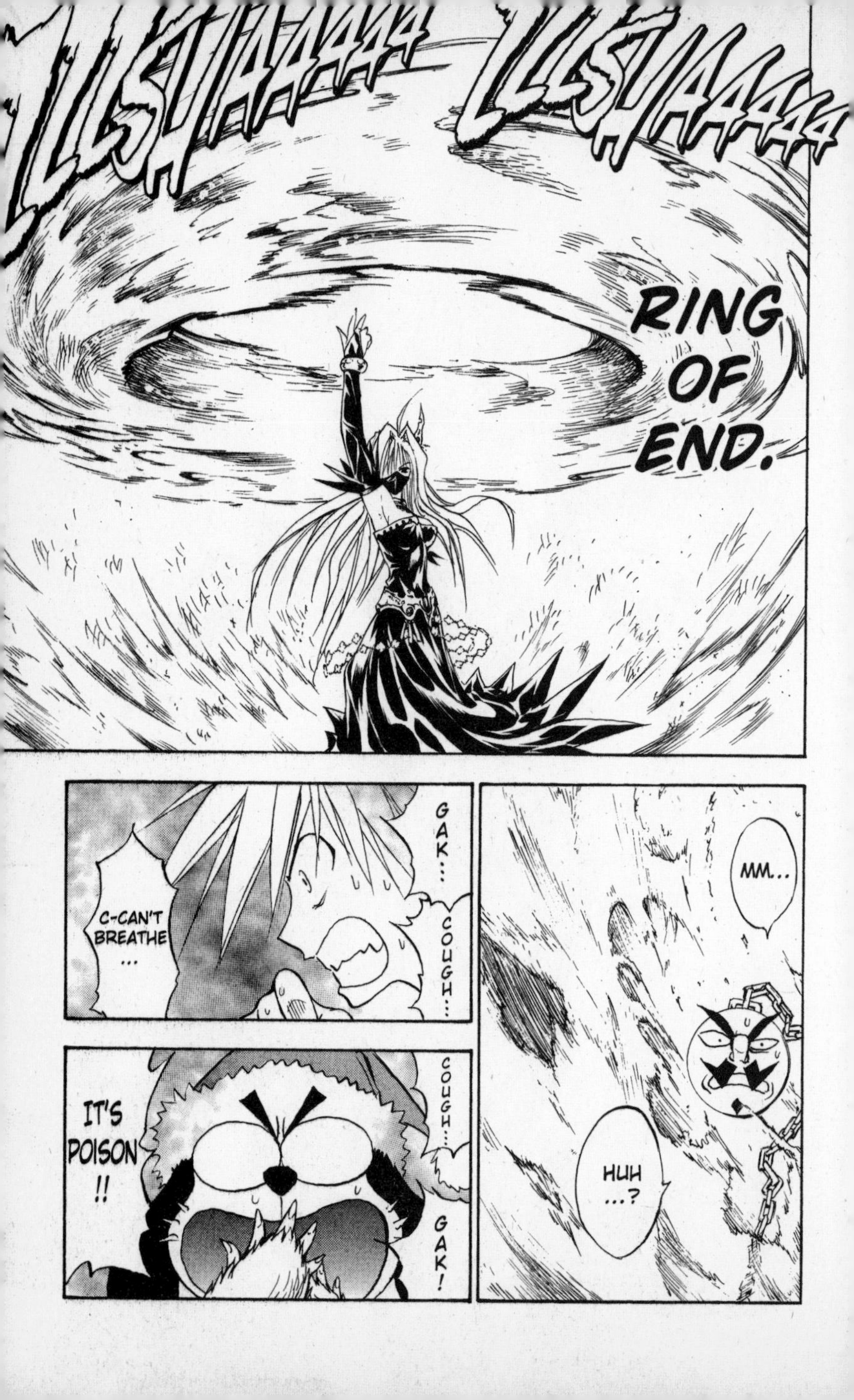
RING OF END.
MM...
HUH ...?
GAK... COUGH...
C-CAN'T BREATHE ...
COUGH... GAK!
IT'S POISON !!

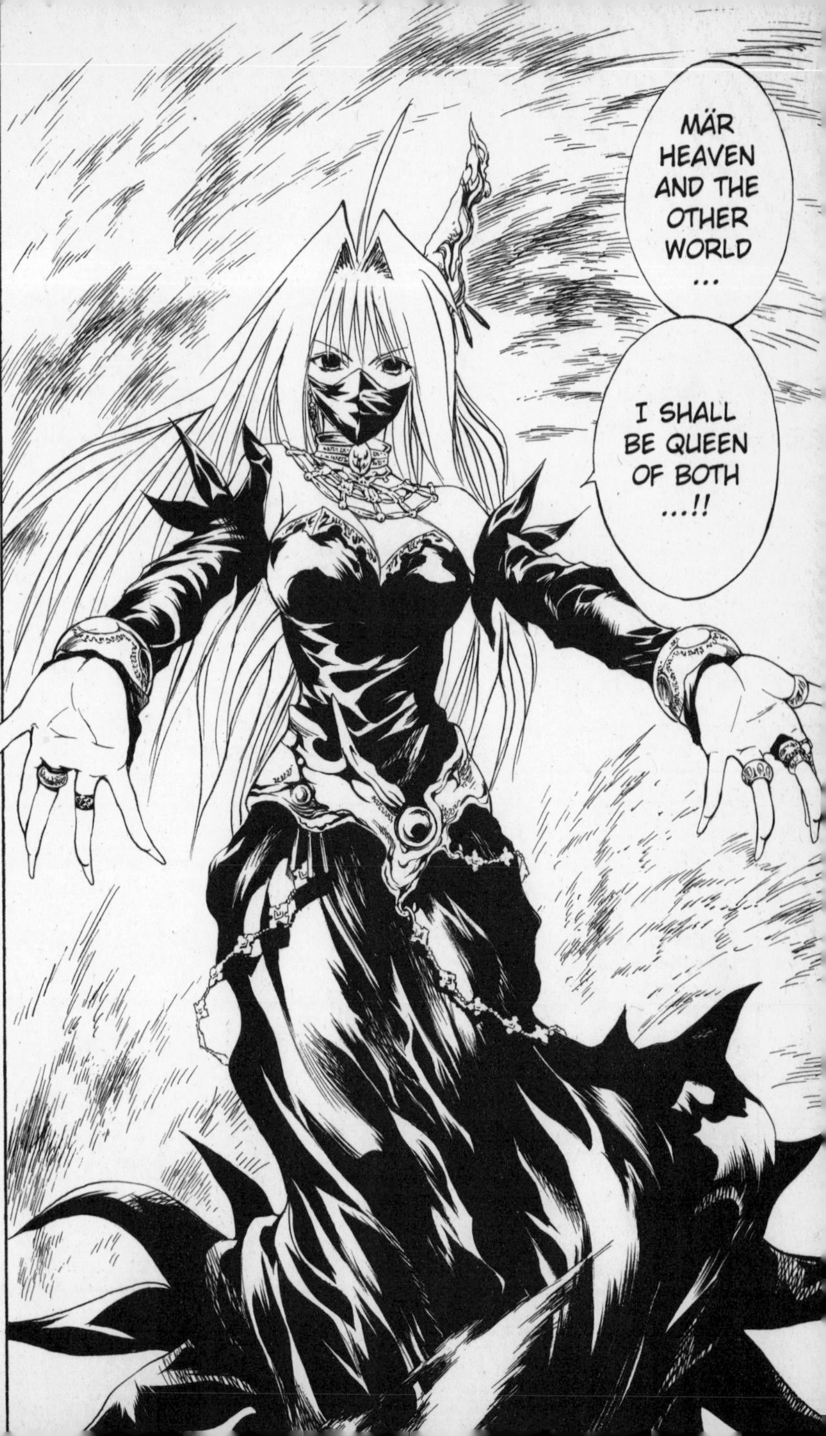
MÄR HEAVEN AND THE OTHER WORLD ...
I SHALL BE QUEEN OF BOTH ...!!

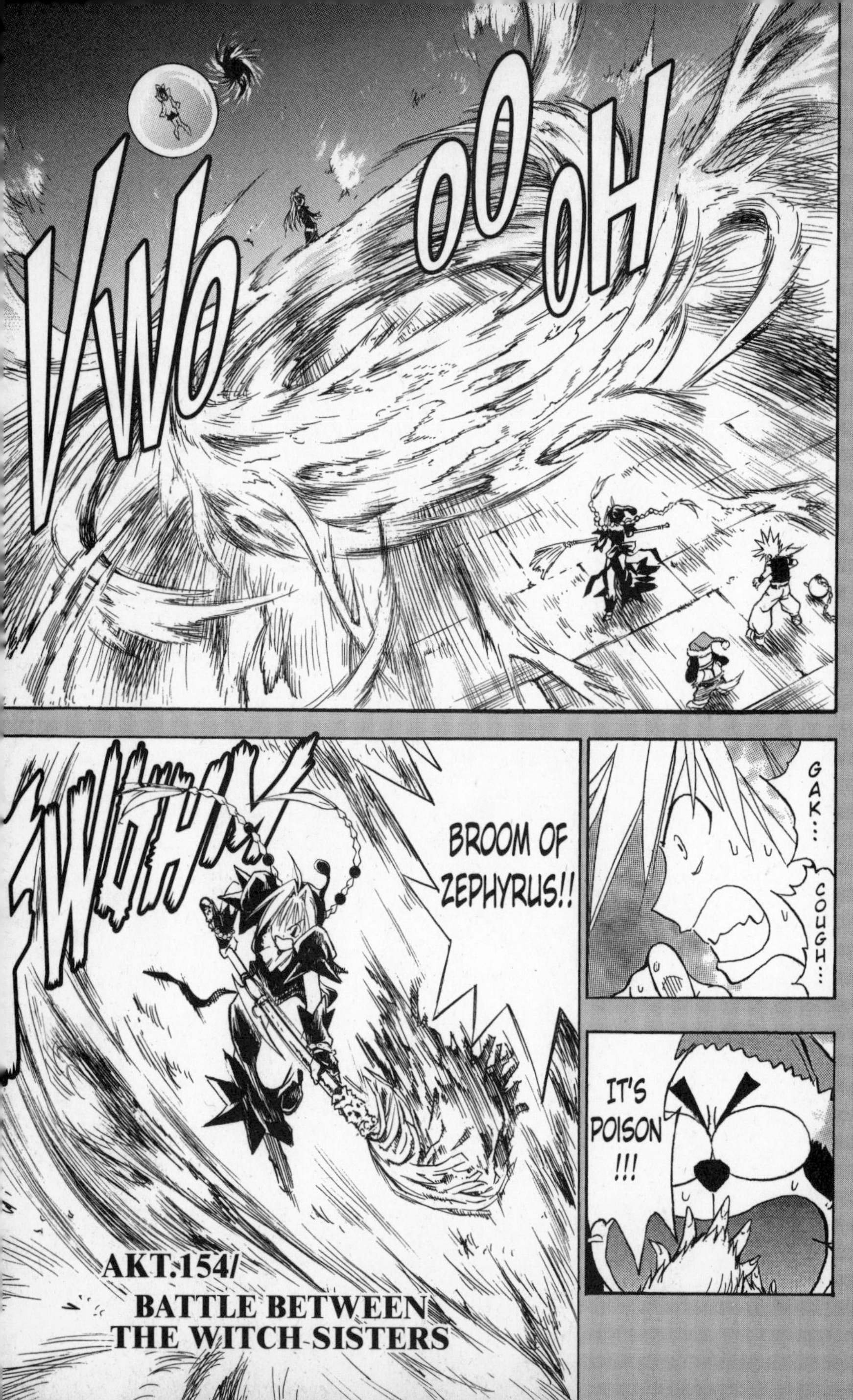
VWOOOOH
GAK... COUGH...
IT'S POISON!!!
BROOM OF ZEPHYRUS!!
AKT.154/
BATTLE BETWEEN THE WITCH SISTERS

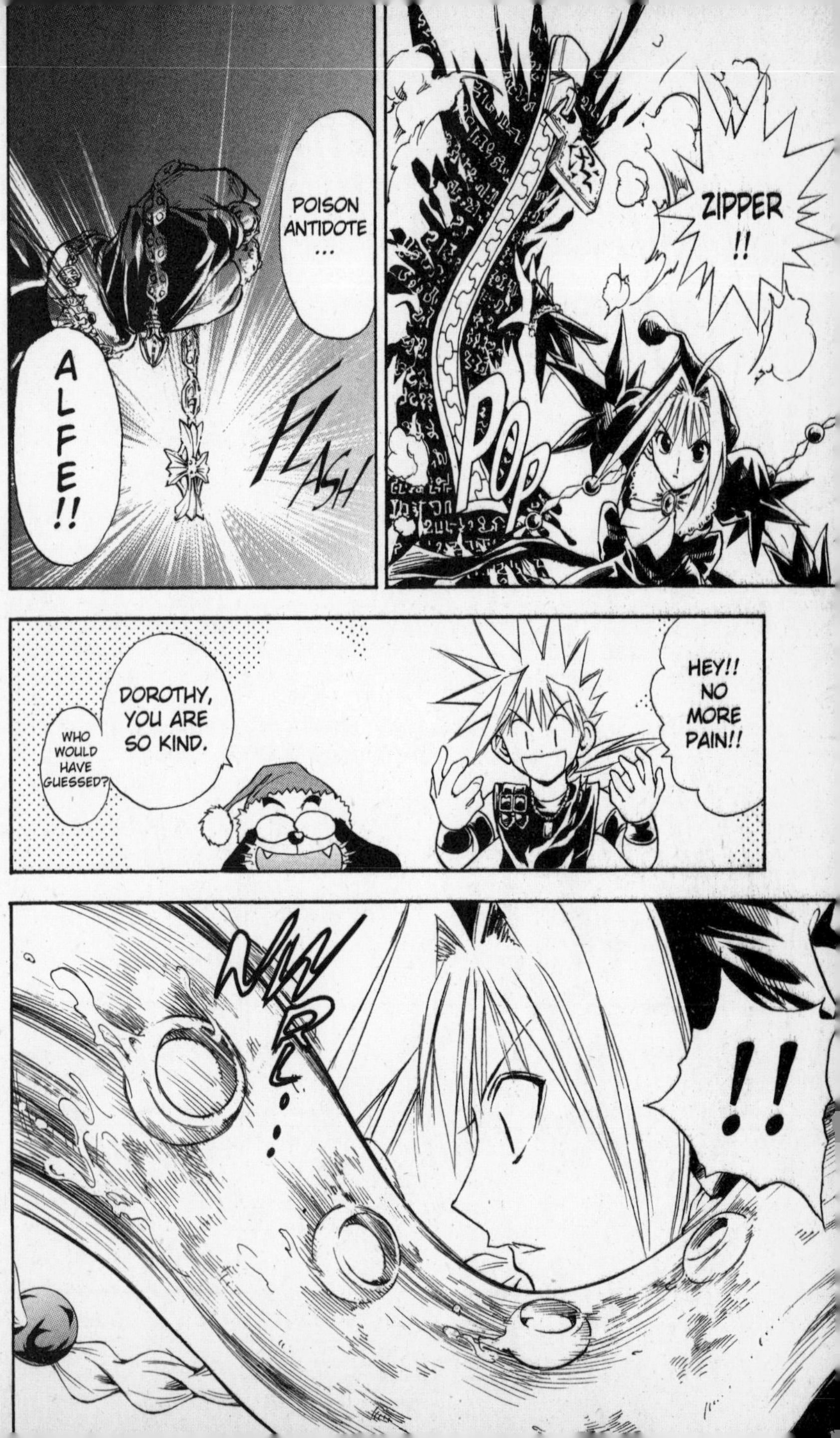
ZIPPER !!
POP
POISON ANTIDOTE ...
ALFE!!
FLASH
HEY!! NO MORE PAIN!!
DOROTHY, YOU ARE SO KIND.
WHO WOULD HAVE GUESSED?
!!
WHIRL...

NGHH....!!

TSK, SO CARELESS.

THAT WAS.... TOO EASY.

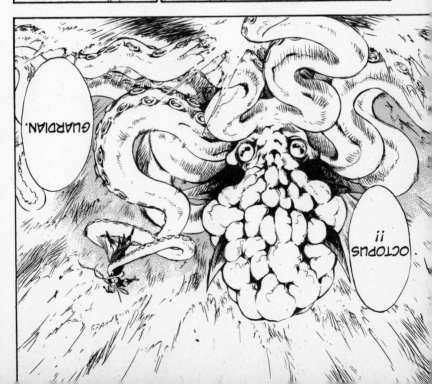

GUARDIAN.

OCTOPUS!!

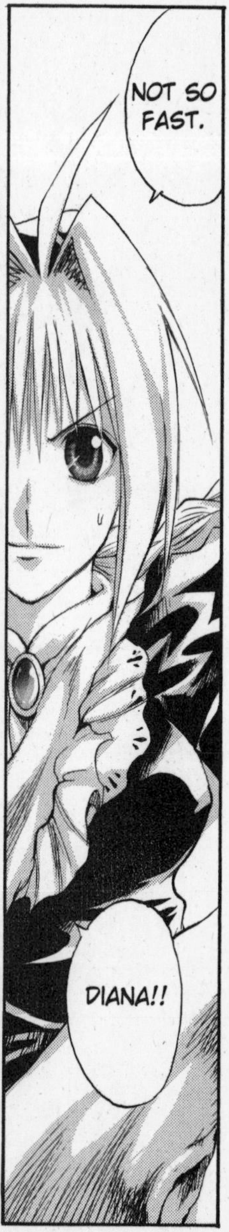
NOT SO FAST.
DIANA!!
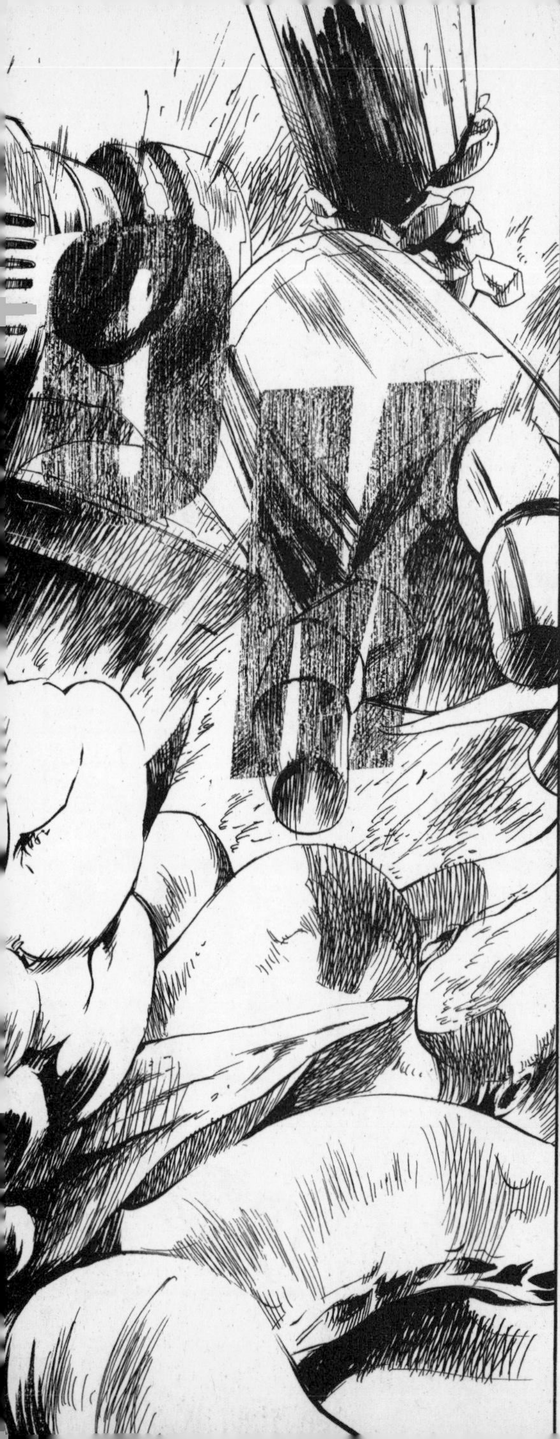

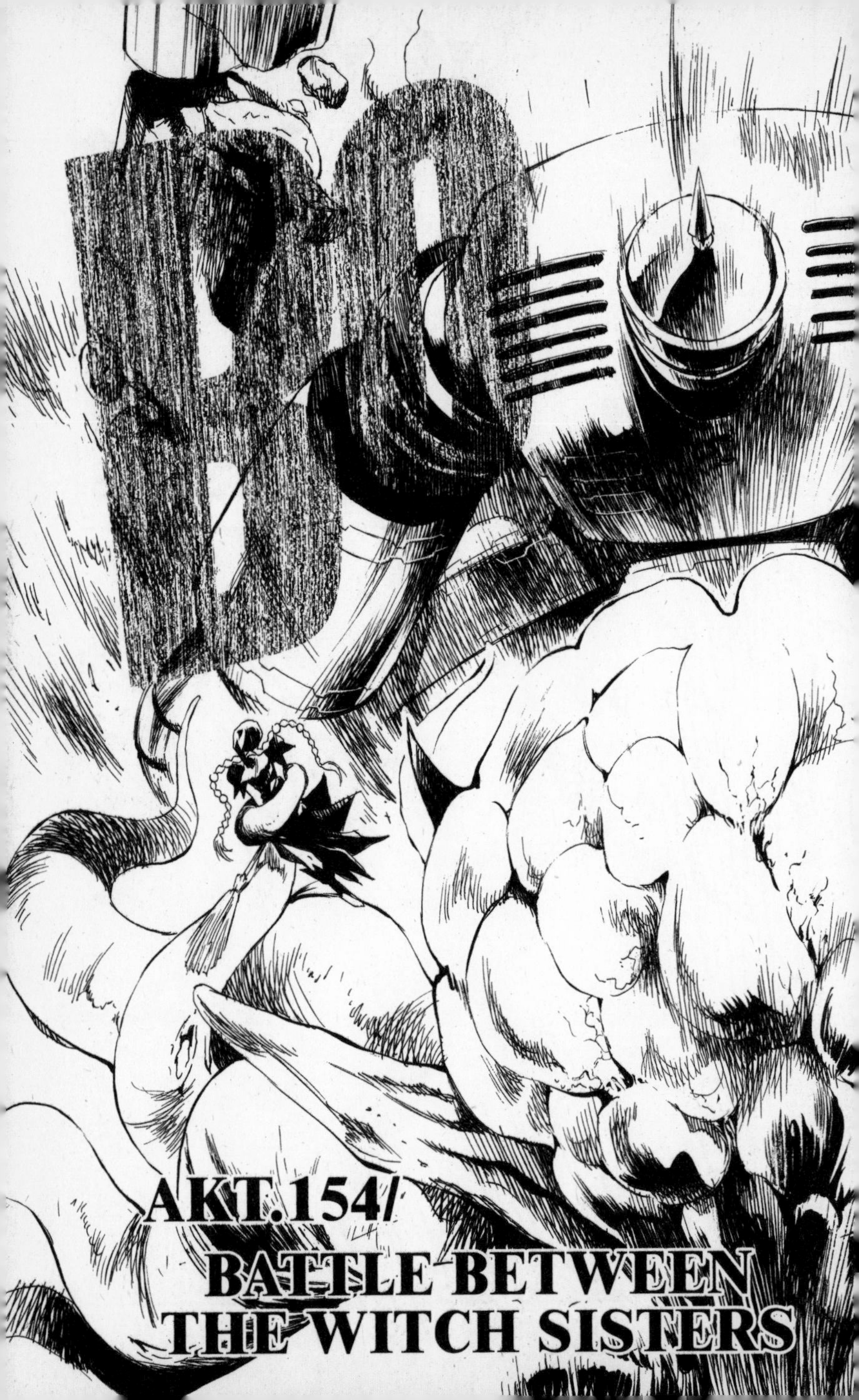
AKT.154/
BATTLE BETWEEN
THE WITCH SISTERS

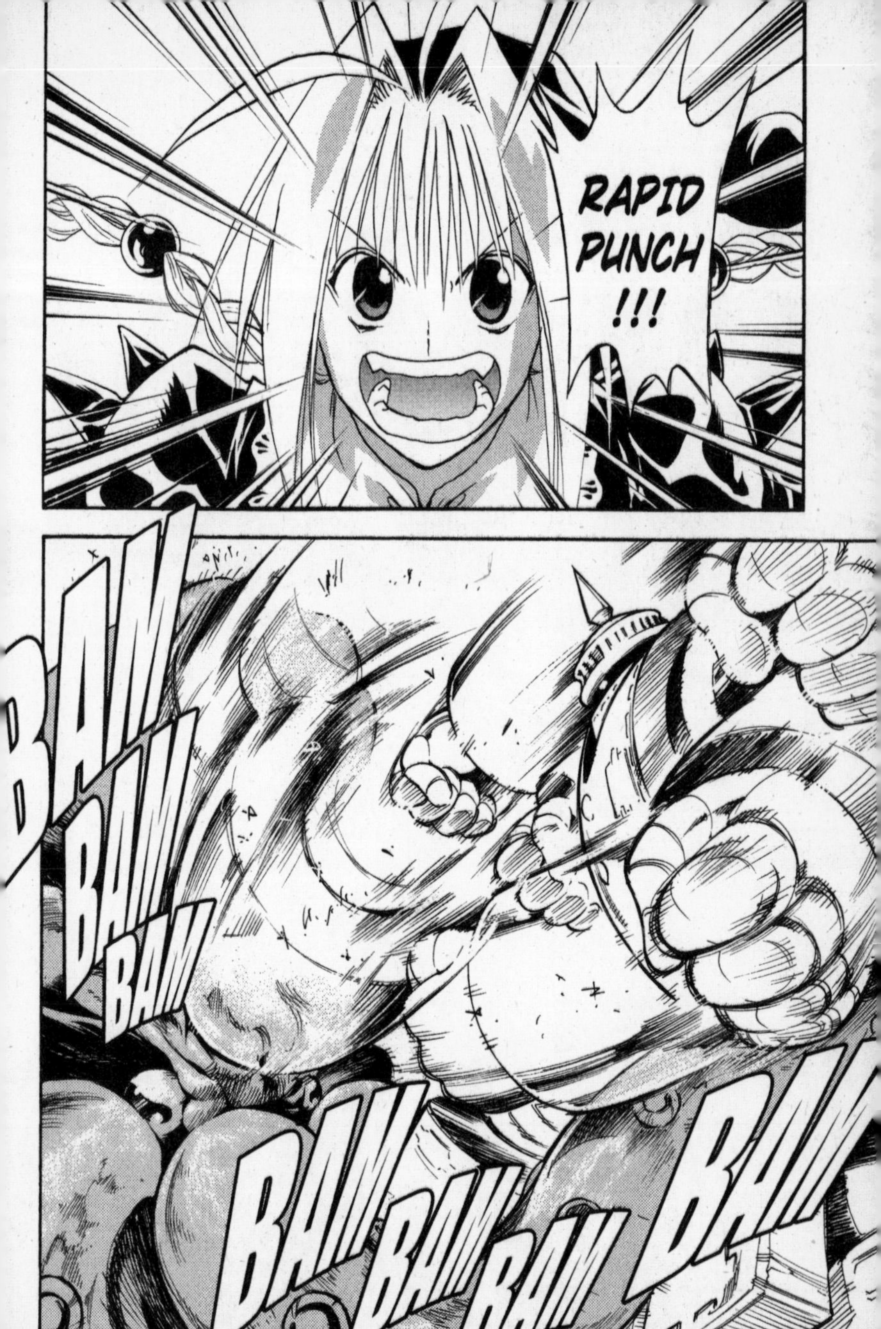
RAPID PUNCH !!!
BAM
BAM
BAM
BAM
BAM
BAM
BAM

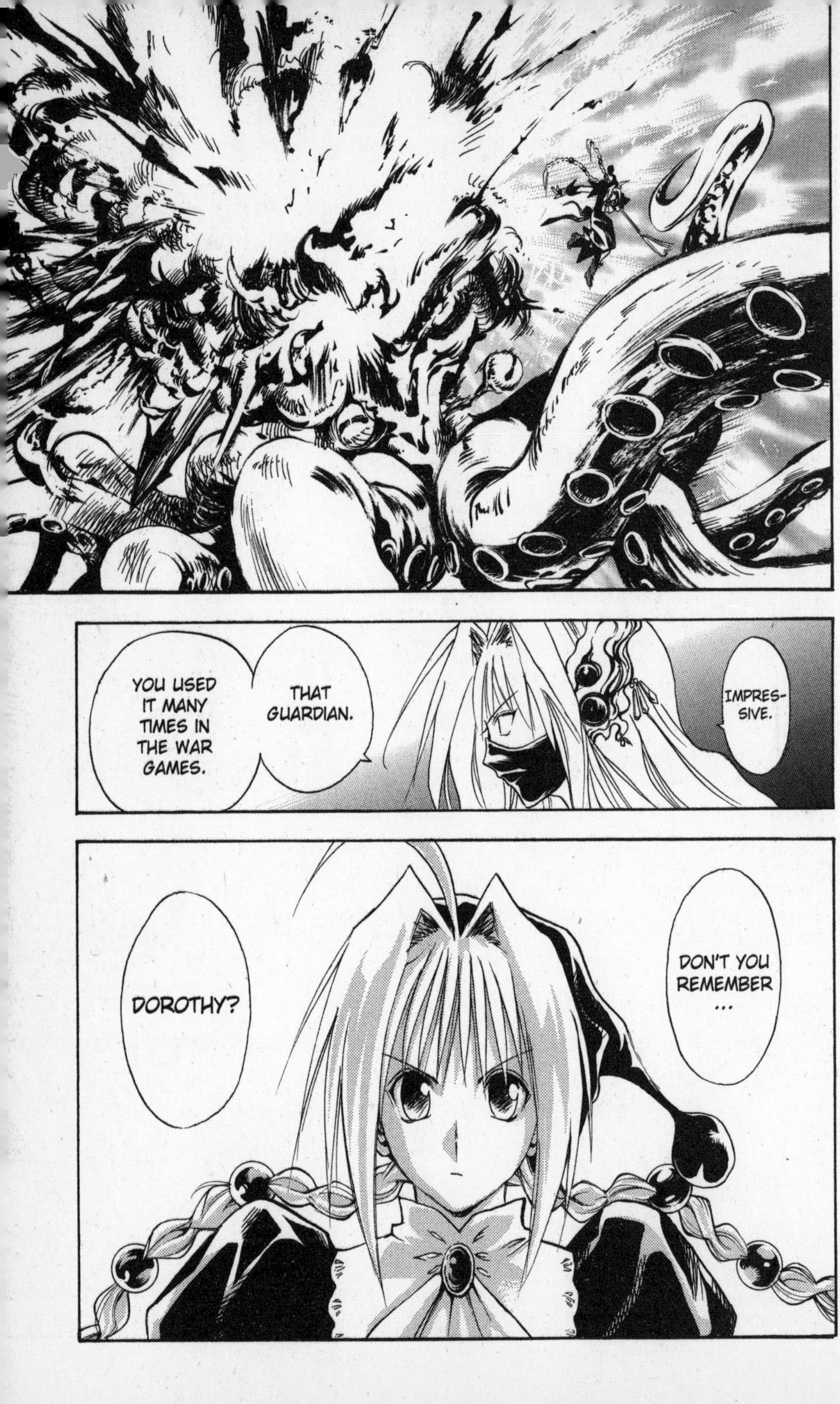
IMPRES-
SIVE.
THAT
GUARDIAN.
YOU USED
IT MANY
TIMES IN
THE WAR
GAMES.
DON'T YOU
REMEMBER
...
DOROTHY?

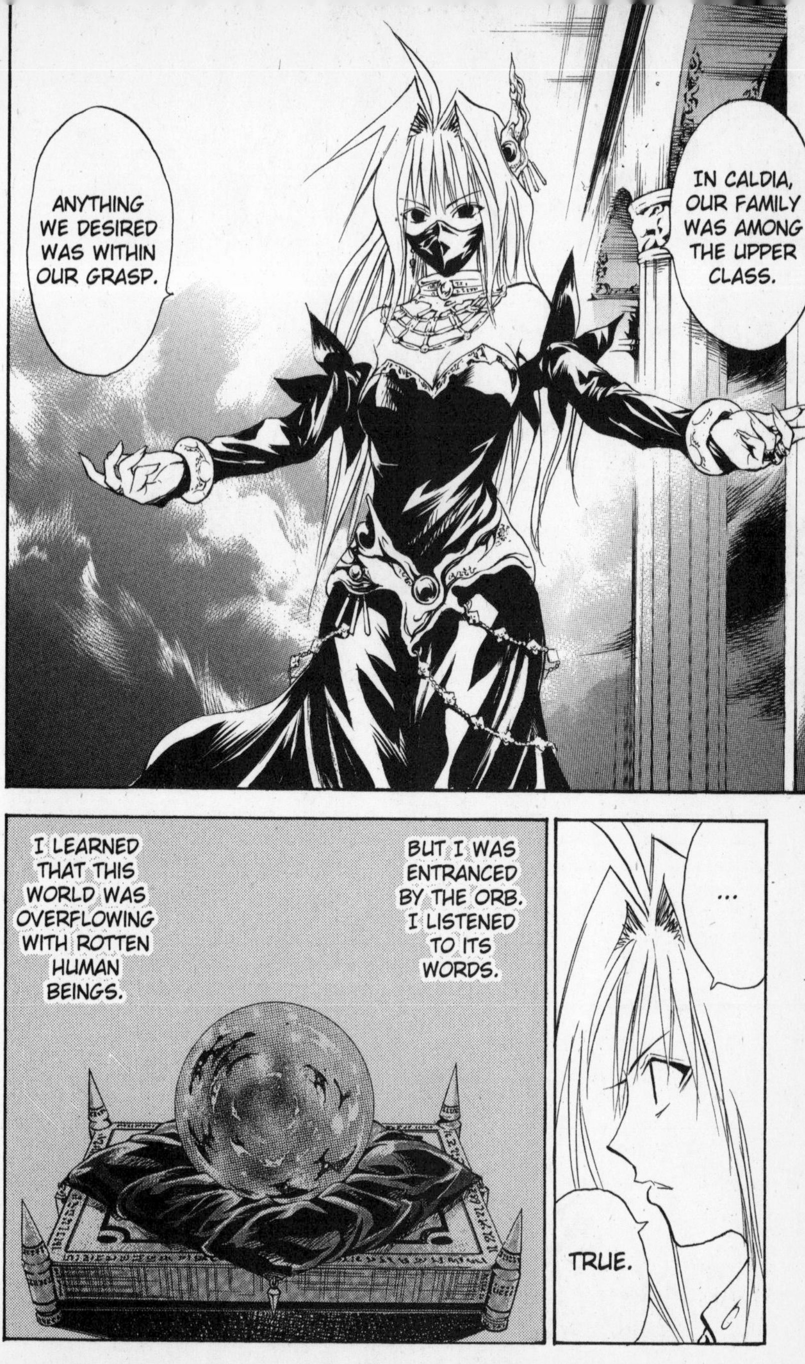
IN CALDIA, OUR FAMILY WAS AMONG THE UPPER CLASS.
ANYTHING WE DESIRED WAS WITHIN OUR GRASP.
...
TRUE.
BUT I WAS ENTRANCED BY THE ORB. I LISTENED TO ITS WORDS.
I LEARNED THAT THIS WORLD WAS OVERFLOWING WITH ROTTEN HUMAN BEINGS.

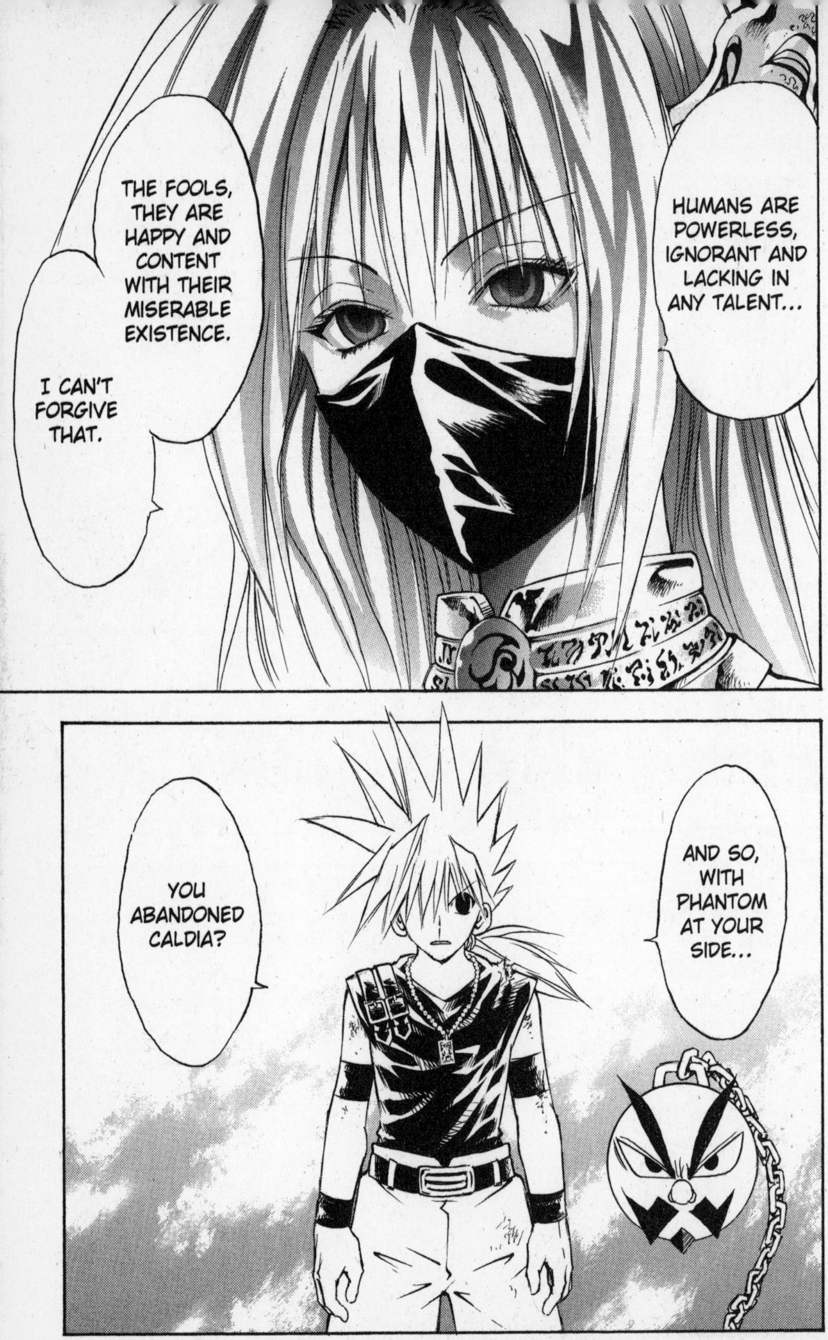
HUMANS ARE POWERLESS, IGNORANT AND LACKING IN ANY TALENT...
THE FOOLS, THEY ARE HAPPY AND CONTENT WITH THEIR MISERABLE EXISTENCE.
I CAN'T FORGIVE THAT.
AND SO, WITH PHANTOM AT YOUR SIDE...
YOU ABANDONED CALDIA?

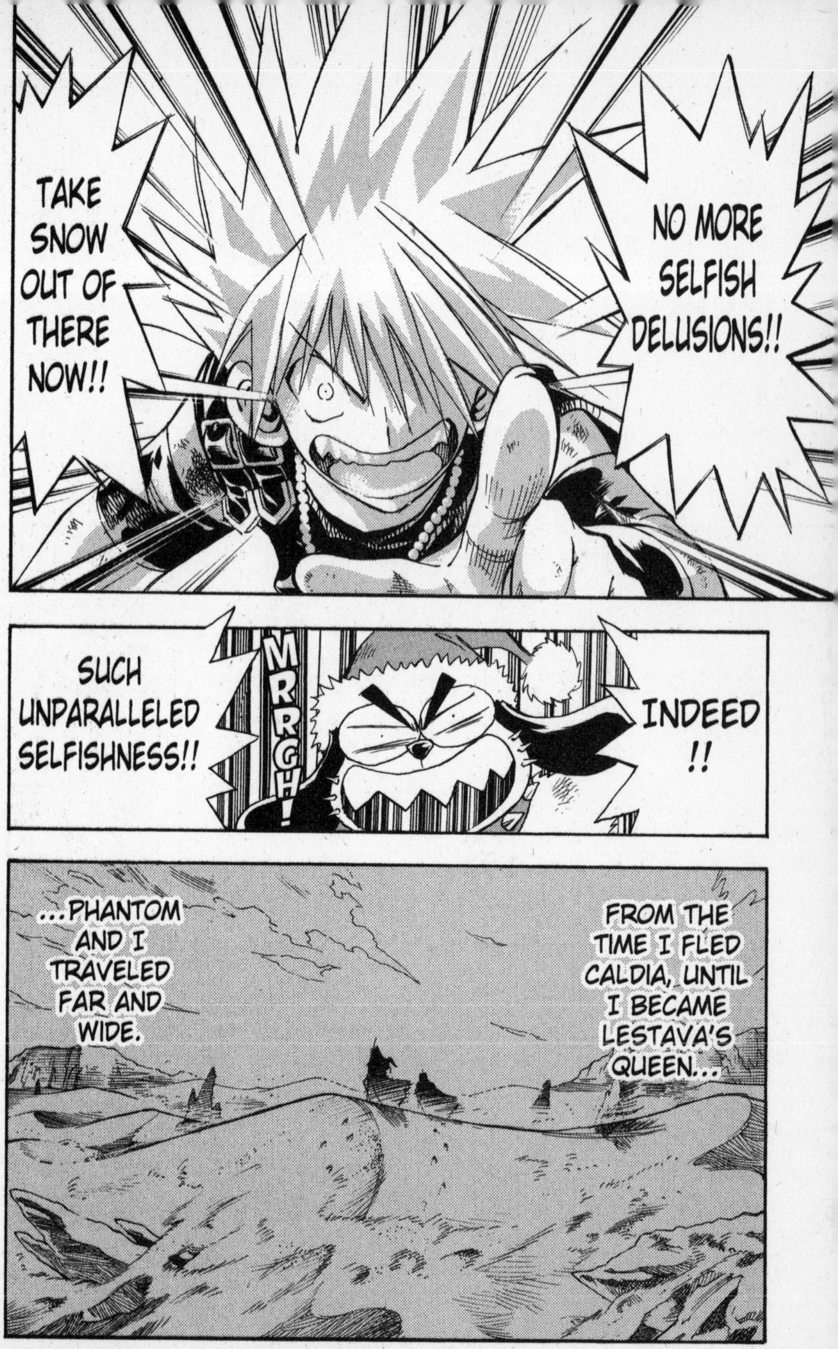
NO MORE SELFISH DELUSIONS!!
TAKE SNOW OUT OF THERE NOW!!
INDEED!!
MRRGH!
SUCH UNPARALLELED SELFISHNESS!!
FROM THE TIME I FLED CALDIA, UNTIL I BECAME LESTAVA'S QUEEN...
...PHANTOM AND I TRAVELED FAR AND WIDE.

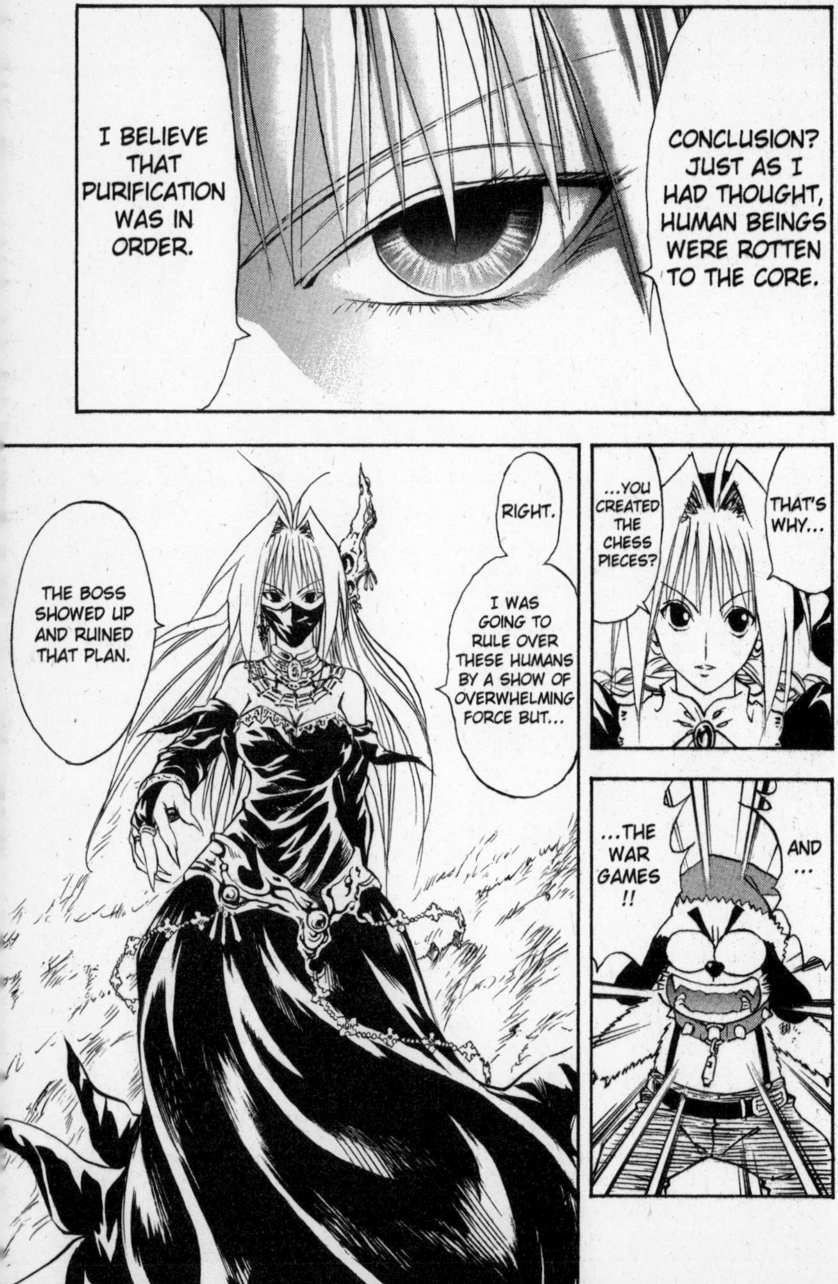
CONCLUSION? JUST AS I HAD THOUGHT, HUMAN BEINGS WERE ROTTEN TO THE CORE.
I BELIEVE THAT PURIFICATION WAS IN ORDER.
THAT'S WHY...
...YOU CREATED THE CHESS PIECES?
AND ...
...THE WAR GAMES !!
RIGHT.
I WAS GOING TO RULE OVER THESE HUMANS BY A SHOW OF OVERWHELMING FORCE BUT...
THE BOSS SHOWED UP AND RUINED THAT PLAN.

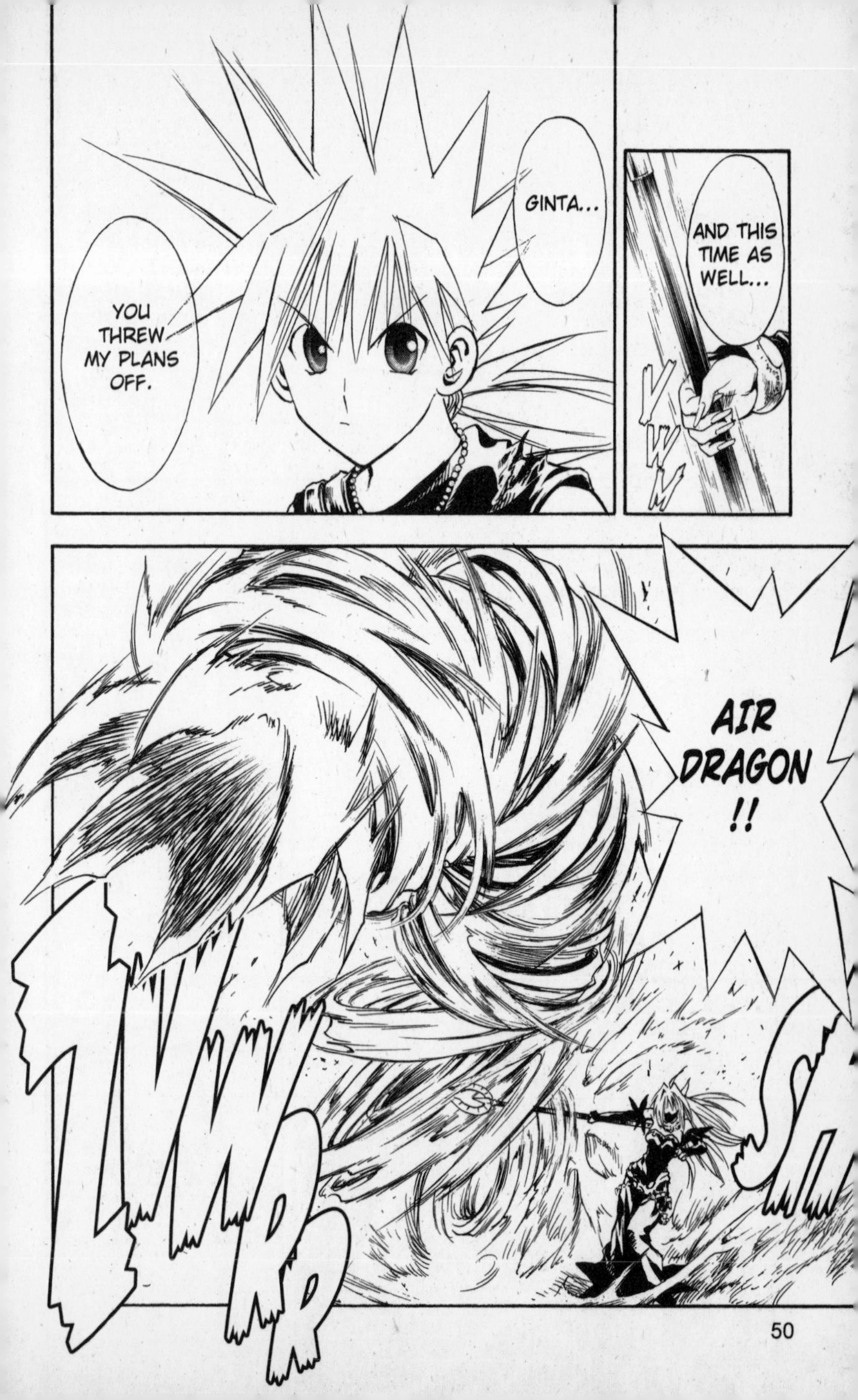
AND THIS TIME AS WELL...
VWM
GINTA...
YOU THREW MY PLANS OFF.
AIR DRAGON !!

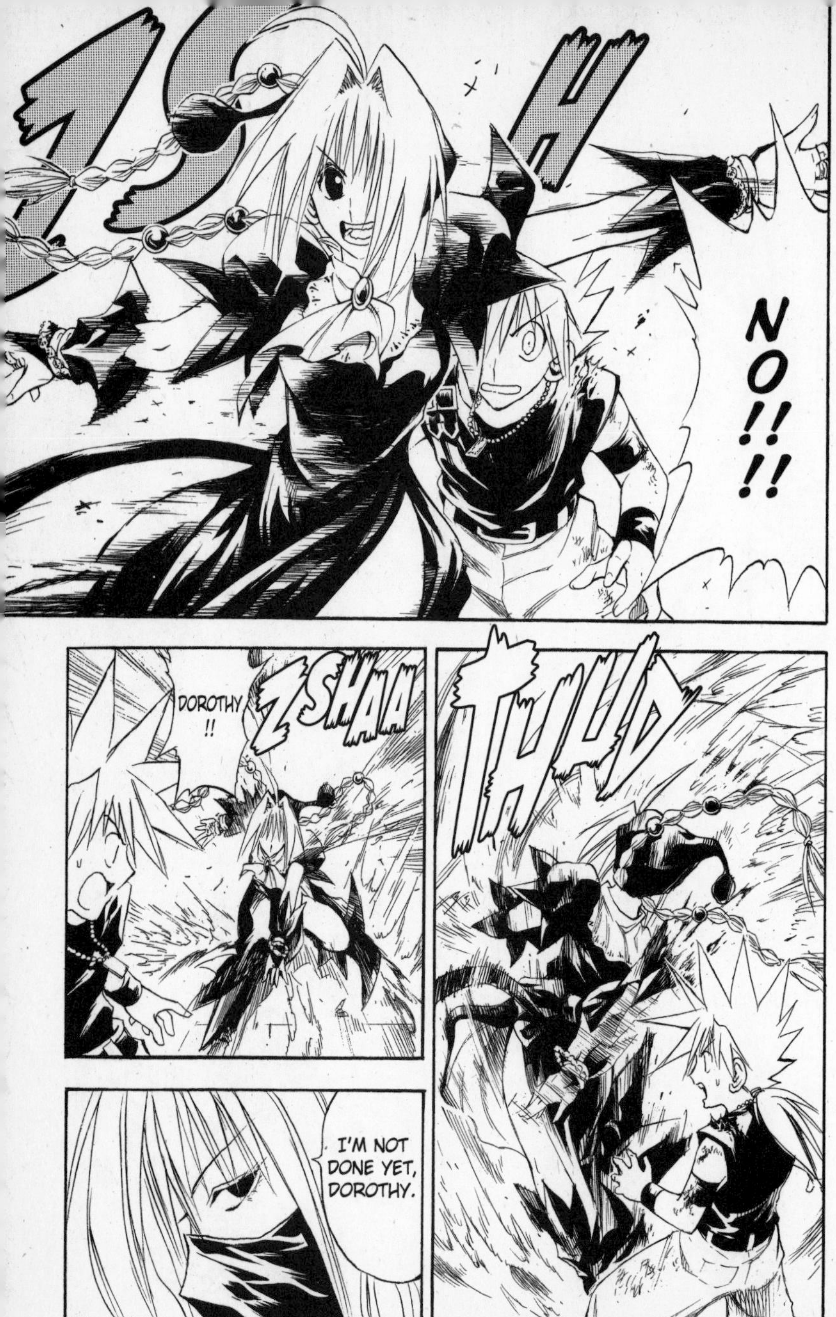
NO!!!!
THUD
DORHOTY !!
ZSHAA
I'M NOT DONE YET, DOROTHY.

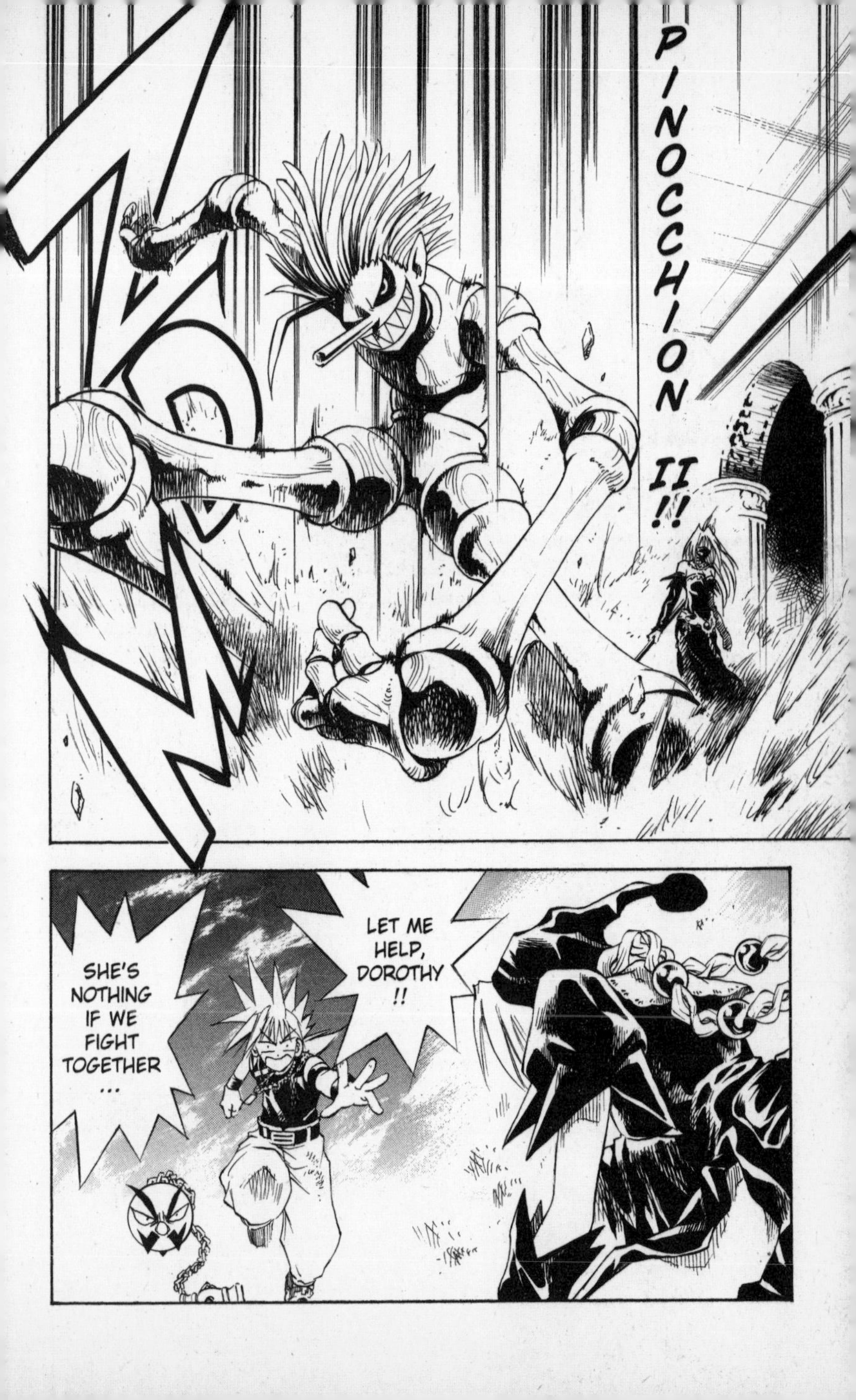
PINOCCHION II!!
LET ME HELP, DOROTHY!!
SHE'S NOTHING IF WE FIGHT TOGETHER...

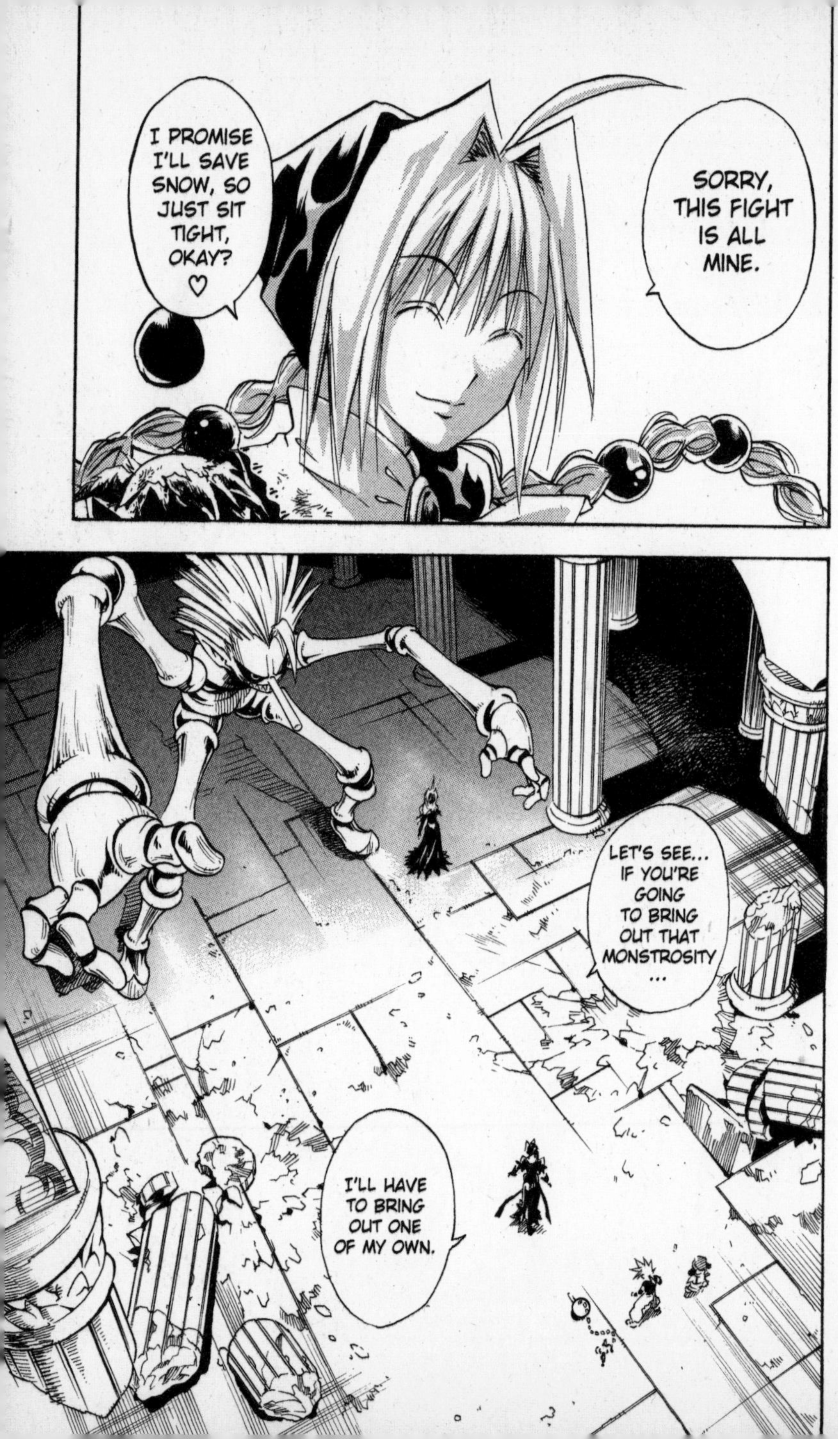
SORRY, THIS FIGHT IS ALL MINE.
I PROMISE I'LL SAVE SNOW, SO JUST SIT TIGHT, OKAY? ♡
LET'S SEE... IF YOU'RE GOING TO BRING OUT THAT MONSTROSITY...
I'LL HAVE TO BRING OUT ONE OF MY OWN.

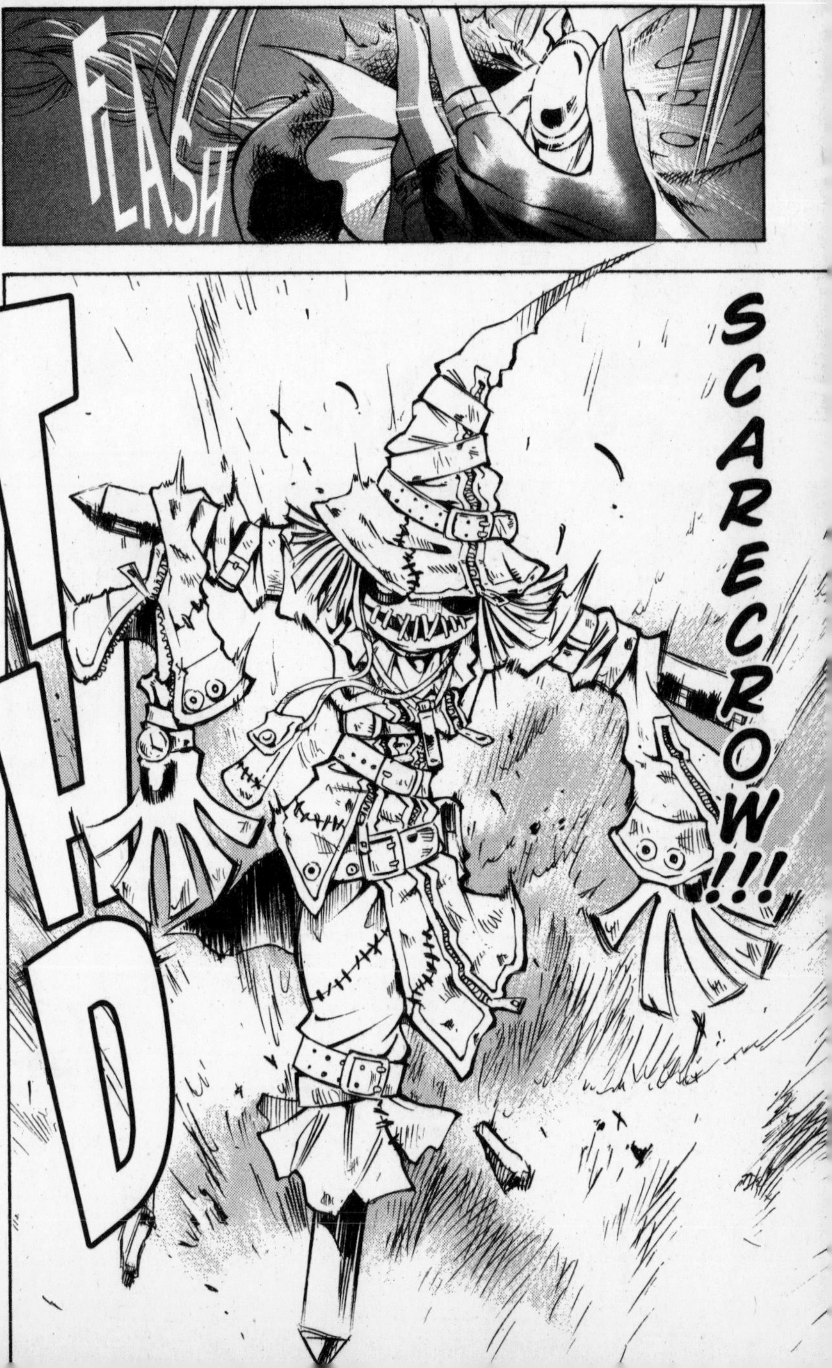
FLASH
SCARECROW!!!

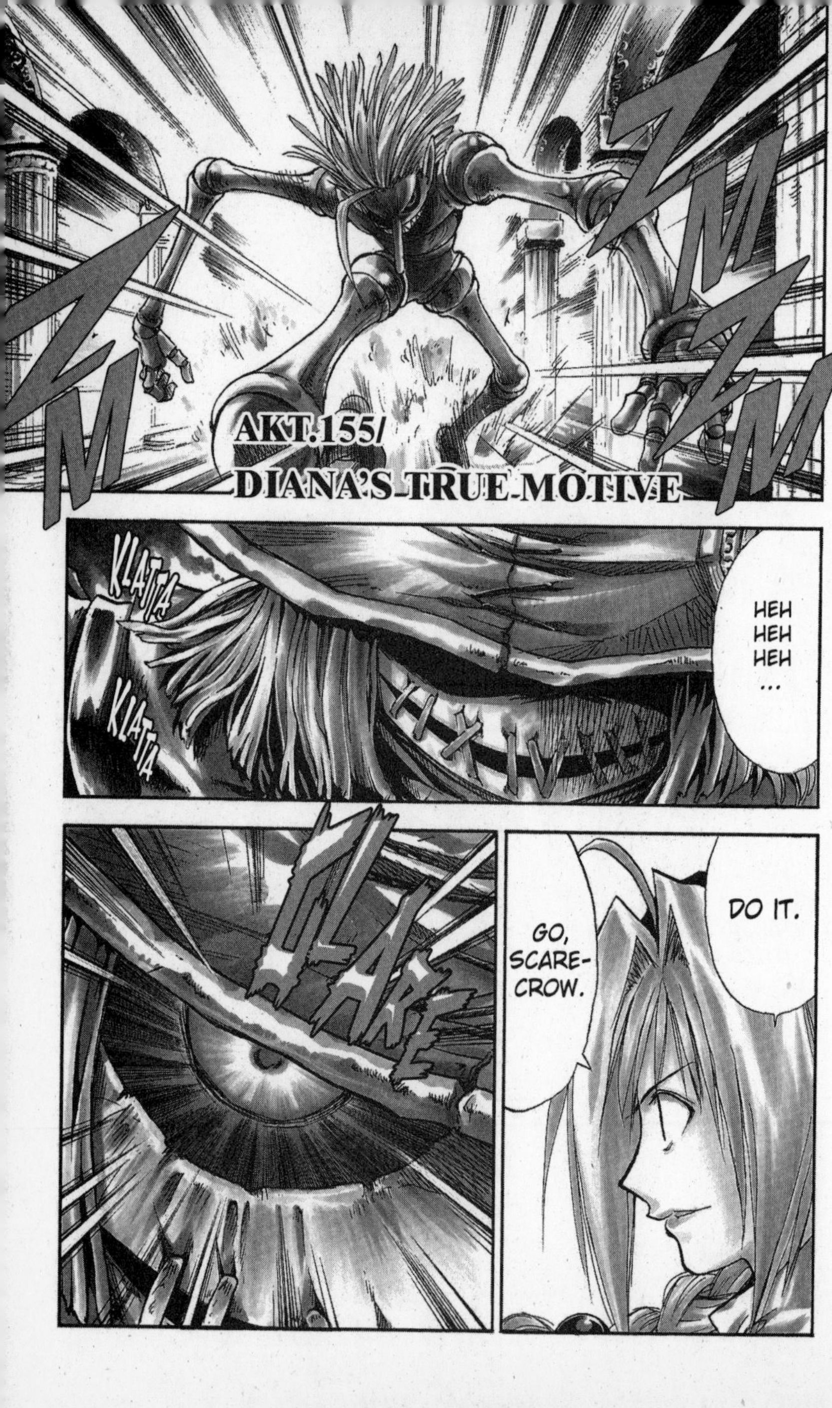
ZMM
ZM
AKT.155/
DIANA'S TRUE MOTIVE
HEH HEH HEH...
KLATTA
KLATTA
DO IT.
GO, SCARE-CROW.
GLARE

AKT.155/ DIANA'S TRUE MOTIVE

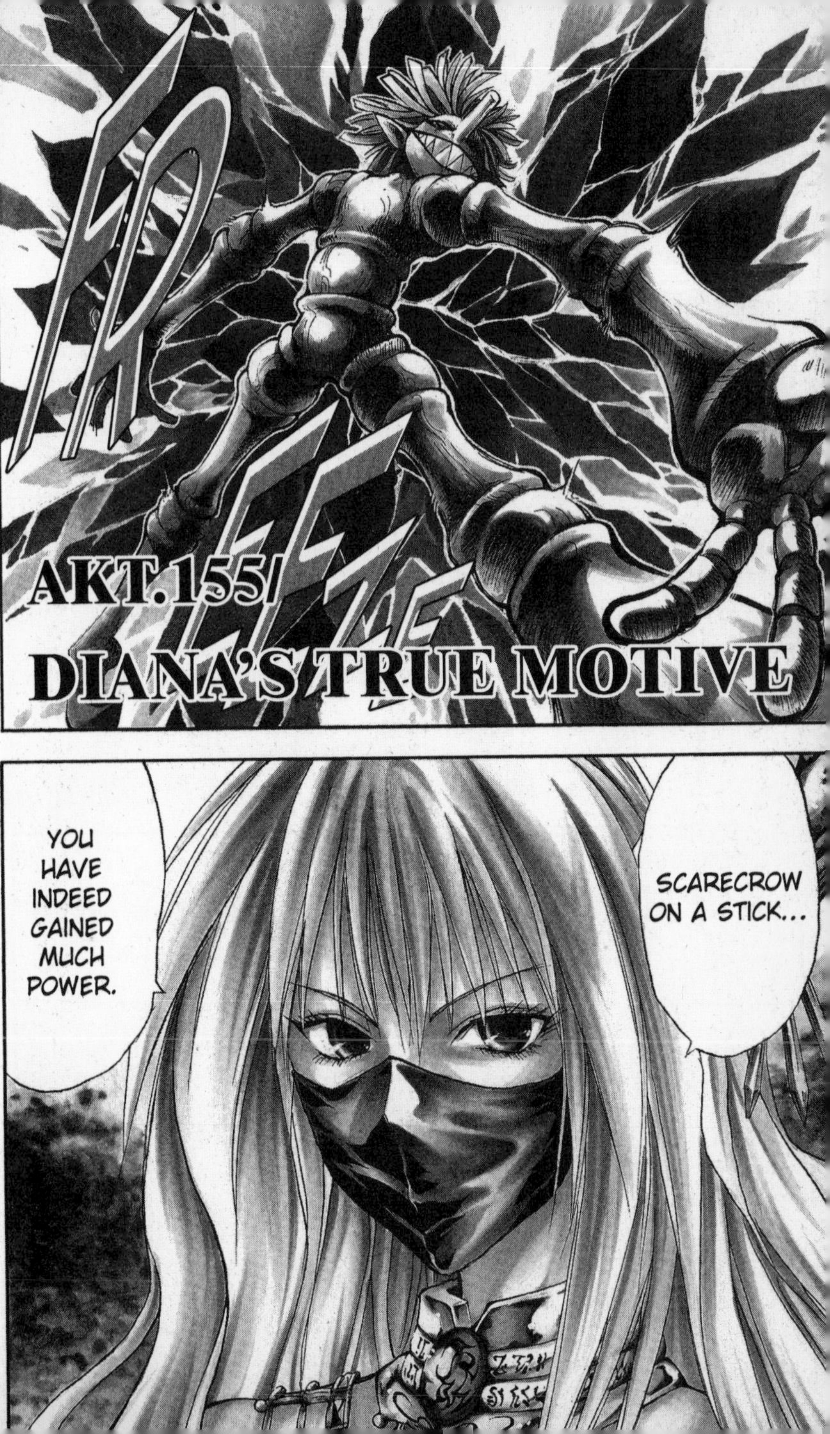
SCARECROW ON A STICK...
YOU HAVE INDEED GAINED MUCH POWER.

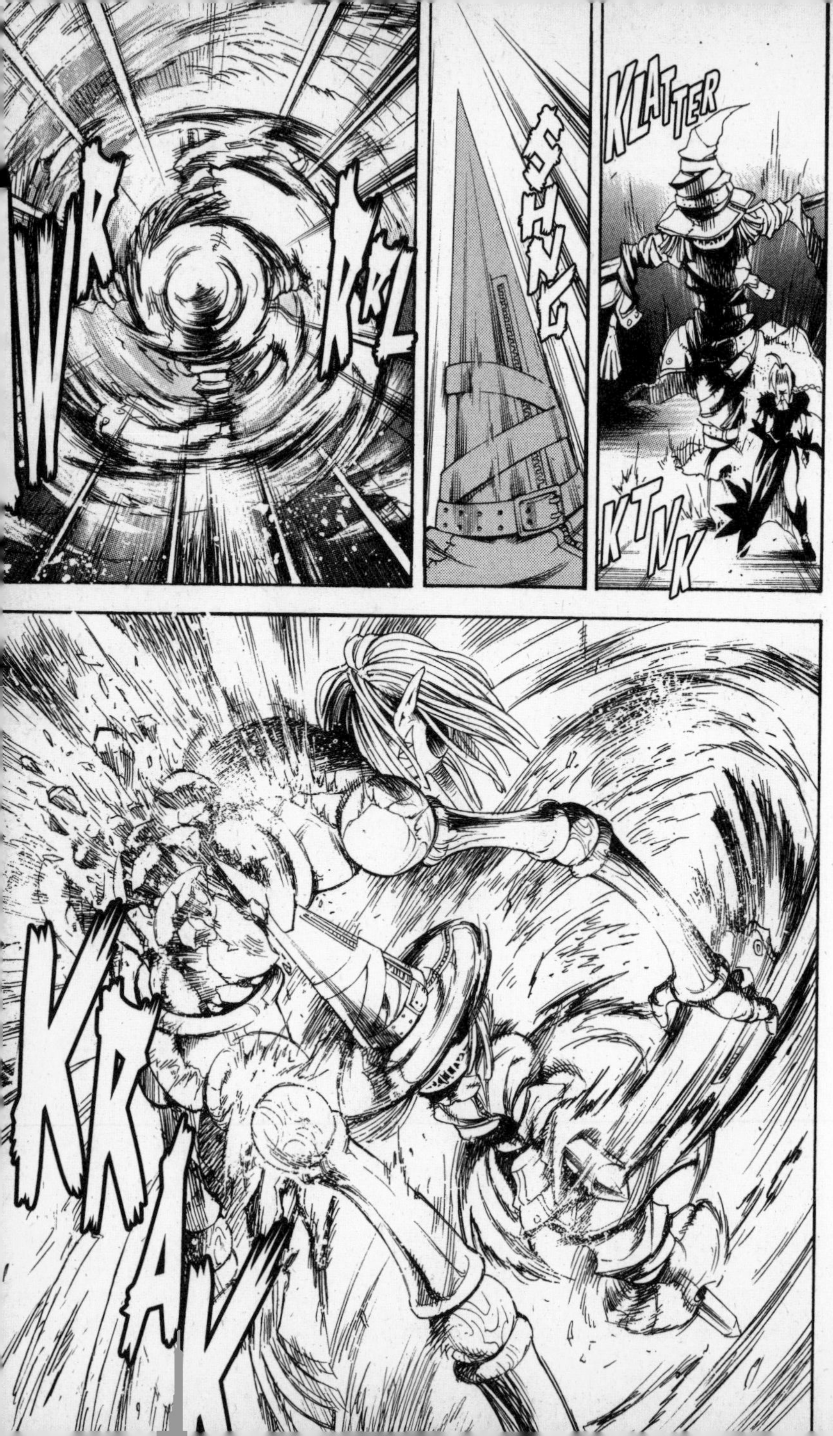
KLATTER
KTNK
SHING
KRL
WR
KRAK

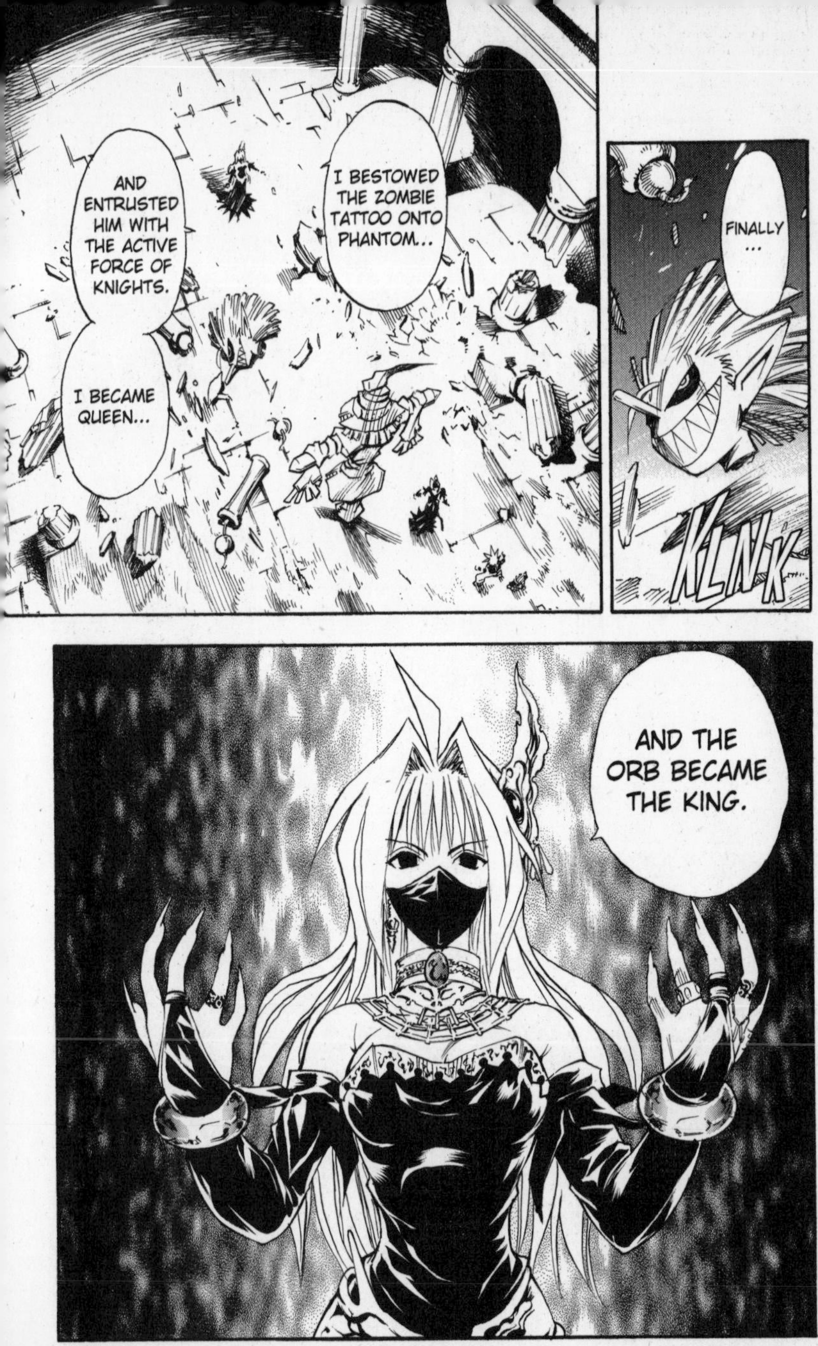
FINALLY ...
KLNK
I BESTOWED THE ZOMBIE TATTOO ONTO PHANTOM...
AND ENTRUSTED HIM WITH THE ACTIVE FORCE OF KNIGHTS.
I BECAME QUEEN...
AND THE ORB BECAME THE KING.

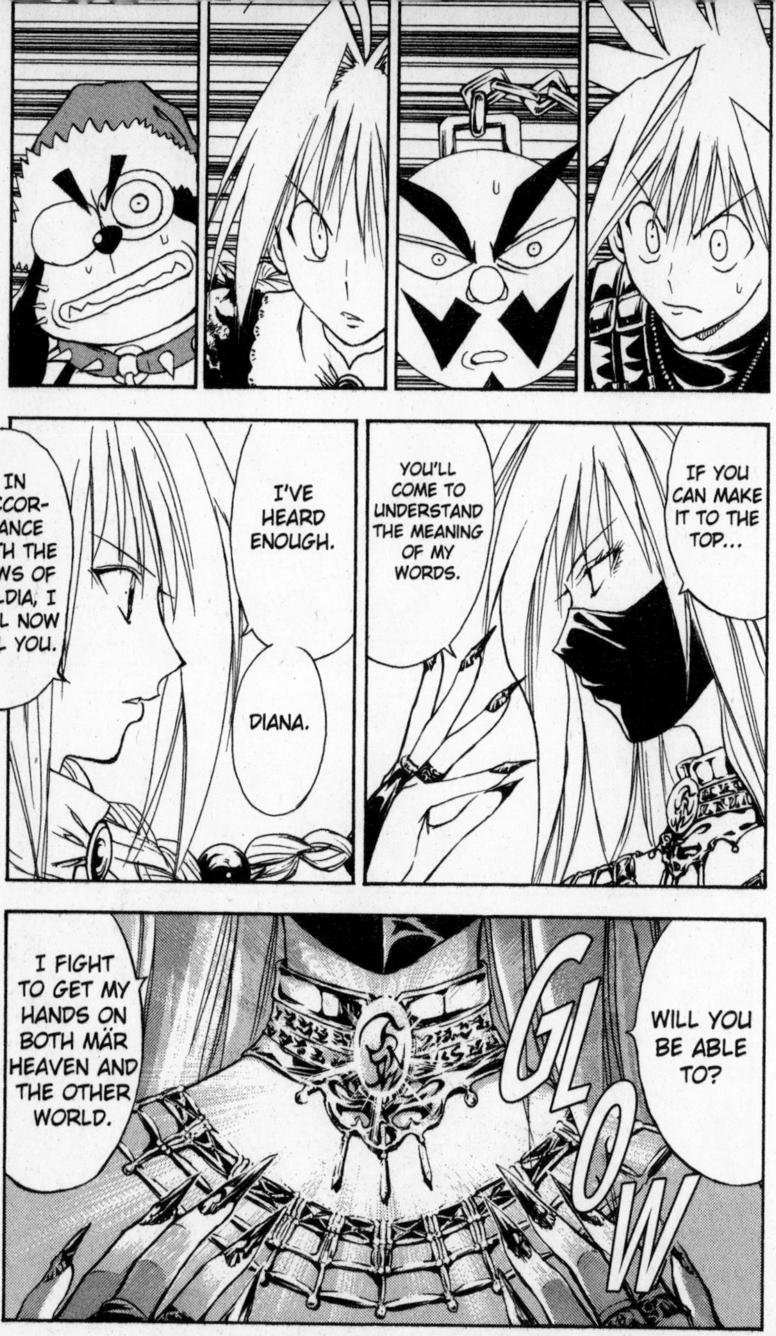
IF YOU CAN MAKE IT TO THE TOP...
YOU'LL COME TO UNDERSTAND THE MEANING OF MY WORDS.
I'VE HEARD ENOUGH.
DIANA.
IN ACCORDANCE WITH THE LAWS OF CALDIA, I WILL NOW KILL YOU.
WILL YOU BE ABLE TO?
GLOW
I FIGHT TO GET MY HANDS ON BOTH MÄR HEAVEN AND THE OTHER WORLD.

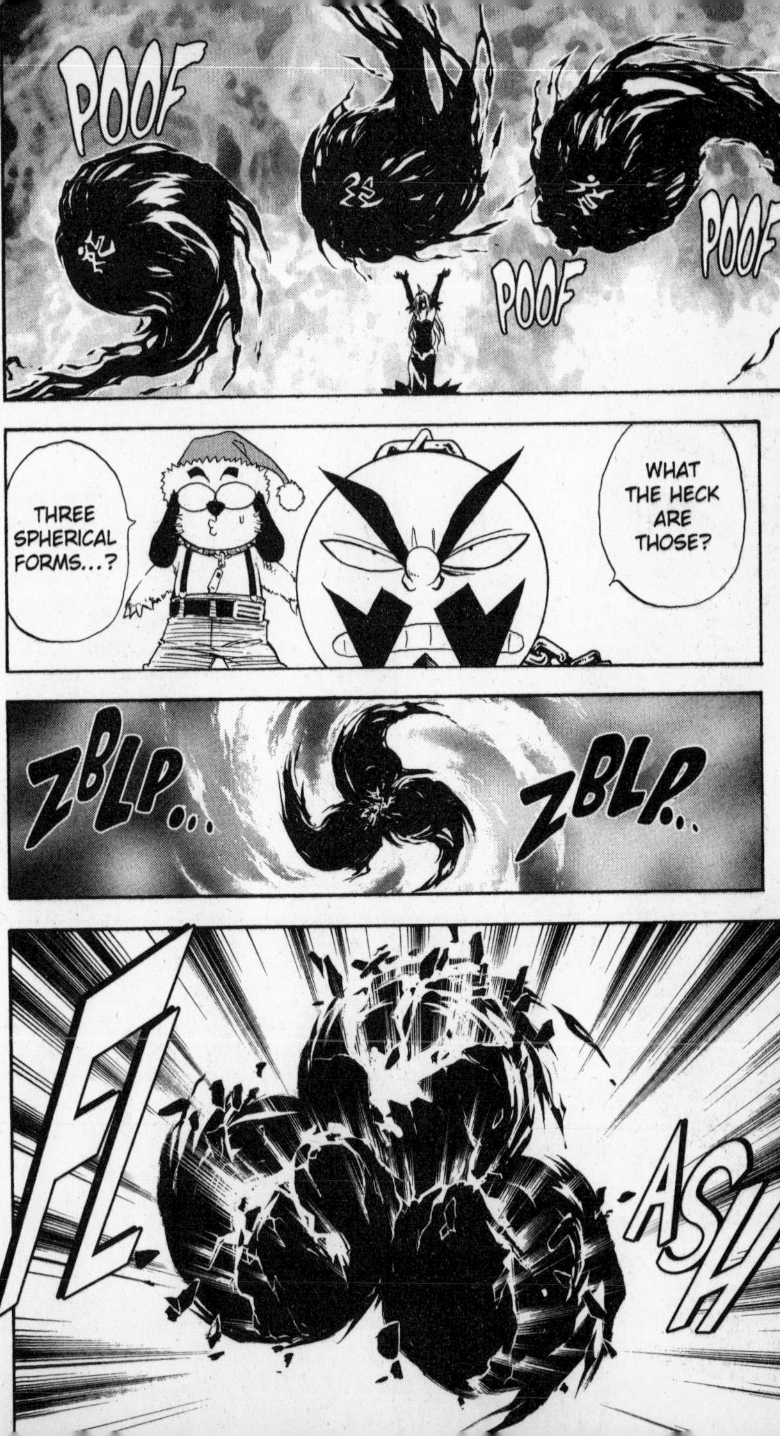
POOF
POOF
POOF
WHAT THE HECK ARE THOSE?
THREE SPHERICAL FORMS...?
ZBLP...
ZBLP...
FL-
-ASH

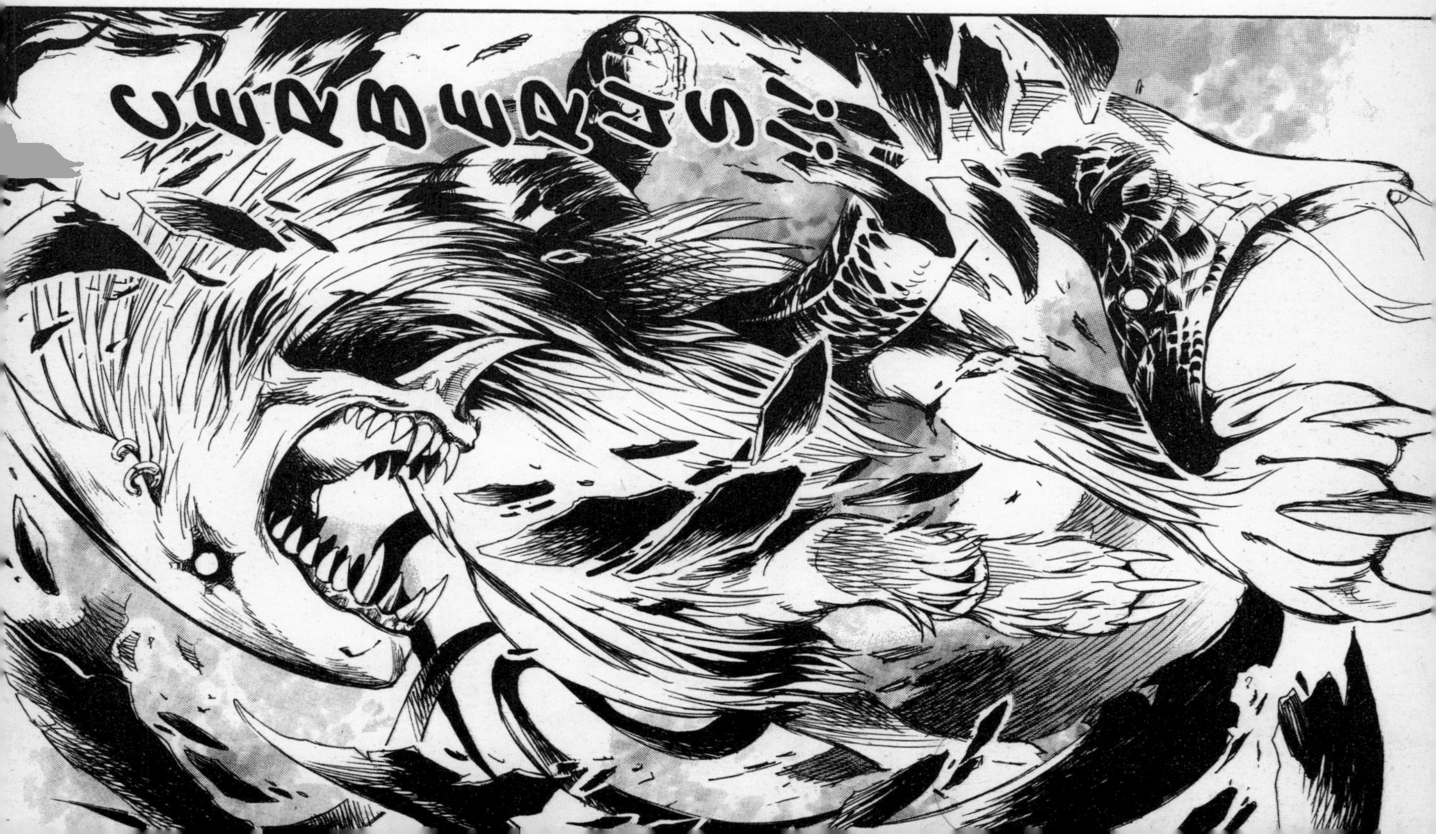
CERBERUS!!

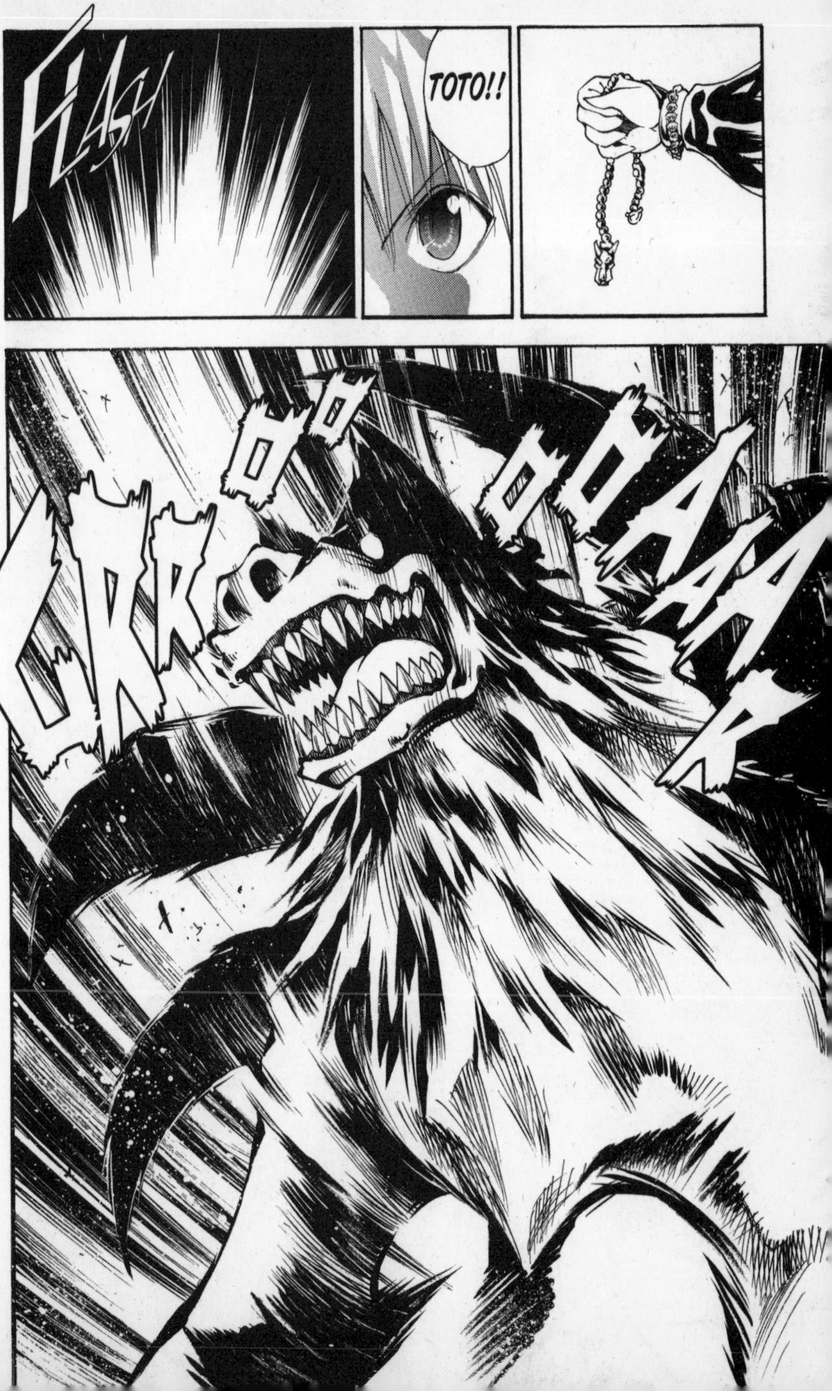
TOTO!!
FLASH
GRROOOOAAAR

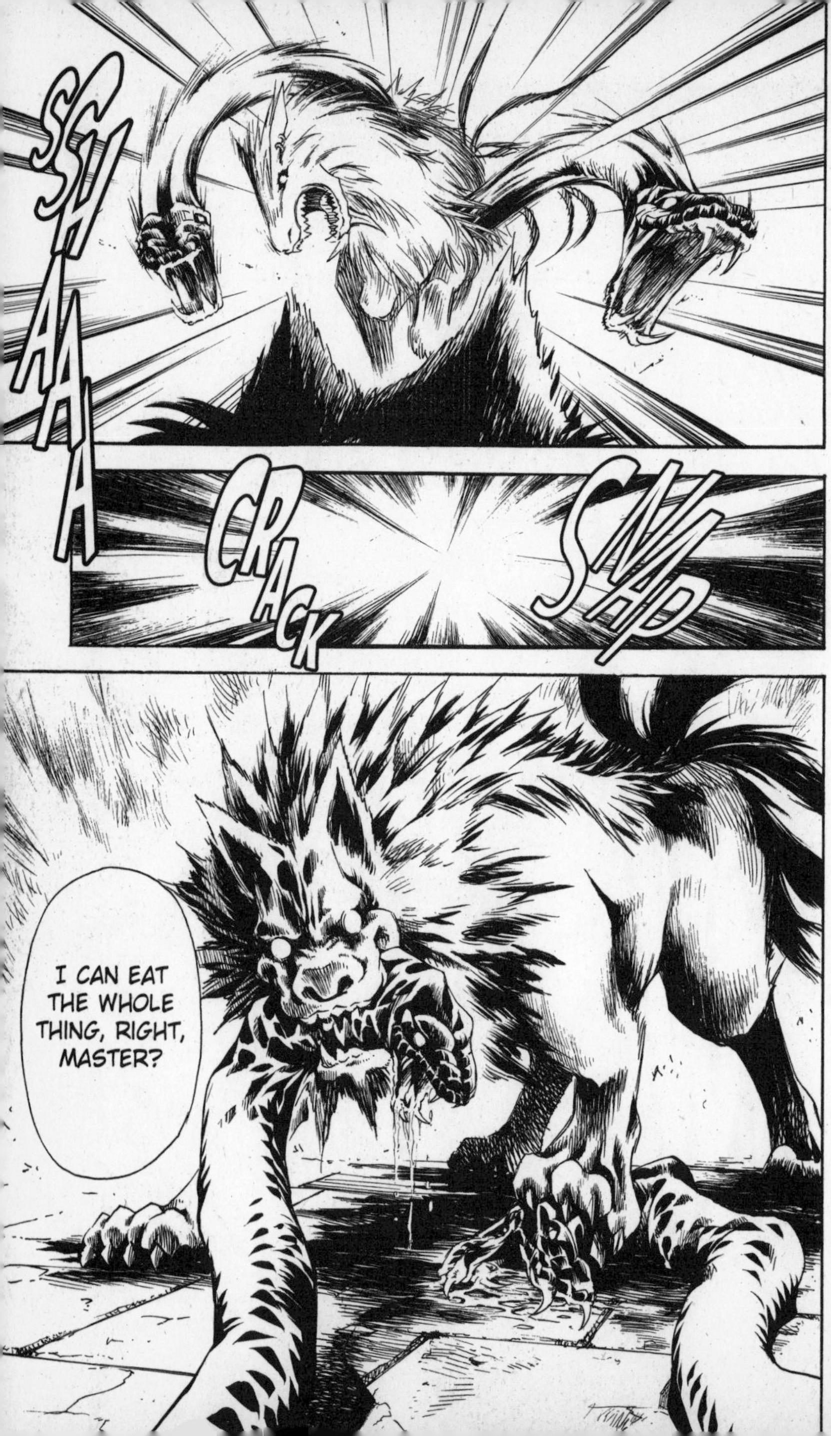
SCHAAAA
SNAP
CRACK
I CAN EAT THE WHOLE THING, RIGHT, MASTER?

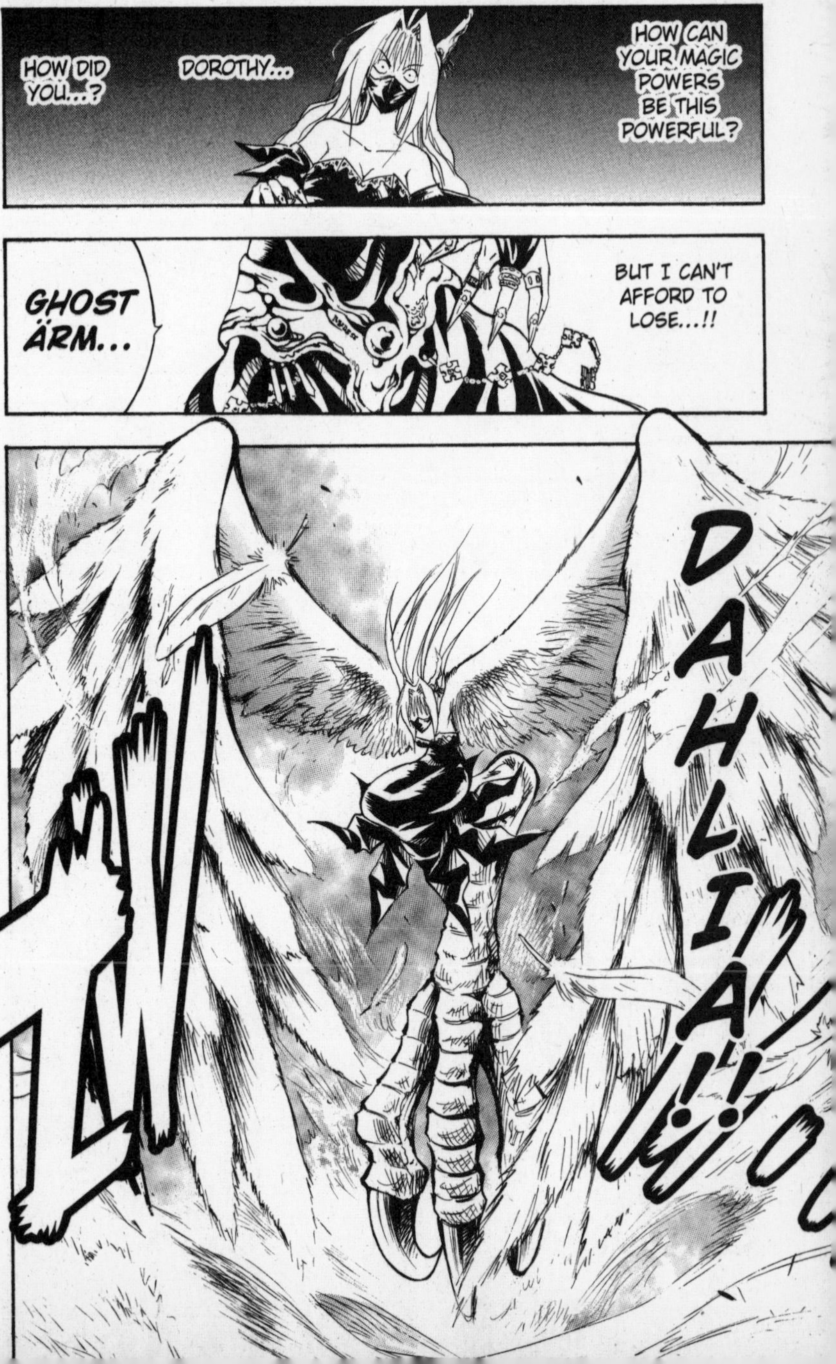
HOW CAN YOUR MAGIC POWERS BE THIS POWERFUL?
DOROTHY...
HOW DID YOU...?
BUT I CAN'T AFFORD TO LOSE...!!
GHOST ÄRM...
DAHLIA!!
OOO

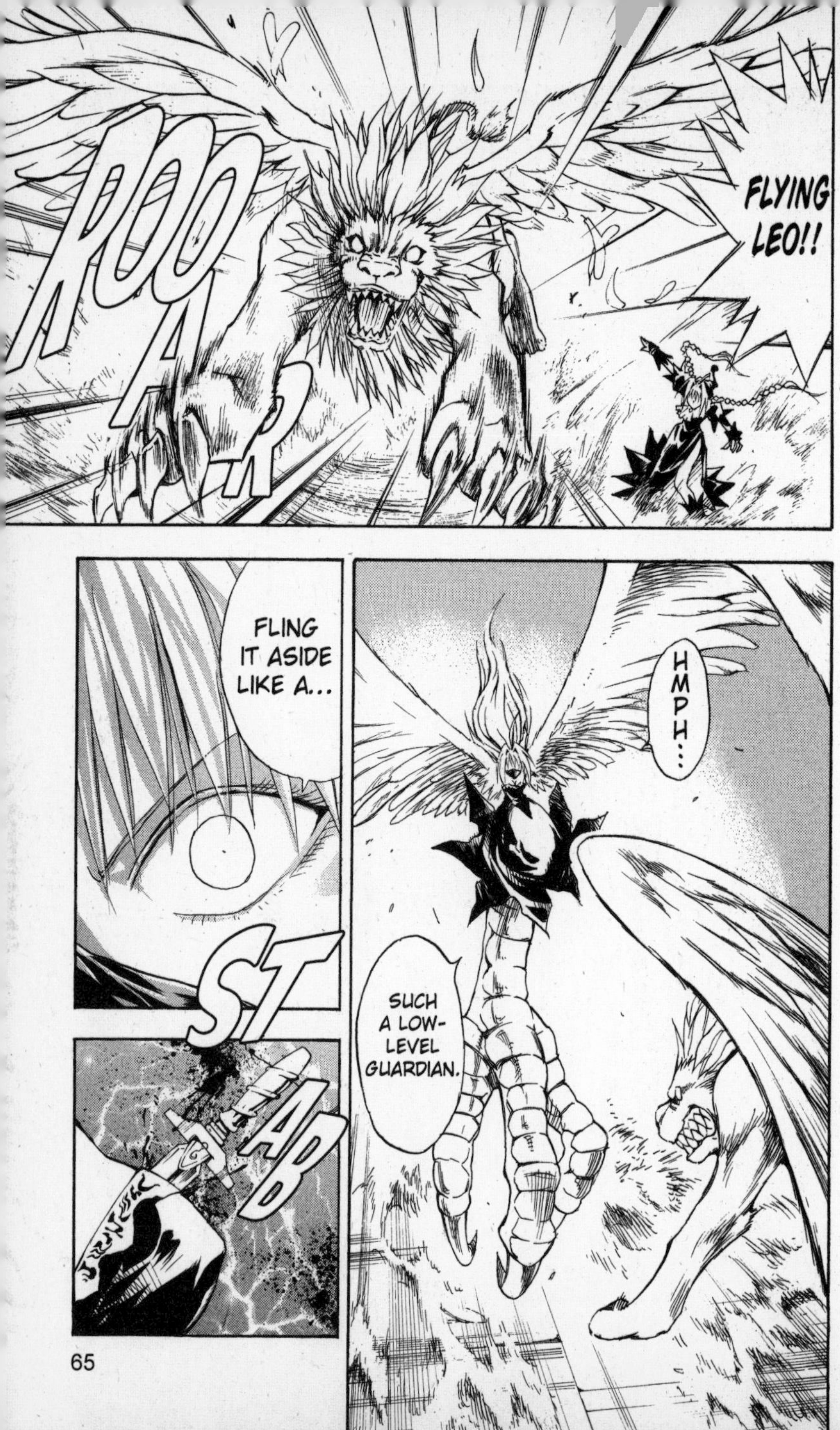
FLYING LEO!!
ROOOAAR
HMPH...
SUCH A LOW-LEVEL GUARDIAN.
FLING IT ASIDE LIKE A...
STAB

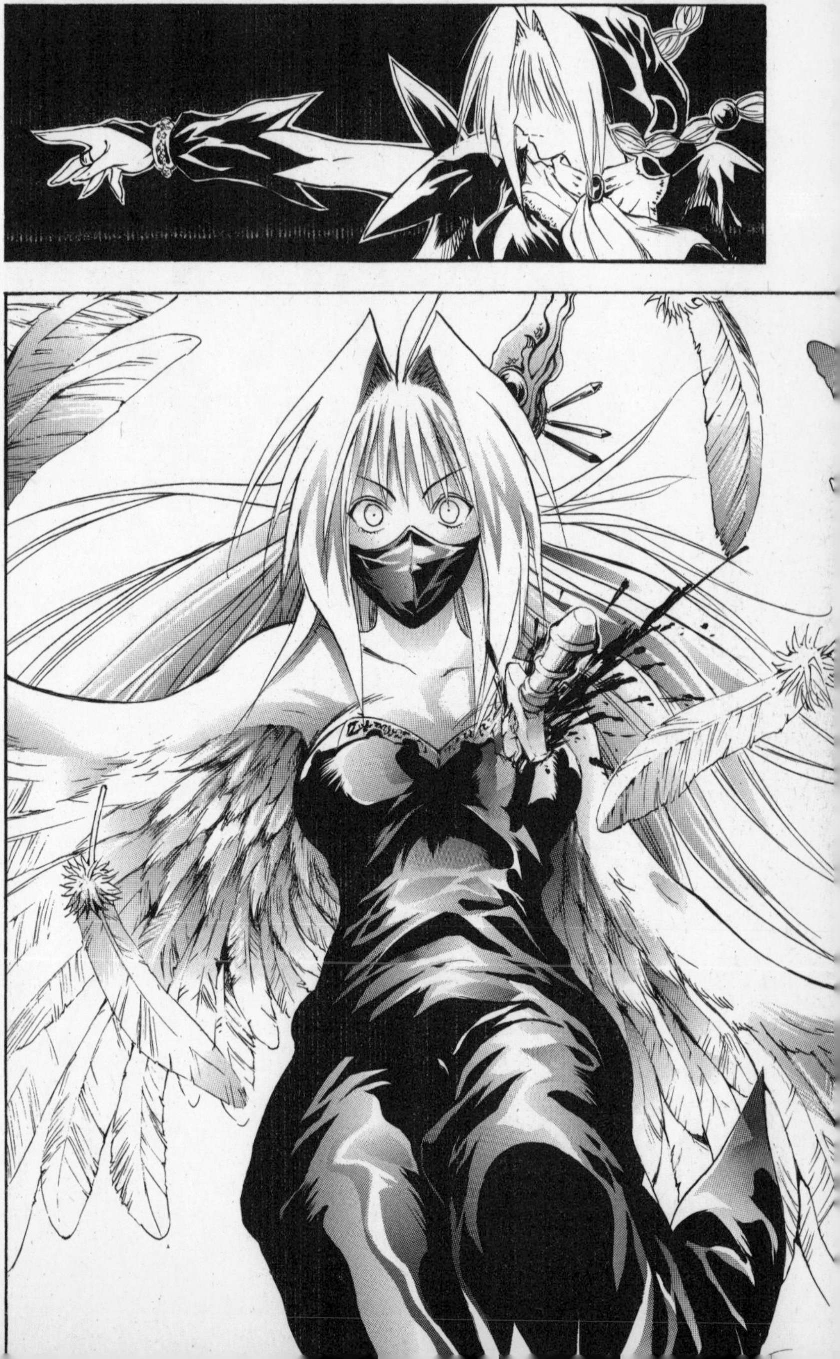

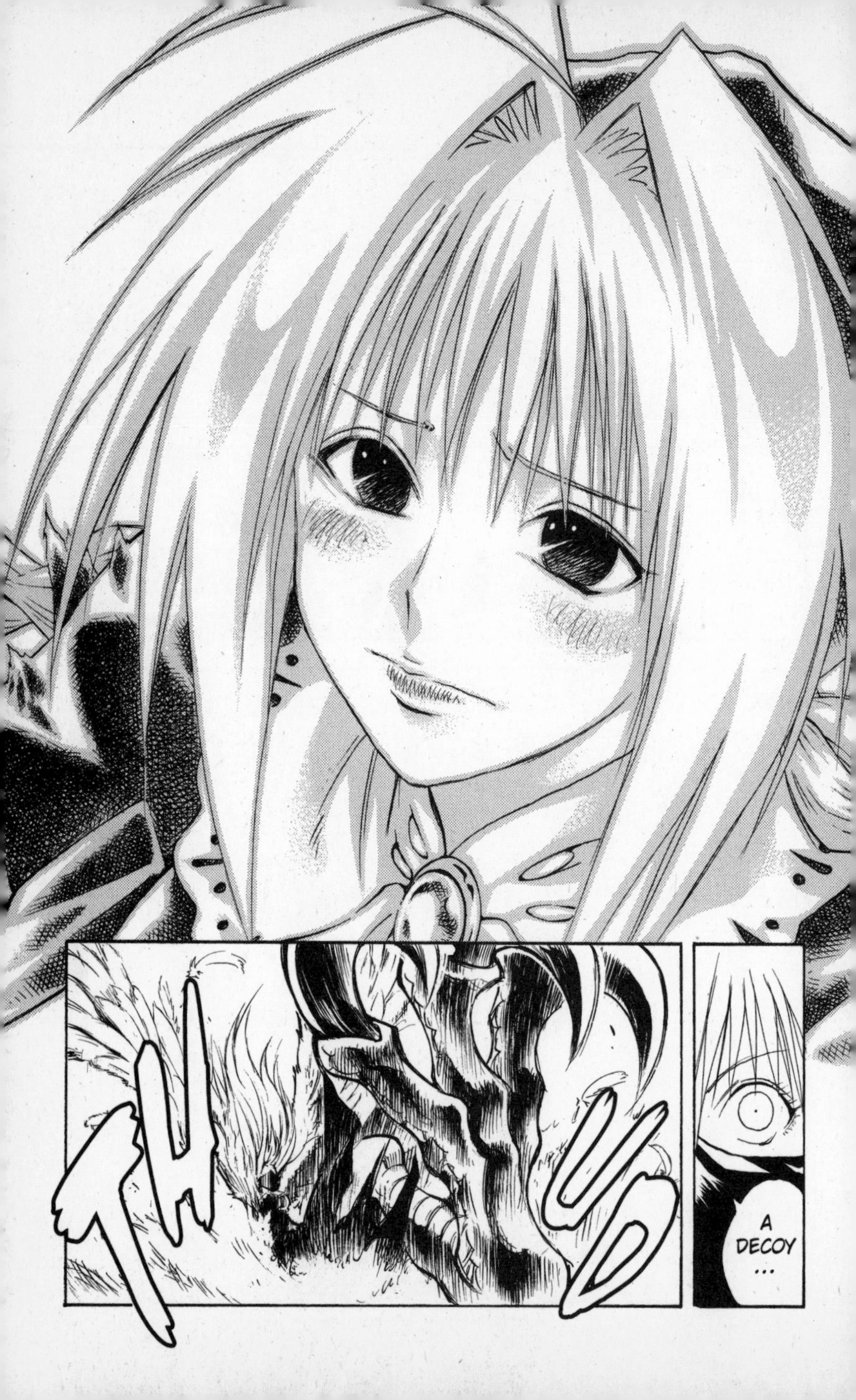
A DECOY ...
THUD

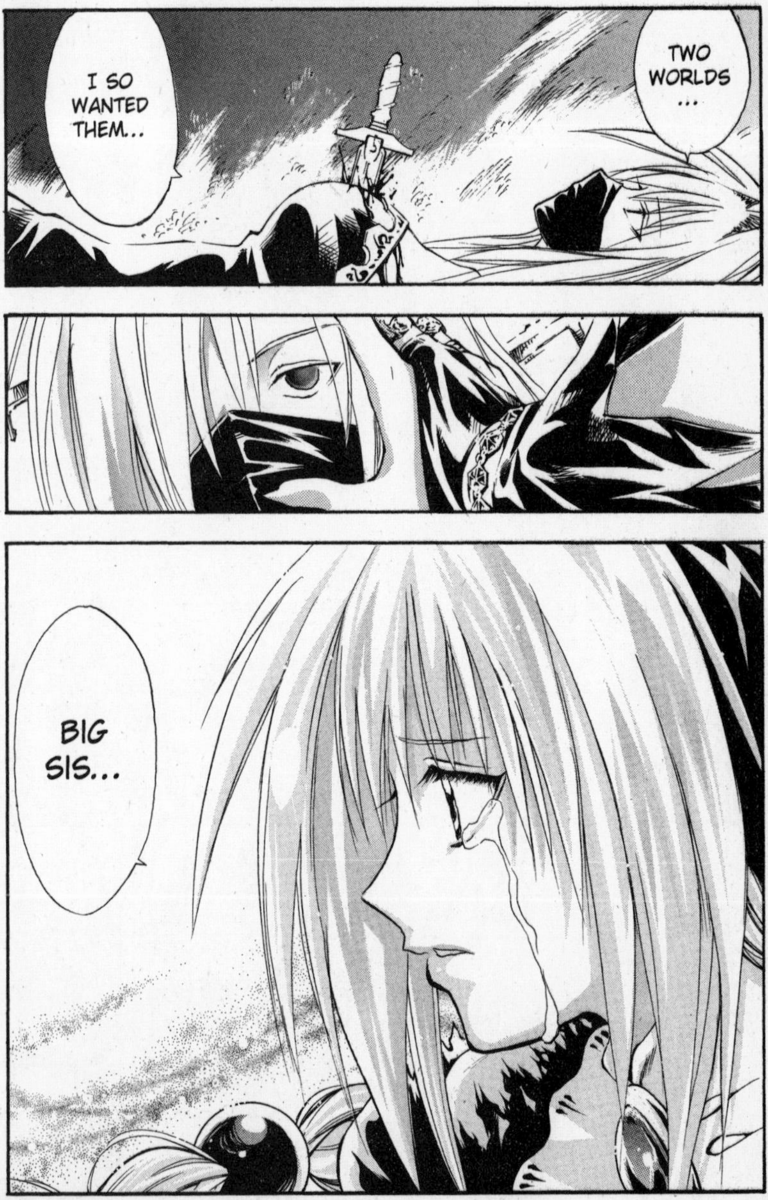
TWO WORLDS ...
I SO WANTED THEM...
BIG SIS...

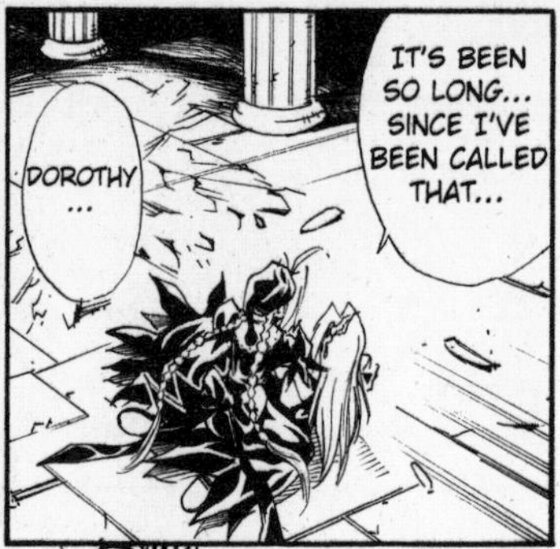
IT'S BEEN SO LONG... SINCE I'VE BEEN CALLED THAT...
DOROTHY...
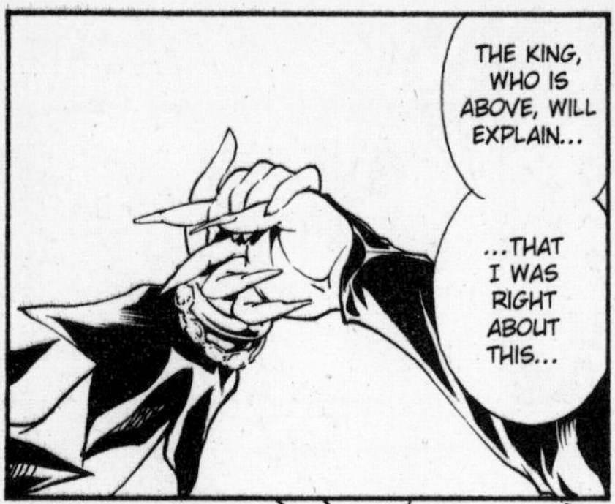
THE KING, WHO IS ABOVE, WILL EXPLAIN...
...THAT I WAS RIGHT ABOUT THIS...
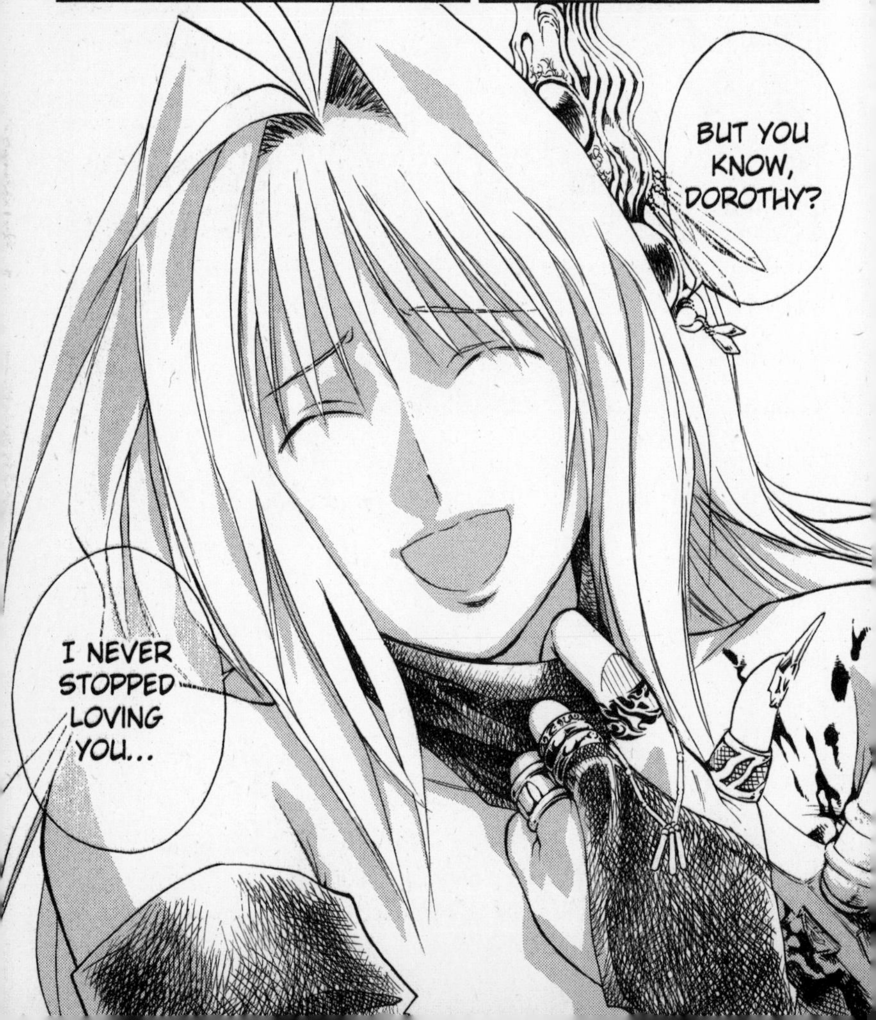
BUT YOU KNOW, DOROTHY?
I NEVER STOPPED LOVING YOU...

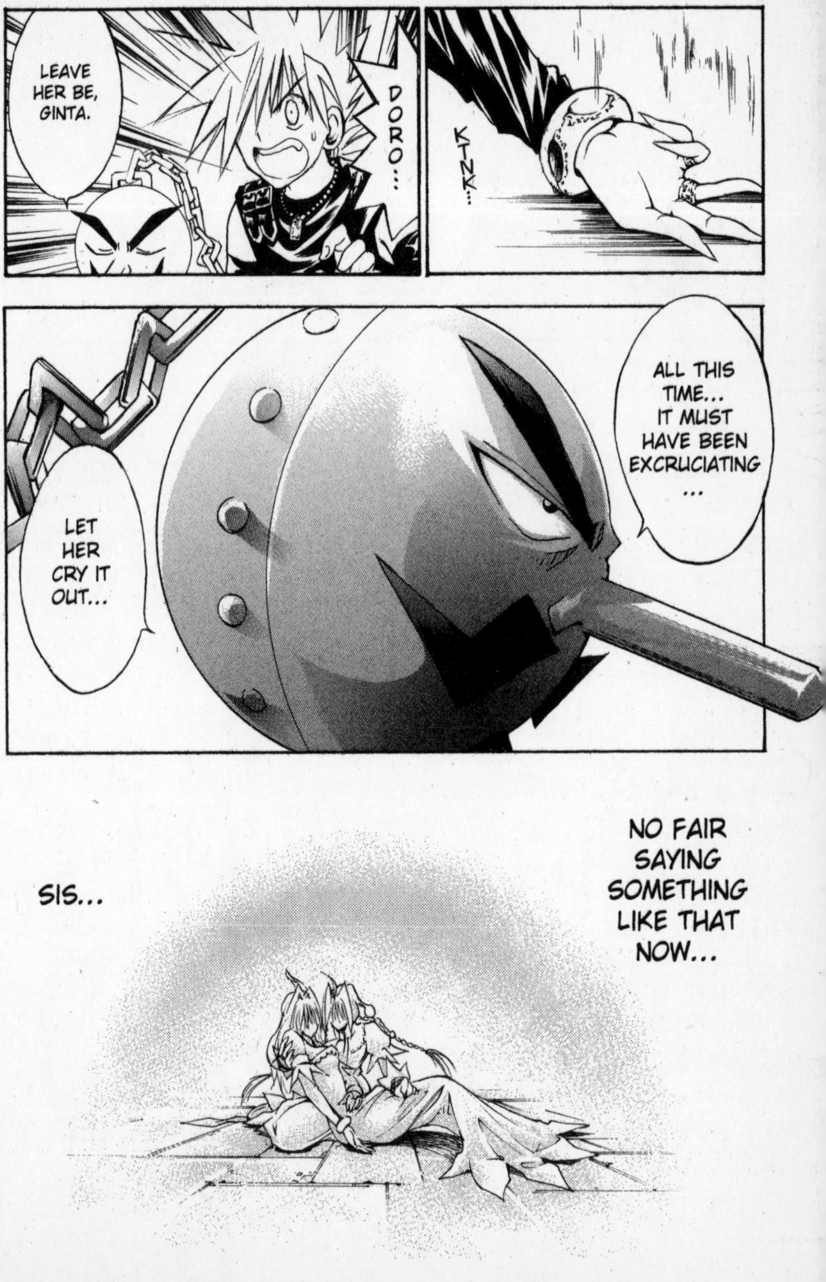
KTNK...
DORO...
LEAVE HER BE, GINTA.
ALL THIS TIME... IT MUST HAVE BEEN EXCRUCIATING...
LET HER CRY IT OUT...
NO FAIR SAYING SOMETHING LIKE THAT NOW...
SIS...

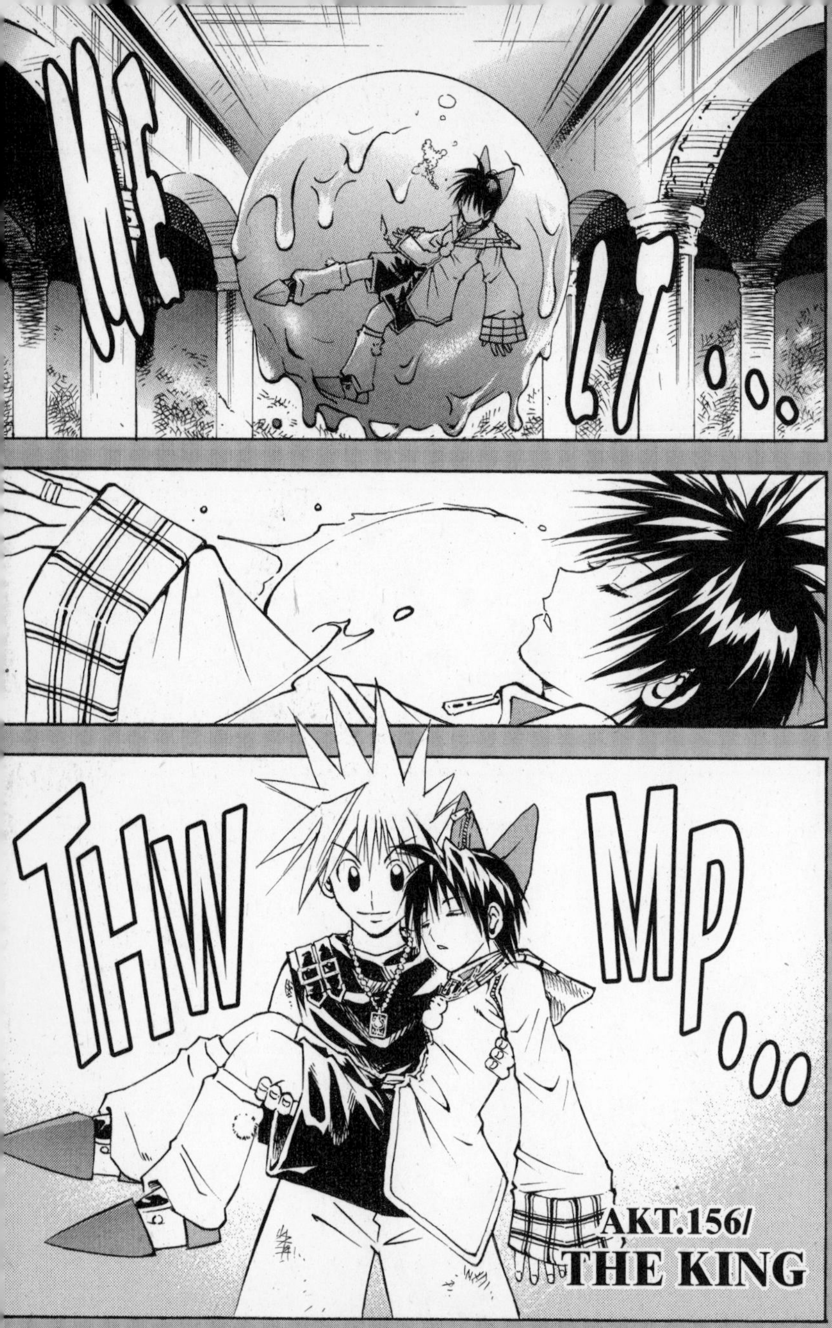
ME
LT...
THW
MP...
AKT.156/
THE KING

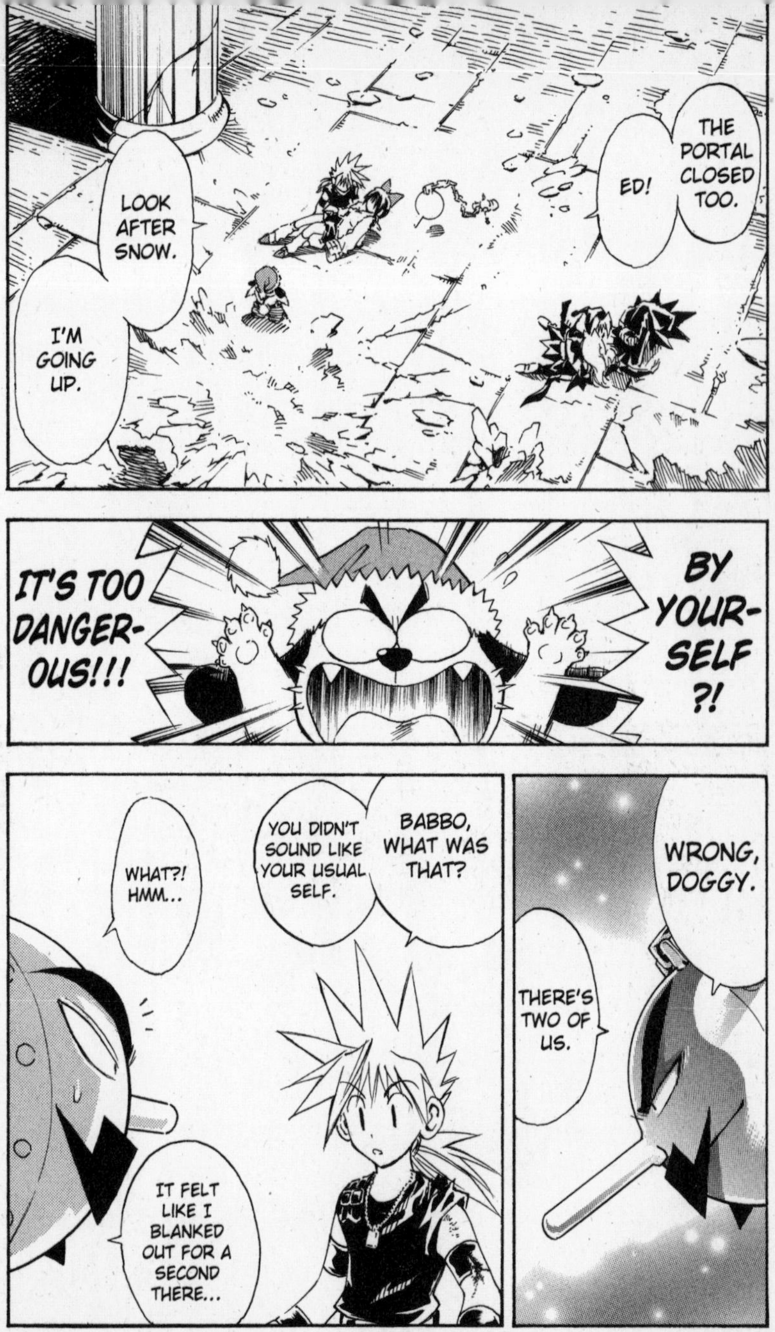
THE PORTAL CLOSED TOO.
ED!
LOOK AFTER SNOW.
I'M GOING UP.
BY YOUR-SELF ?!
IT'S TOO DANGER-OUS!!!
WRONG, DOGGY.
THERE'S TWO OF US.
BABBO, WHAT WAS THAT?
YOU DIDN'T SOUND LIKE YOUR USUAL SELF.
WHAT?! HMM...
IT FELT LIKE I BLANKED OUT FOR A SECOND THERE...

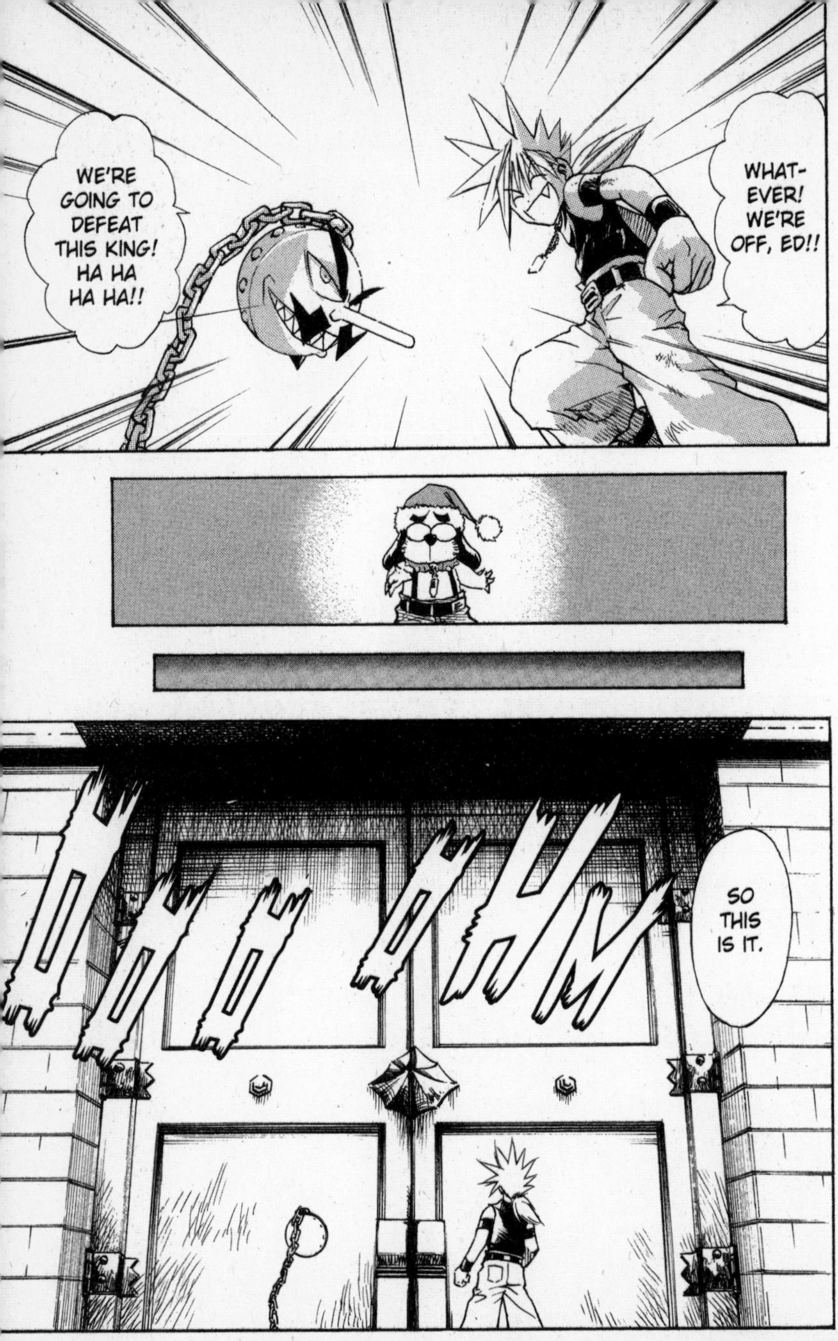
WHAT-EVER! WE'RE OFF, ED!!
WE'RE GOING TO DEFEAT THIS KING! HA HA HA HA!!
SO THIS IS IT.

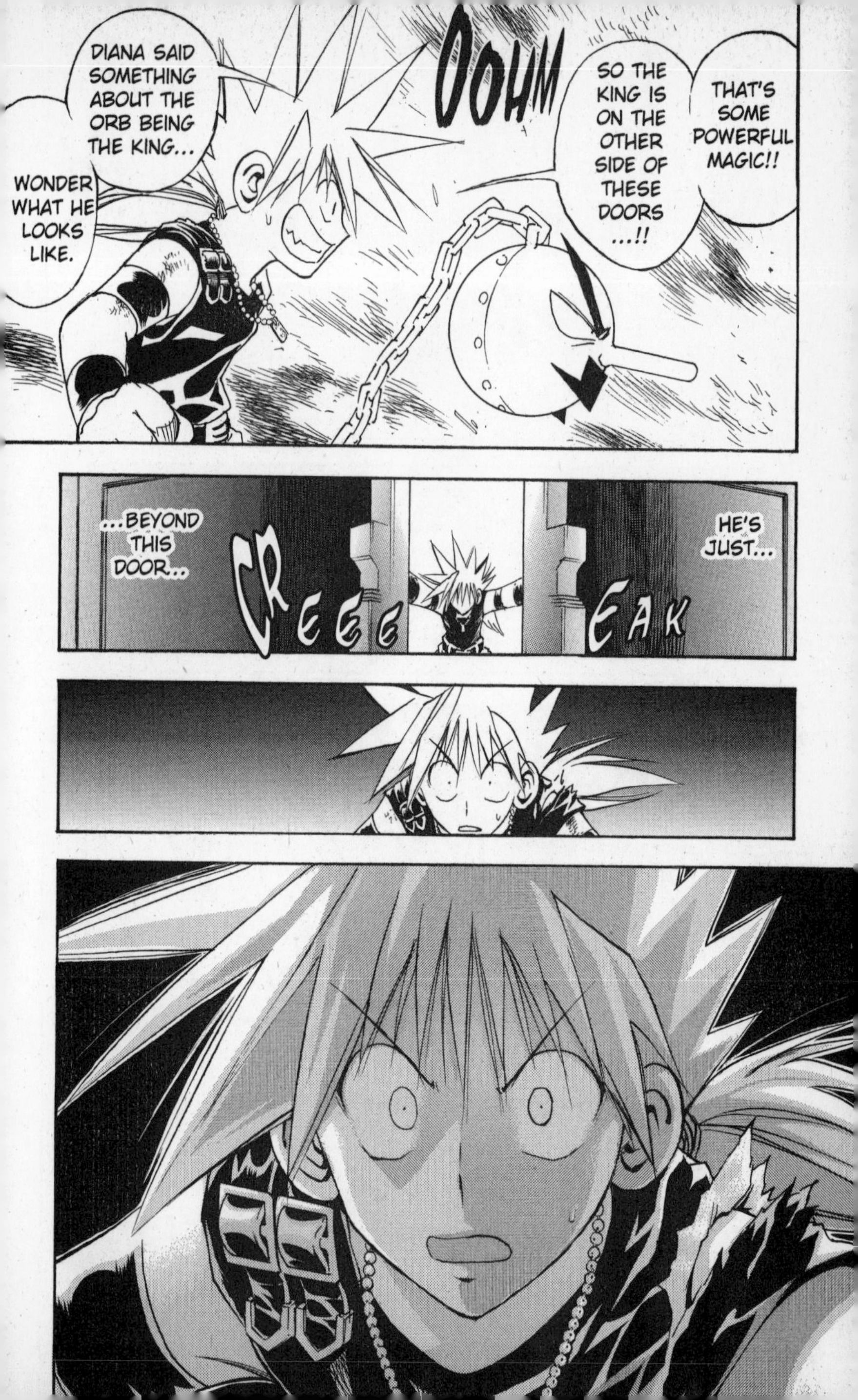
THAT'S SOME POWERFUL MAGIC!!
SO THE KING IS ON THE OTHER SIDE OF THESE DOORS ...!!
OOHM
DIANA SAID SOMETHING ABOUT THE ORB BEING THE KING...
WONDER WHAT HE LOOKS LIKE.
HE'S JUST...
...BEYOND THIS DOOR...
CREEEEAK

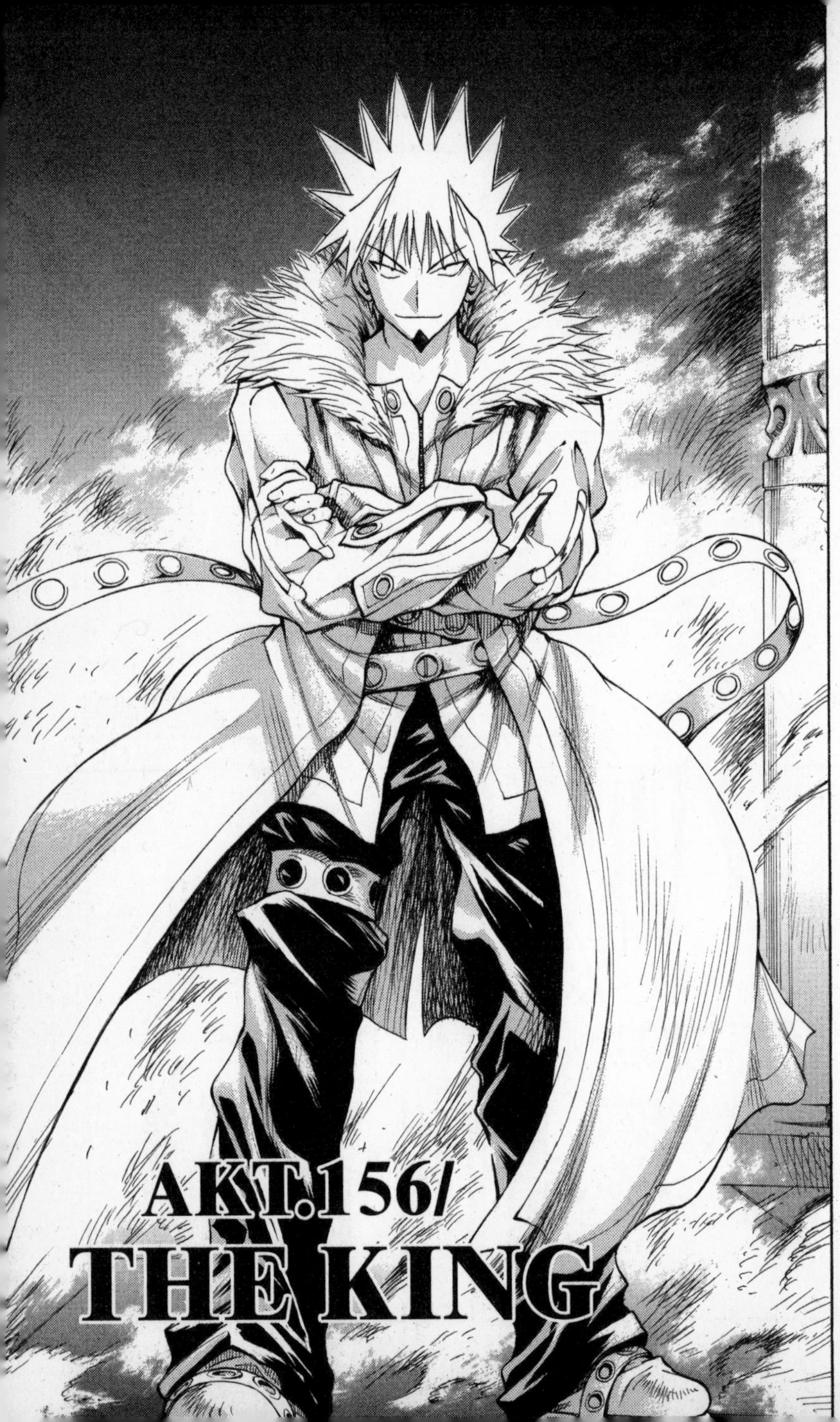
AKT.156/
THE KING

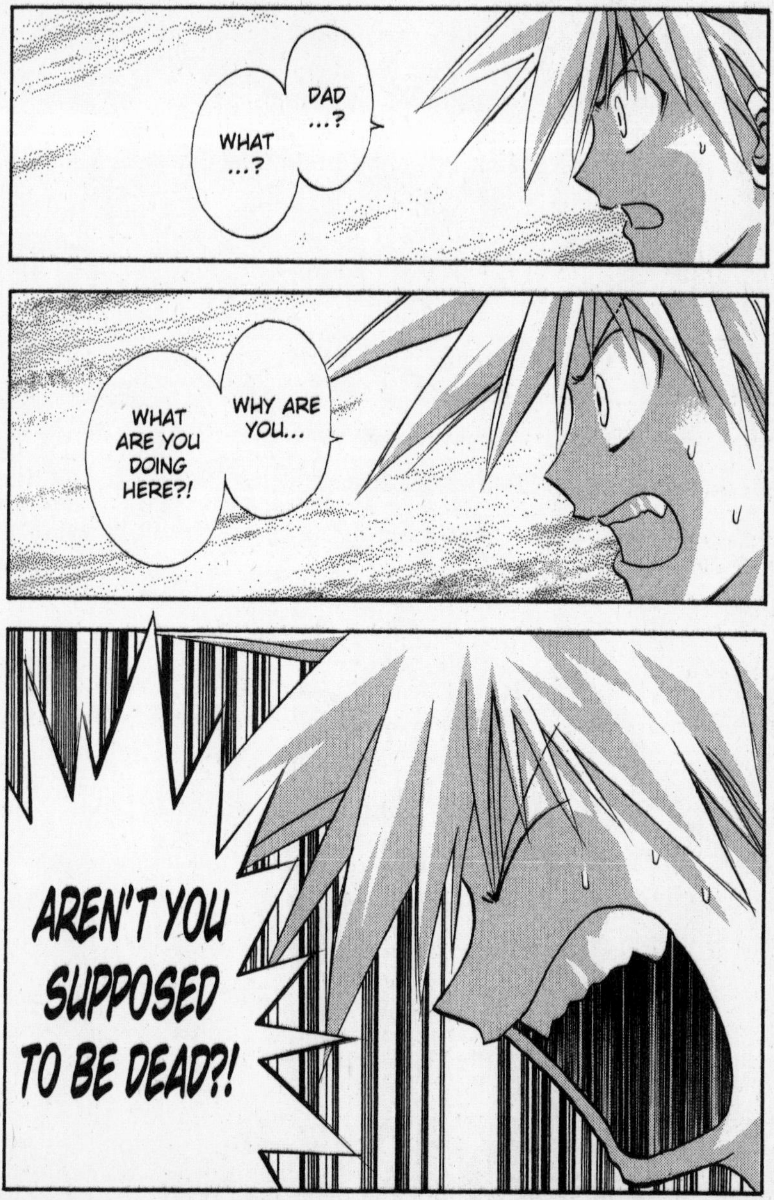
DAD ...?
WHAT ...?
WHY ARE YOU...
WHAT ARE YOU DOING HERE?!
AREN'T YOU SUPPOSED TO BE DEAD?!

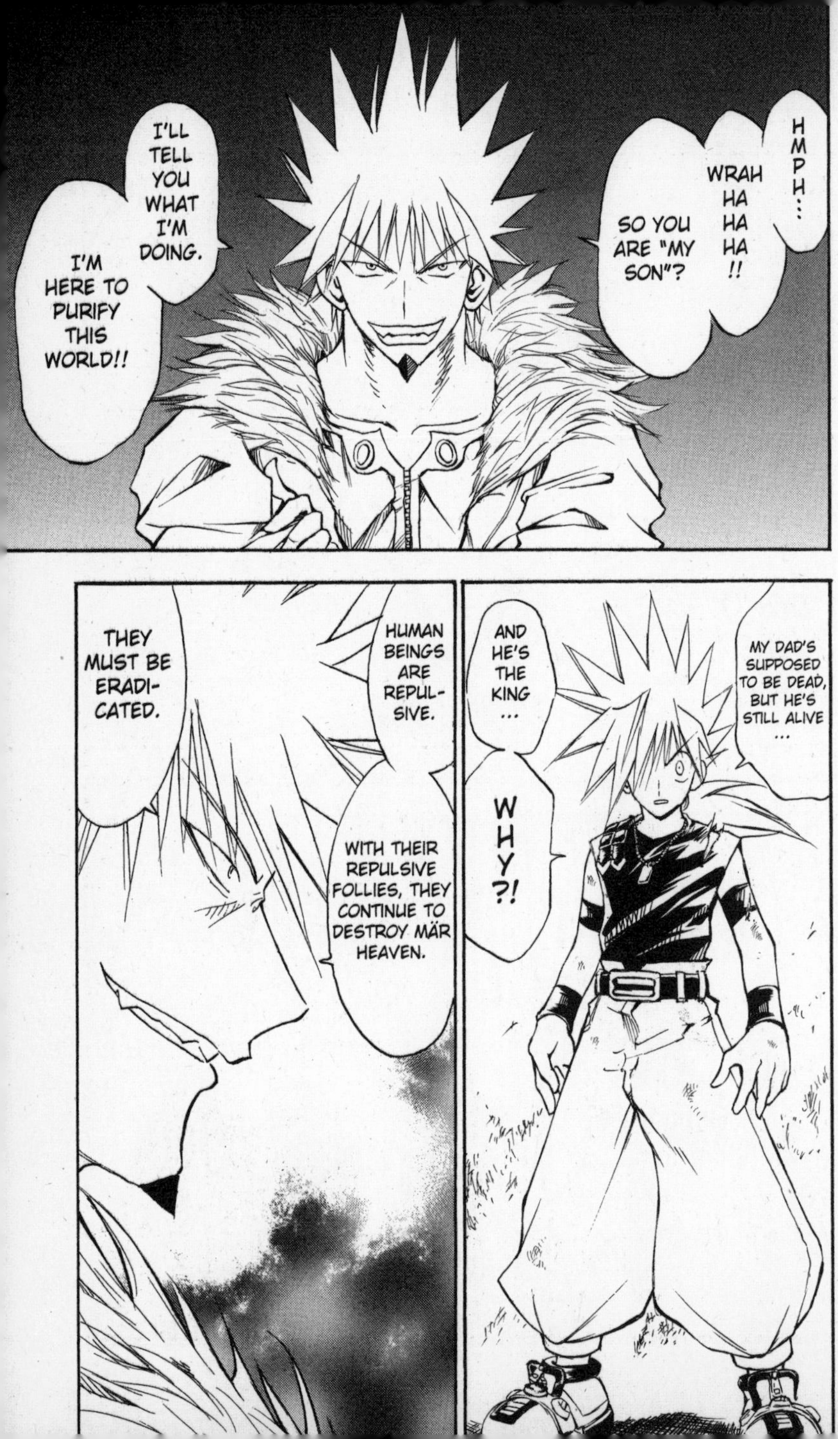
HMPH...
WRAH HA HA HA!!
SO YOU ARE "MY SON"?
I'LL TELL YOU WHAT I'M DOING.
I'M HERE TO PURIFY THIS WORLD!!
MY DAD'S SUPPOSED TO BE DEAD, BUT HE'S STILL ALIVE...
AND HE'S THE KING...
WHY?!
HUMAN BEINGS ARE REPULSIVE.
WITH THEIR REPULSIVE FOLLIES, THEY CONTINUE TO DESTROY MÄR HEAVEN.
THEY MUST BE ERADICATED.

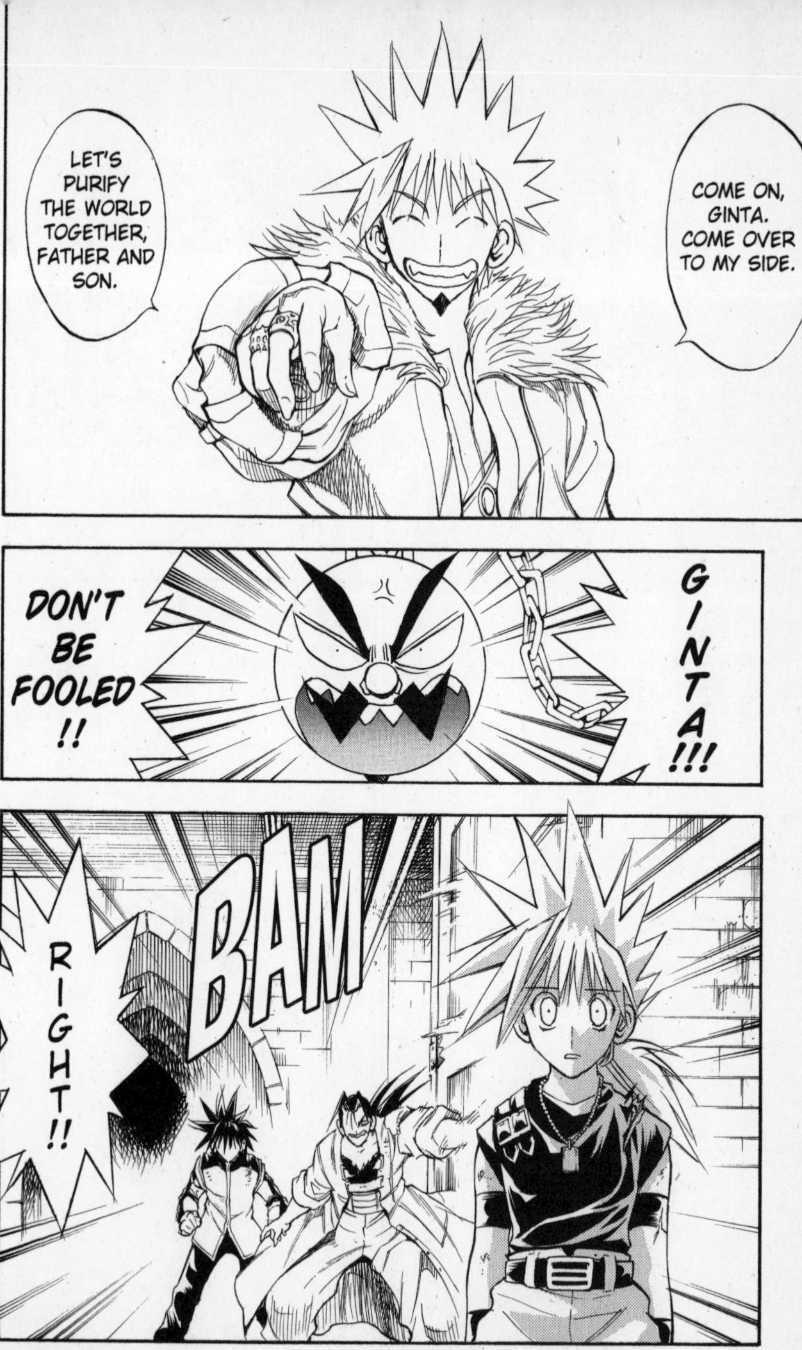
COME ON, GINTA. COME OVER TO MY SIDE.
LET'S PURIFY THE WORLD TOGETHER, FATHER AND SON.
GINTA!!!
DON'T BE FOOLED!!
BAM
RIGHT!!

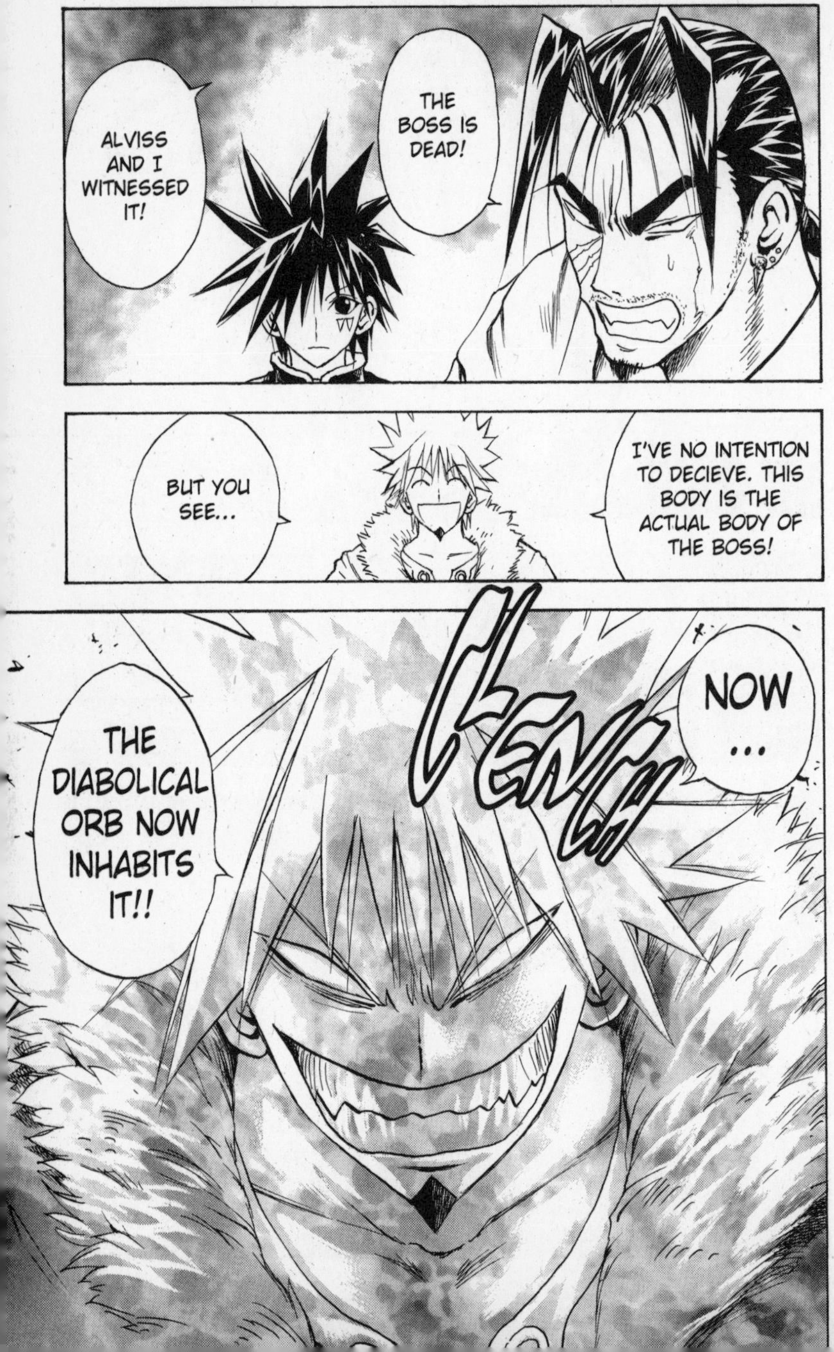
THE BOSS IS DEAD!
ALVISS AND I WITNESSED IT!
I'VE NO INTENTION TO DECIEVE. THIS BODY IS THE ACTUAL BODY OF THE BOSS!
BUT YOU SEE...
NOW ...
CLENCH
THE DIABOLICAL ORB NOW INHABITS IT!!

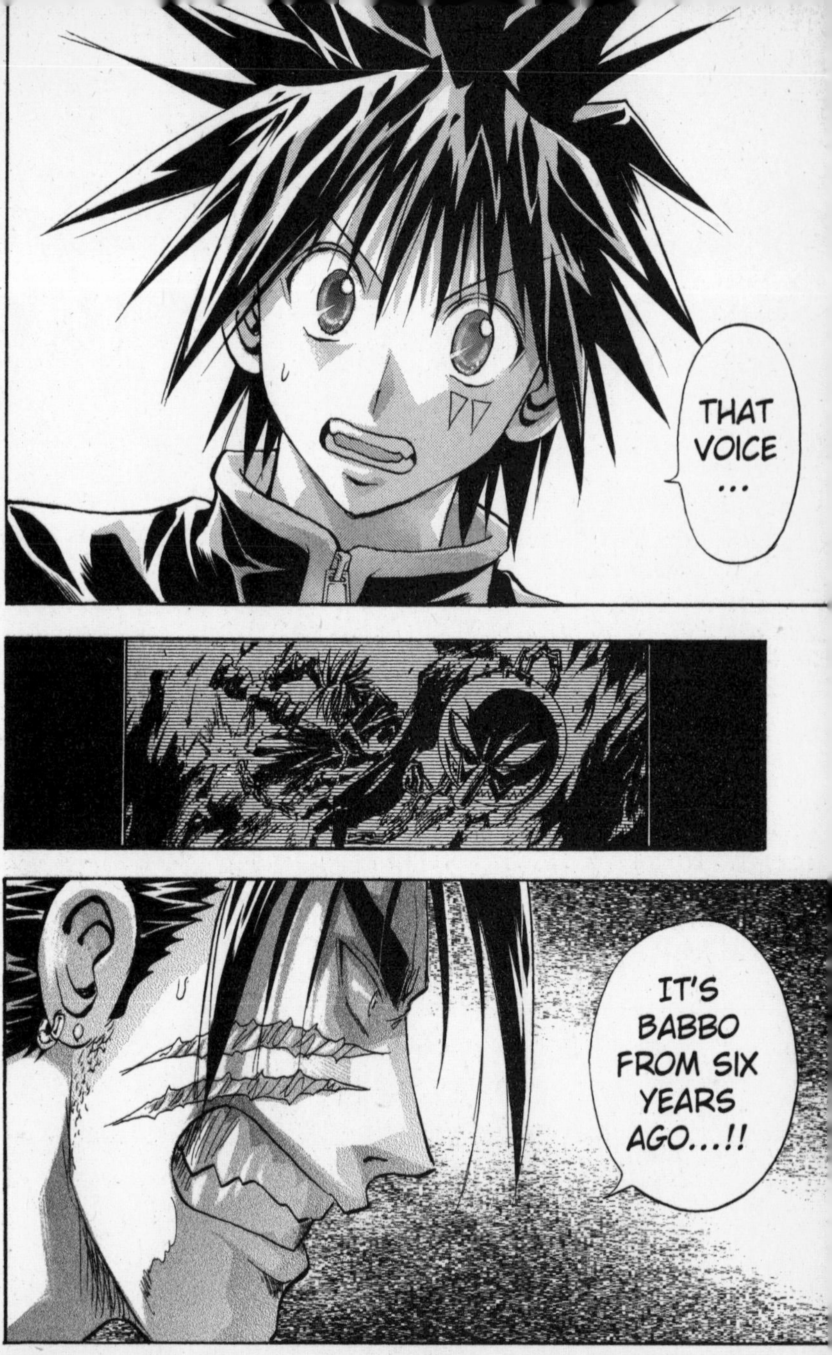
THAT VOICE ...
IT'S BABBO FROM SIX YEARS AGO...!!

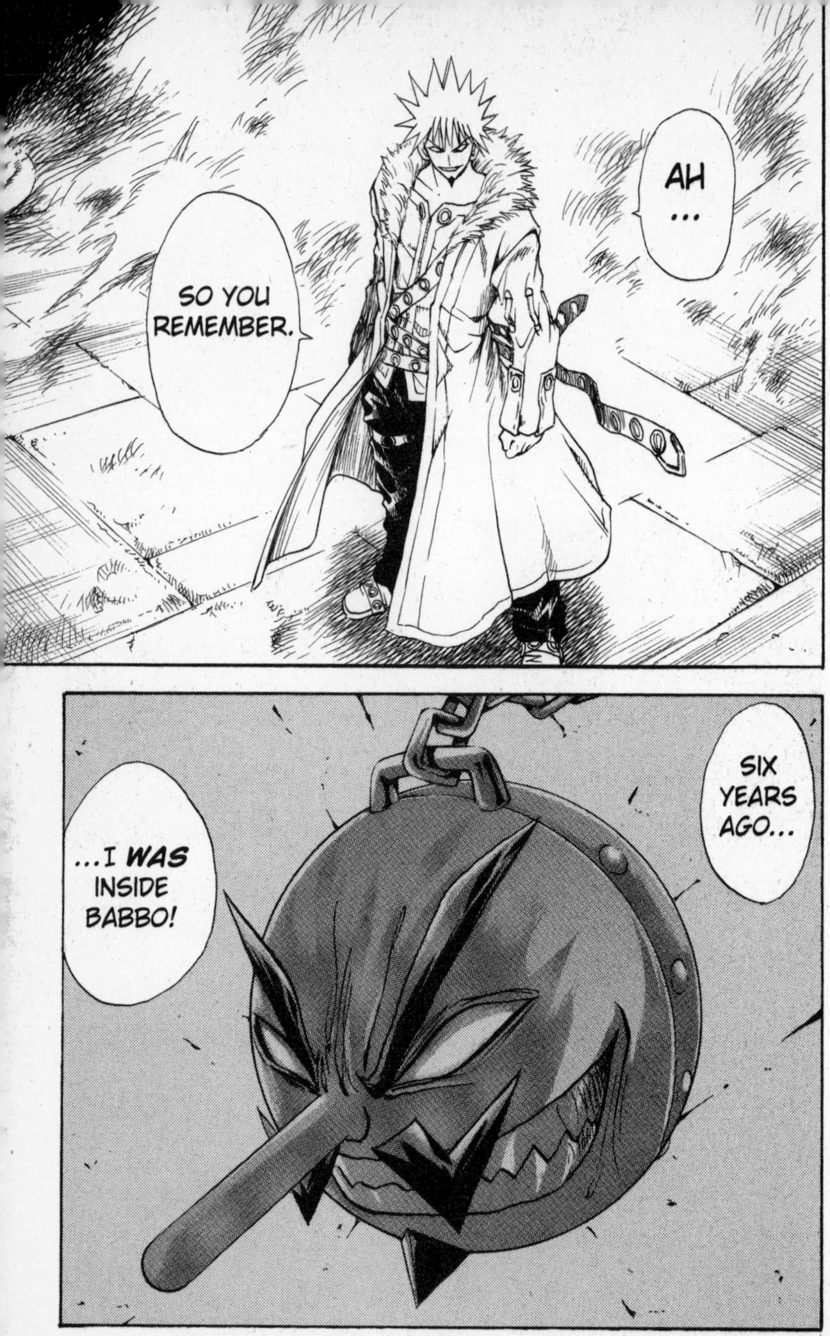
AH
...
SO YOU REMEMBER.
SIX YEARS AGO...
...I **WAS** INSIDE BABBO!

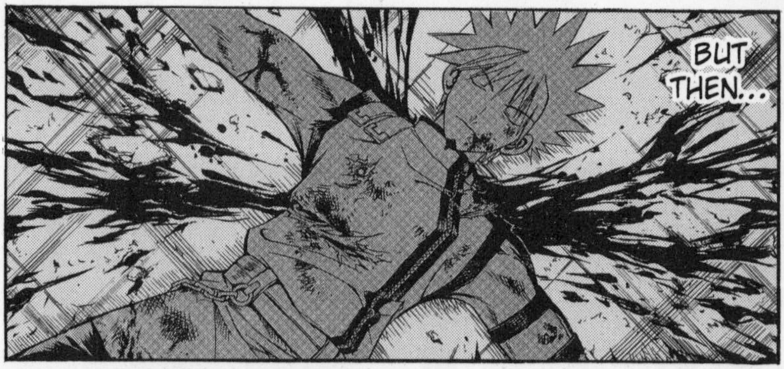
BUT THEN...
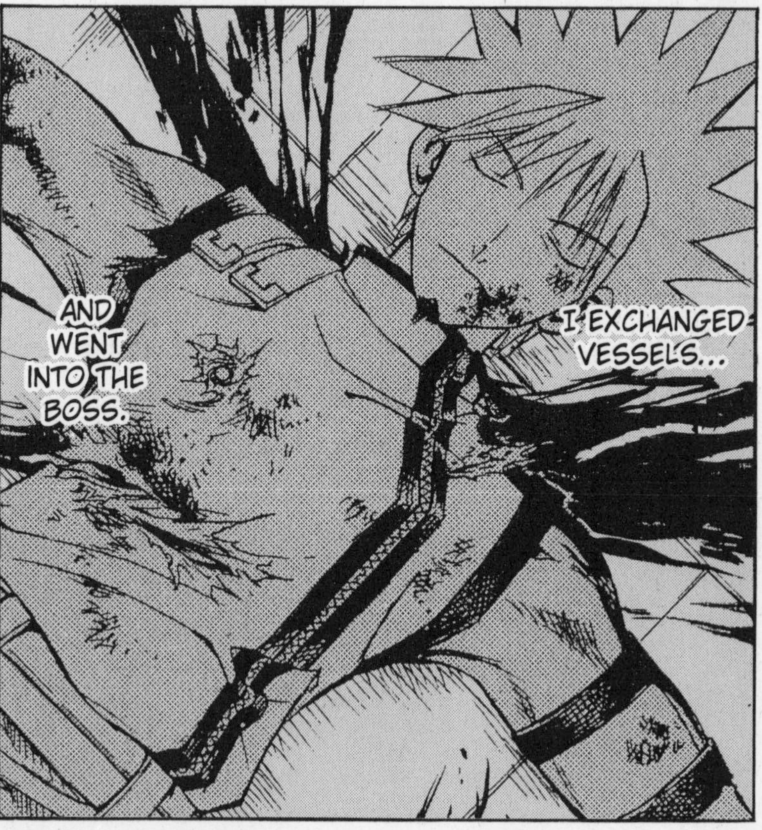
I EXCHANGED VESSELS...
AND WENT INTO THE BOSS.

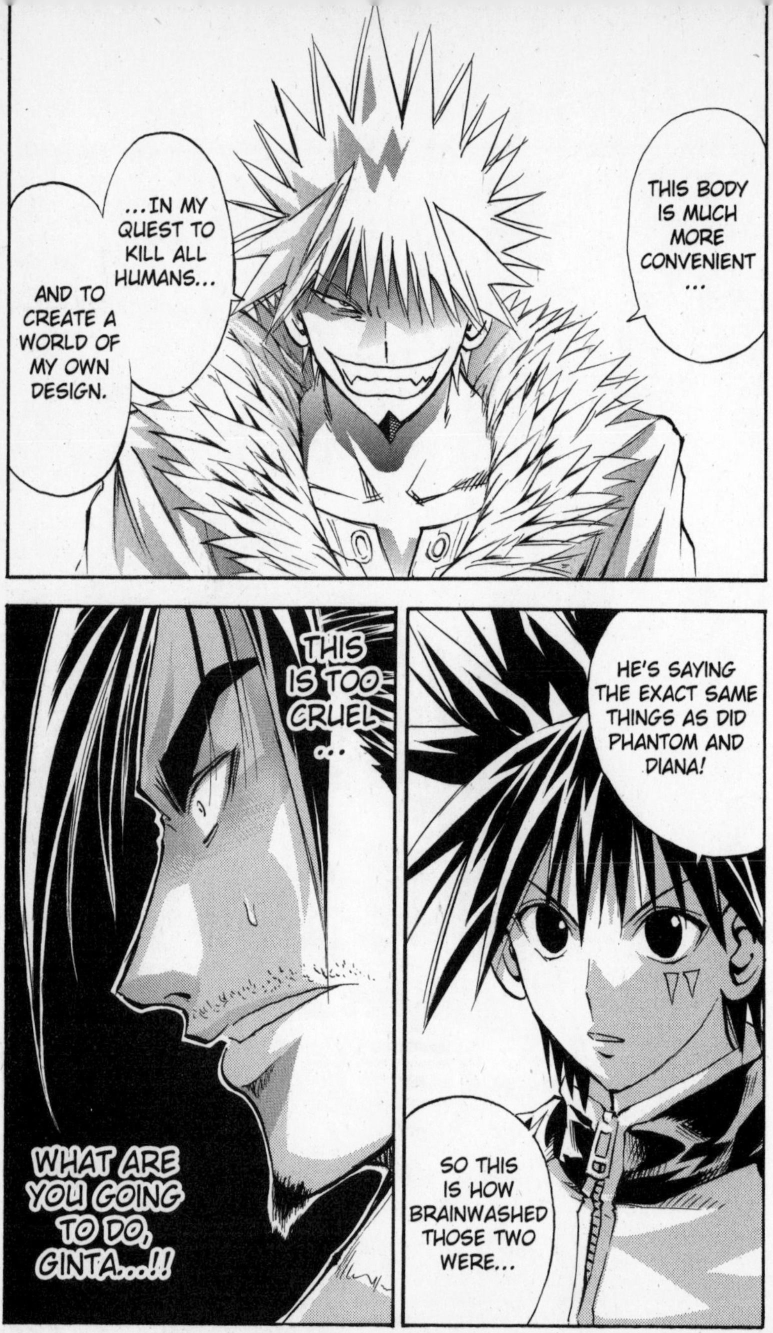
THIS BODY IS MUCH MORE CONVENIENT ...
...IN MY QUEST TO KILL ALL HUMANS...
AND TO CREATE A WORLD OF MY OWN DESIGN.
HE'S SAYING THE EXACT SAME THINGS AS DID PHANTOM AND DIANA!
SO THIS IS HOW BRAINWASHED THOSE TWO WERE...
THIS IS TOO CRUEL ...
WHAT ARE YOU GOING TO DO, GINTA...!!

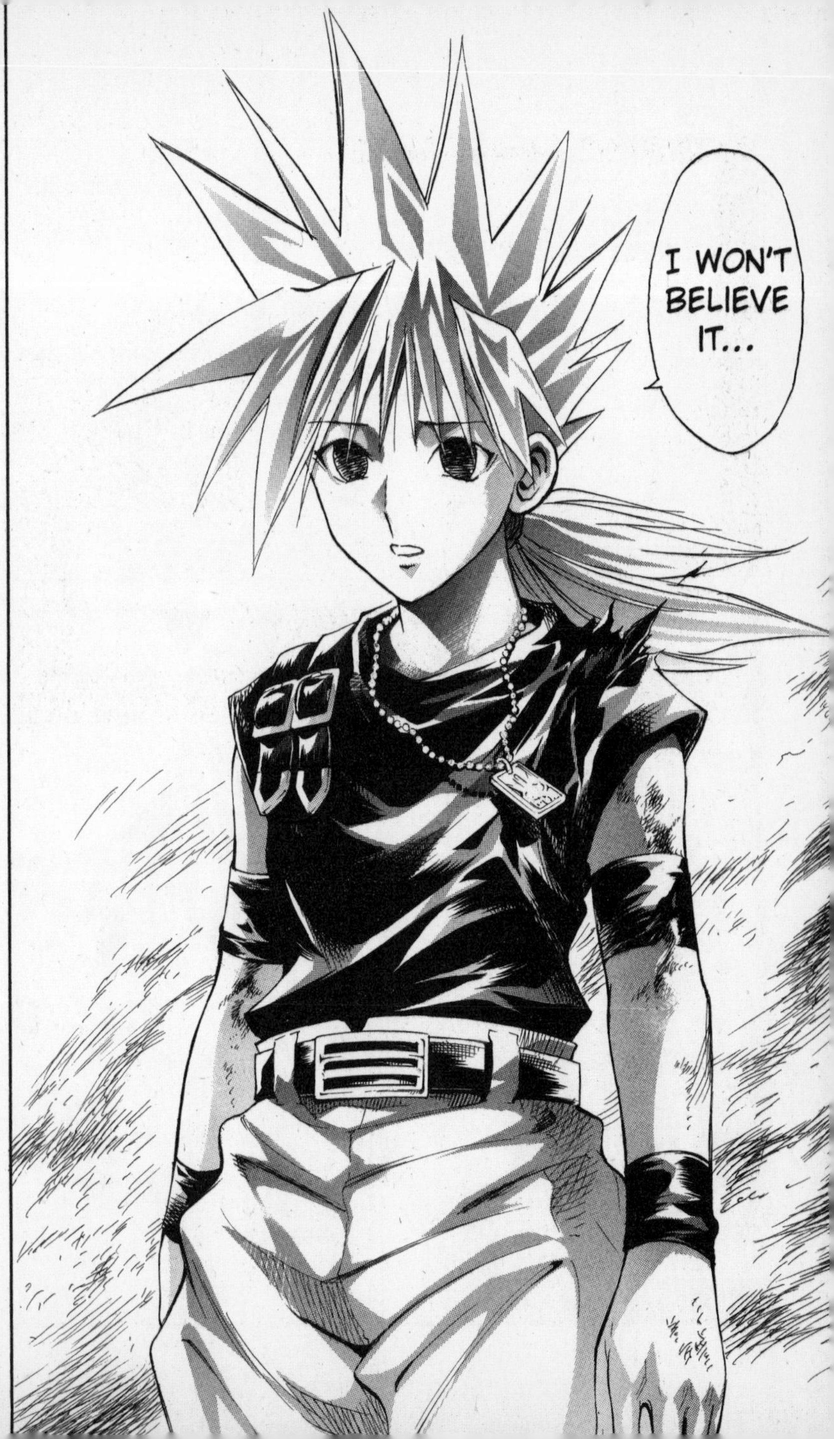
I WON'T BELIEVE IT...

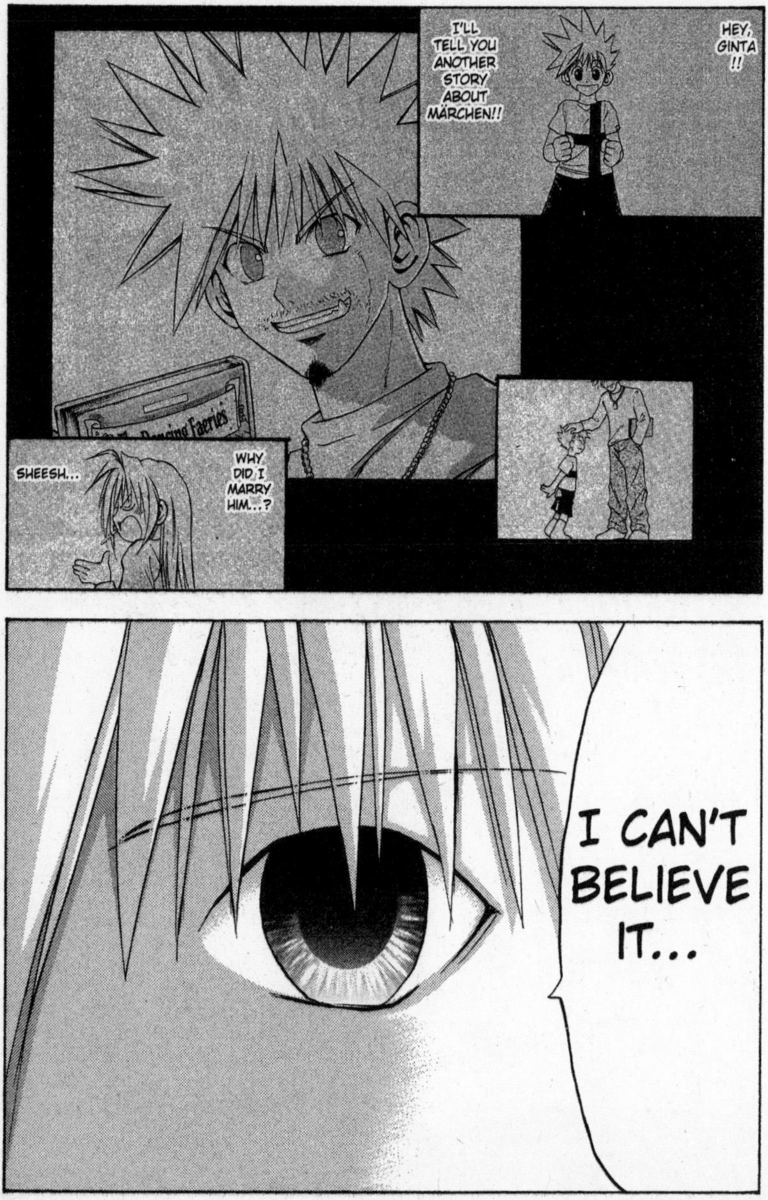
HEY, GINTA !!
I'LL TELL YOU ANOTHER STORY ABOUT MÄRCHEN!!
The Dancing Faeries
WHY DID I MARRY HIM...?
SHEESH...
I CAN'T BELIEVE IT...

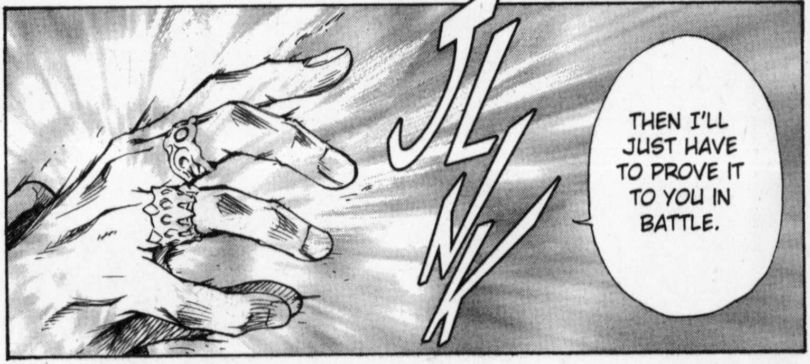
THEN I'LL JUST HAVE TO PROVE IT TO YOU IN BATTLE.
JINX
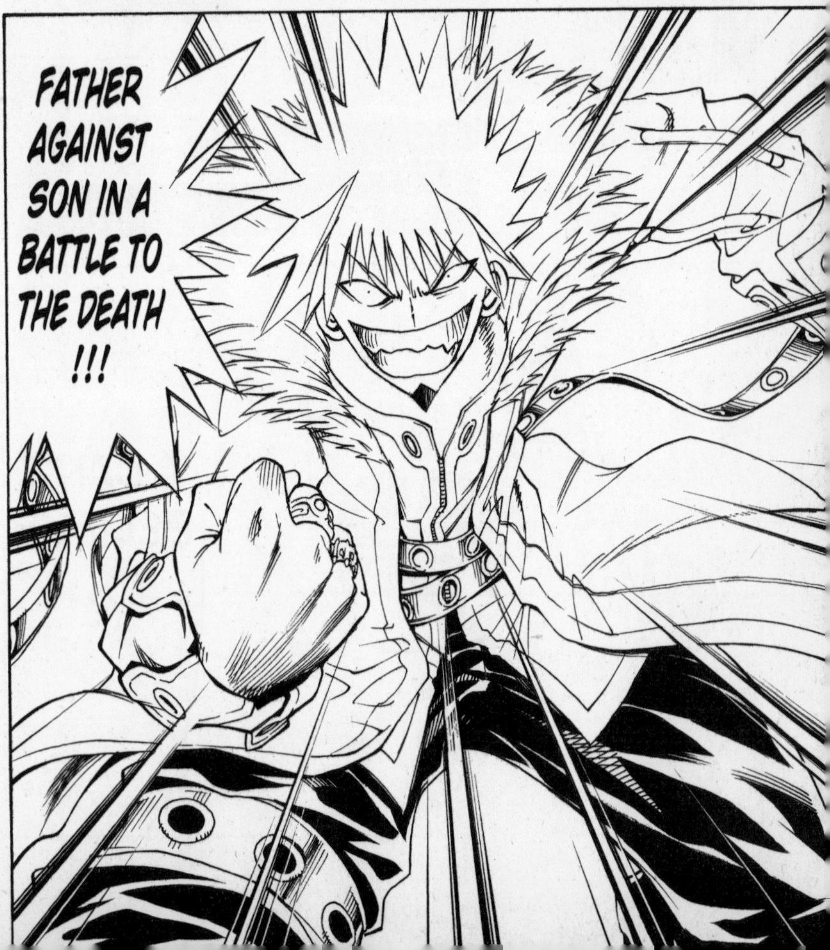
FATHER AGAINST SON IN A BATTLE TO THE DEATH !!!

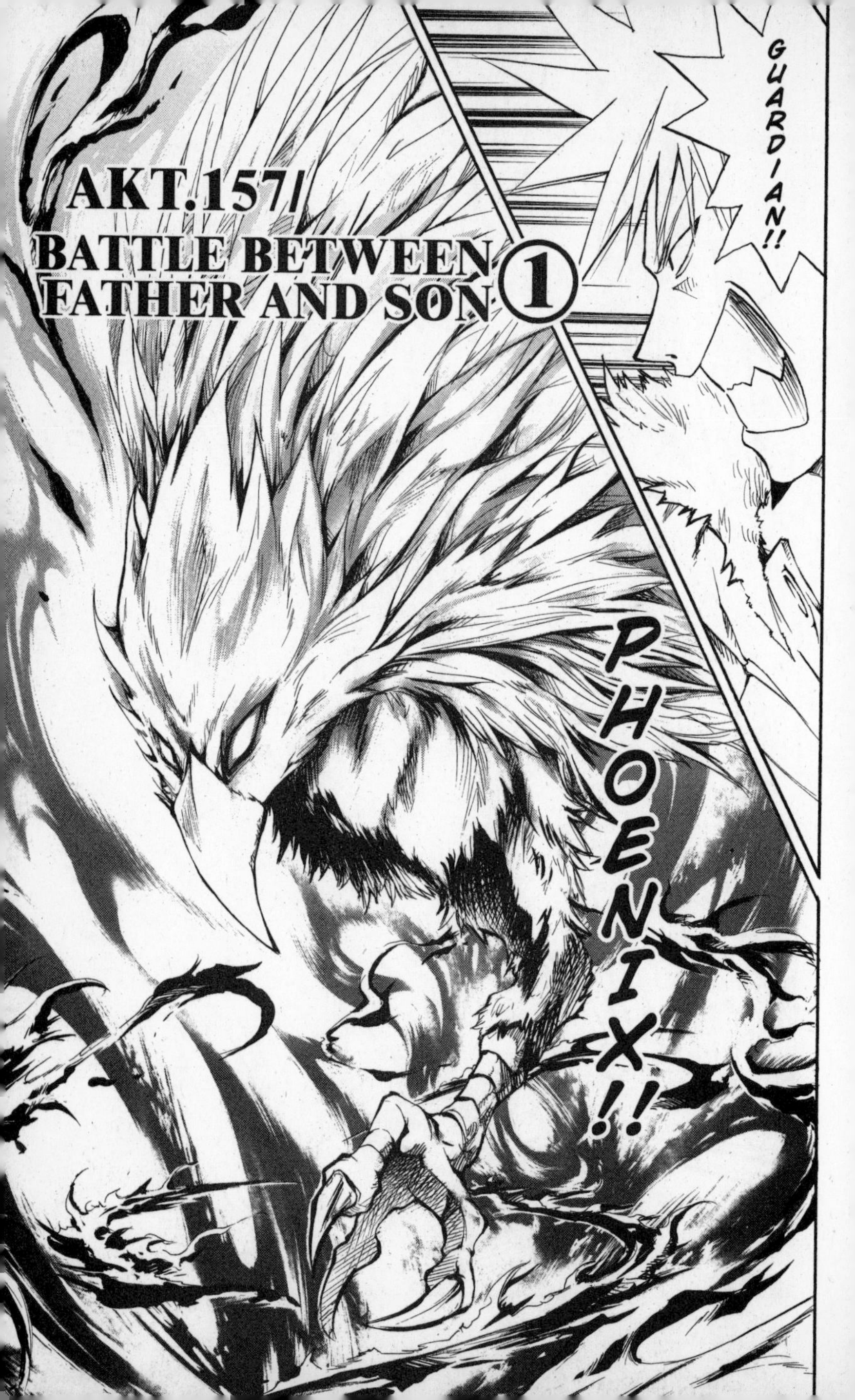
GUARDIAN!!
AKT.157/
BATTLE BETWEEN FATHER AND SON ①
PHOENIX!!

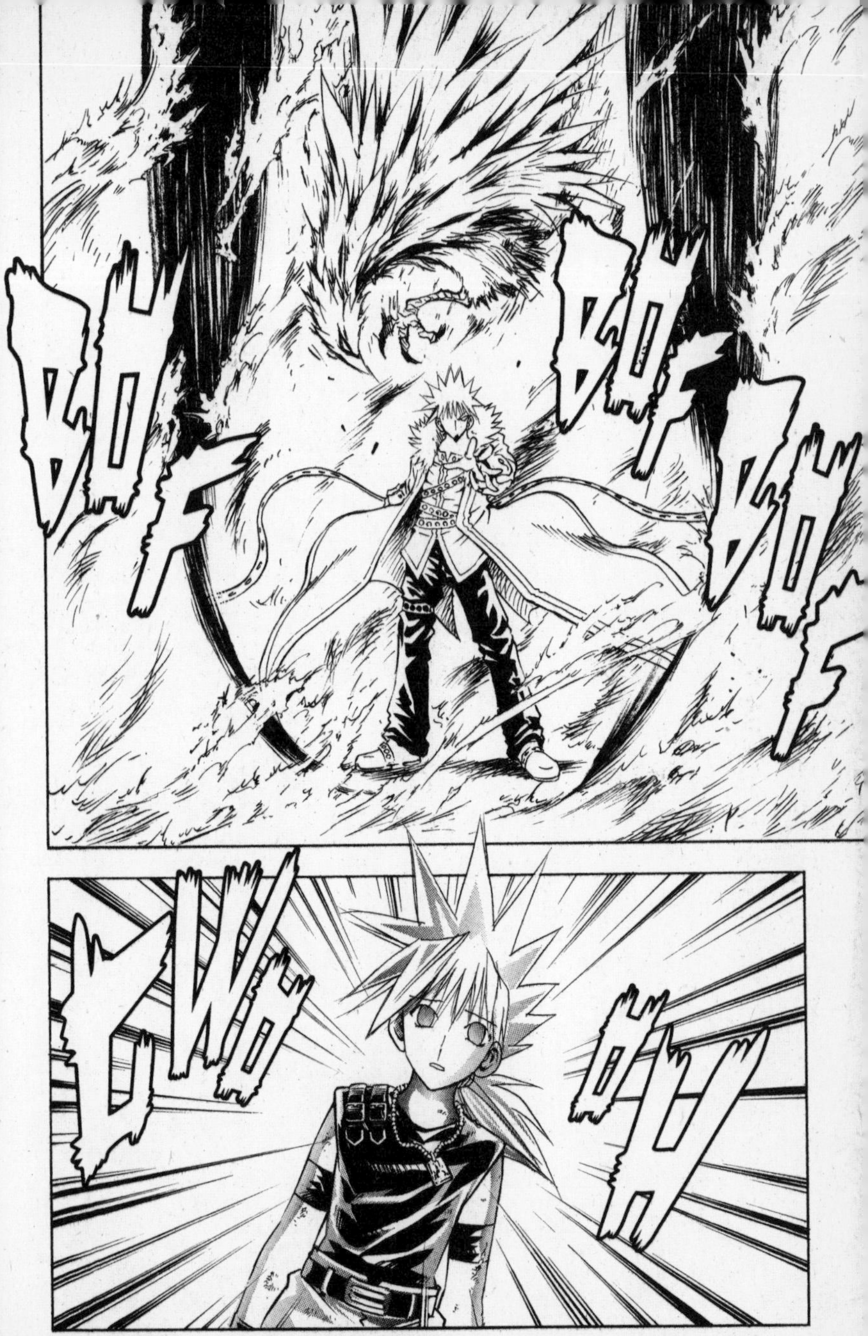
BUF
BUF
BUF
AH
GWA

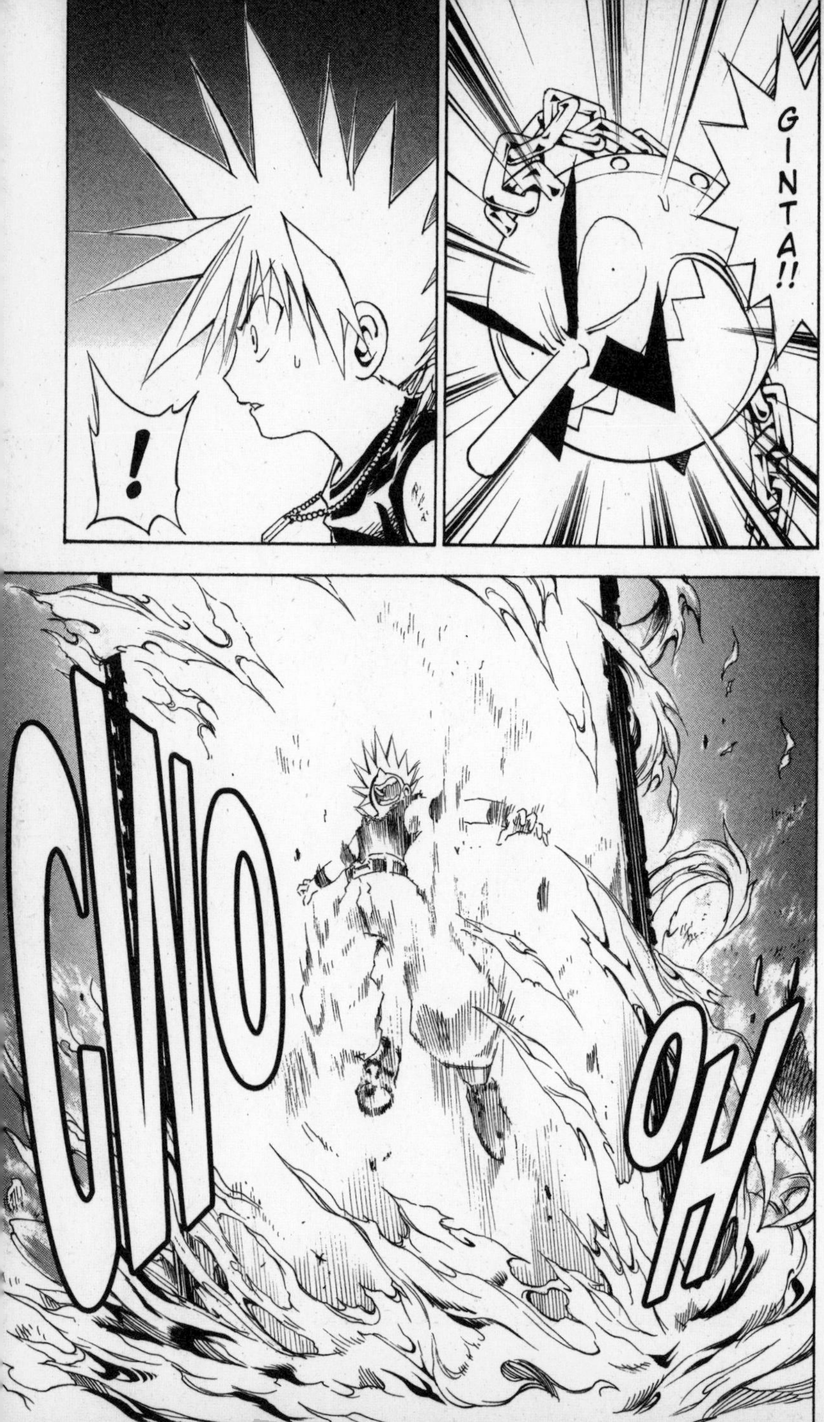
GINTA!!
!
GWO
OH

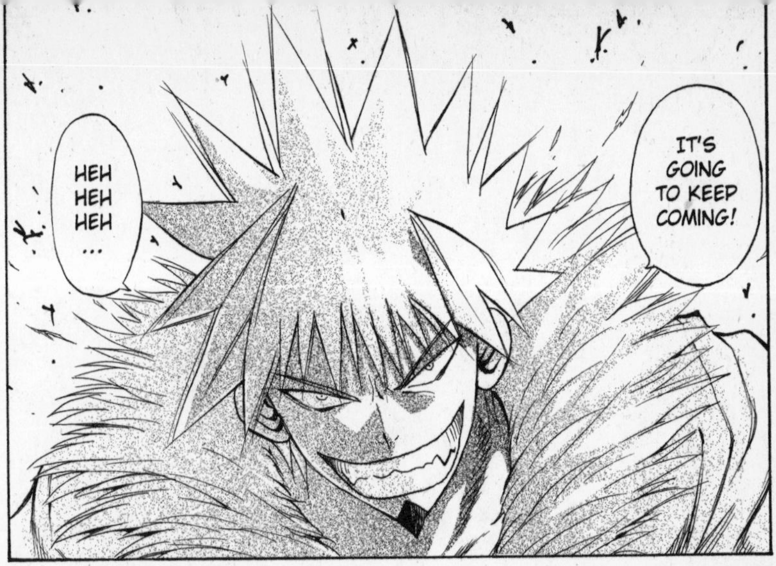
IT'S GOING TO KEEP COMING!
HEH HEH HEH ...

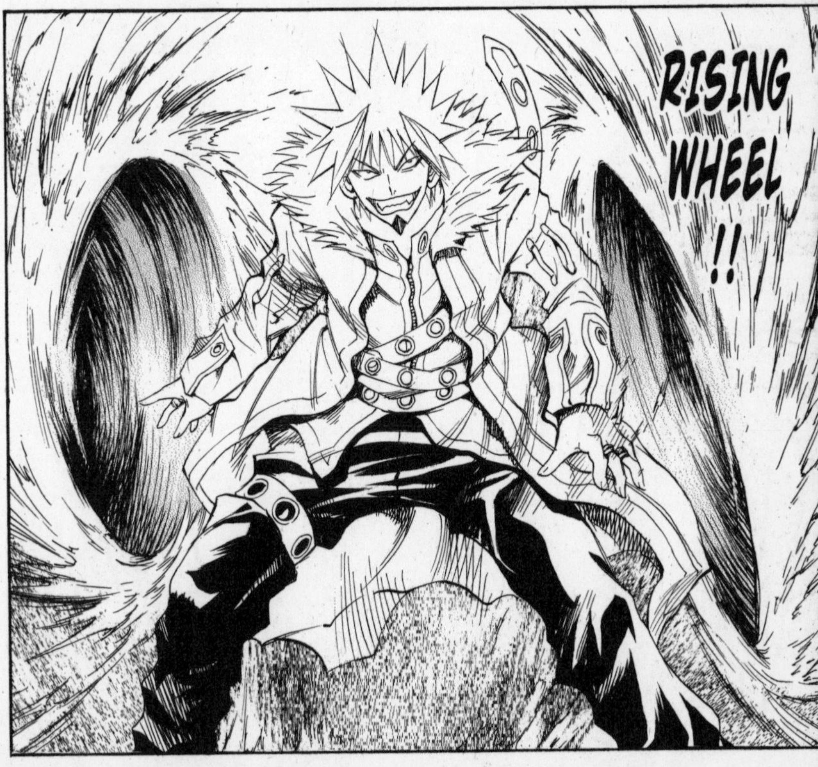
RISING WHEEL !!

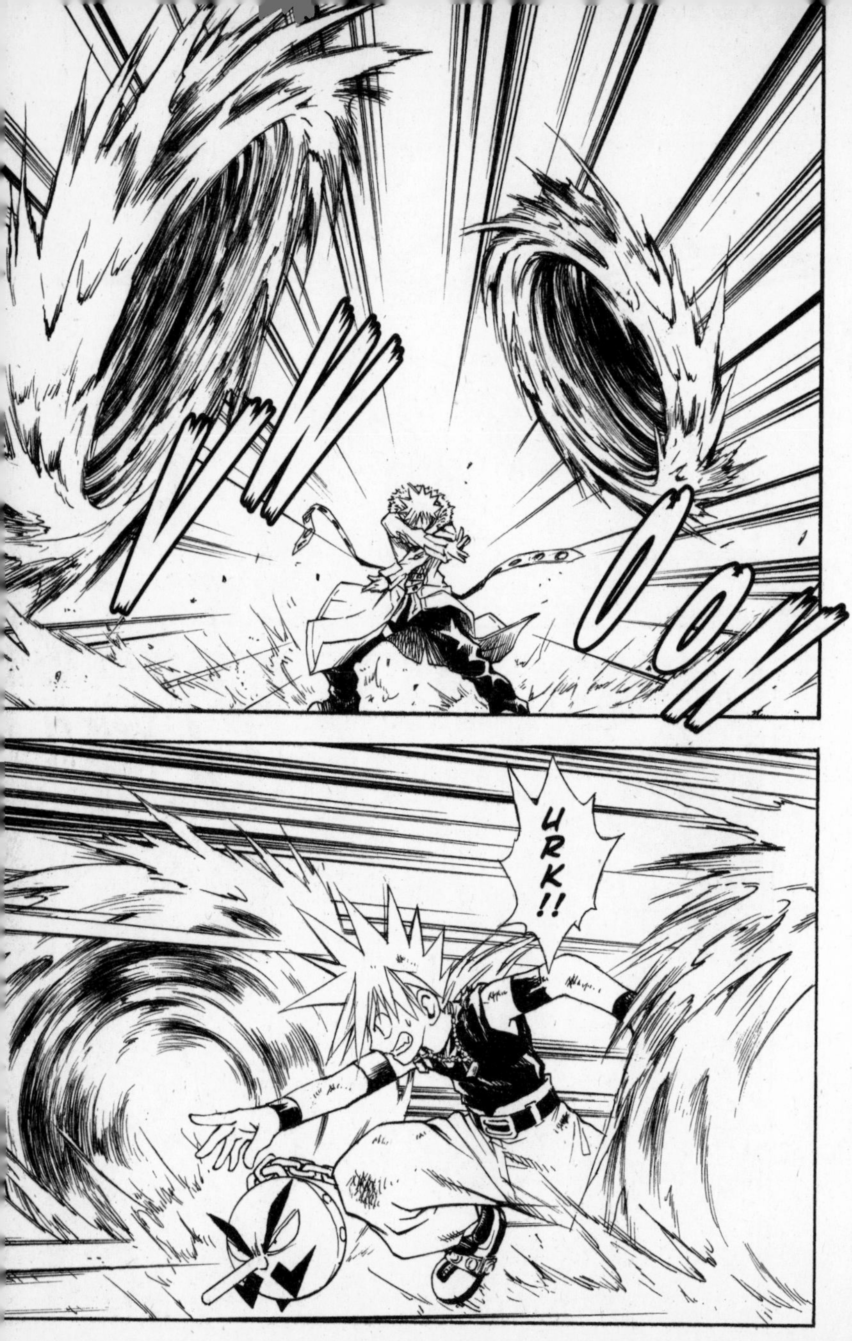
URK!!

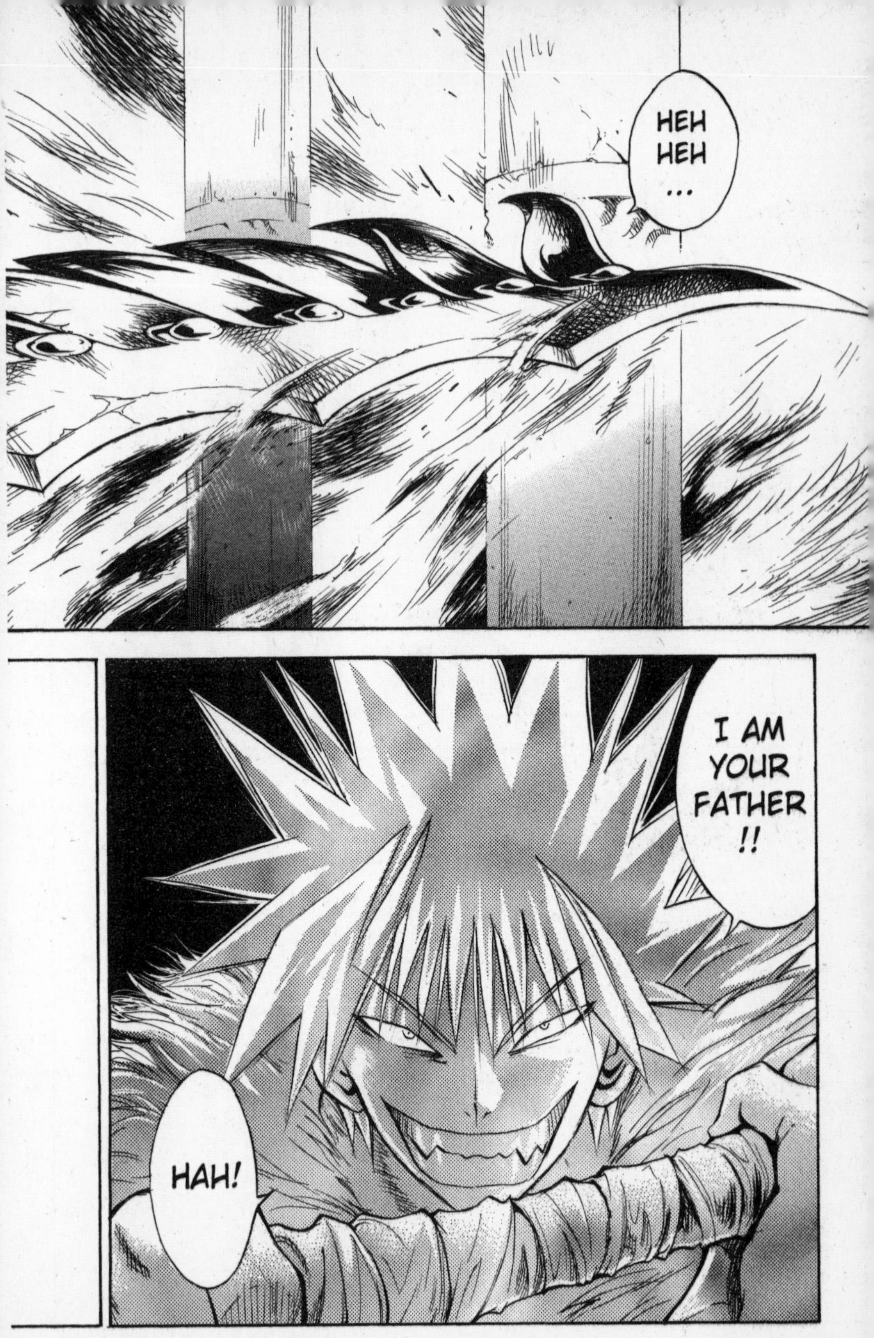
HEH HEH ...
I AM YOUR FATHER !!
HAH!

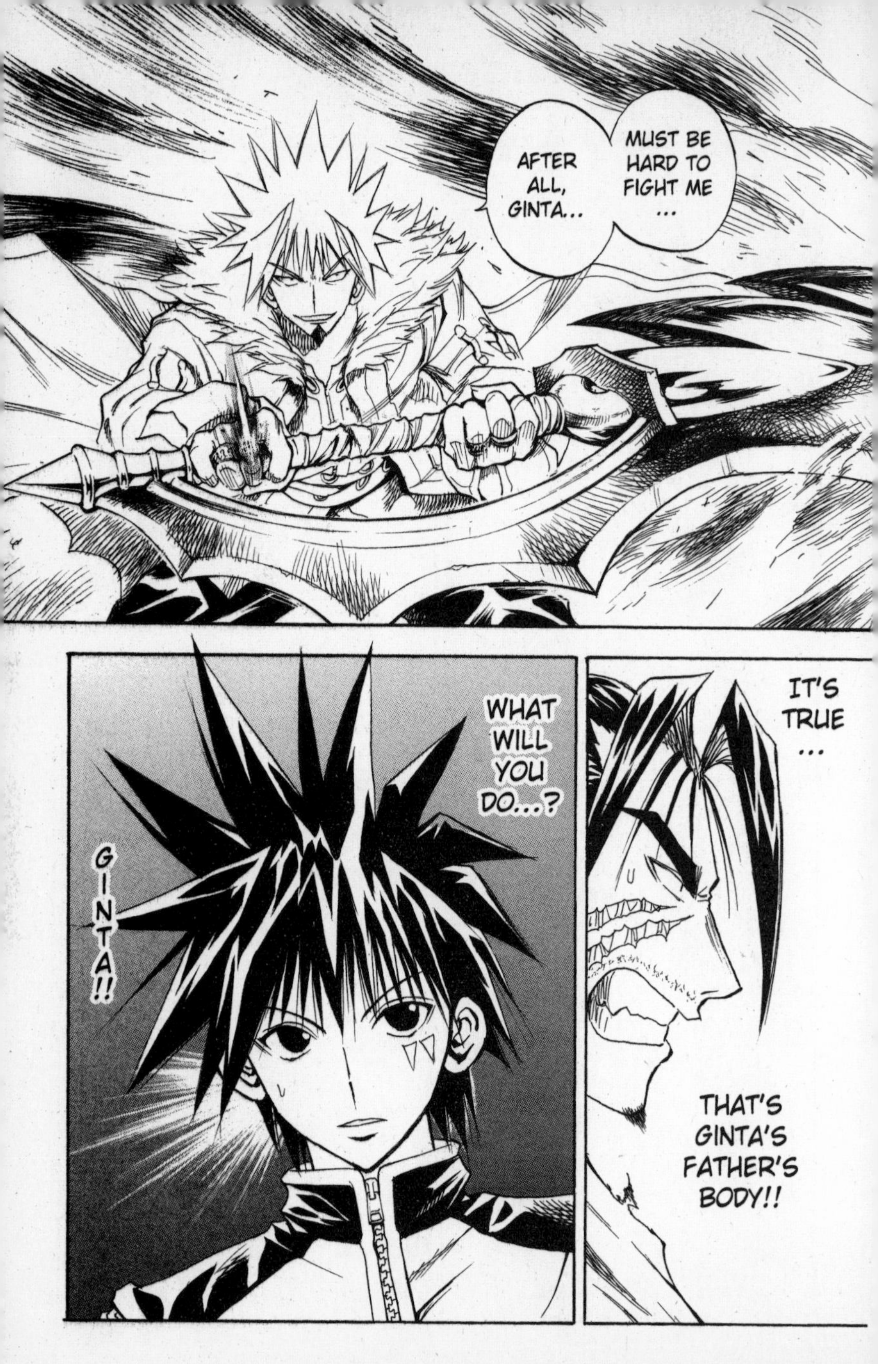
MUST BE HARD TO FIGHT ME ...
AFTER ALL, GINTA...
IT'S TRUE ...
THAT'S GINTA'S FATHER'S BODY!!
WHAT WILL YOU DO...?
GINTA!!

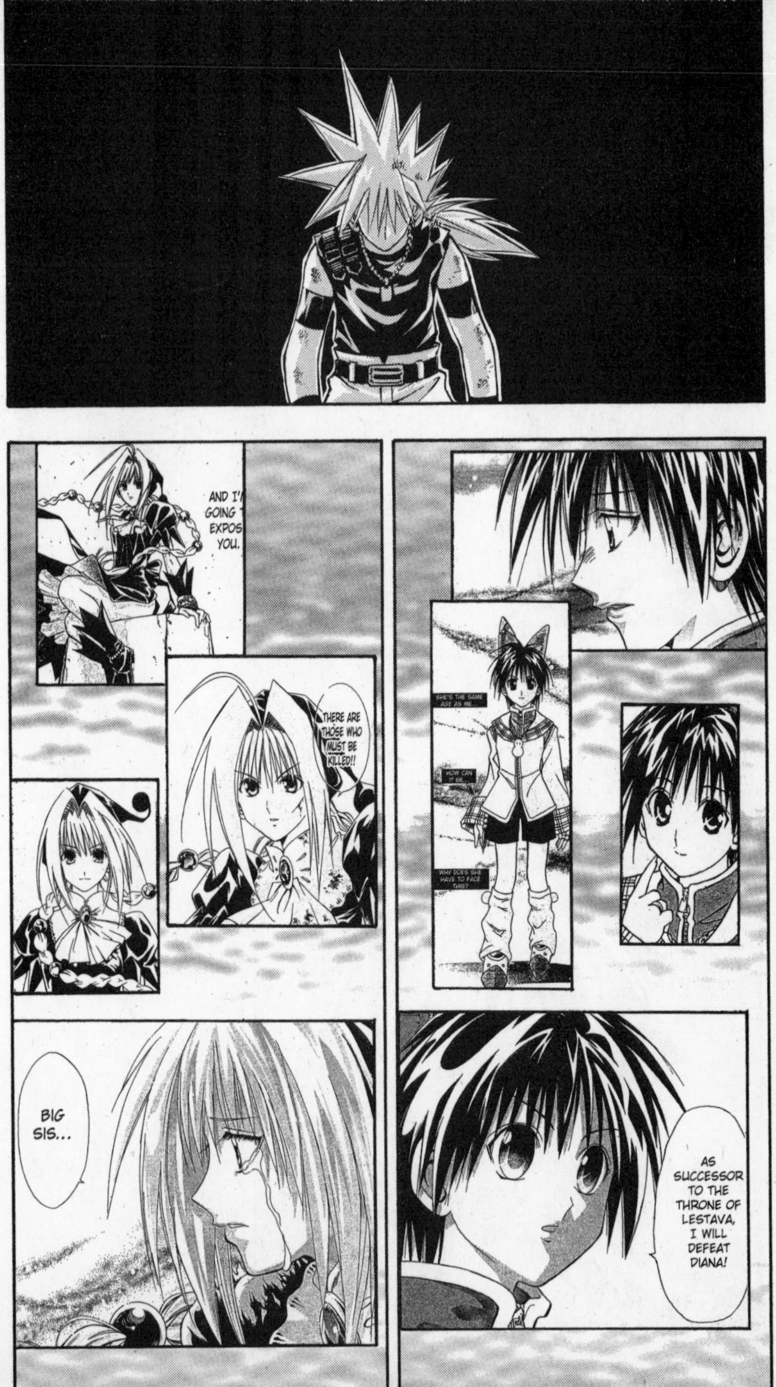
SHE'S THE SAME AGE AS ME...
HOW CAN IT BE...
WHY DOES SHE HAVE TO FACE THIS?
AS SUCCESSOR TO THE THRONE OF LESTAVA, I WILL DEFEAT DIANA!
AND I' GOING EXPOS YOU.
THERE ARE THOSE WHO MUST BE KILLED!!
BIG SIS...

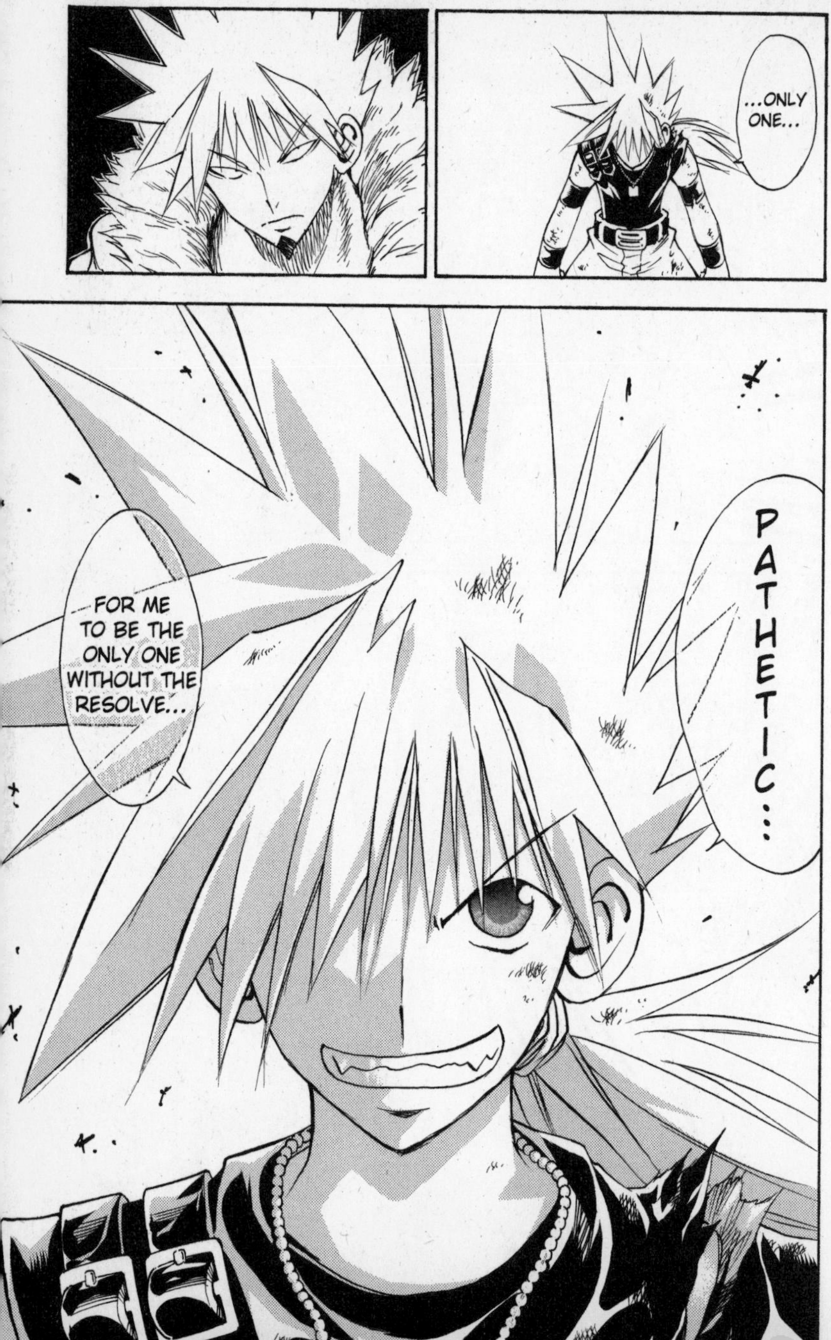
...ONLY ONE...
PATHETIC...
FOR ME TO BE THE ONLY ONE WITHOUT THE RESOLVE...

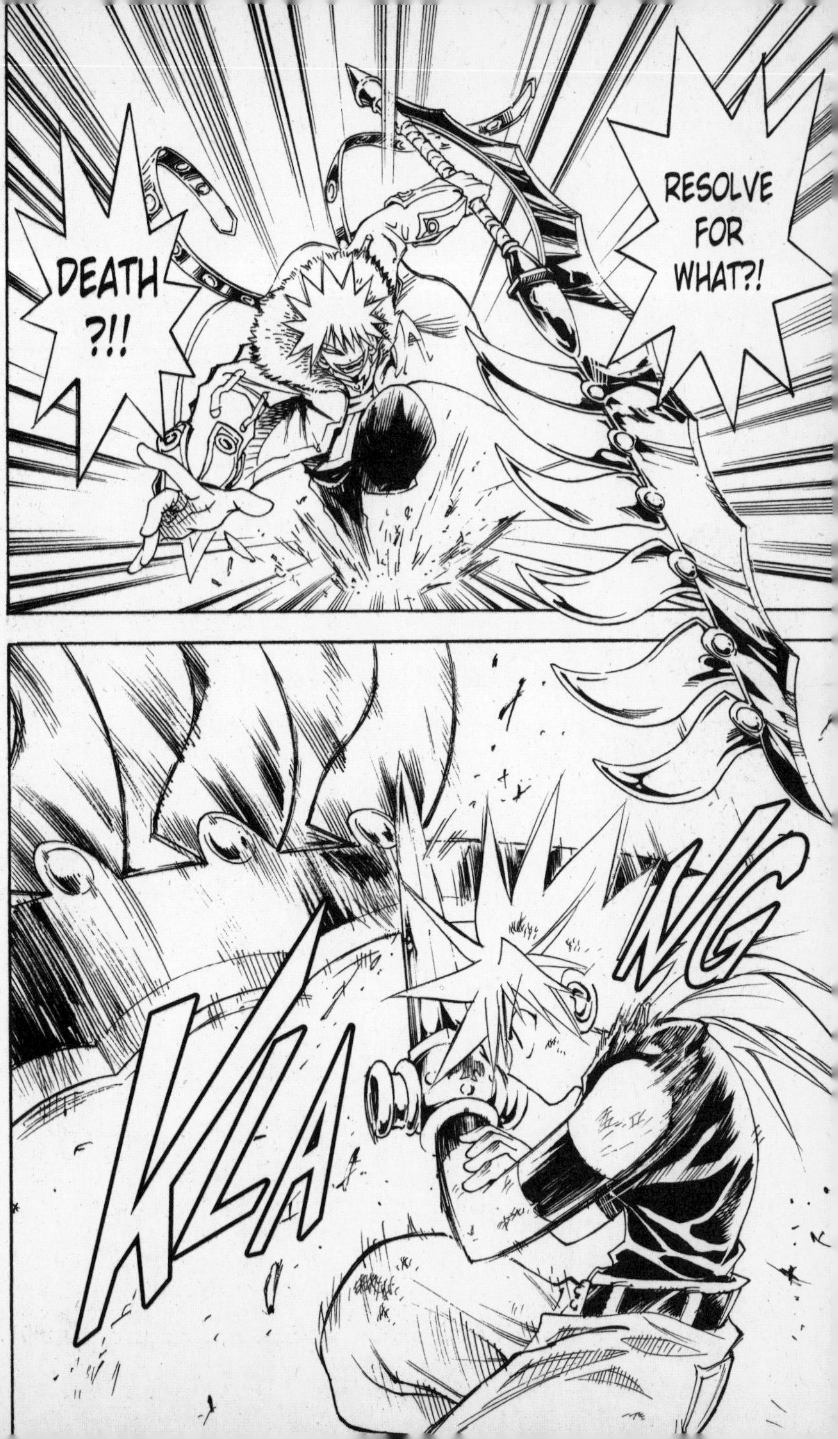
RESOLVE FOR WHAT?!
DEATH ?!!
KLA
NG

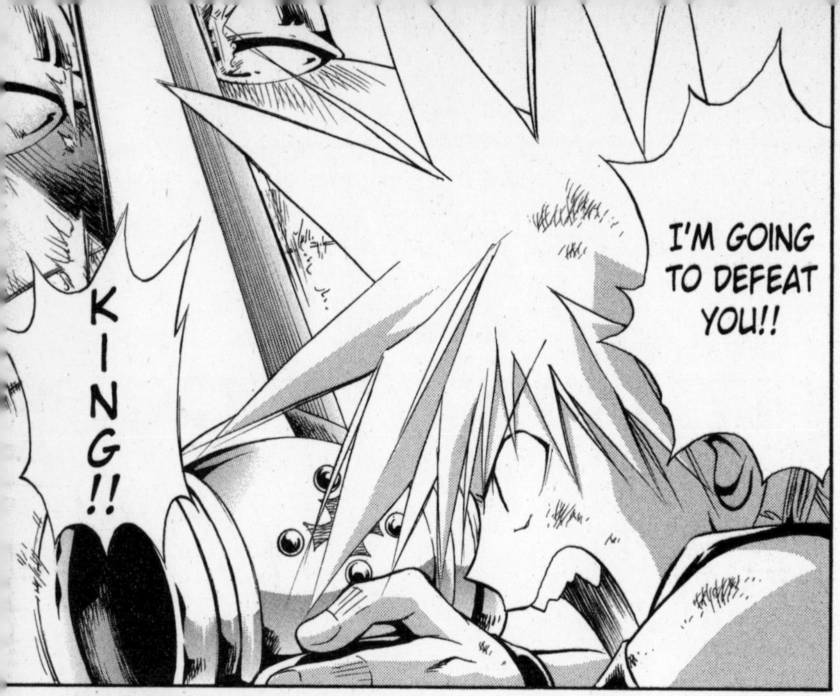
I'M GOING TO DEFEAT YOU!!
KING!!

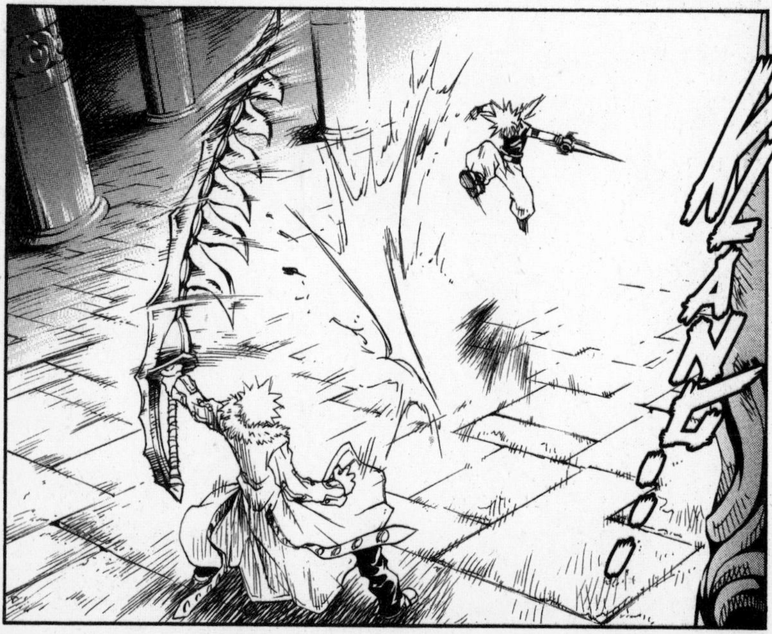
WANG....

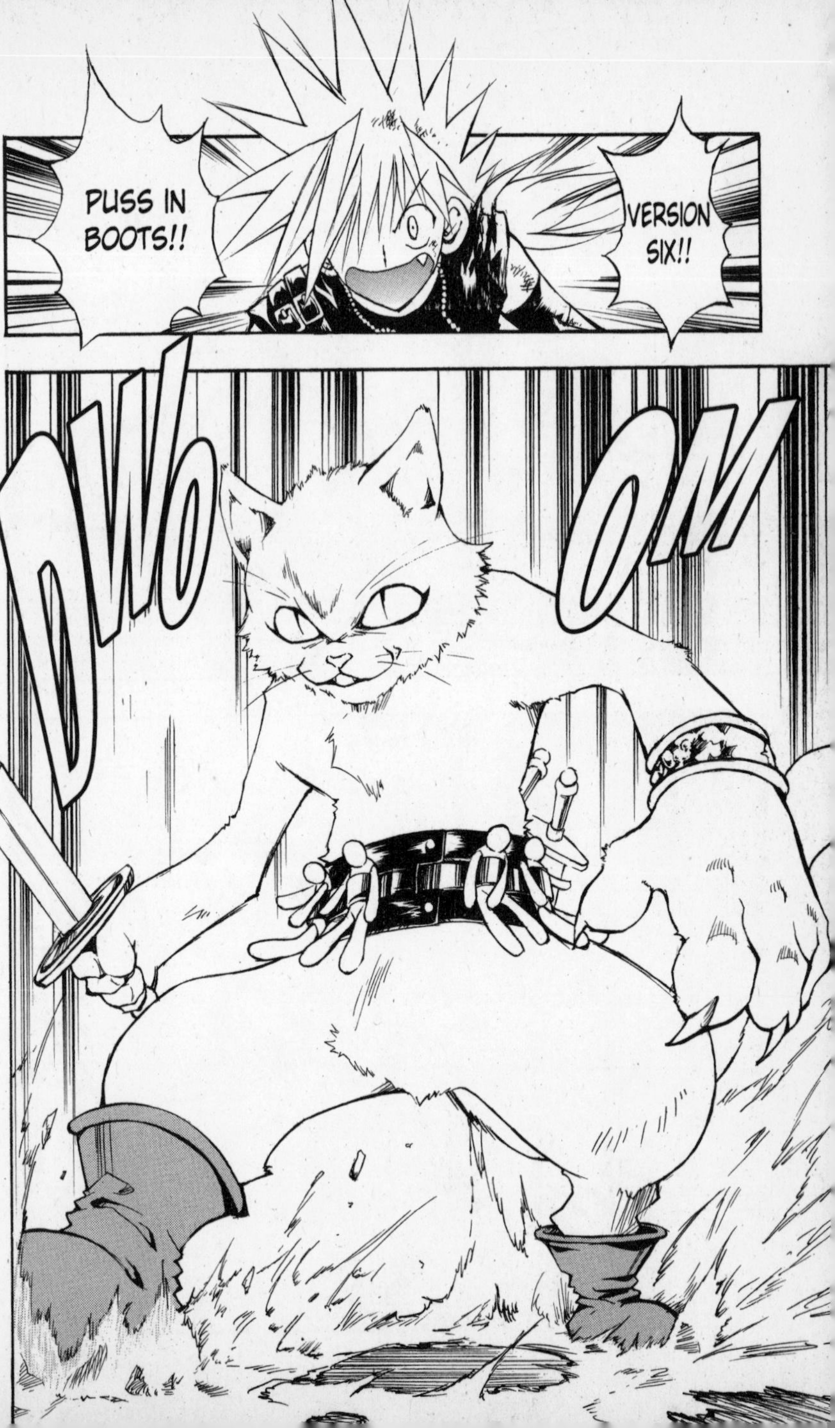
VERSION SIX!!
PUSS IN BOOTS!!
DWOOM

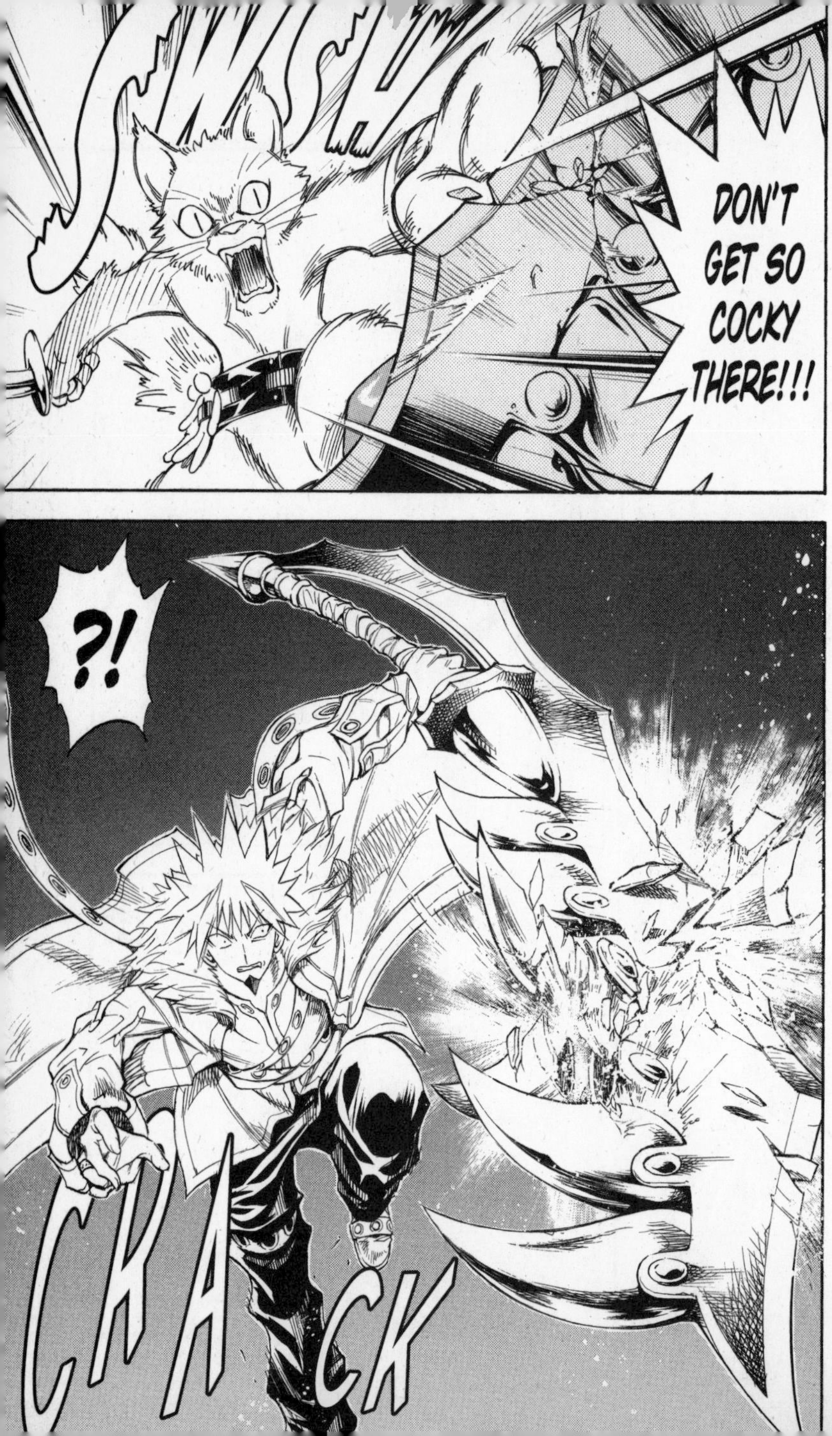
DON'T GET SO COCKY THERE!!!
?!
CRACK

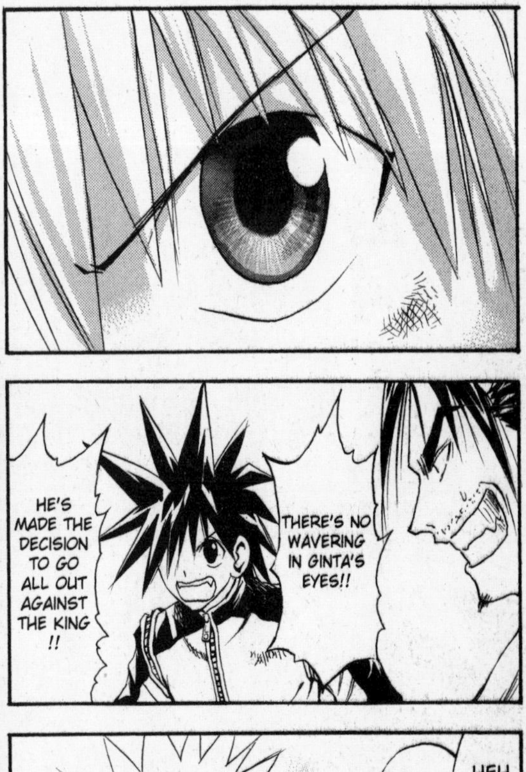
THERE'S NO WAVERING IN GINTA'S EYES!!
HE'S MADE THE DECISION TO GO ALL OUT AGAINST THE KING !!
HEH HEH ...
I'LL FINISH YOU WITH THIS.
FLASH
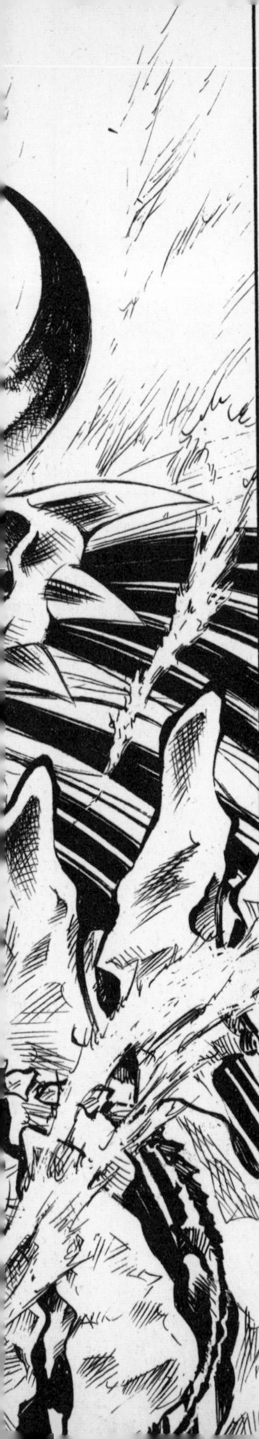

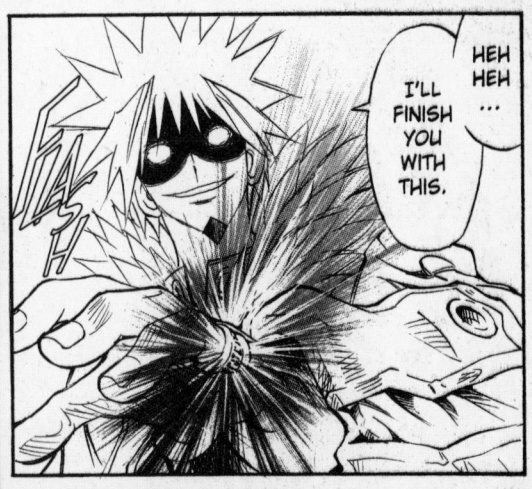

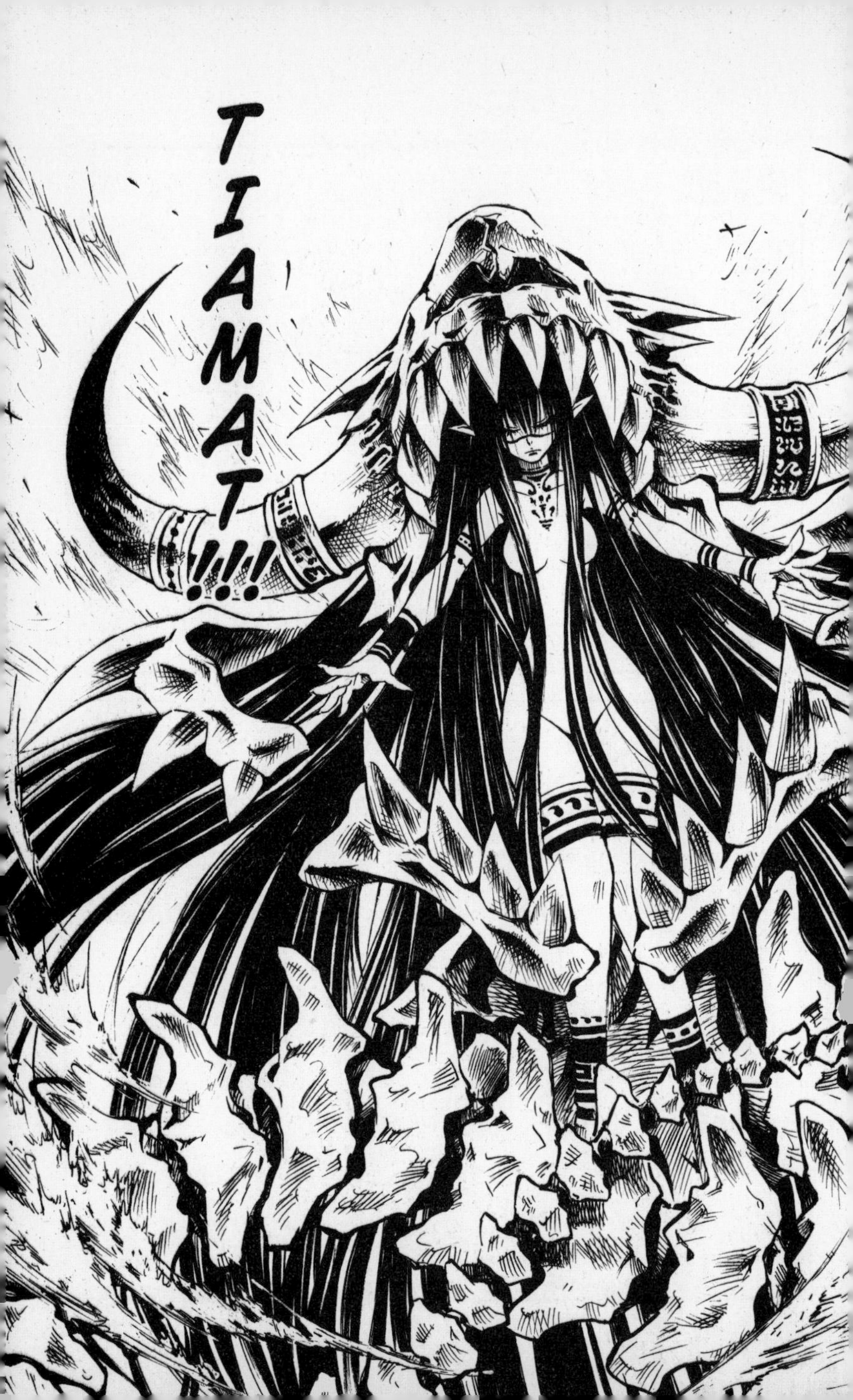
TIAMAT!!!!

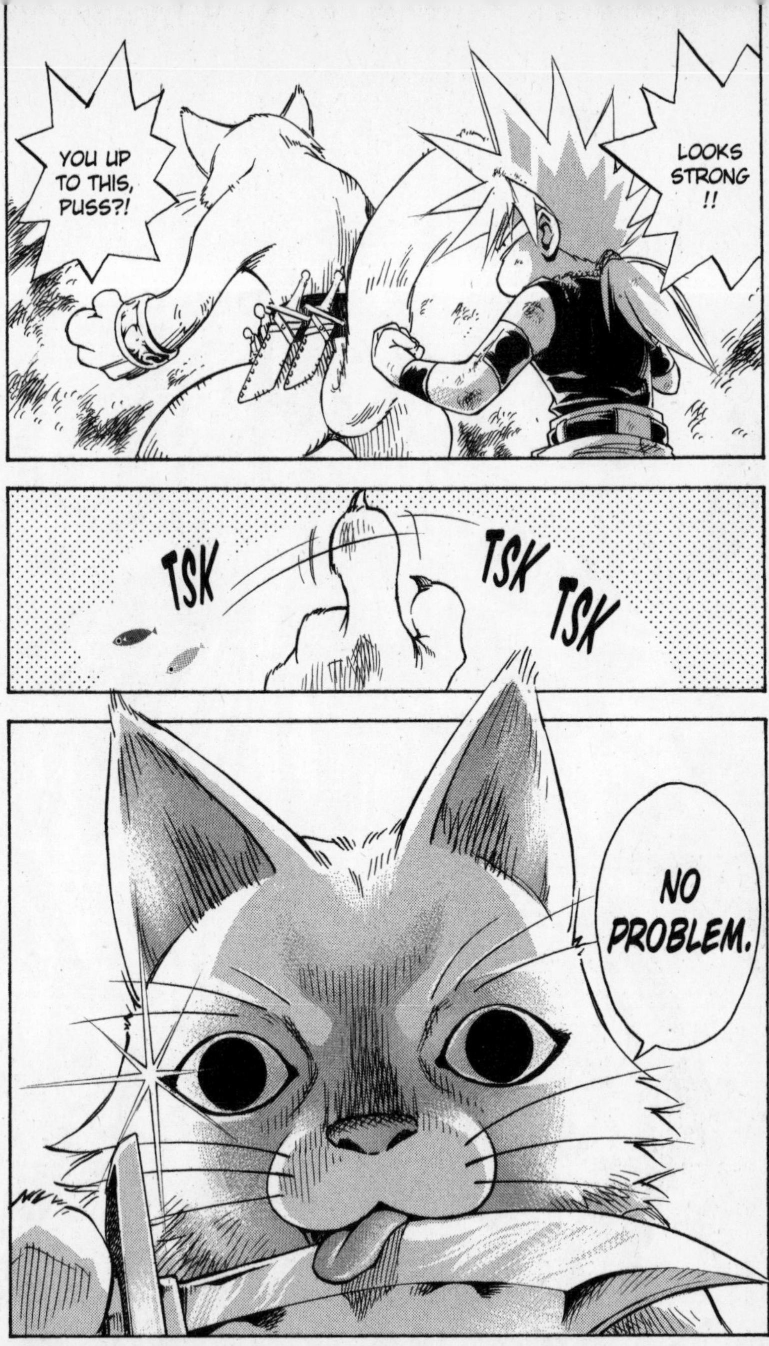
LOOKS STRONG!!
YOU UP TO THIS, PUSS?!
TSK TSK
TSK
NO PROBLEM.

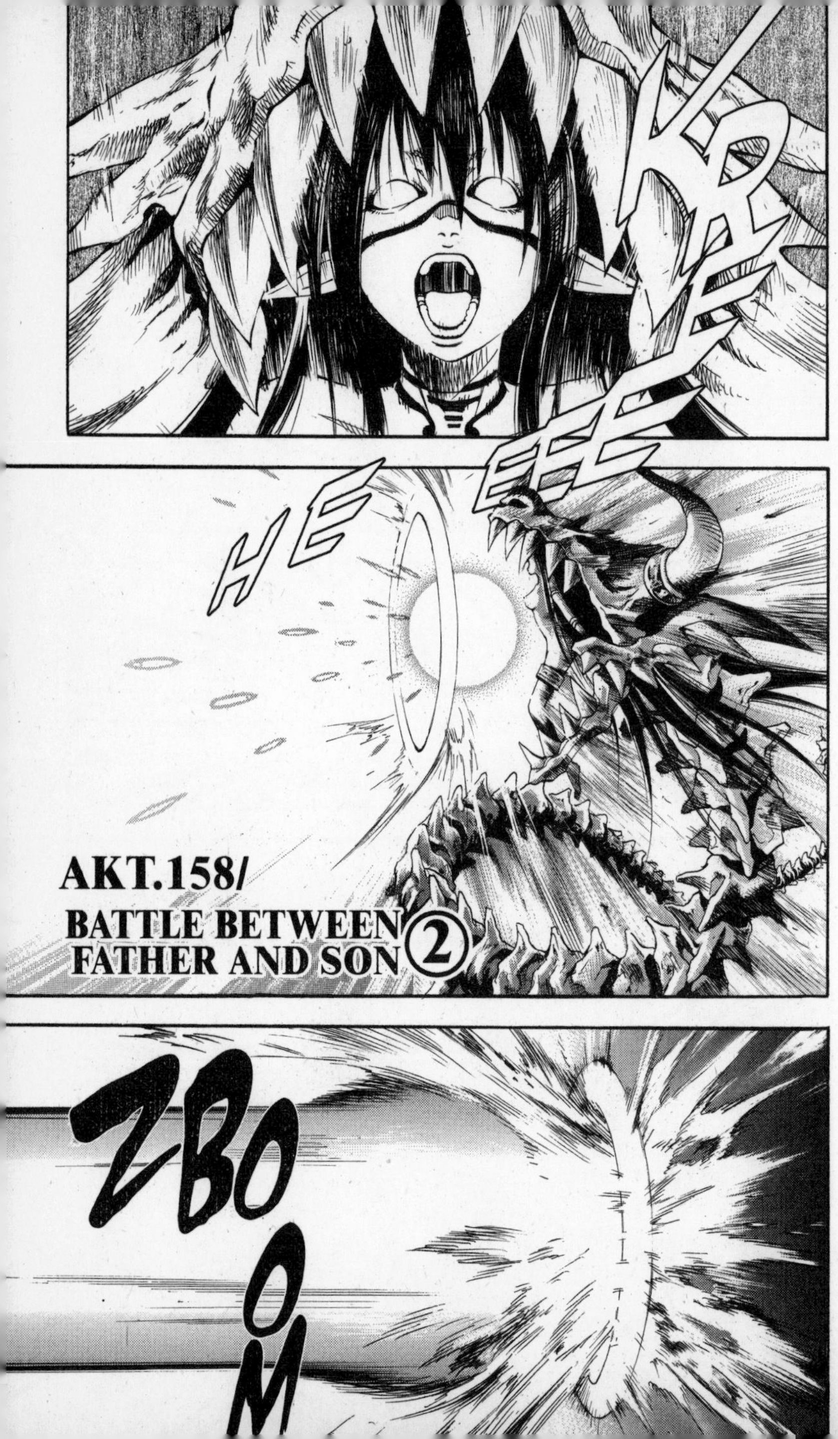
KRYEEE
HE
AKT.158/
BATTLE BETWEEN FATHER AND SON ②
ZBOOM

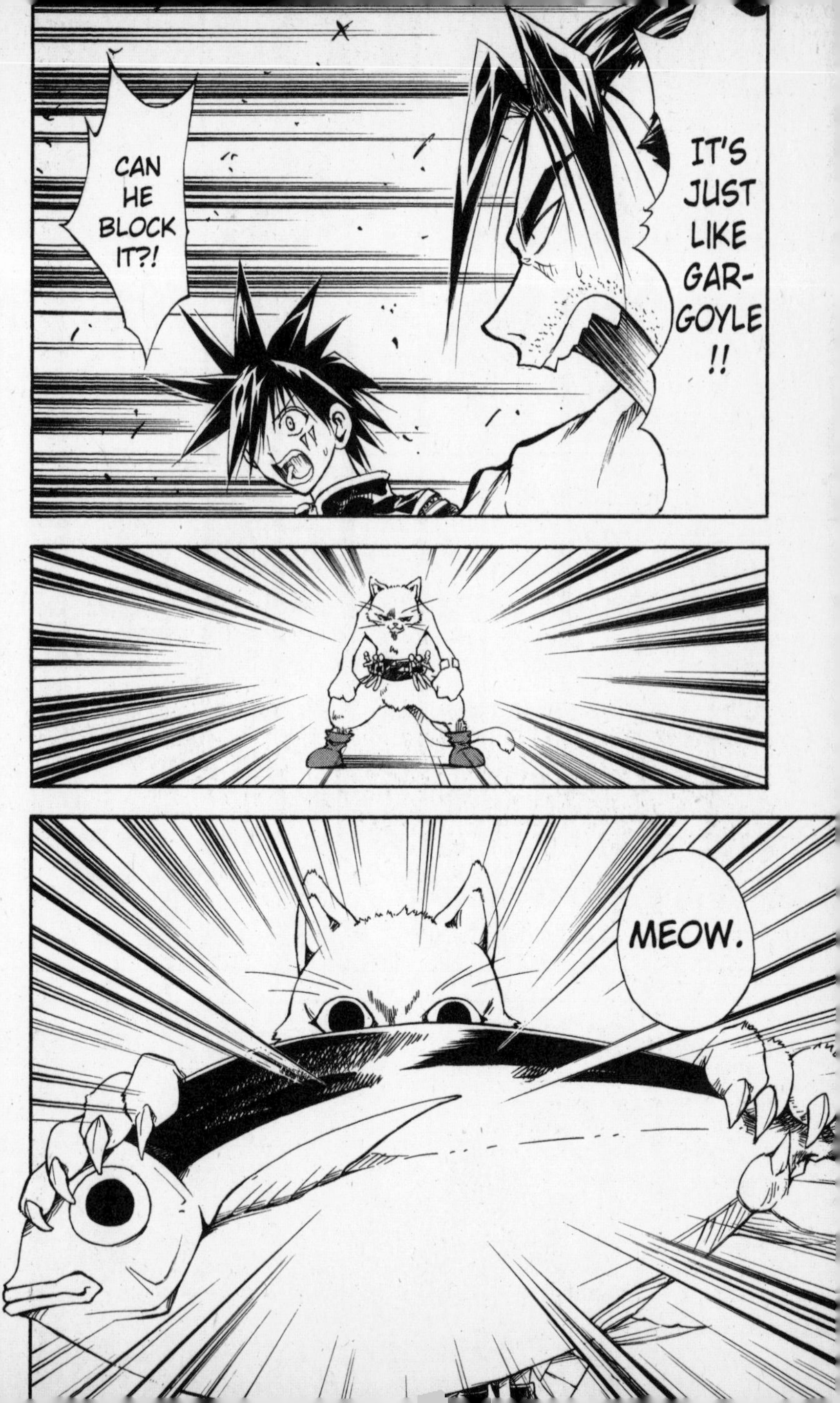
IT'S JUST LIKE GAR-GOYLE !!
CAN HE BLOCK IT?!
MEOW.

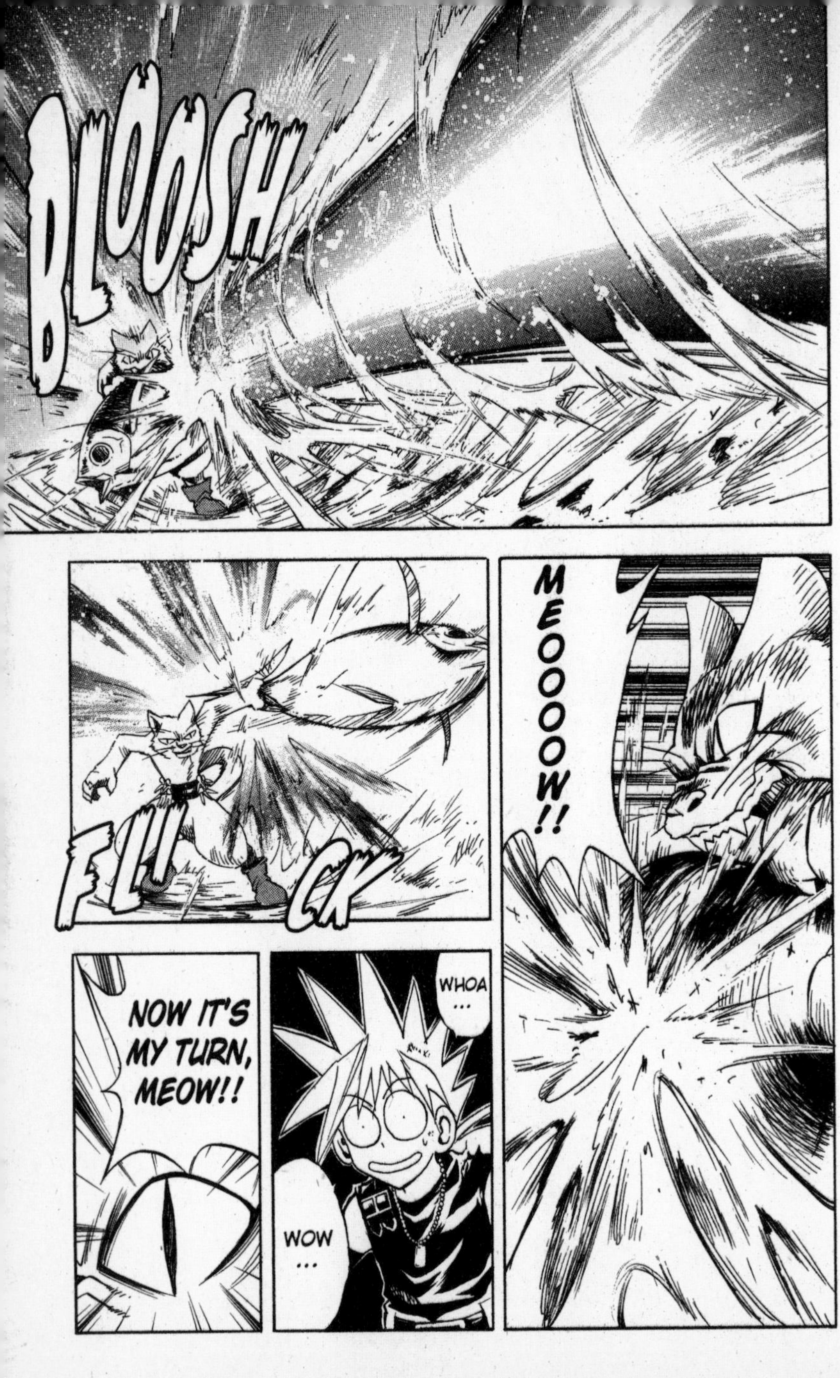
BLOOSH
MEOOOOOW!!
FLICK
WHOA ...
WOW ...
NOW IT'S MY TURN, MEOW!!

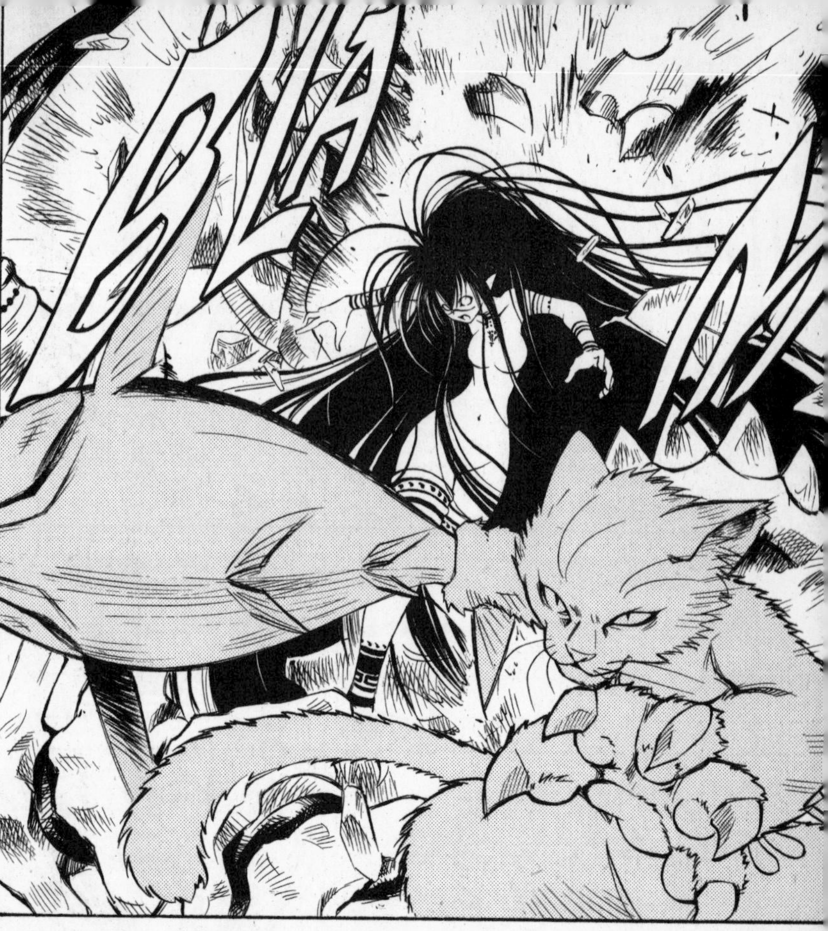
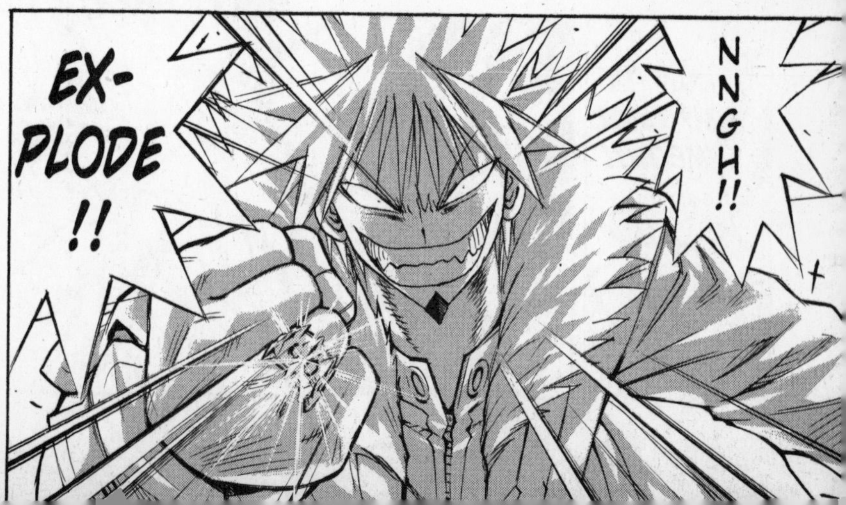
NNGH!!
EX-
PLODE
!!

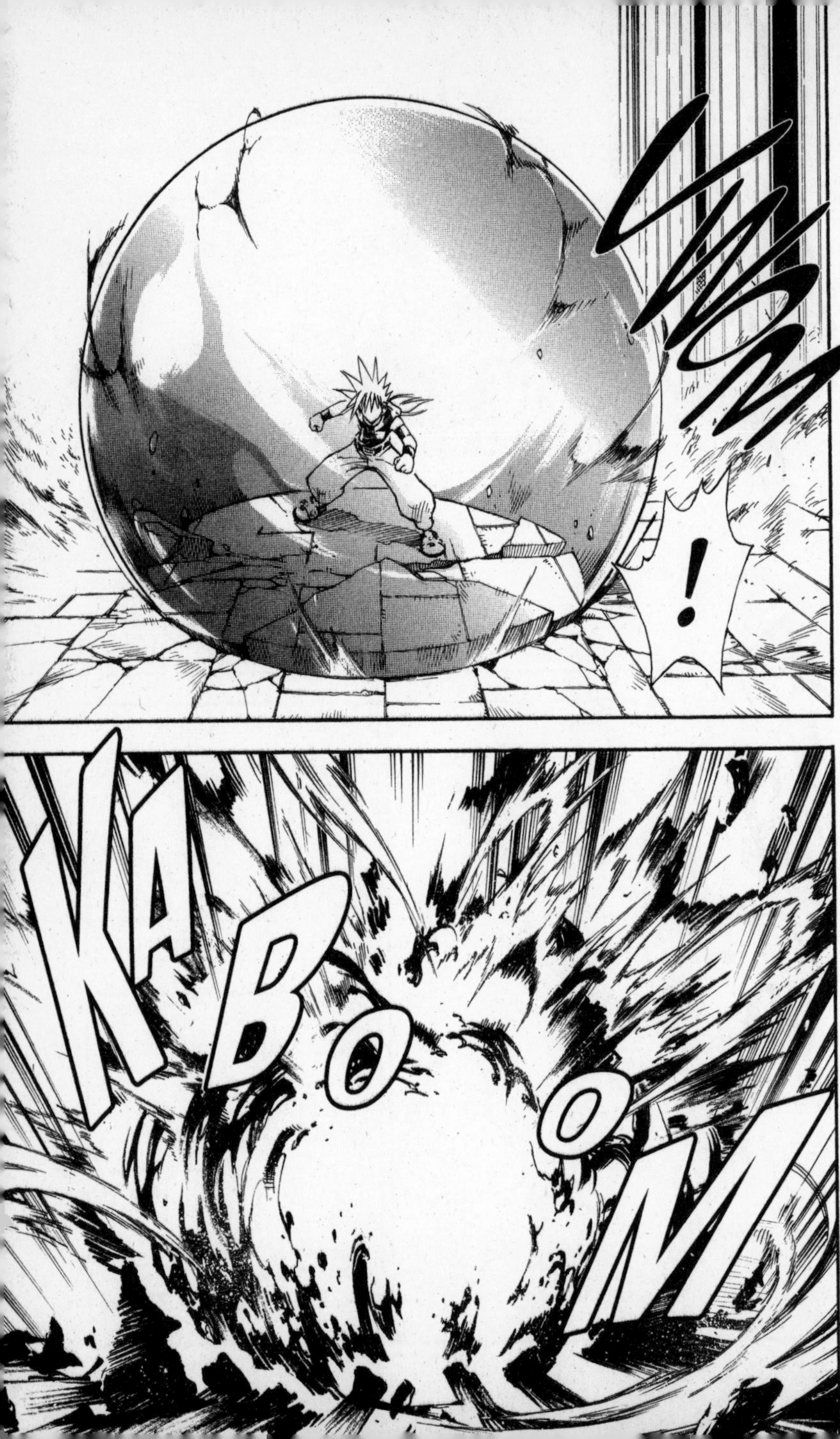
!
KABOOM

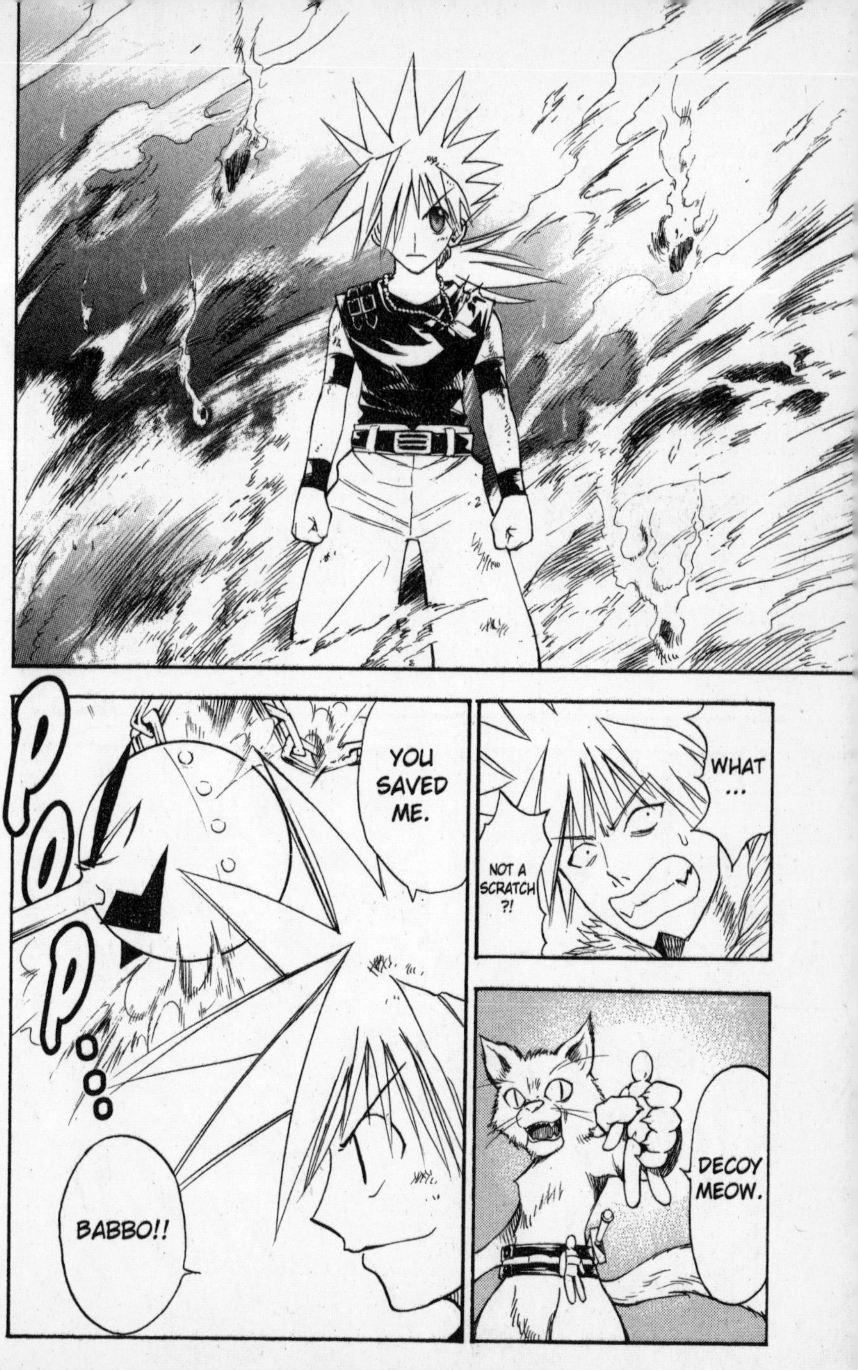
WHAT ...
NOT A SCRATCH ?!
DECOY MEOW.
YOU SAVED ME.
POPPOOO
BABBO!!

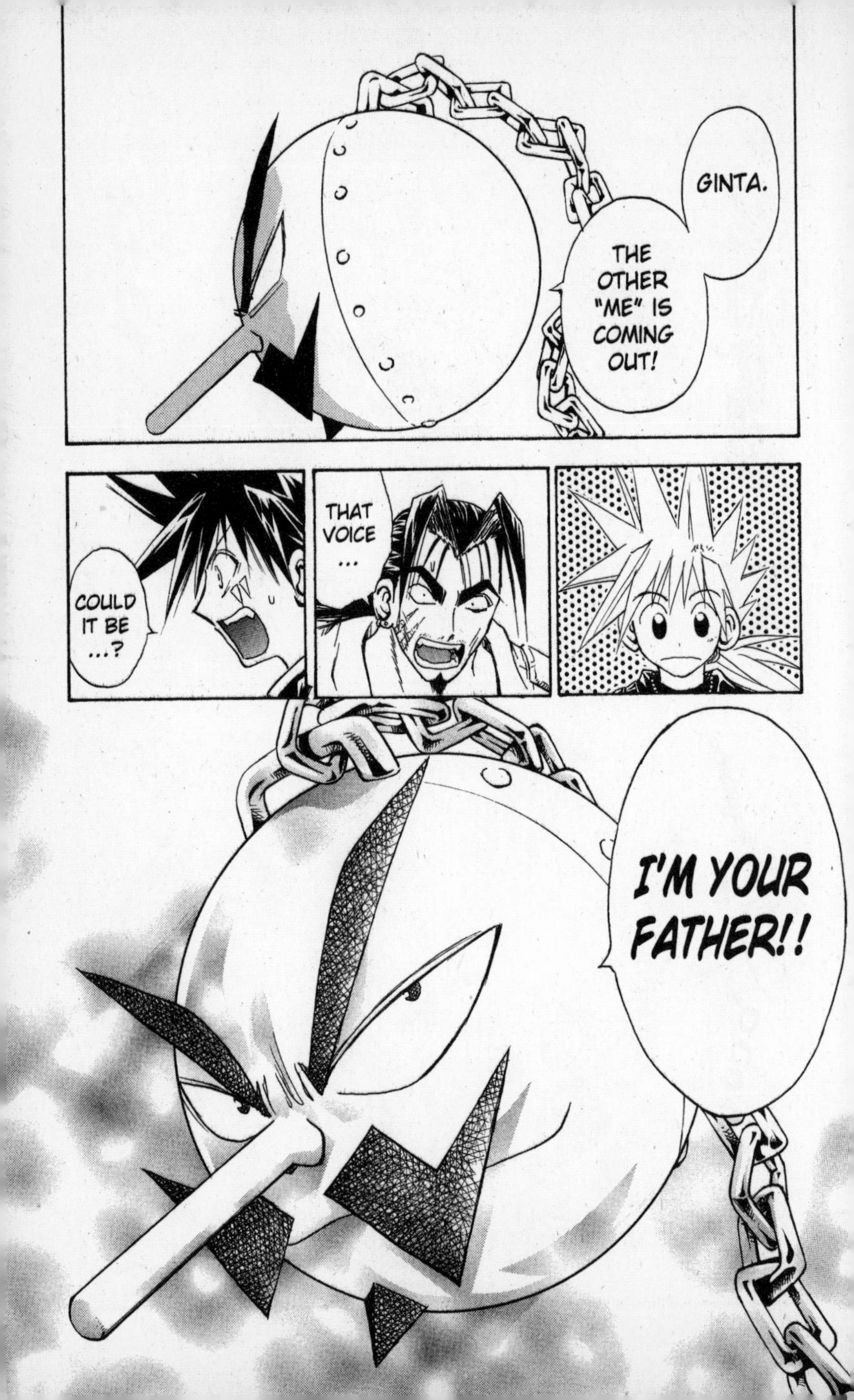
GINTA.
THE OTHER "ME" IS COMING OUT!
THAT VOICE ...
COULD IT BE ...?
I'M YOUR FATHER!!

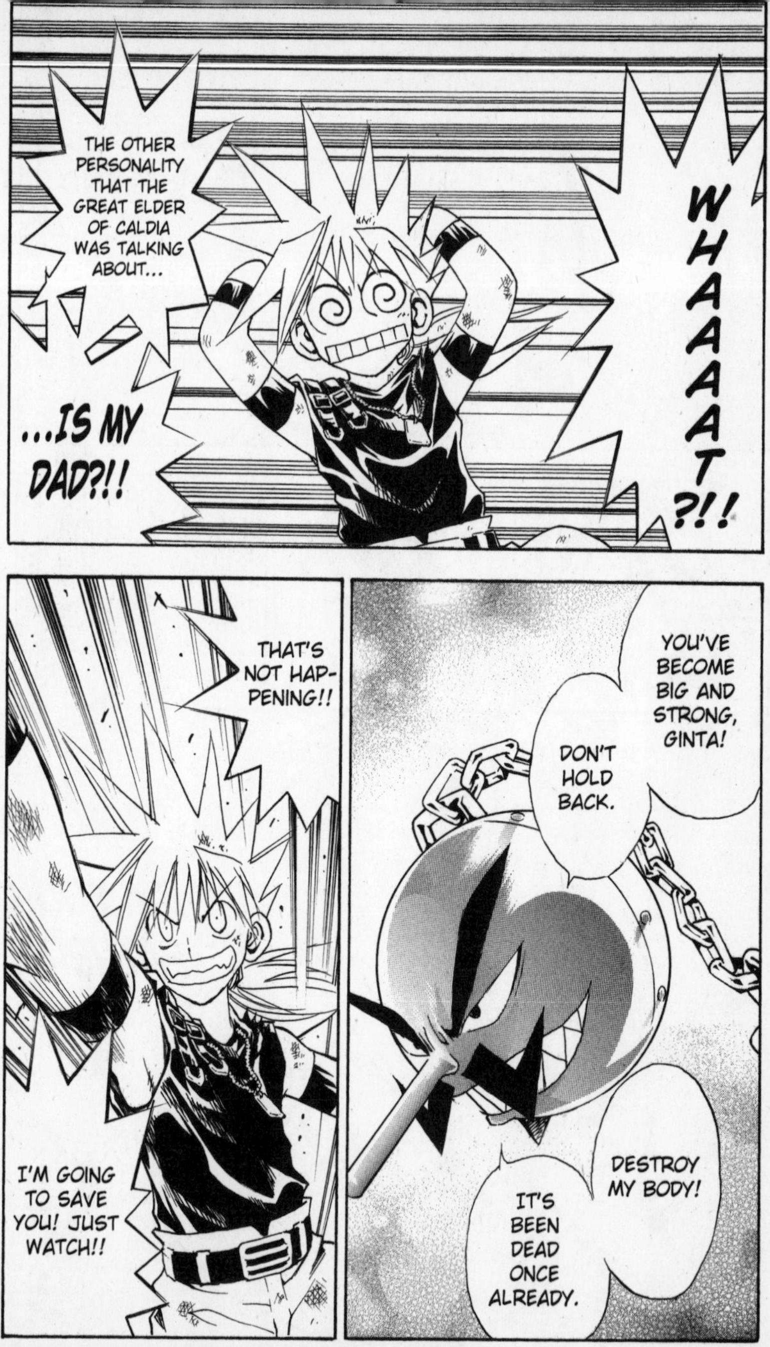
THE OTHER PERSONALITY THAT THE GREAT ELDER OF CALDIA WAS TALKING ABOUT...
...IS MY DAD?!!
WHAAAAAT?!!
YOU'VE BECOME BIG AND STRONG, GINTA!
DON'T HOLD BACK.
DESTROY MY BODY!
IT'S BEEN DEAD ONCE ALREADY.
THAT'S NOT HAP-PENING!!
I'M GOING TO SAVE YOU! JUST WATCH!!

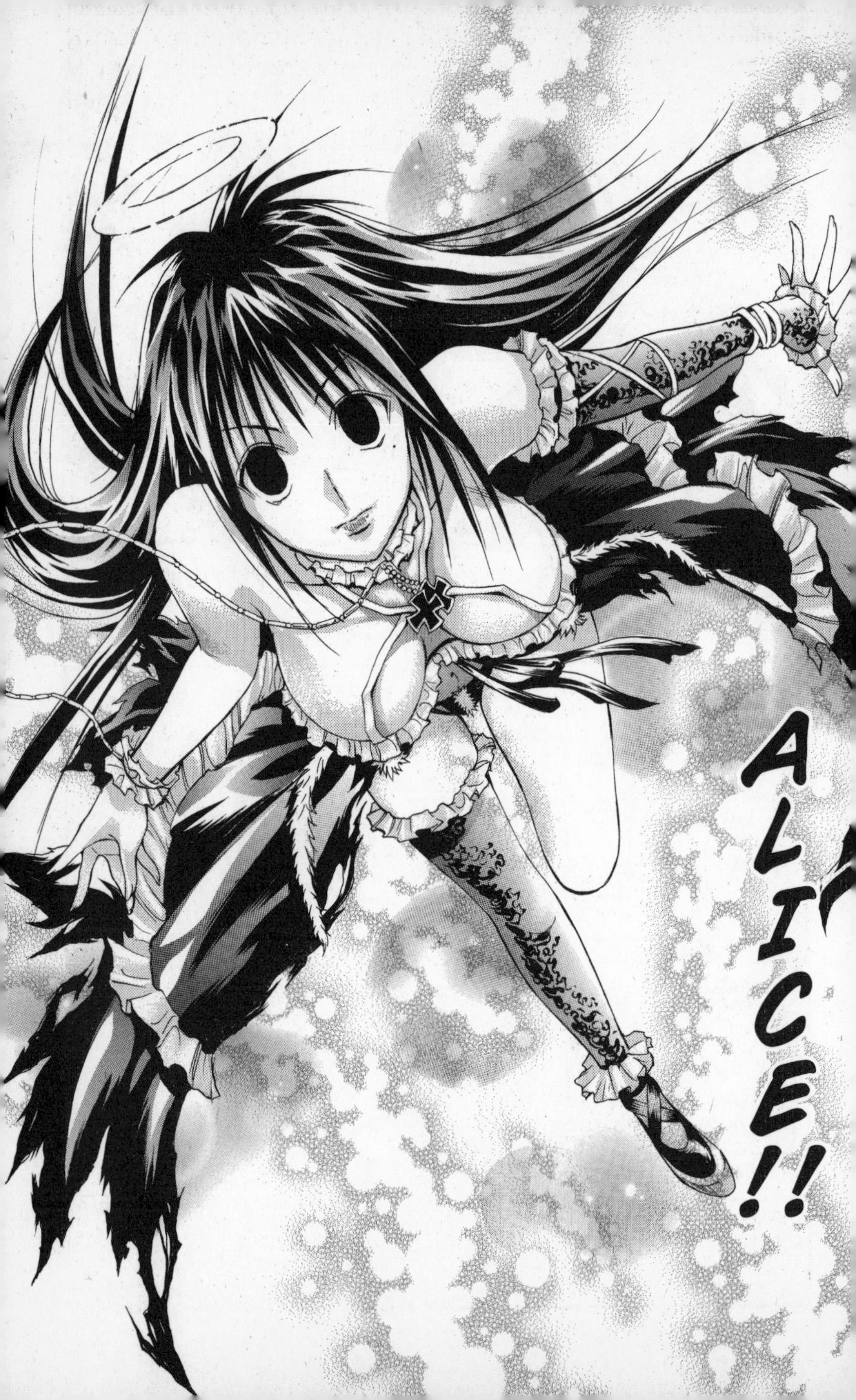
ALICE!!

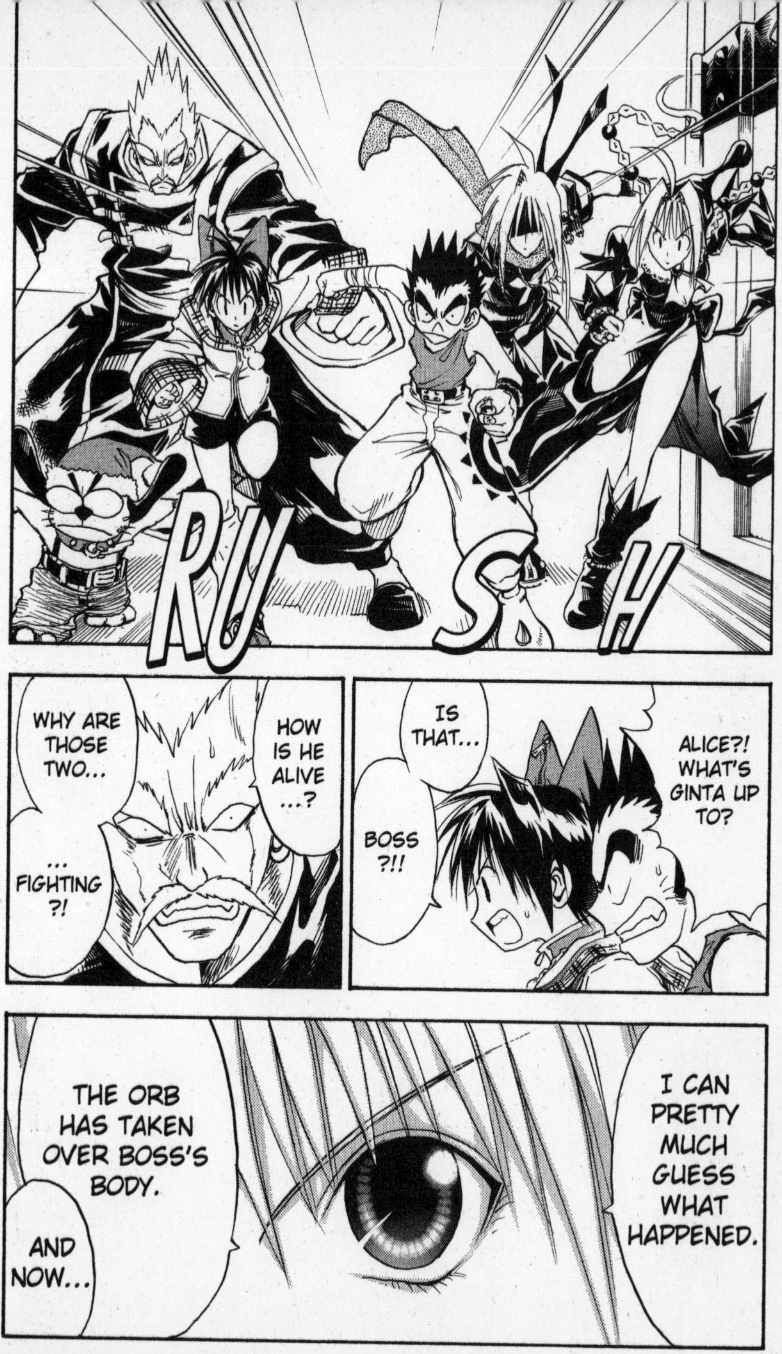
RUSH
IS THAT...
BOSS ?!!
ALICE?! WHAT'S GINTA UP TO?
HOW IS HE ALIVE ...?
WHY ARE THOSE TWO...
... FIGHTING ?!
I CAN PRETTY MUCH GUESS WHAT HAPPENED.
THE ORB HAS TAKEN OVER BOSS'S BODY.
AND NOW...

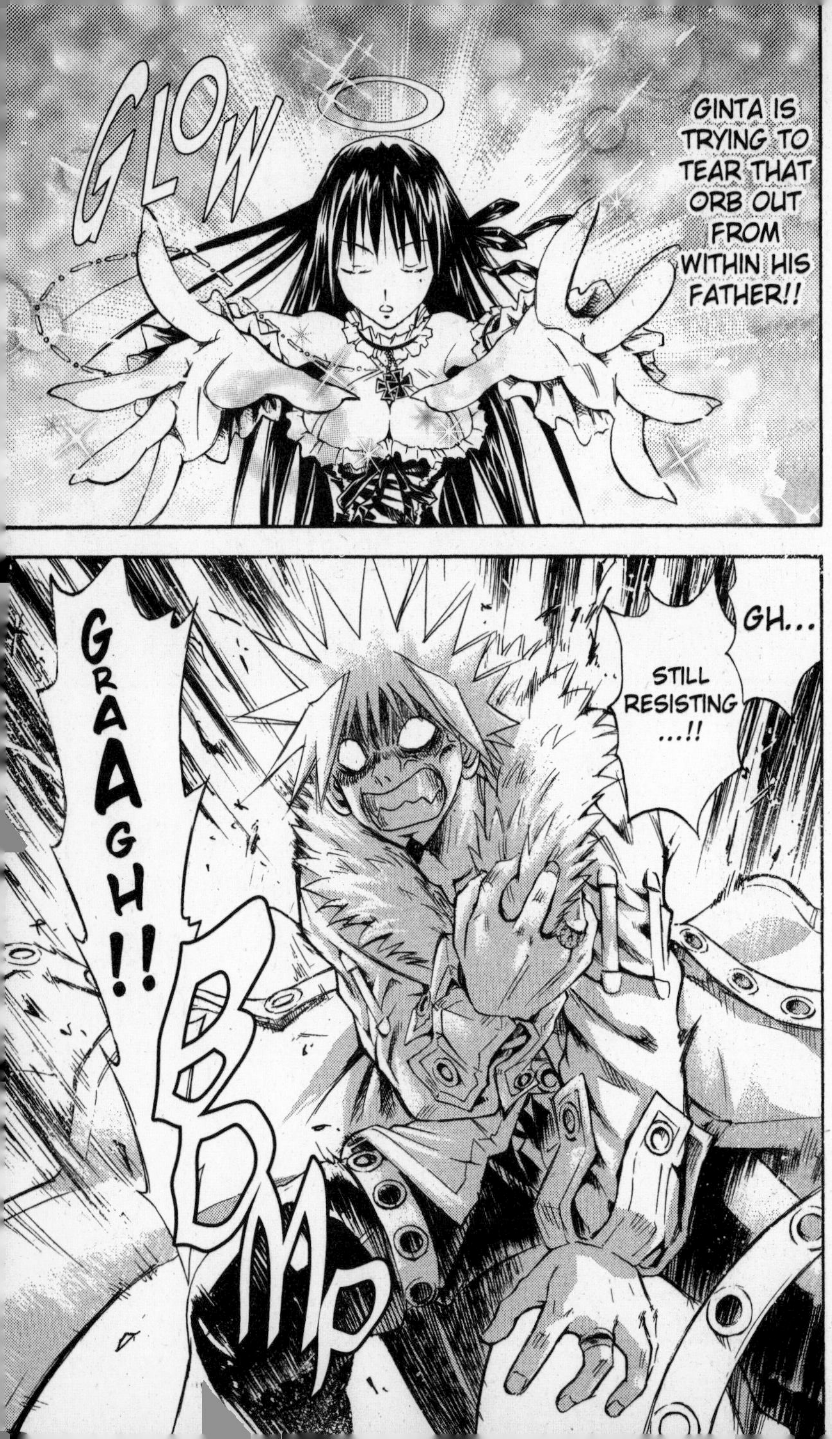
GINTA IS TRYING TO TEAR THAT ORB OUT FROM WITHIN HIS FATHER!!
GLOW
GH...
STILL RESISTING ...!!
GRAAGH!!
BOMP

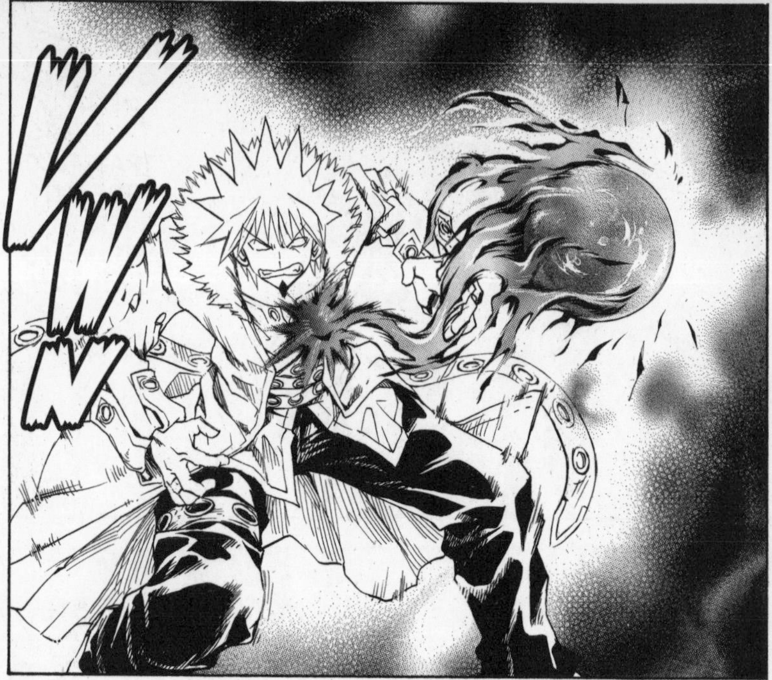
VWN

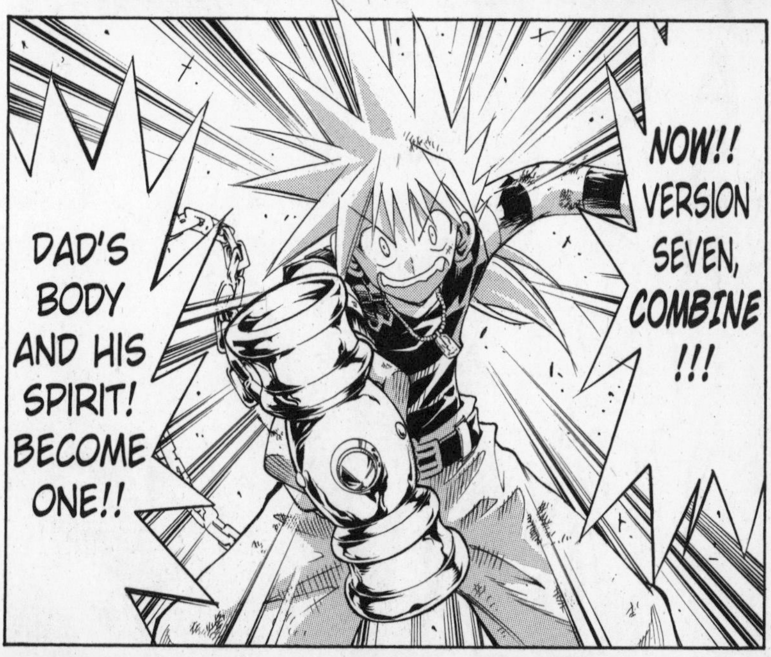
NOW!! VERSION SEVEN, COMBINE !!!
DAD'S BODY AND HIS SPIRIT! BECOME ONE!!

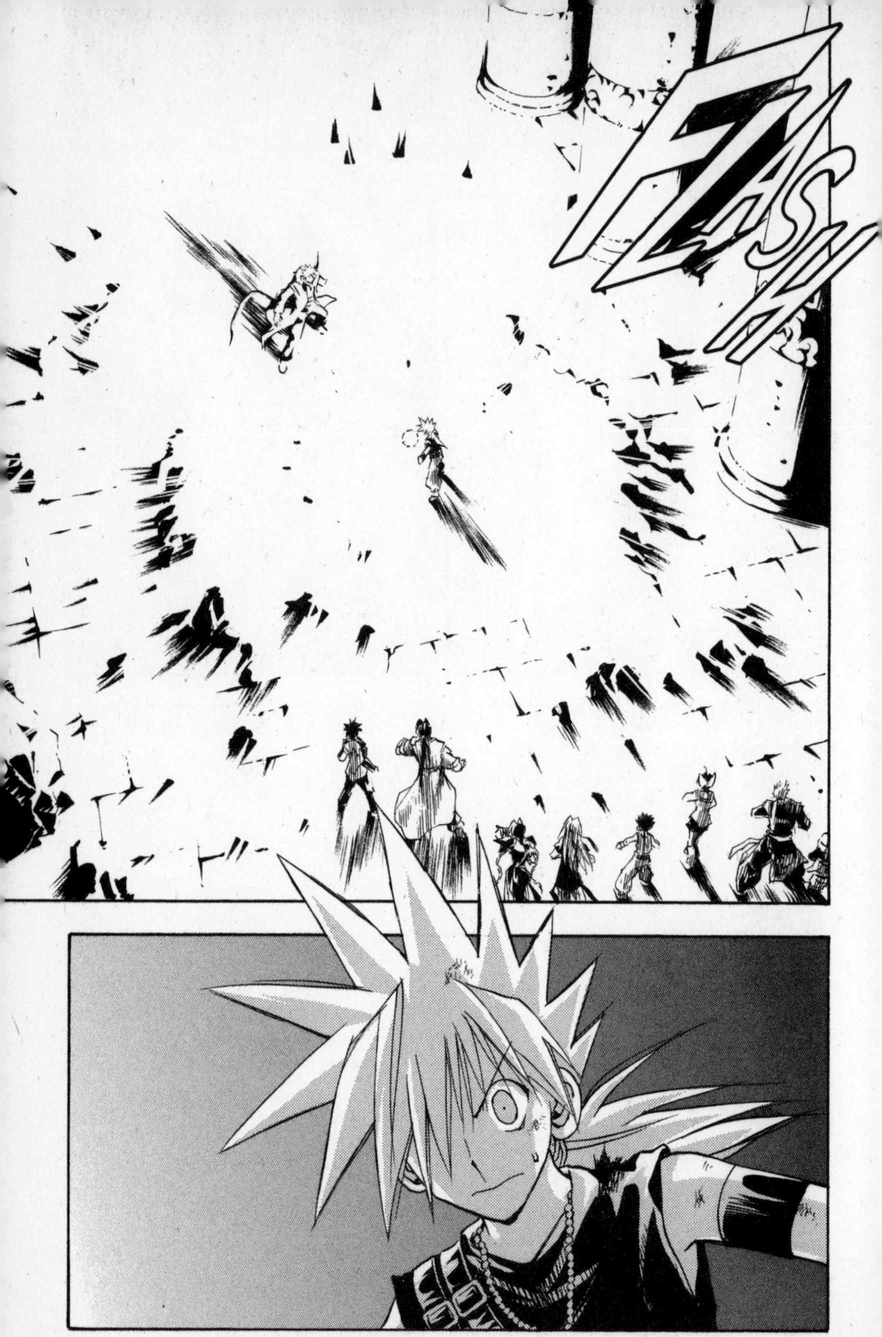
ZASH

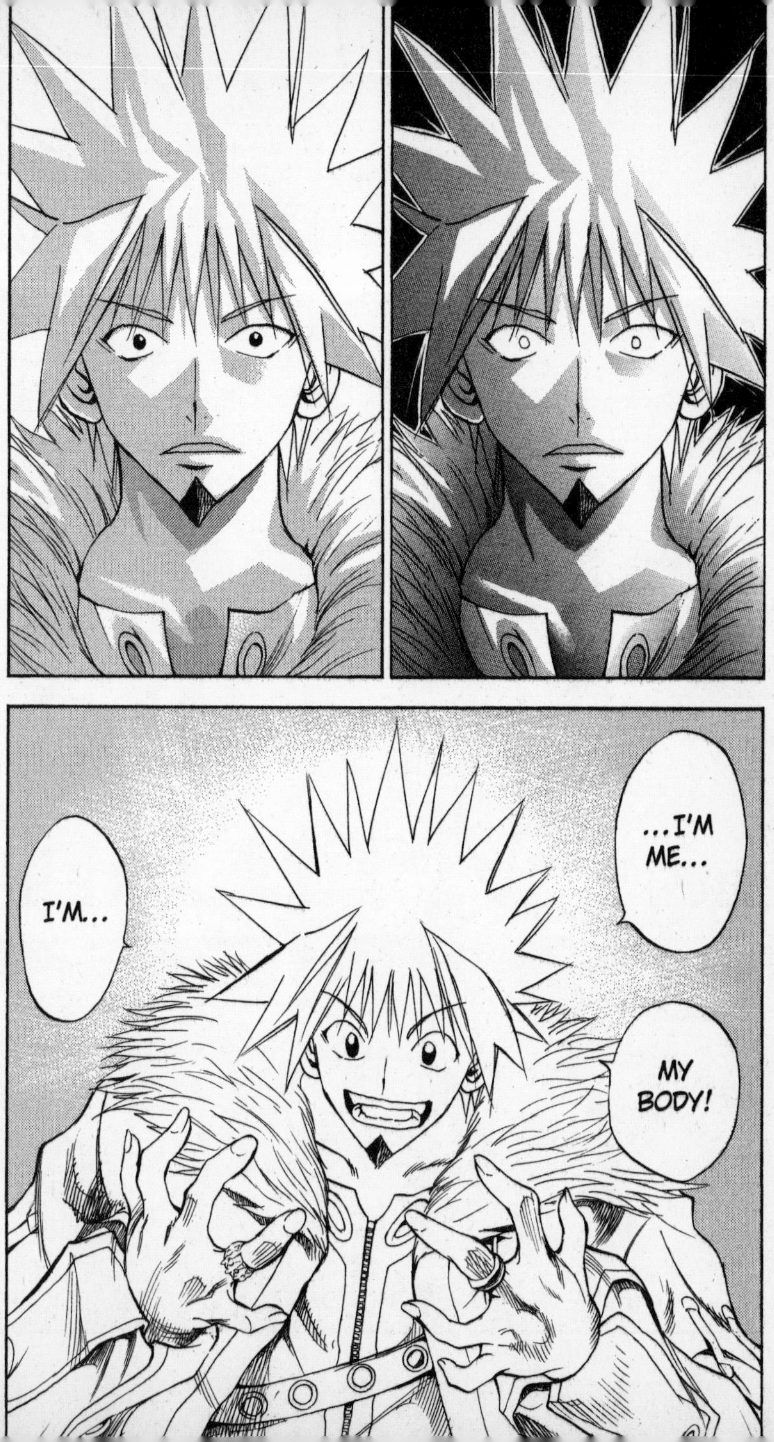
...I'M ME...
I'M...
MY BODY!

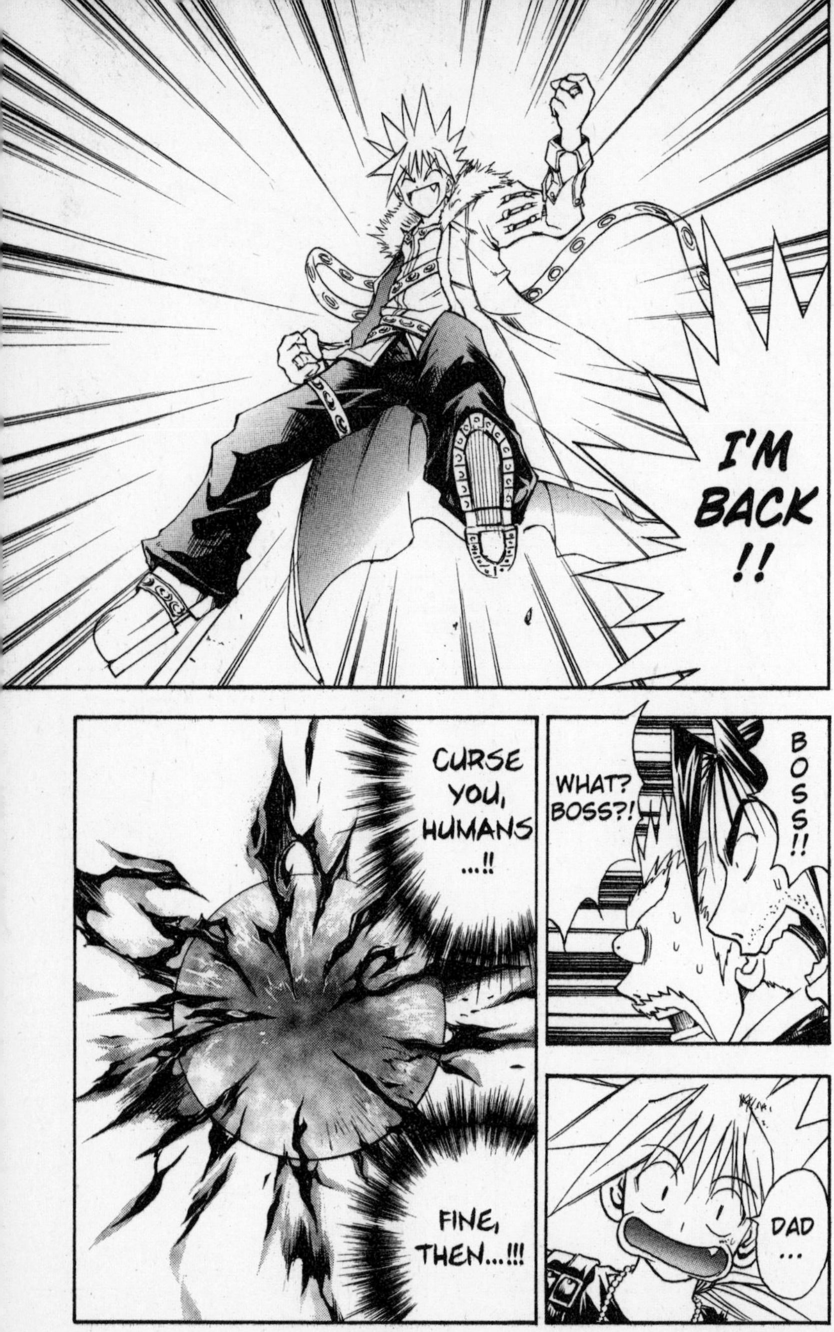
I'M BACK !!
BOSS!!
WHAT? BOSS?!
DAD ...
CURSE YOU, HUMANS ...!!
FINE, THEN...!!!

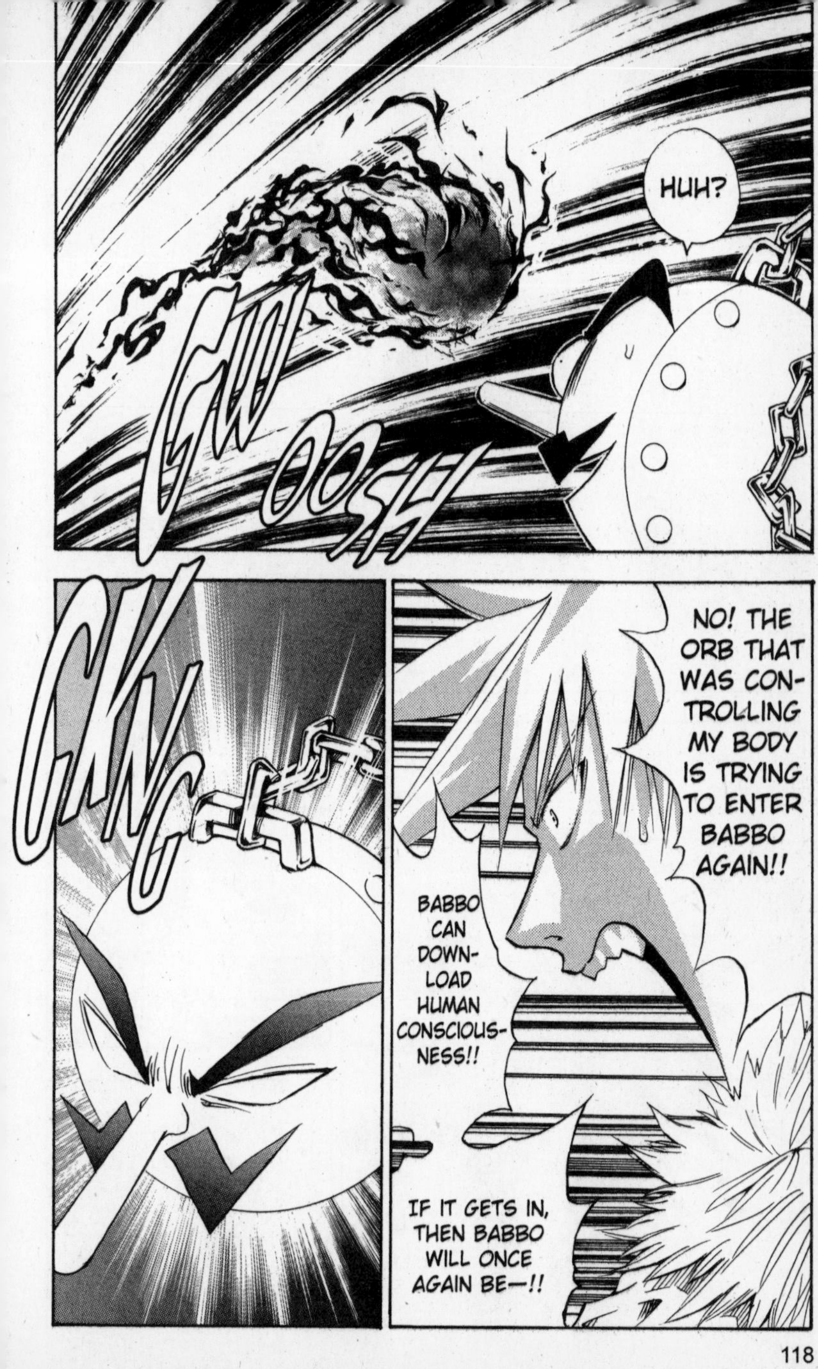
HUH?
GWOOSH
NO! THE ORB THAT WAS CONTROLLING MY BODY IS TRYING TO ENTER BABBO AGAIN!!
BABBO CAN DOWNLOAD HUMAN CONSCIOUSNESS!!
IF IT GETS IN, THEN BABBO WILL ONCE AGAIN BE—!!
CLANG

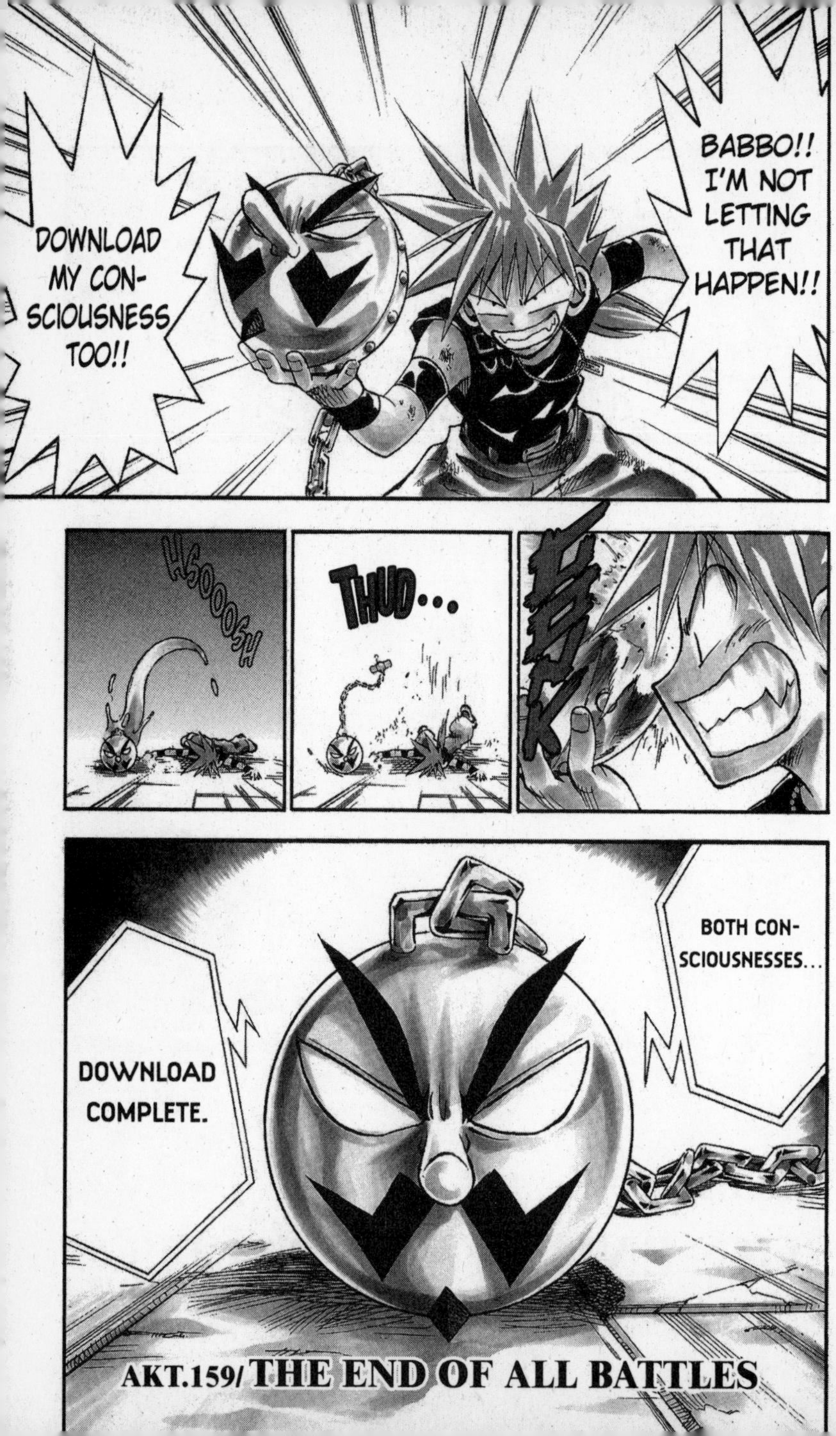
BABBO!! I'M NOT LETTING THAT HAPPEN!!
DOWNLOAD MY CON-SCIOUSNESS TOO!!
THUD...
BOTH CON-SCIOUSNESSES...
DOWNLOAD COMPLETE.
AKT.159/ THE END OF ALL BATTLES

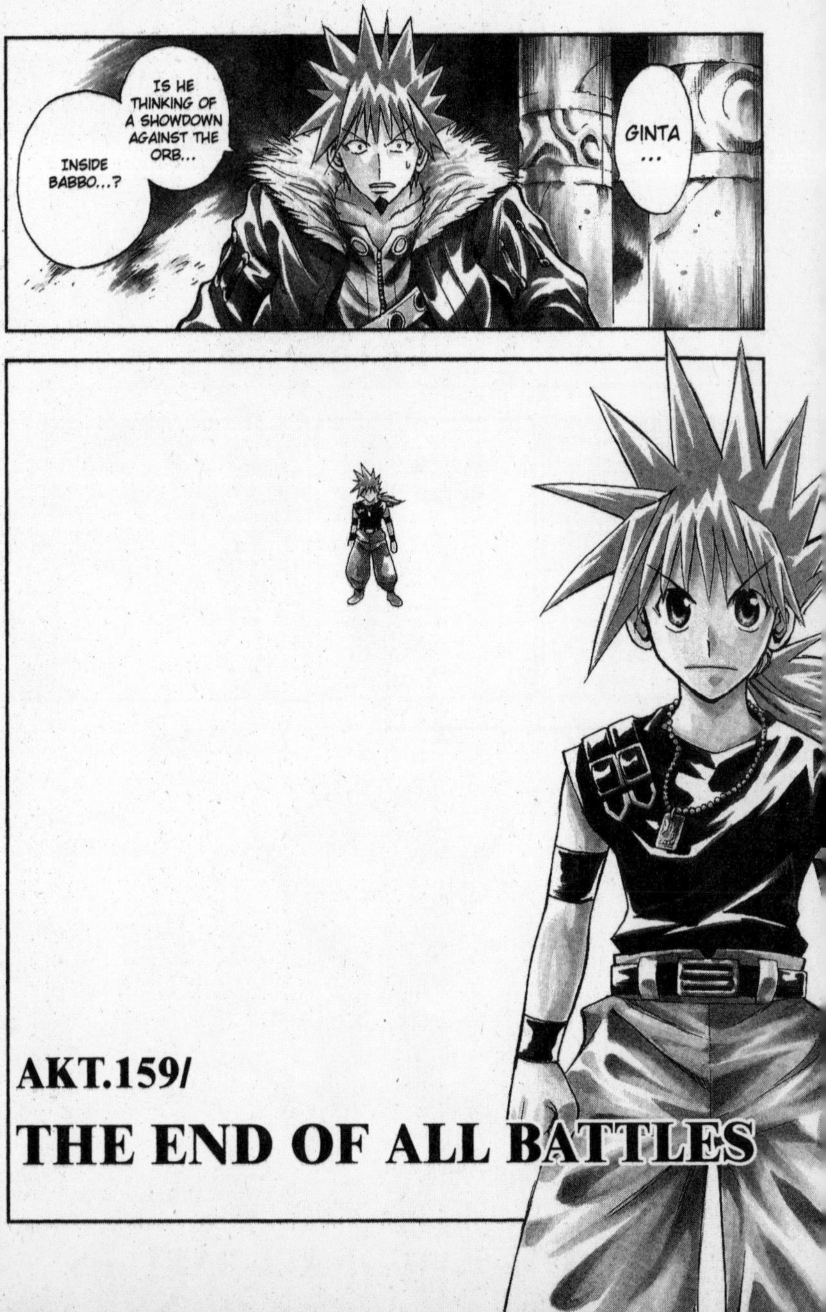
GINTA ...
IS HE THINKING OF A SHOWDOWN AGAINST THE ORB... INSIDE BABBO...?

AKT.159/ THE END OF ALL BATTLES

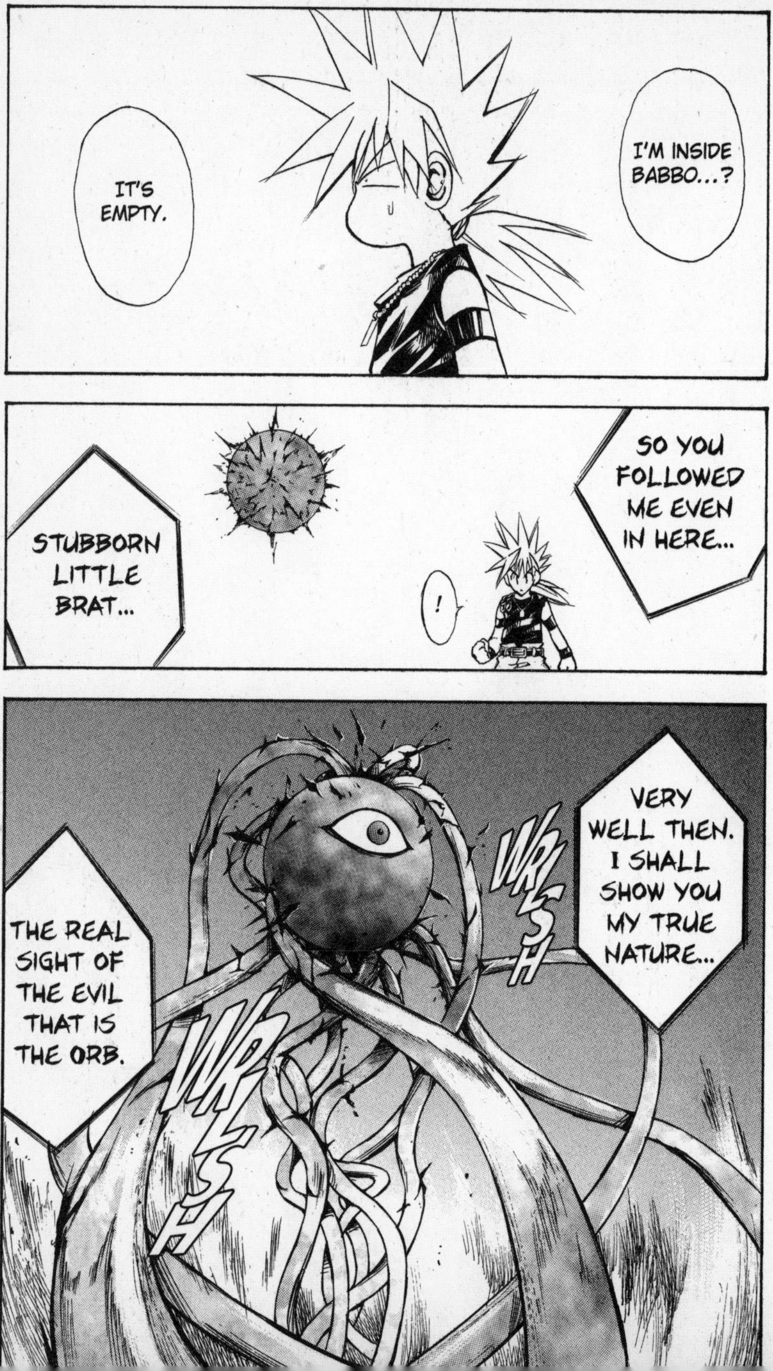
I'M INSIDE BABBO...?
IT'S EMPTY.
SO YOU FOLLOWED ME EVEN IN HERE...
!
STUBBORN LITTLE BRAT...
VERY WELL THEN. I SHALL SHOW YOU MY TRUE NATURE...
VWRSH
VWRSH
THE REAL SIGHT OF THE EVIL THAT IS THE ORB.

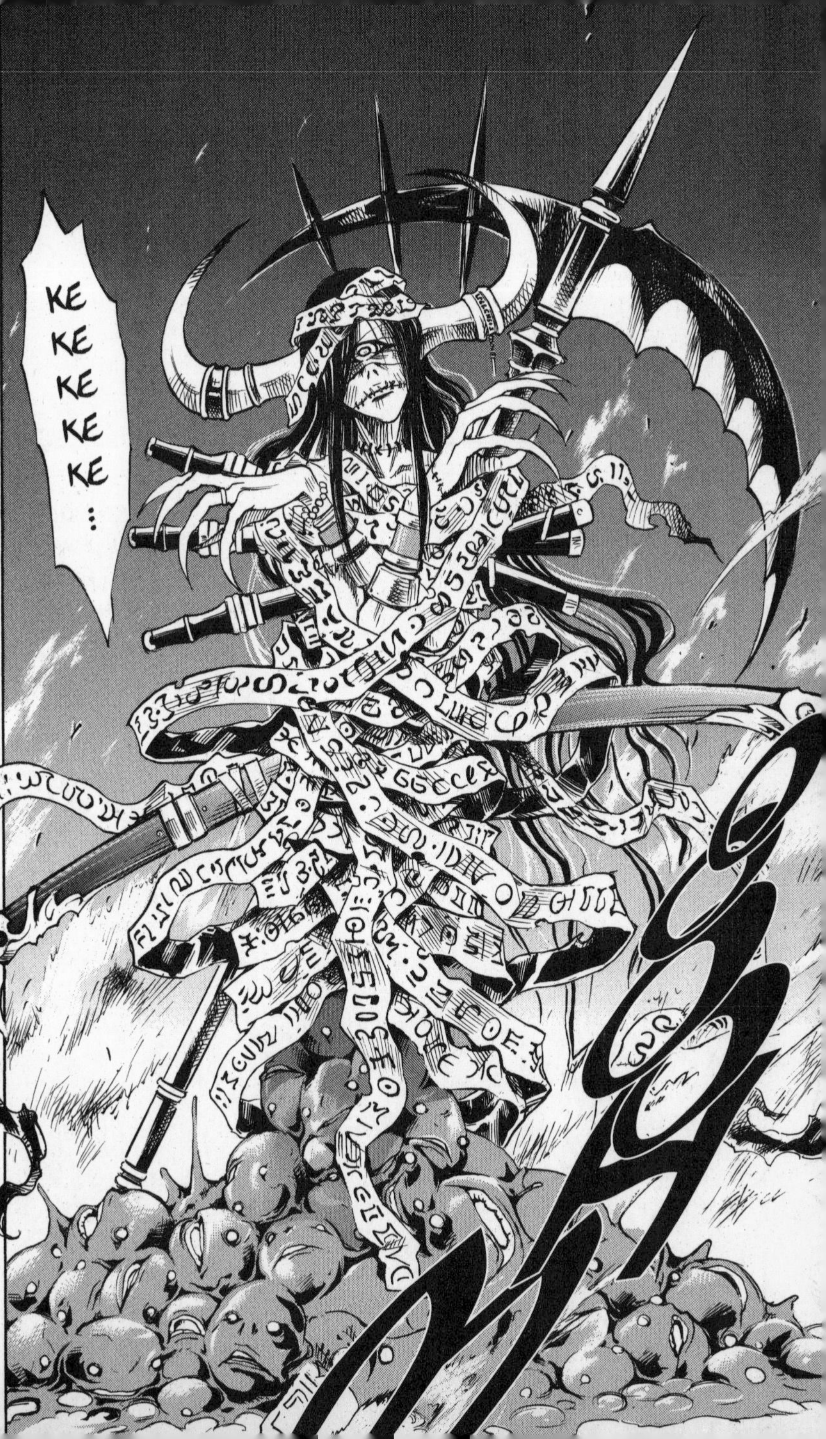
KE KE KE KE KE ...

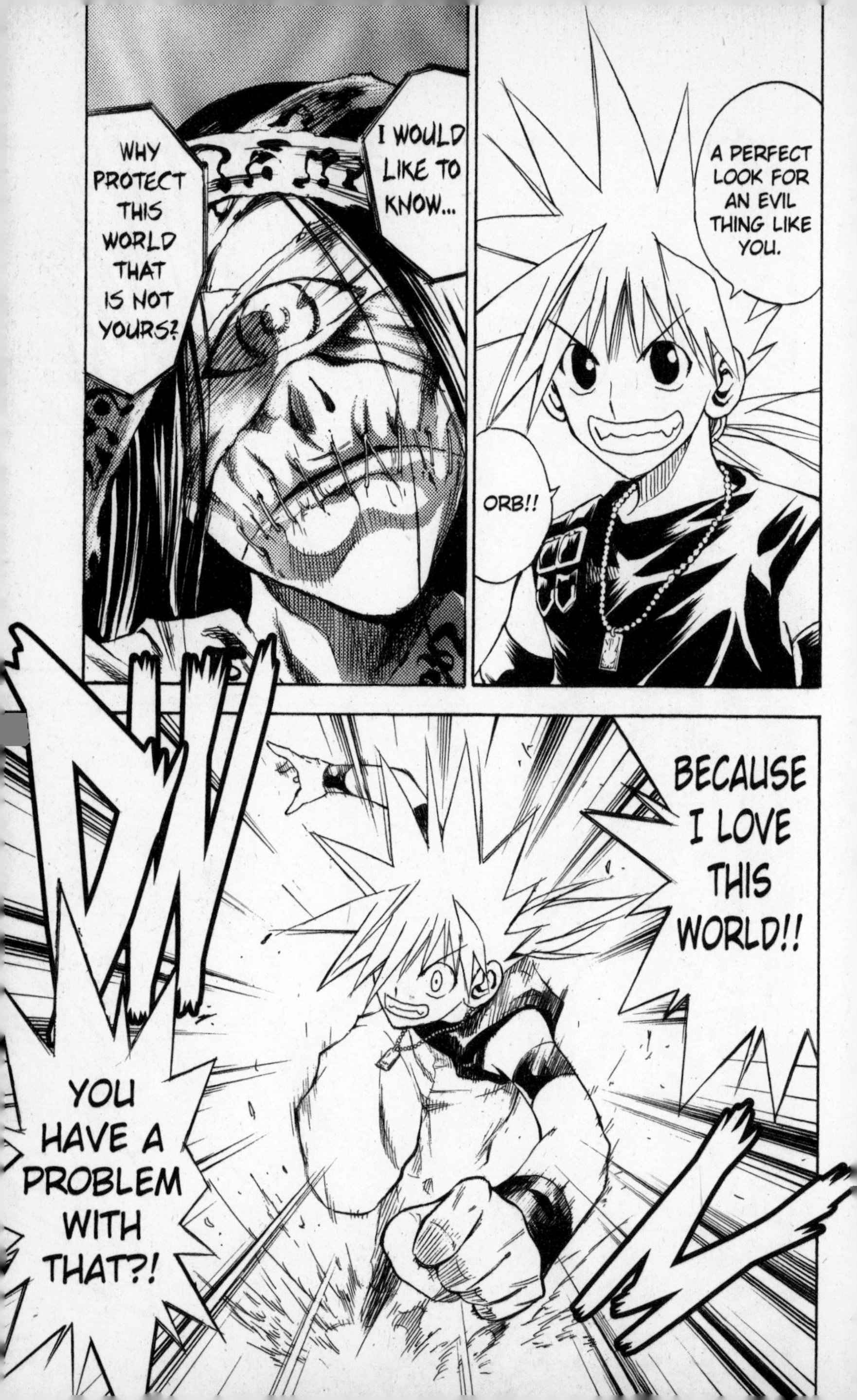
A PERFECT LOOK FOR AN EVIL THING LIKE YOU.
ORB!!
I WOULD LIKE TO KNOW...
WHY PROTECT THIS WORLD THAT IS NOT YOURS?
BECAUSE I LOVE THIS WORLD!!
YOU HAVE A PROBLEM WITH THAT?!

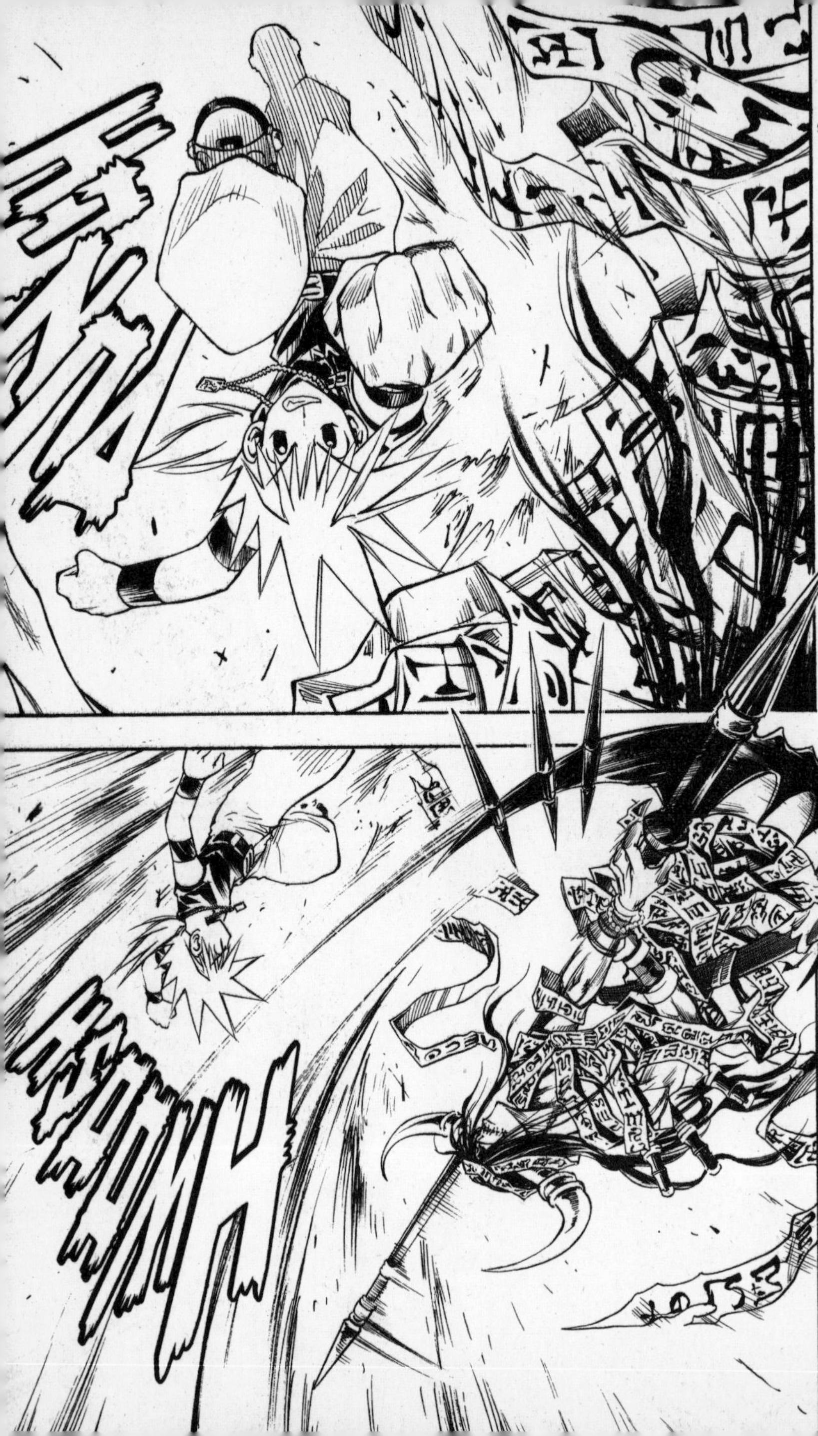

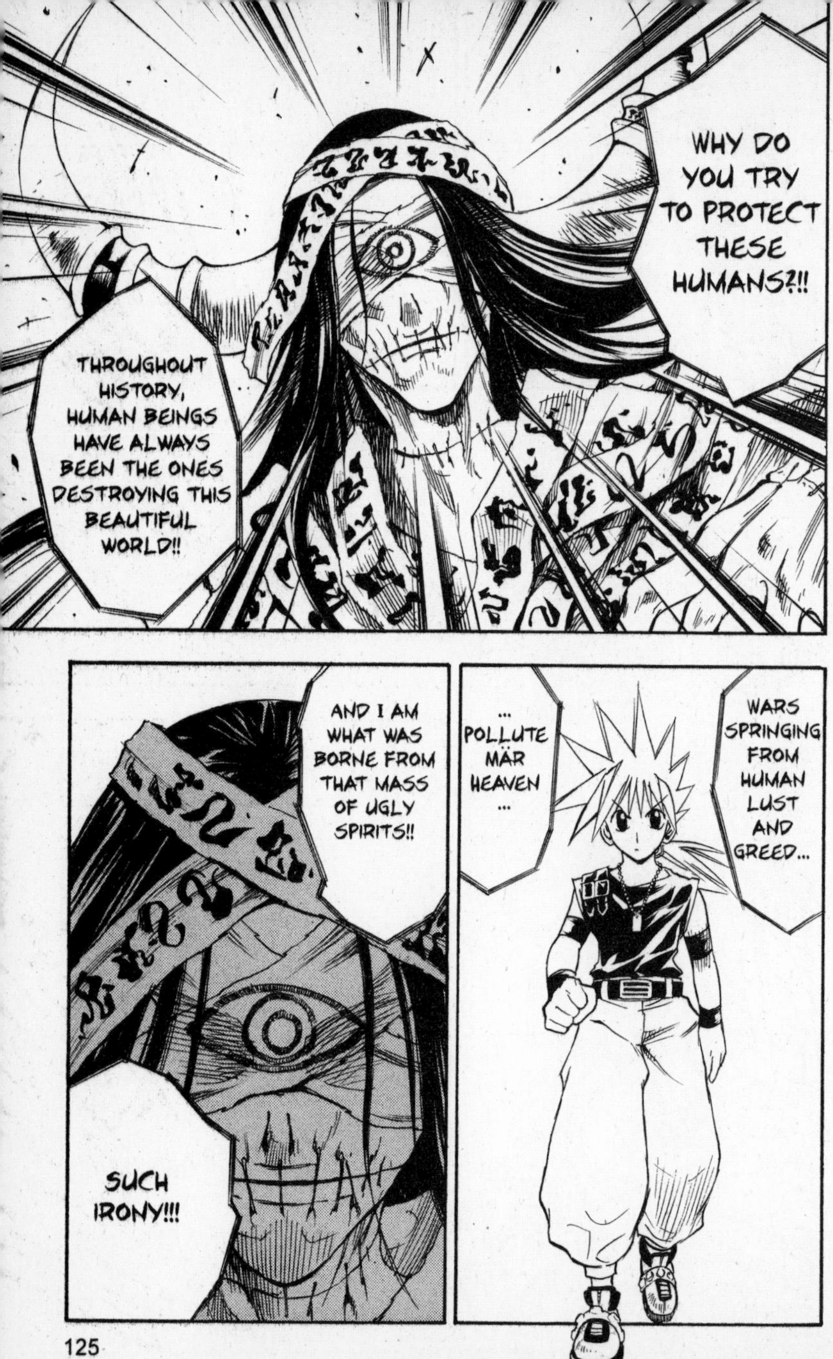
WHY DO YOU TRY TO PROTECT THESE HUMANS?!!
THROUGHOUT HISTORY, HUMAN BEINGS HAVE ALWAYS BEEN THE ONES DESTROYING THIS BEAUTIFUL WORLD!!
WARS SPRINGING FROM HUMAN LUST AND GREED...
... POLLUTE MÄR HEAVEN ...
AND I AM WHAT WAS BORNE FROM THAT MASS OF UGLY SPIRITS!!
SUCH IRONY!!!

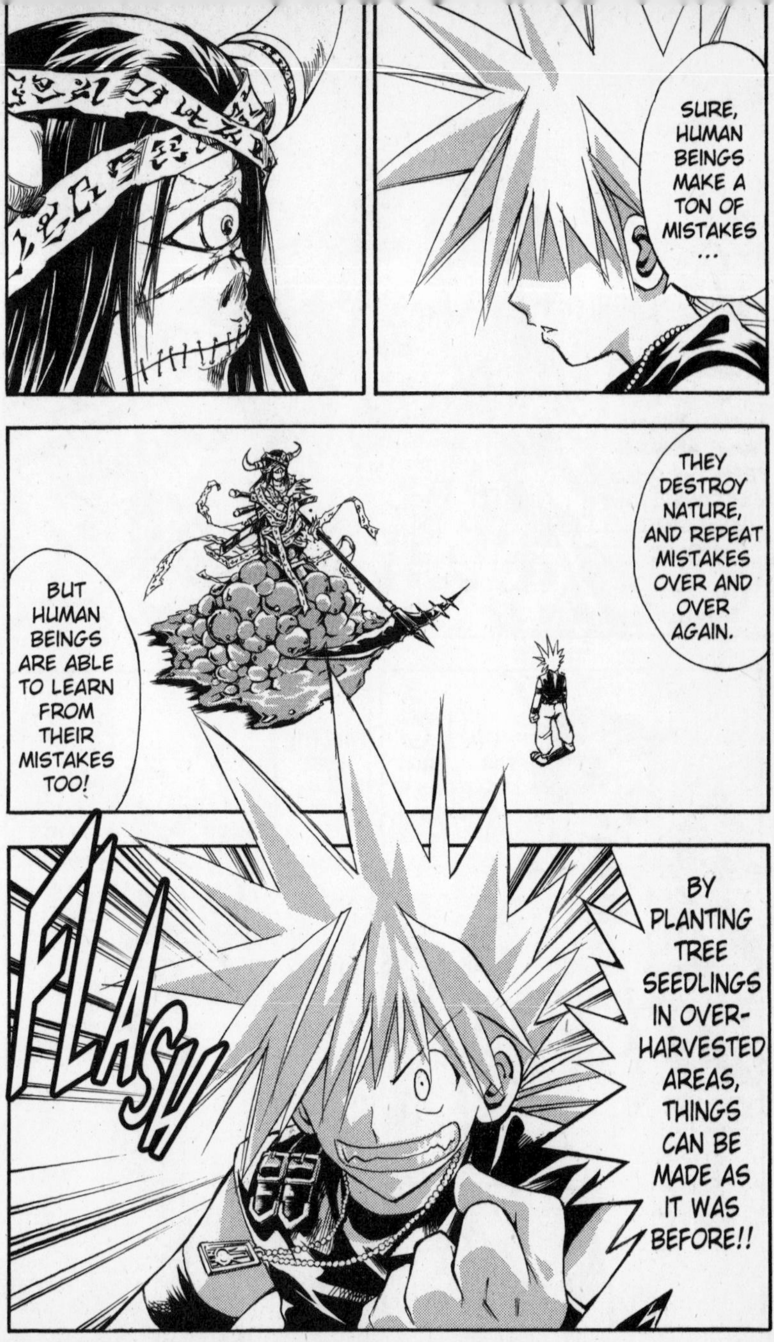
SURE, HUMAN BEINGS MAKE A TON OF MISTAKES ...
THEY DESTROY NATURE, AND REPEAT MISTAKES OVER AND OVER AGAIN.
BUT HUMAN BEINGS ARE ABLE TO LEARN FROM THEIR MISTAKES TOO!
BY PLANTING TREE SEEDLINGS IN OVER-HARVESTED AREAS, THINGS CAN BE MADE AS IT WAS BEFORE!!
FLASH

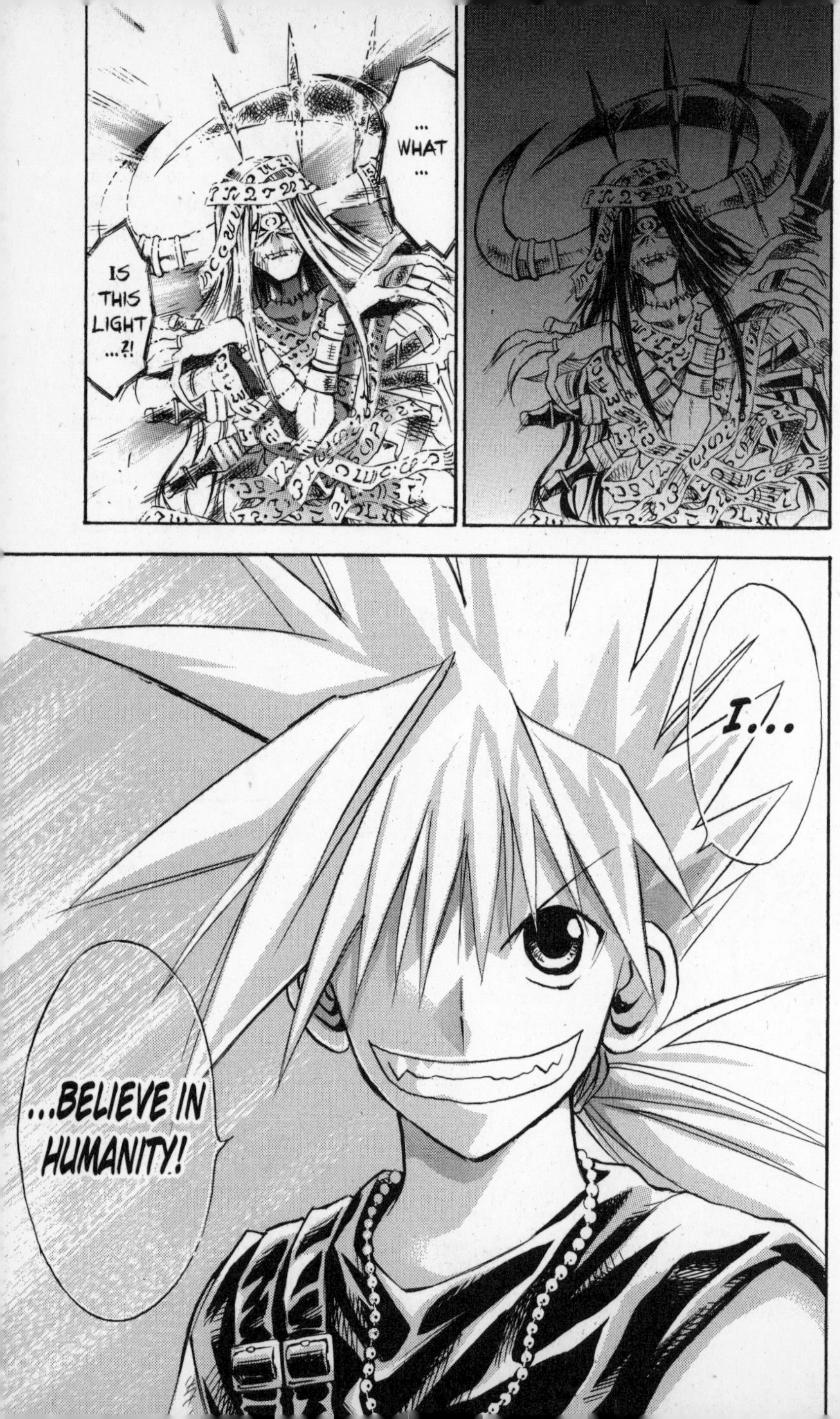
...WHAT...
IS THIS LIGHT...?!
I...
...BELIEVE IN HUMANITY!

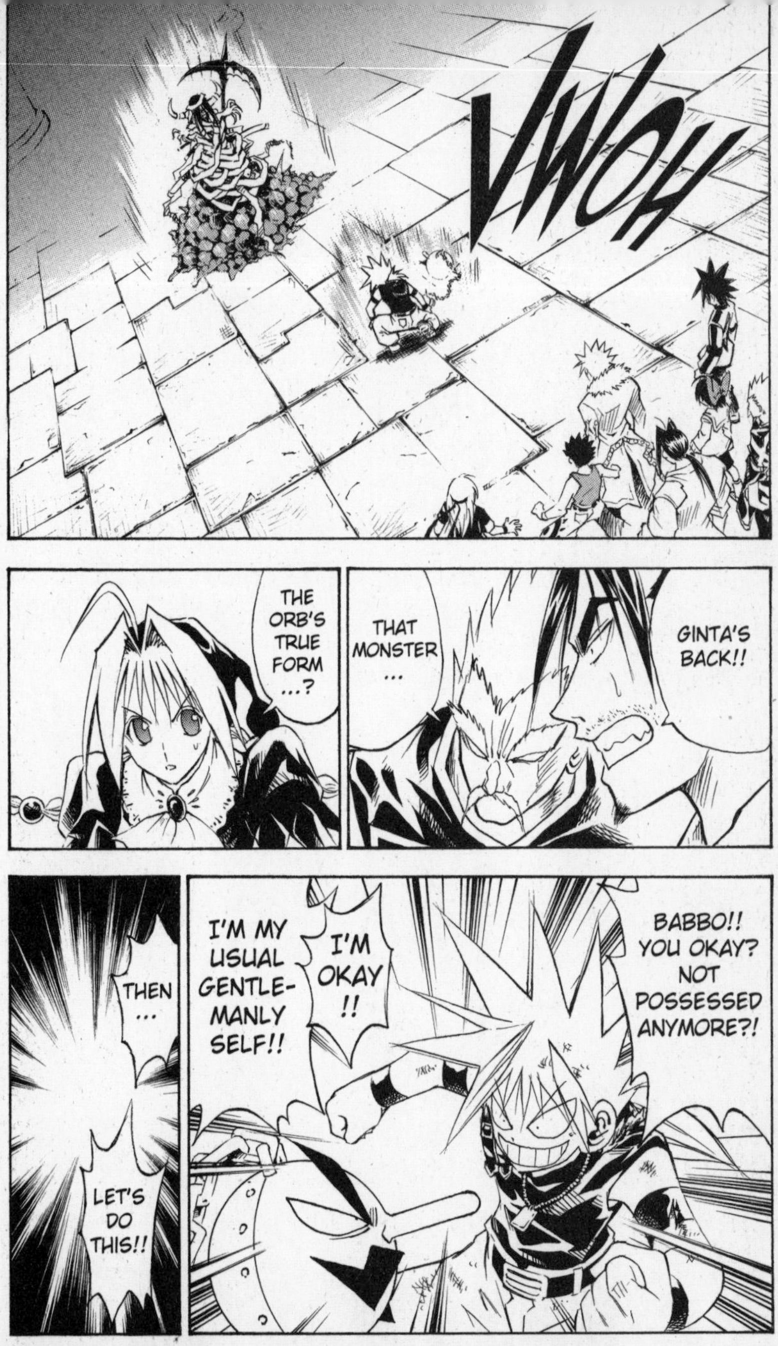
VWOH
GINTA'S BACK!!
THAT MONSTER ...
THE ORB'S TRUE FORM ...?
BABBO!! YOU OKAY? NOT POSSESSED ANYMORE?!
I'M OKAY !!
I'M MY USUAL GENTLE-MANLY SELF!!
THEN ...
LET'S DO THIS!!

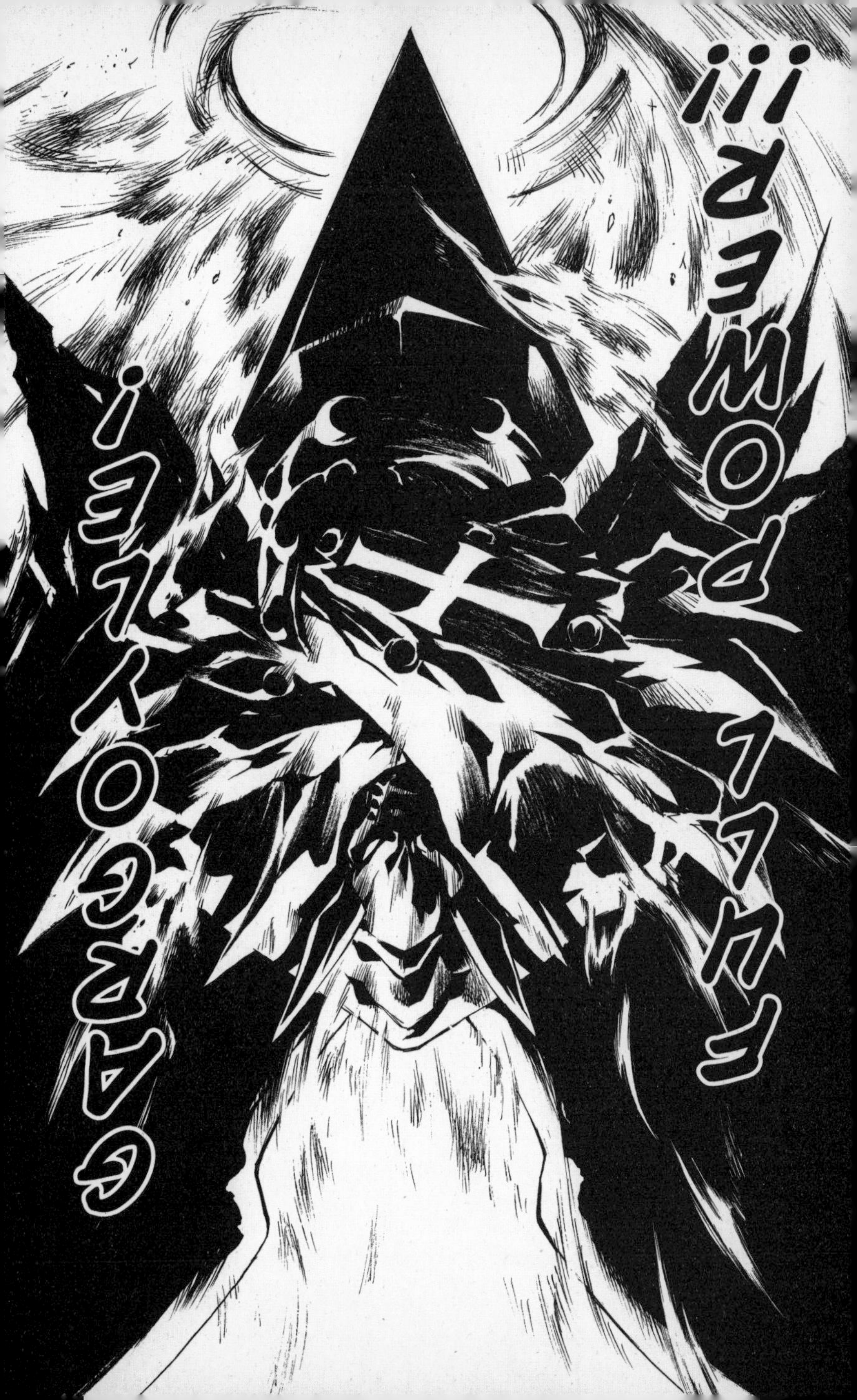
GARGOYLE!
FULL POWER!!!

ONE DAY,
HUMANITY
WILL BE
DESTROYED
BY ITS OWN
HANDS!!

DO NOT
FORGET!!

GYAAAAAAH!!

KRBOOM

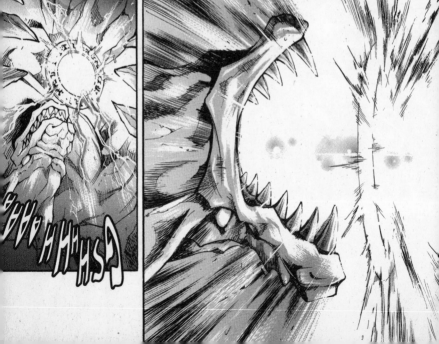

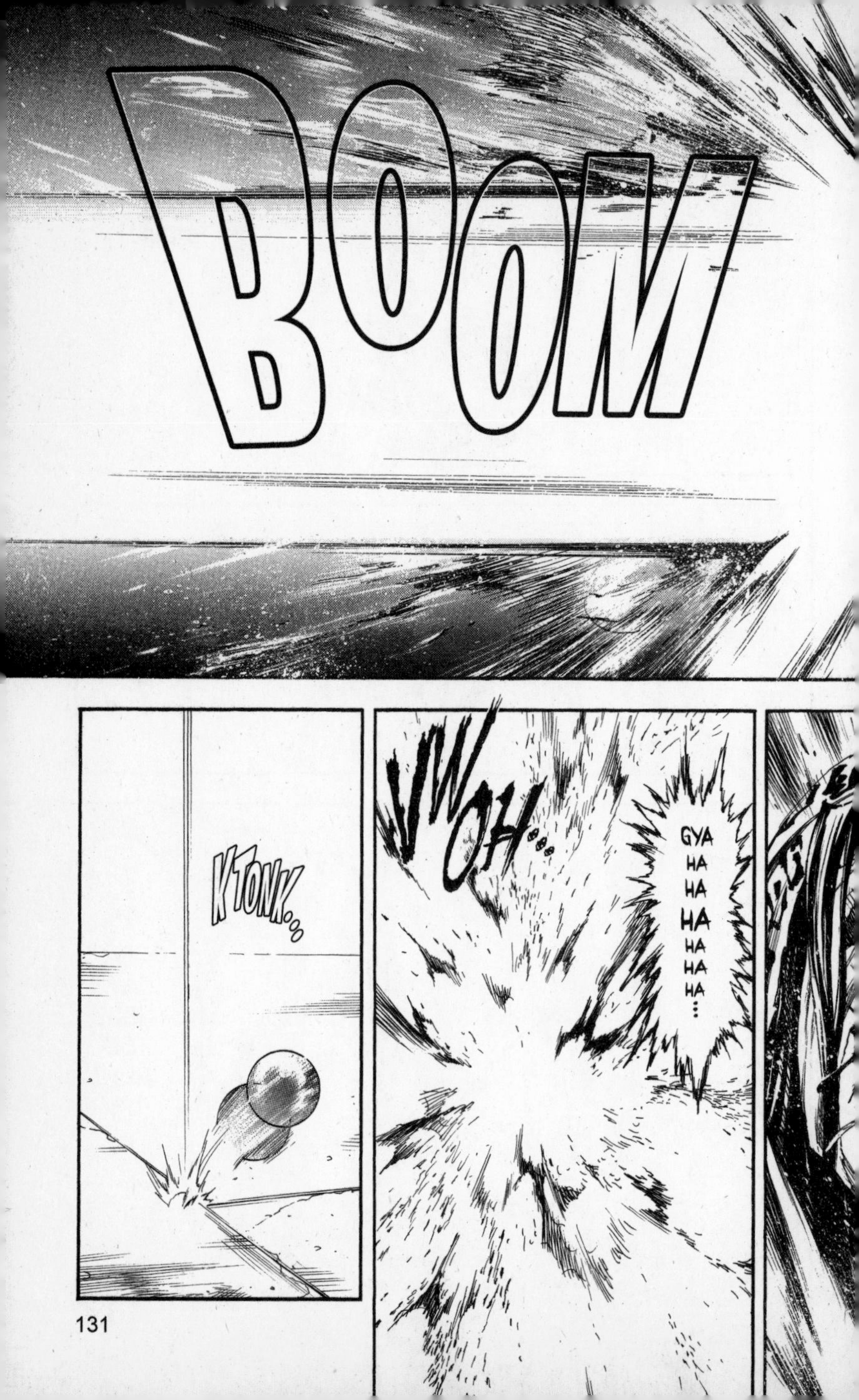
BOOM
GYA HA HA HA HA HA HA...
VWOH...
K'TONK...

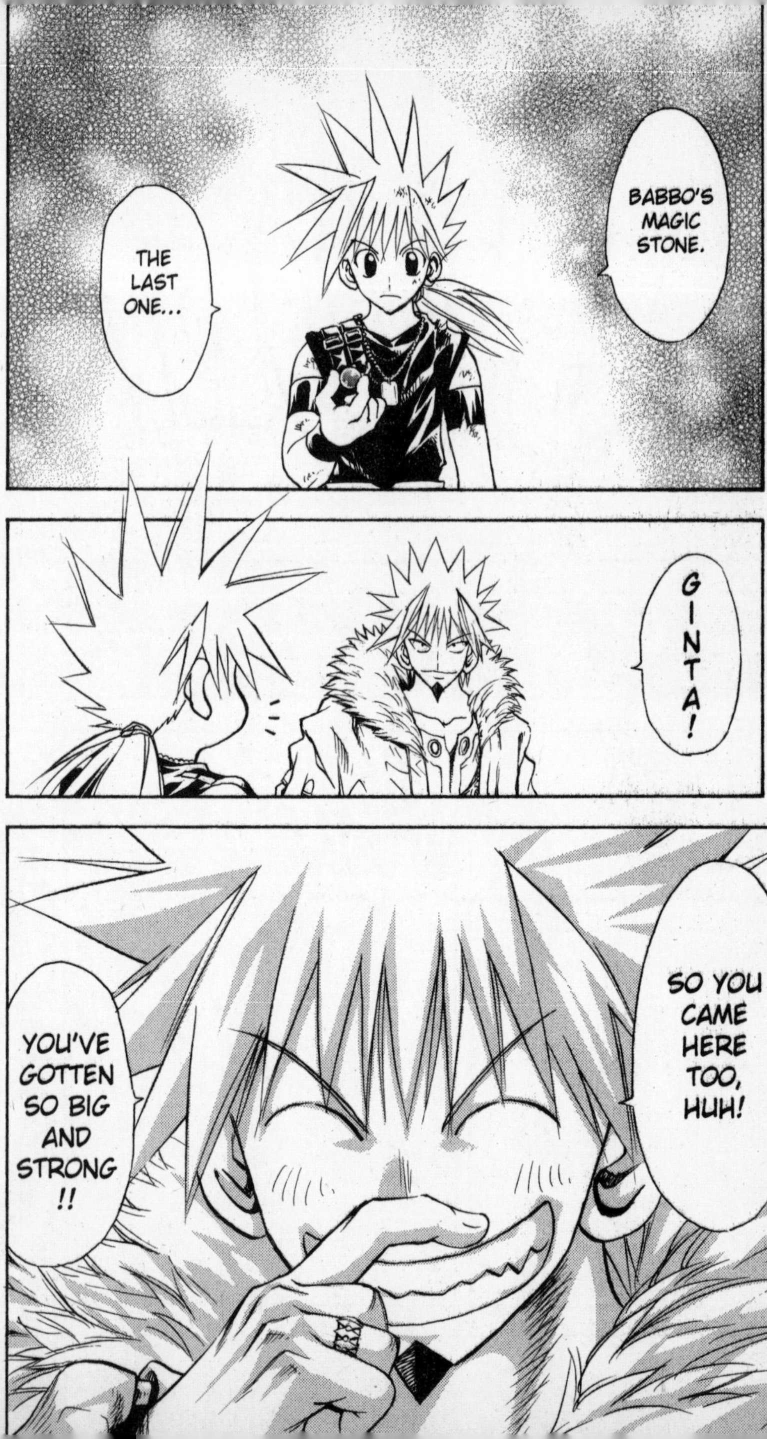
BABBO'S MAGIC STONE.
THE LAST ONE...
GINTA!
SO YOU CAME HERE TOO, HUH!
YOU'VE GOTTEN SO BIG AND STRONG!!

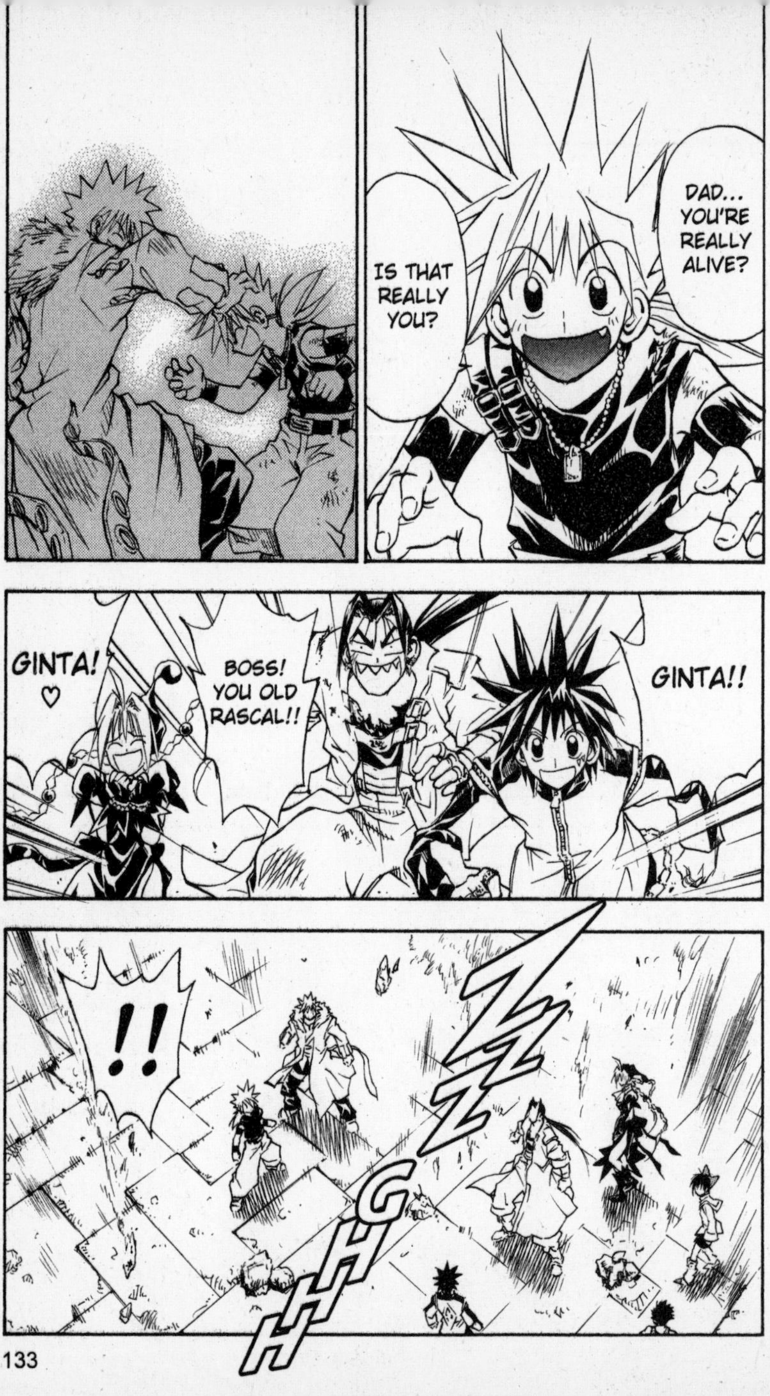
DAD... YOU'RE REALLY ALIVE?
IS THAT REALLY YOU?
GINTA!!
BOSS! YOU OLD RASCAL!!
GINTA! ♡
!!
ZZZGHHHH

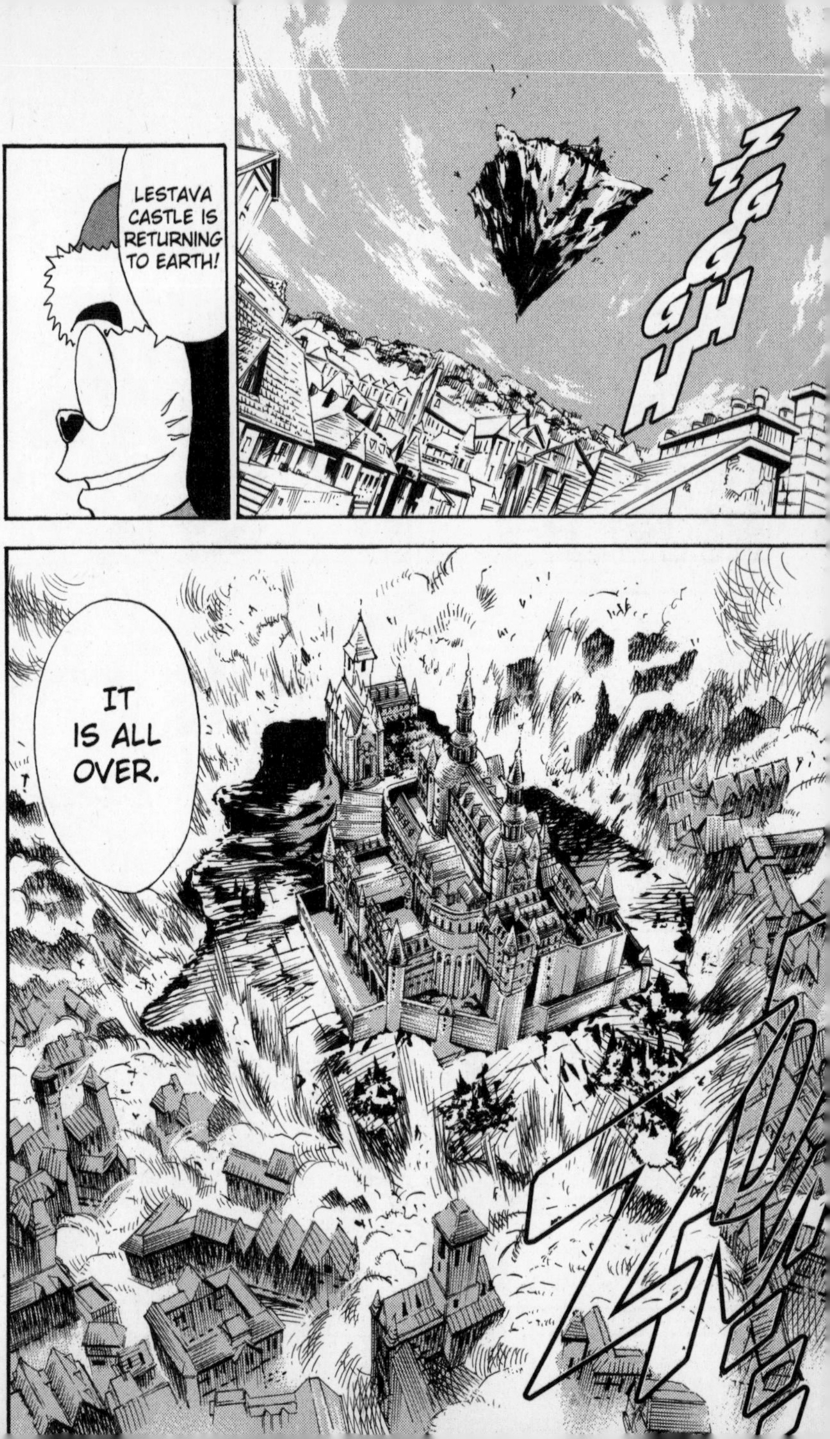
ZGGHH
LESTAVA CASTLE IS RETURNING TO EARTH!
IT IS ALL OVER.

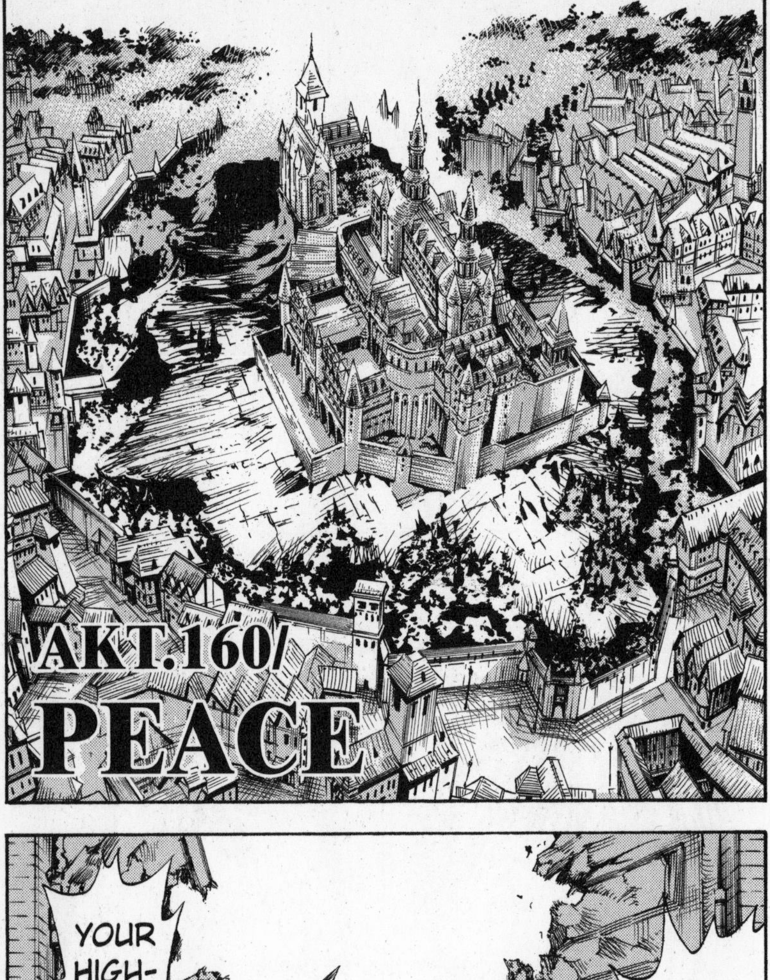
AKT. 160/
PEACE

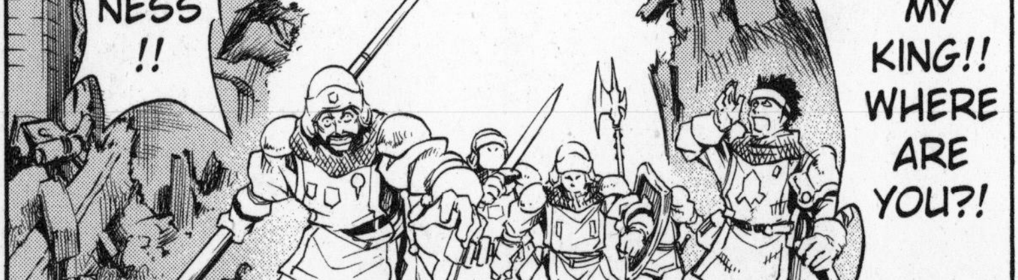
MY KING!! WHERE ARE YOU?!
YOUR HIGH-NESS!!

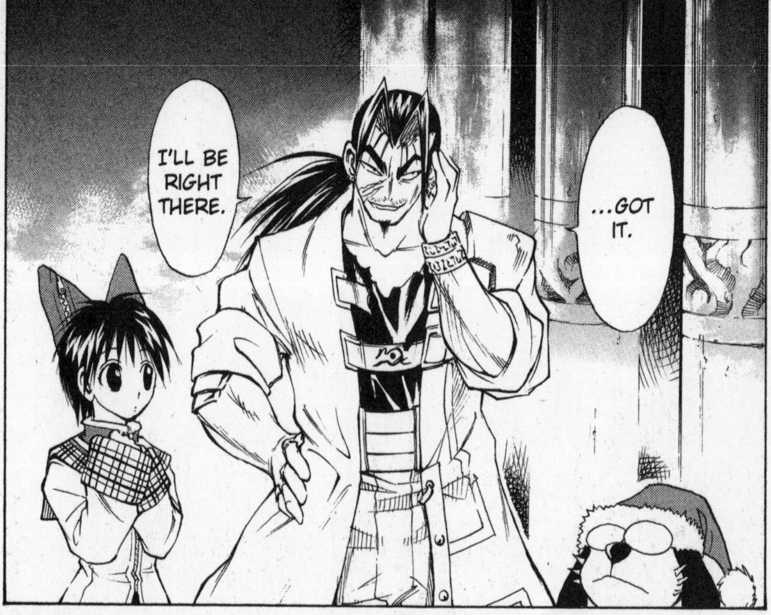
...GOT IT.
I'LL BE RIGHT THERE.
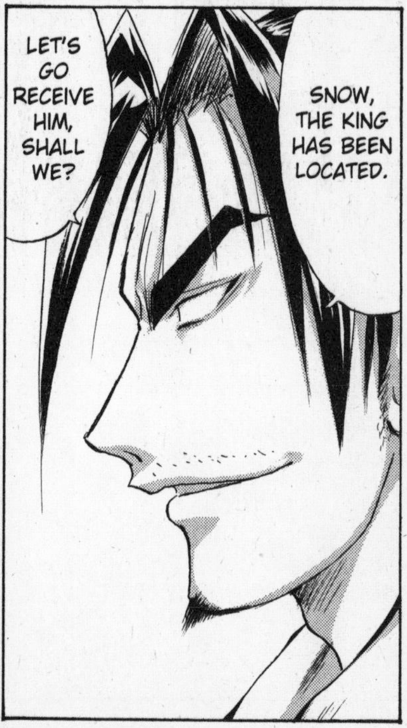
SNOW, THE KING HAS BEEN LOCATED.
LET'S GO RECEIVE HIM, SHALL WE?
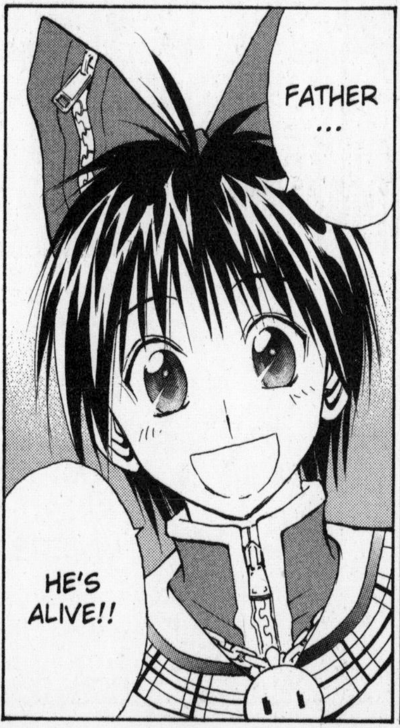
FATHER ...
HE'S ALIVE!!

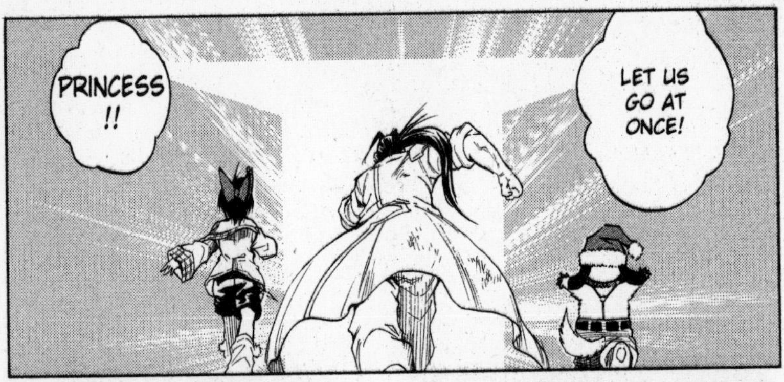
LET US GO AT ONCE!
PRINCESS !!
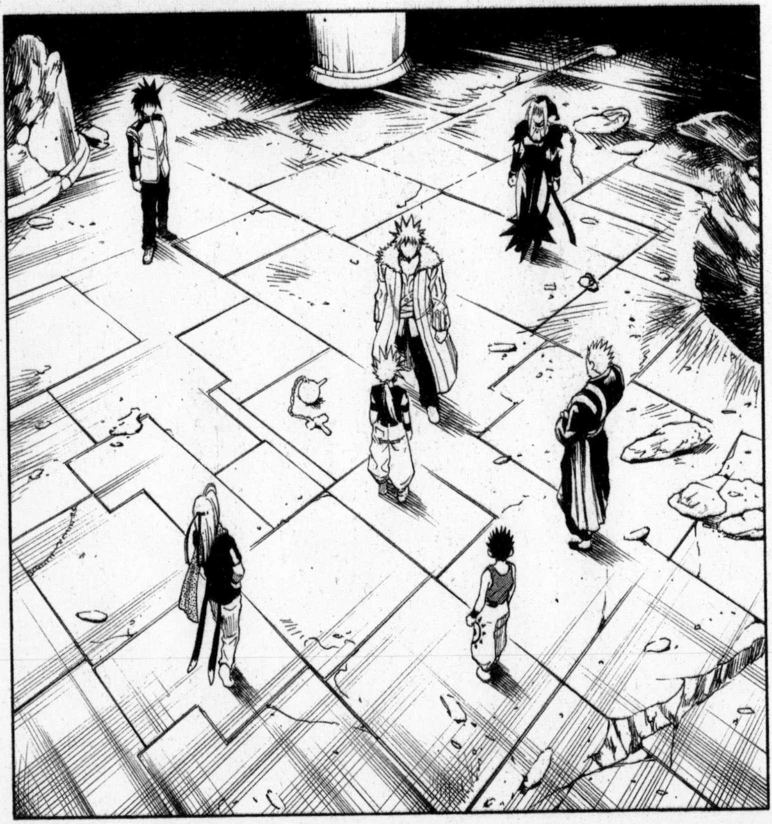

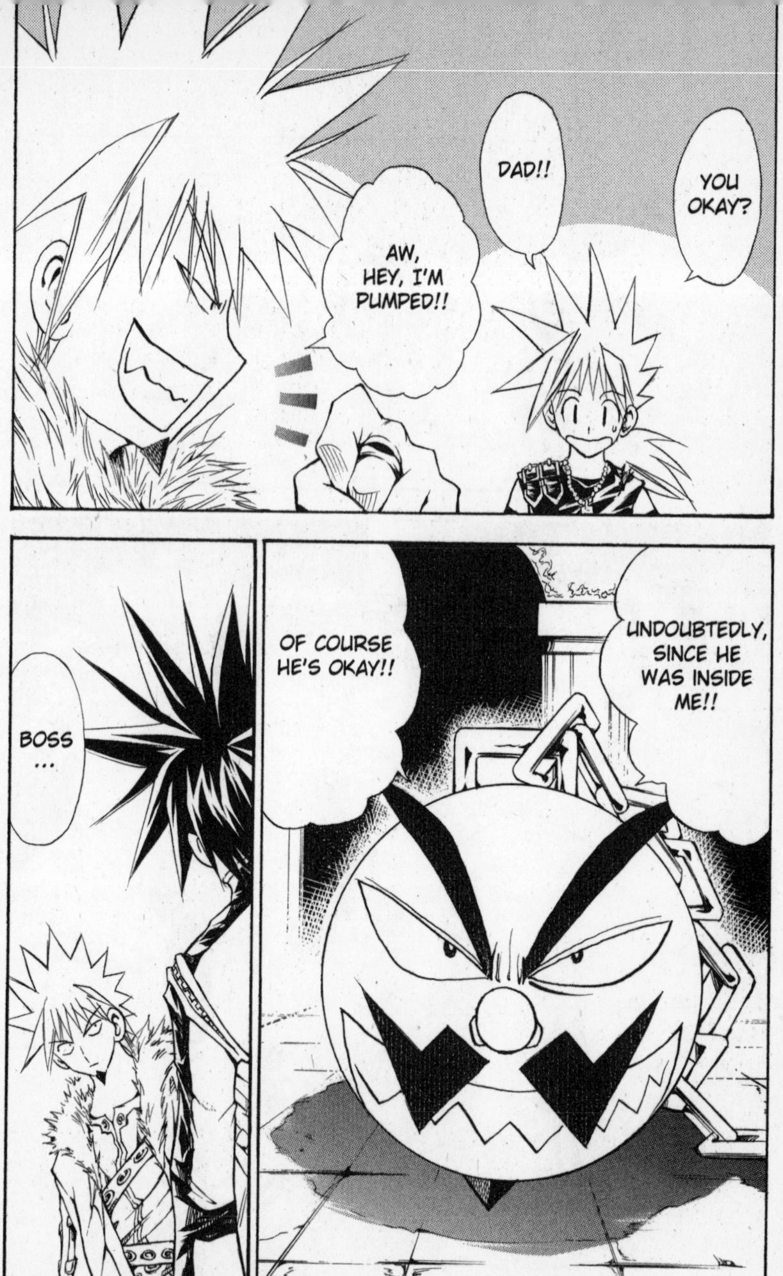
YOU OKAY?
DAD!!
AW, HEY, I'M PUMPED!!
UNDOUBTEDLY, SINCE HE WAS INSIDE ME!!
OF COURSE HE'S OKAY!!
BOSS ...

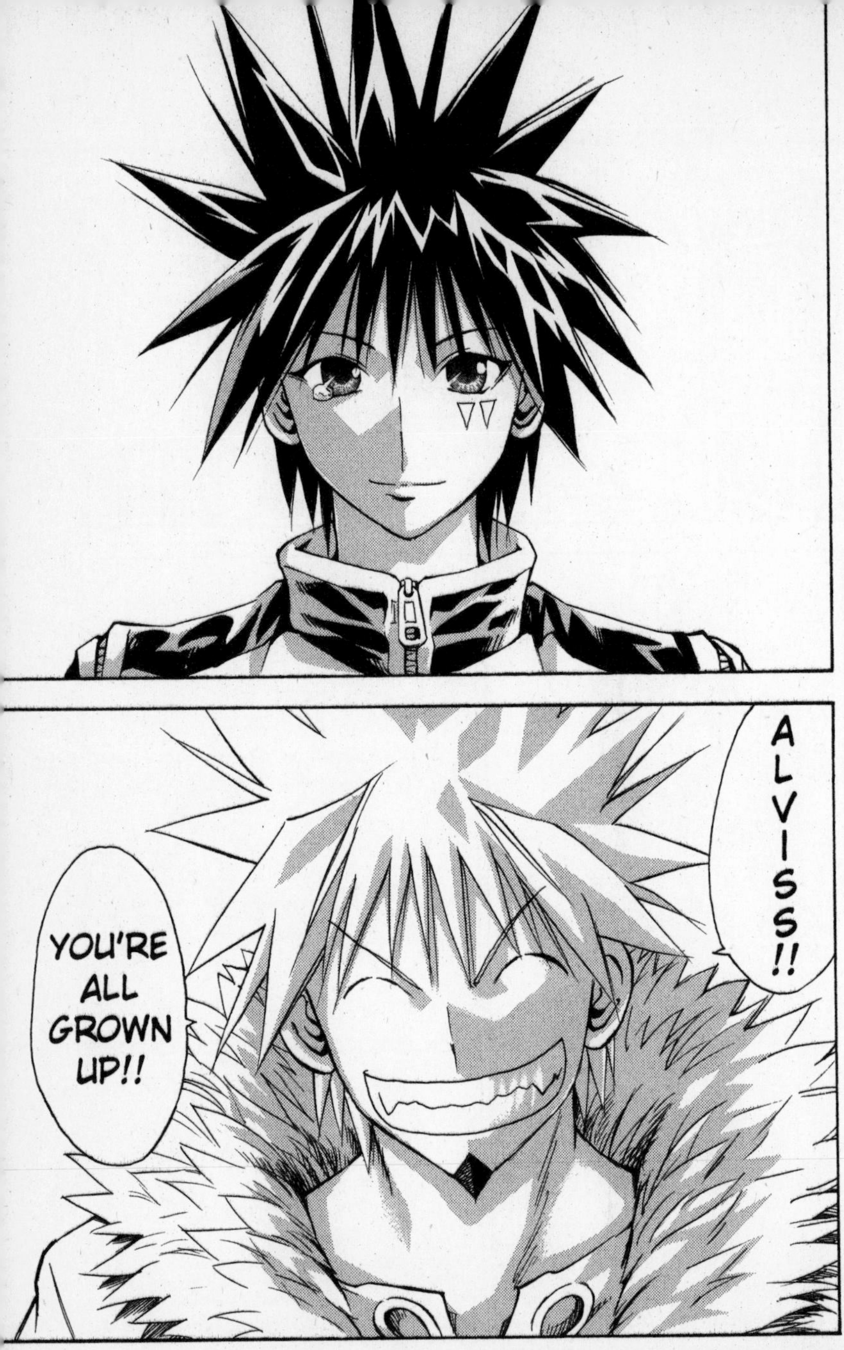
ALVISS!!
YOU'RE ALL GROWN UP!!

...S...

SNOW!!

FATHER...

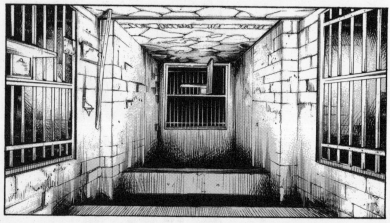

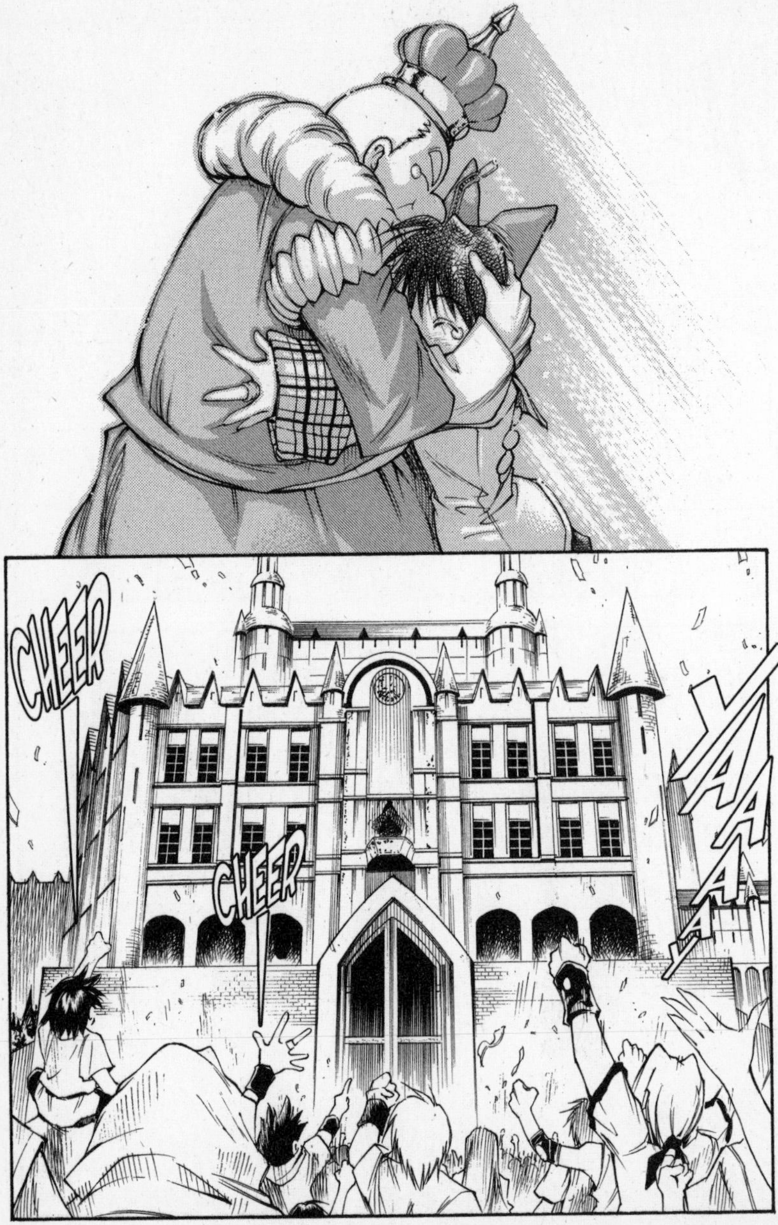
YAAAA
CHEER
CHEER

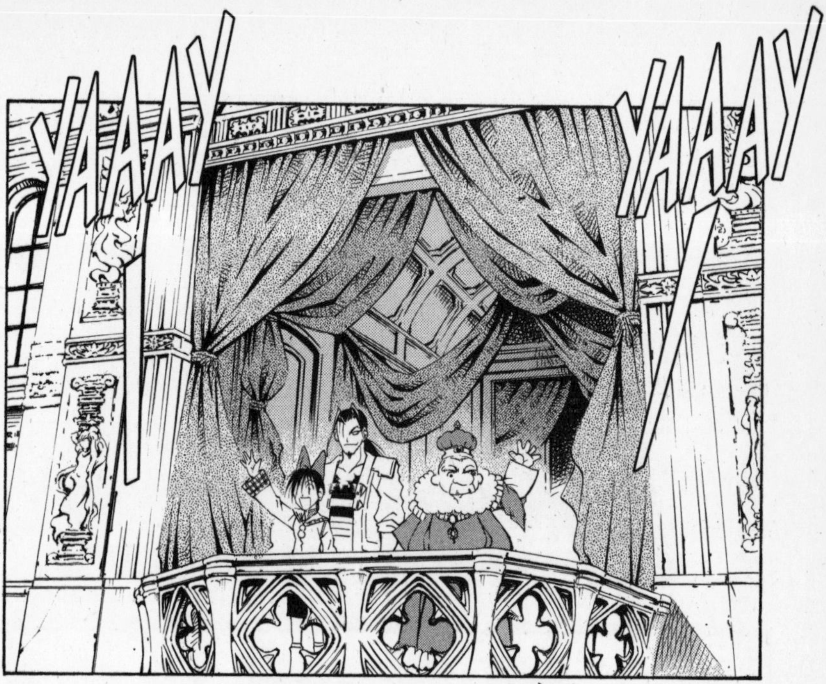
YAAAY
YAAAY

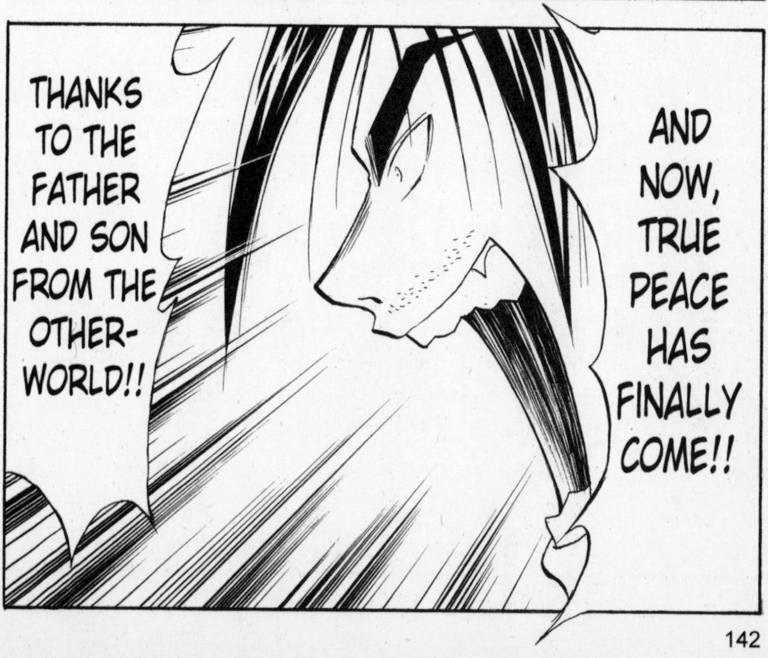
AND NOW, TRUE PEACE HAS FINALLY COME!!
THANKS TO THE FATHER AND SON FROM THE OTHER-WORLD!!

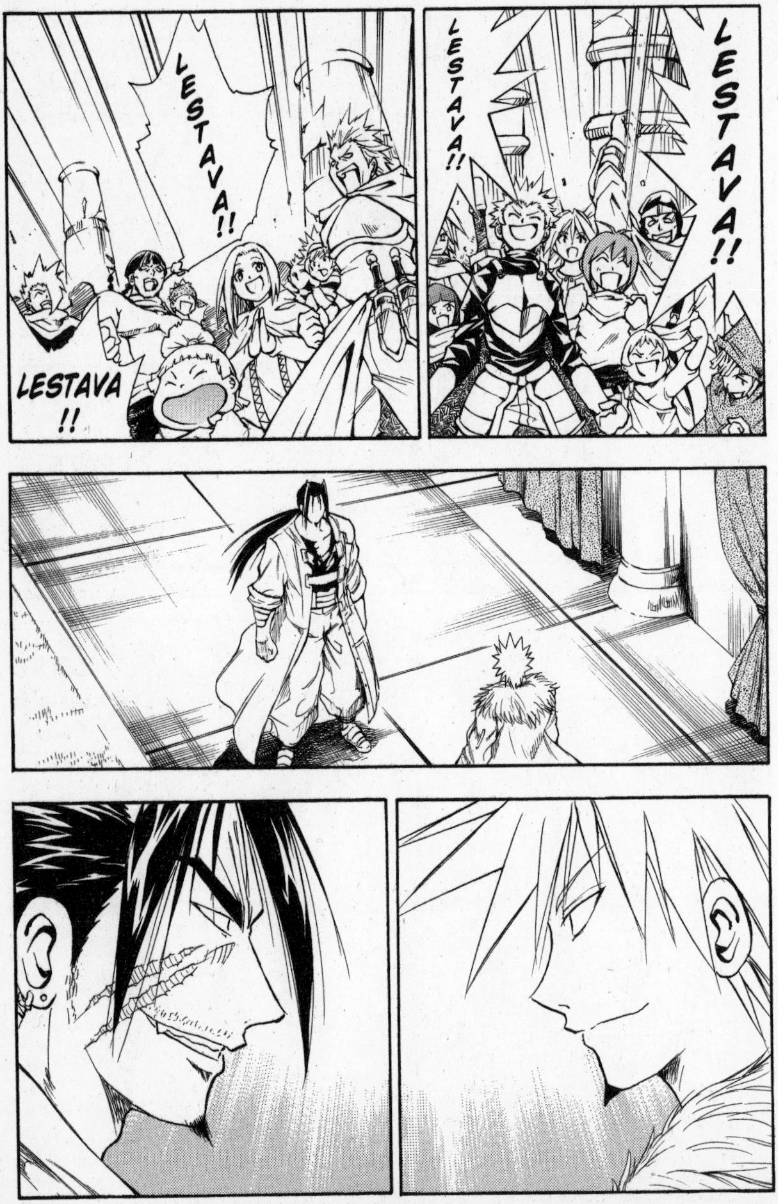
LESTAVA!!
LESTAVA!!
LESTAVA!!
LESTAVA!!

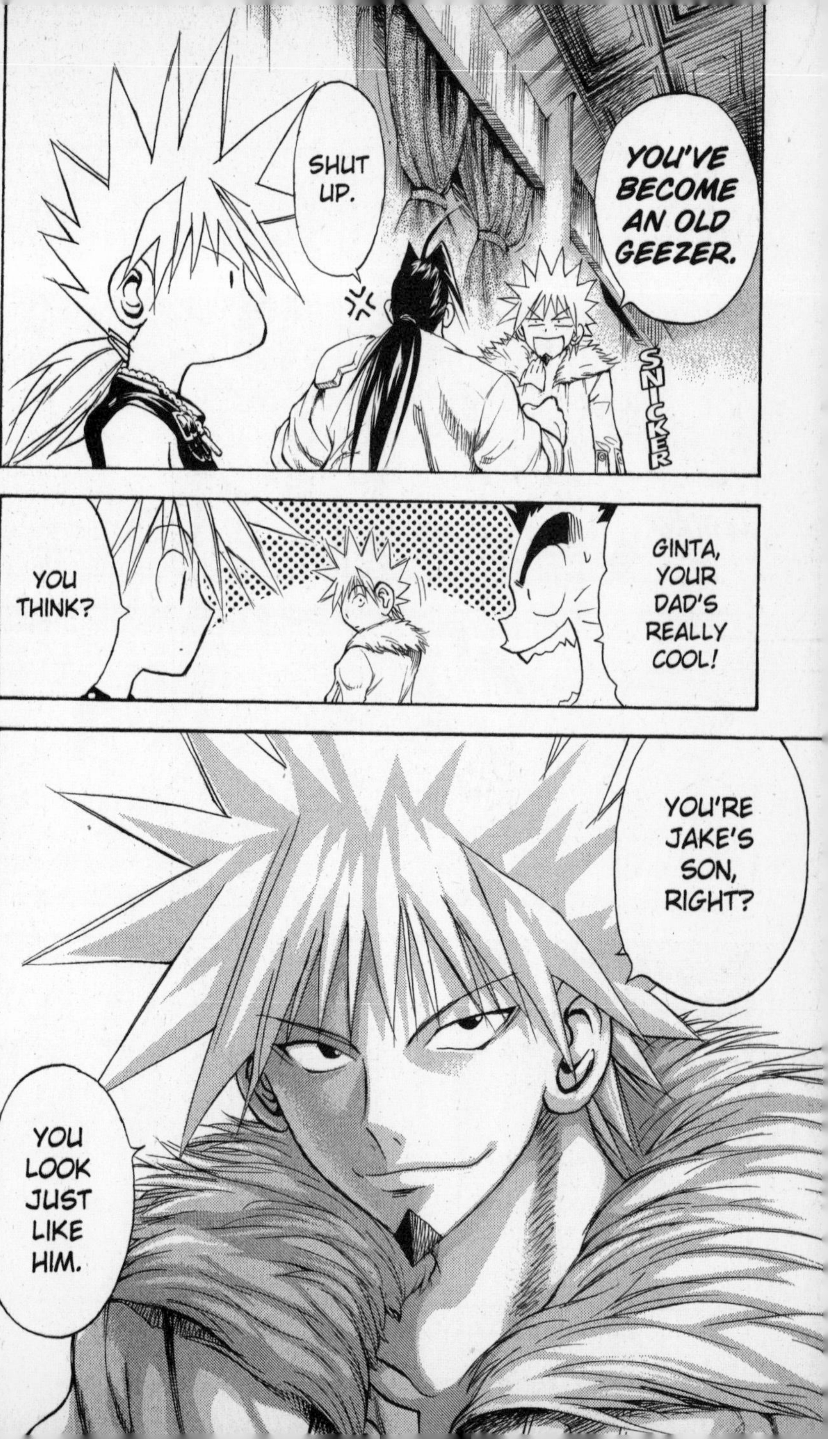
YOU'VE BECOME AN OLD GEEZER.
SNICKER
SHUT UP.
GINTA, YOUR DAD'S REALLY COOL!
YOU THINK?
YOU'RE JAKE'S SON, RIGHT?
YOU LOOK JUST LIKE HIM.

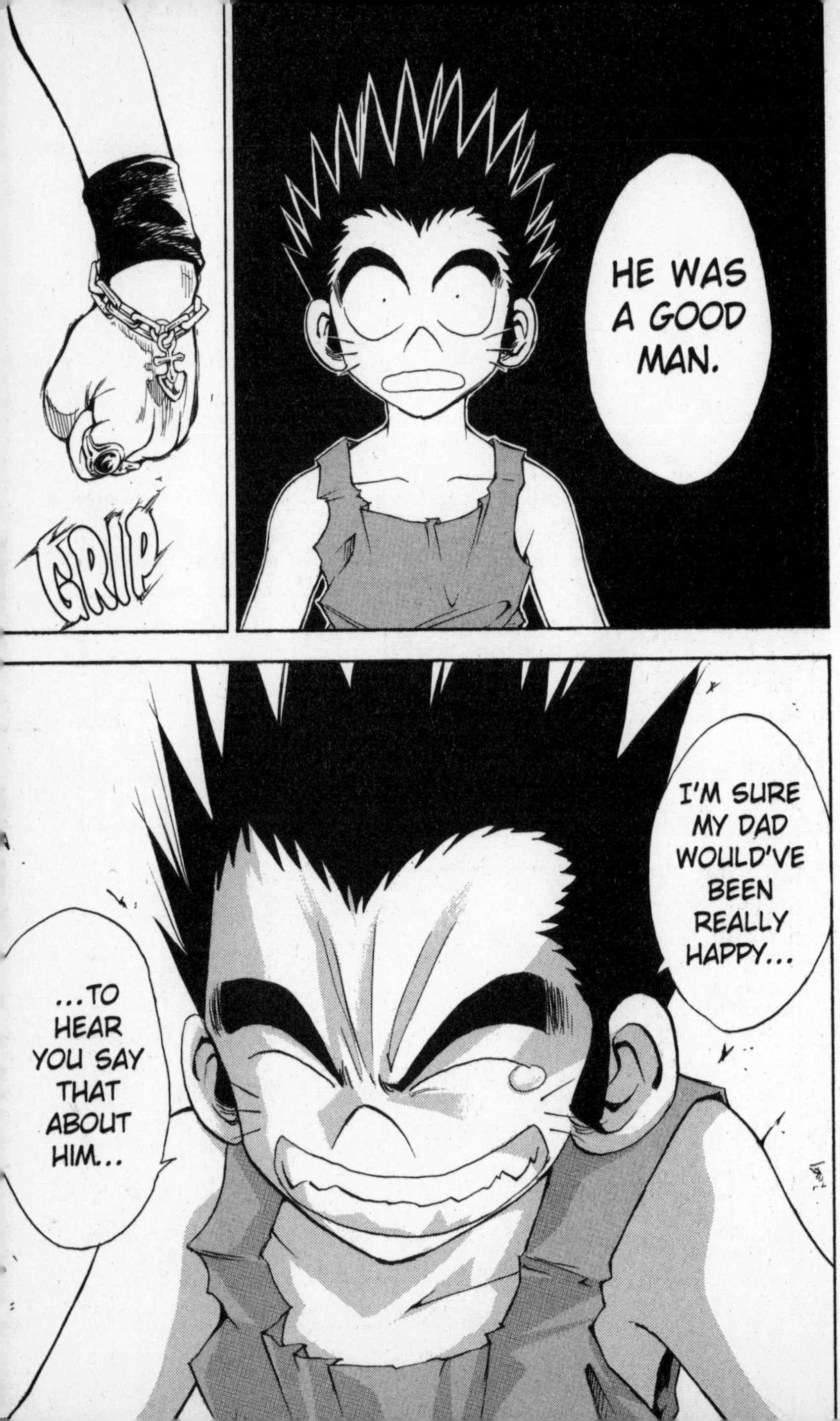
HE WAS A GOOD MAN.
GRIP
I'M SURE MY DAD WOULD'VE BEEN REALLY HAPPY...
...TO HEAR YOU SAY THAT ABOUT HIM...

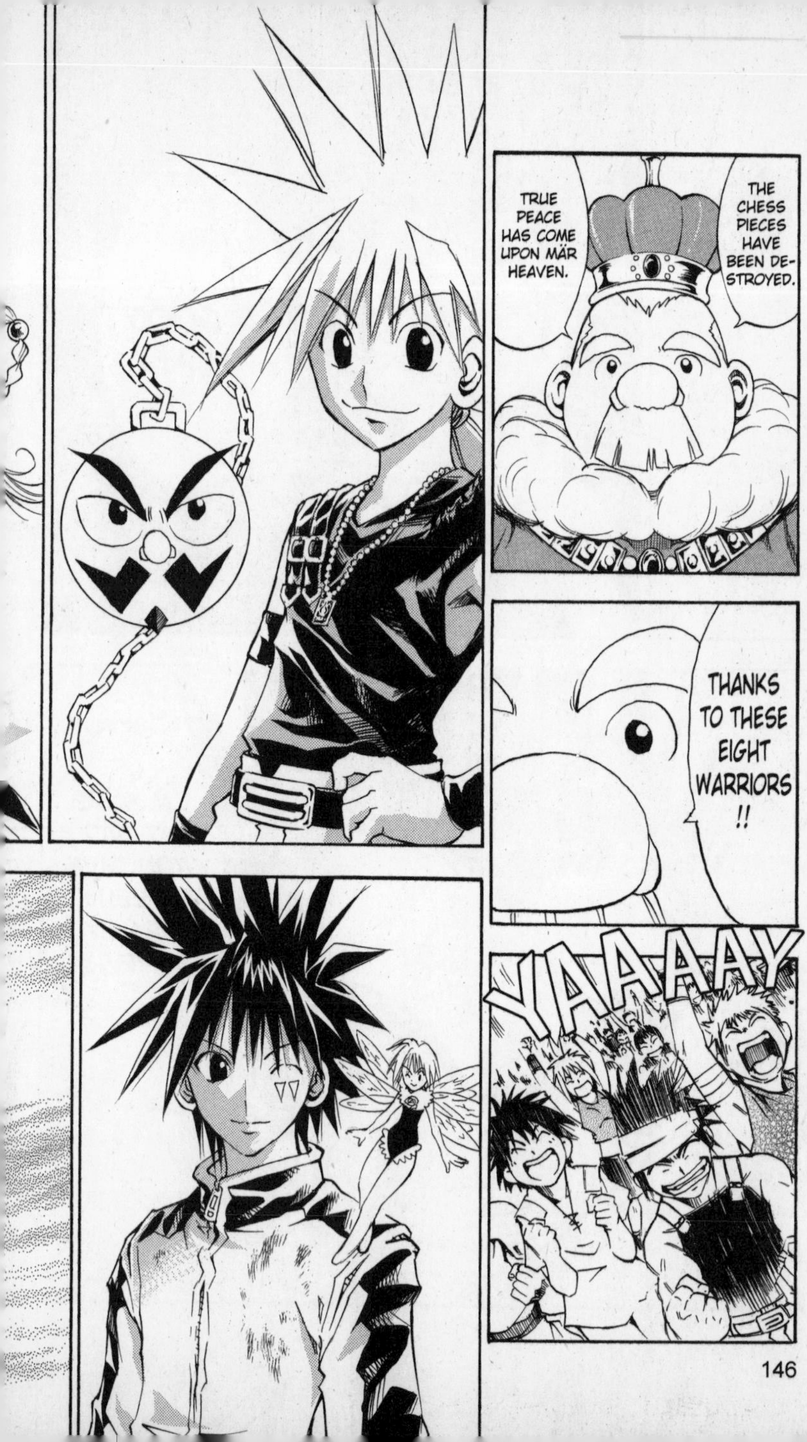
THE CHESS PIECES HAVE BEEN DE-STROYED.
TRUE PEACE HAS COME UPON MÄR HEAVEN.
THANKS TO THESE EIGHT WARRIORS !!
YAAAAY

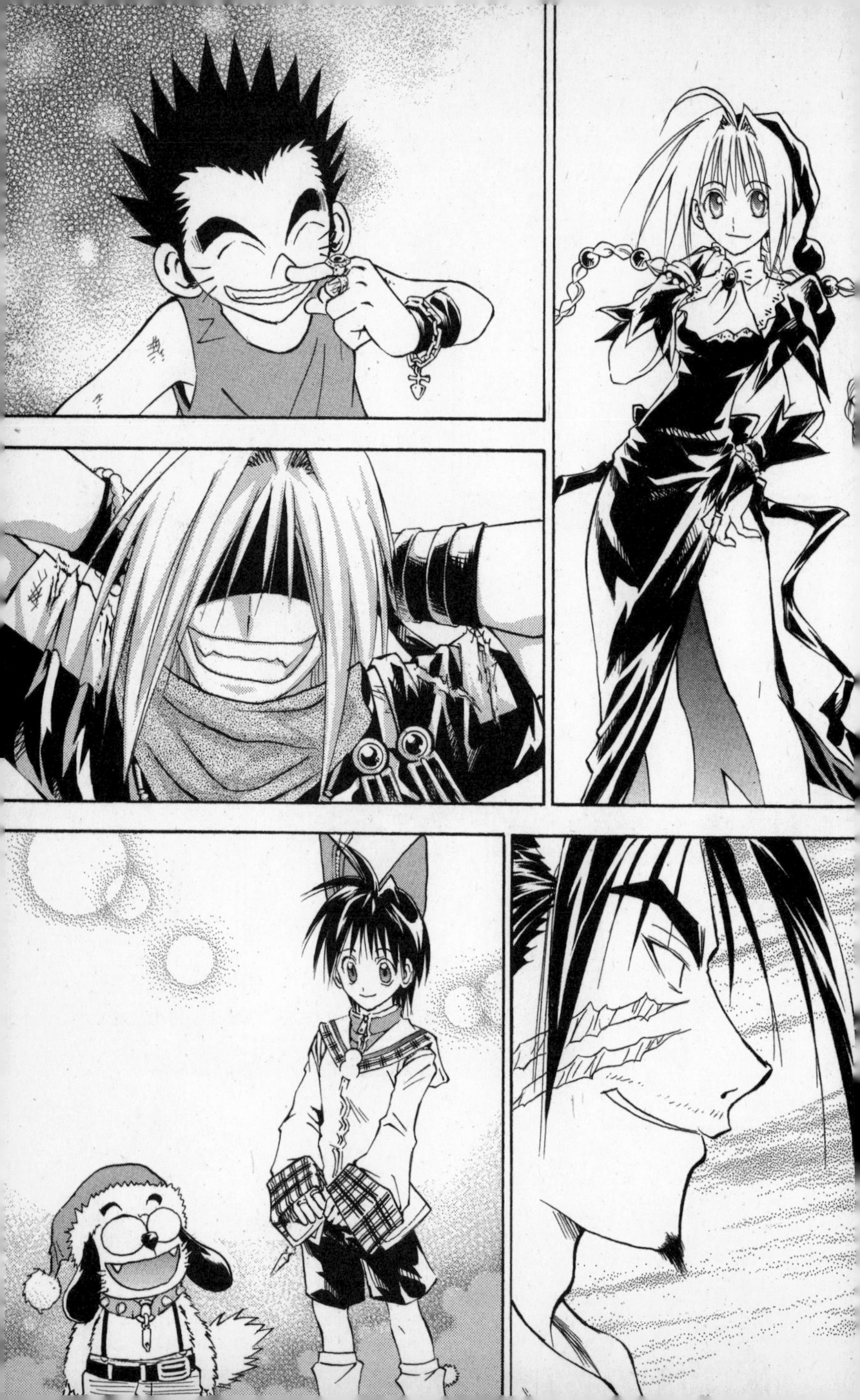

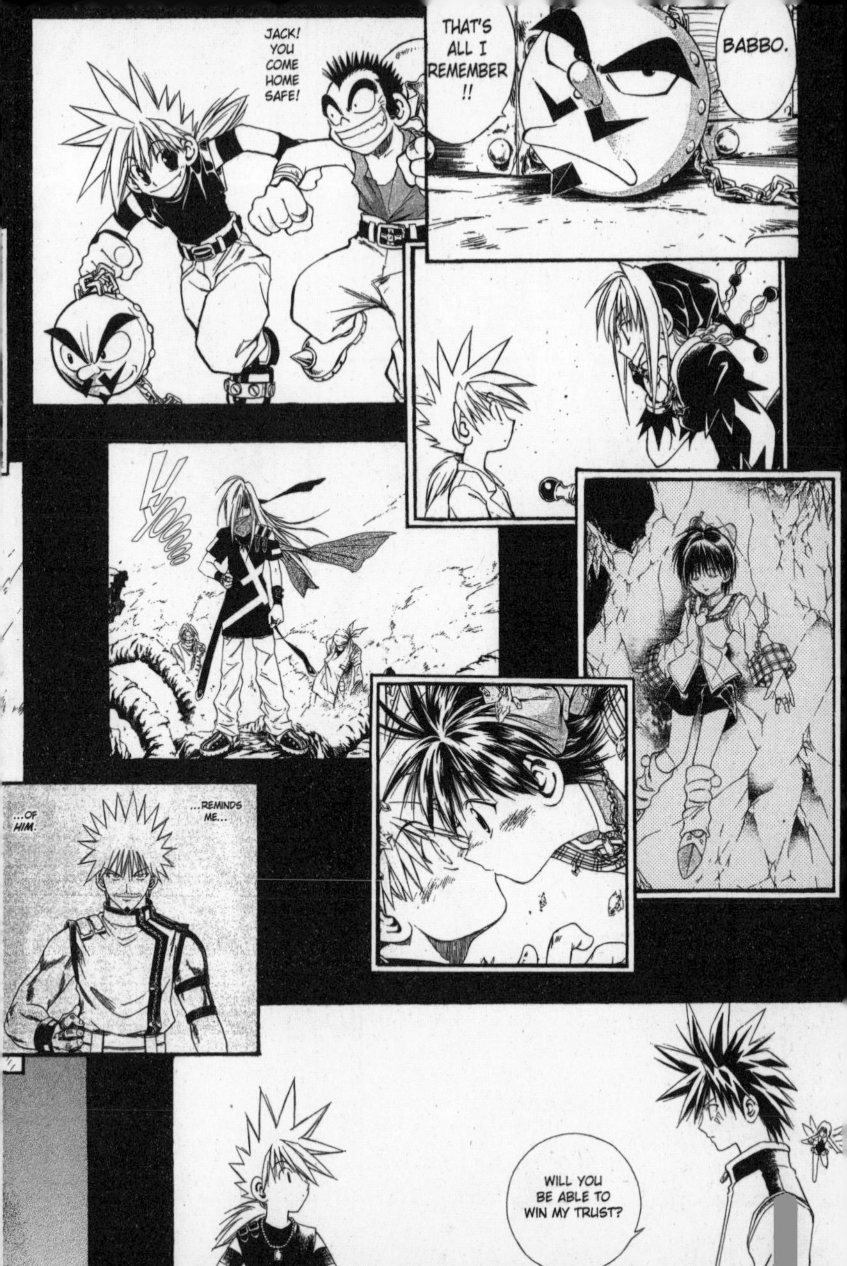
BABBO.
THAT'S ALL I REMEMBER !!
JACK! YOU COME HOME SAFE!
...REMINDS ME...
...OF HIM.
WILL YOU BE ABLE TO WIN MY TRUST?

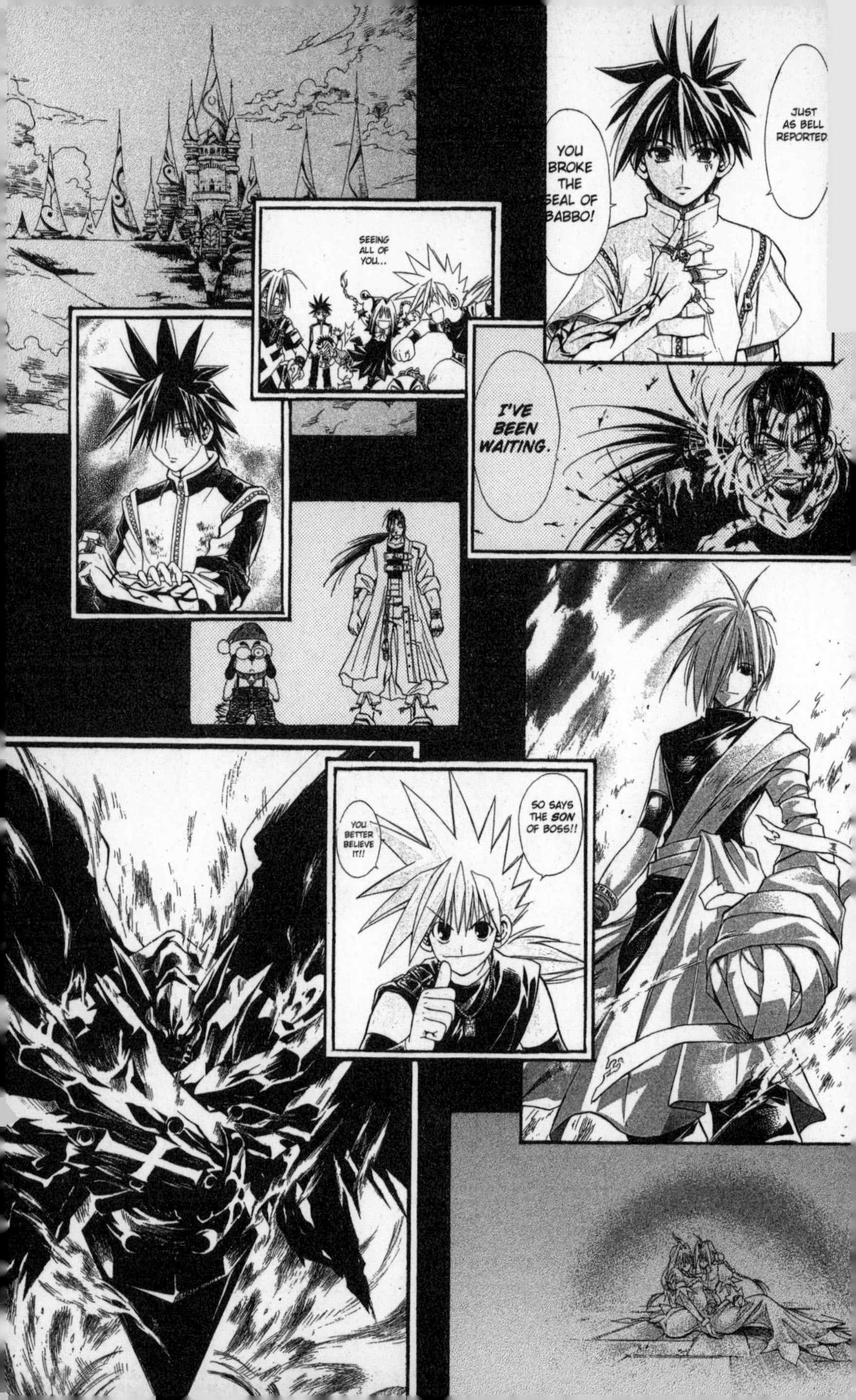
JUST AS BELL REPORTED.
YOU BROKE THE SEAL OF BABBO!
I'VE BEEN WAITING.
SEEING ALL OF YOU...
SO SAYS THE SON OF BOSS!!
YOU BETTER BELIEVE IT!!

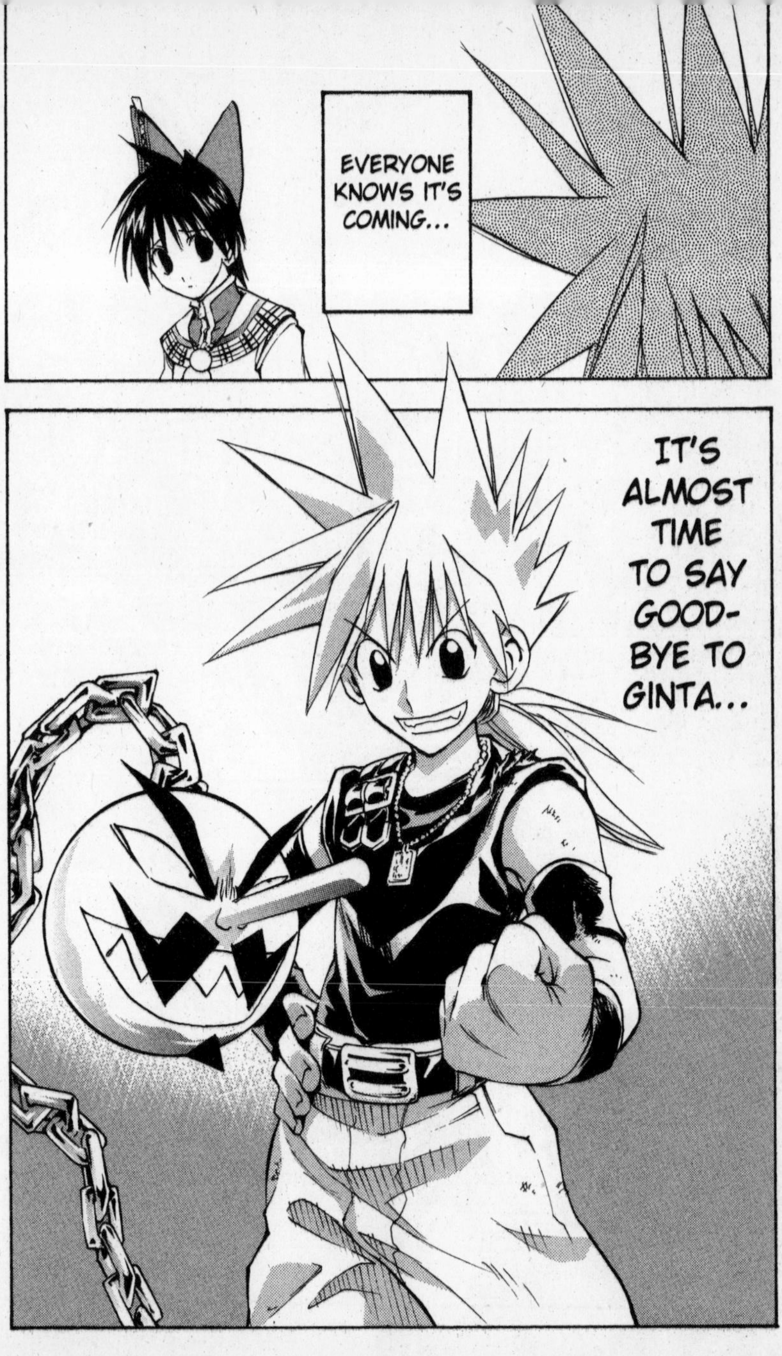
EVERYONE KNOWS IT'S COMING...
IT'S ALMOST TIME TO SAY GOOD-BYE TO GINTA...

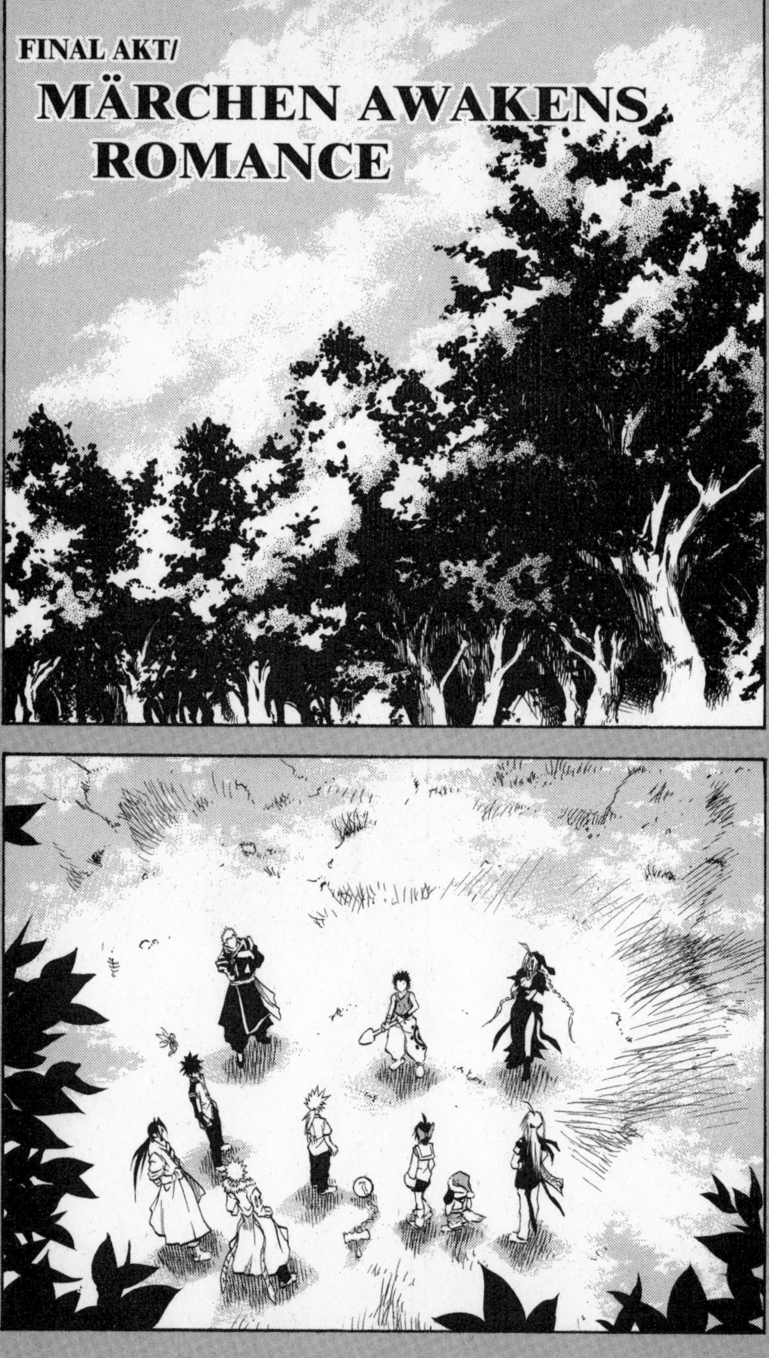
FINAL AKT/
MÄRCHEN AWAKENS ROMANCE

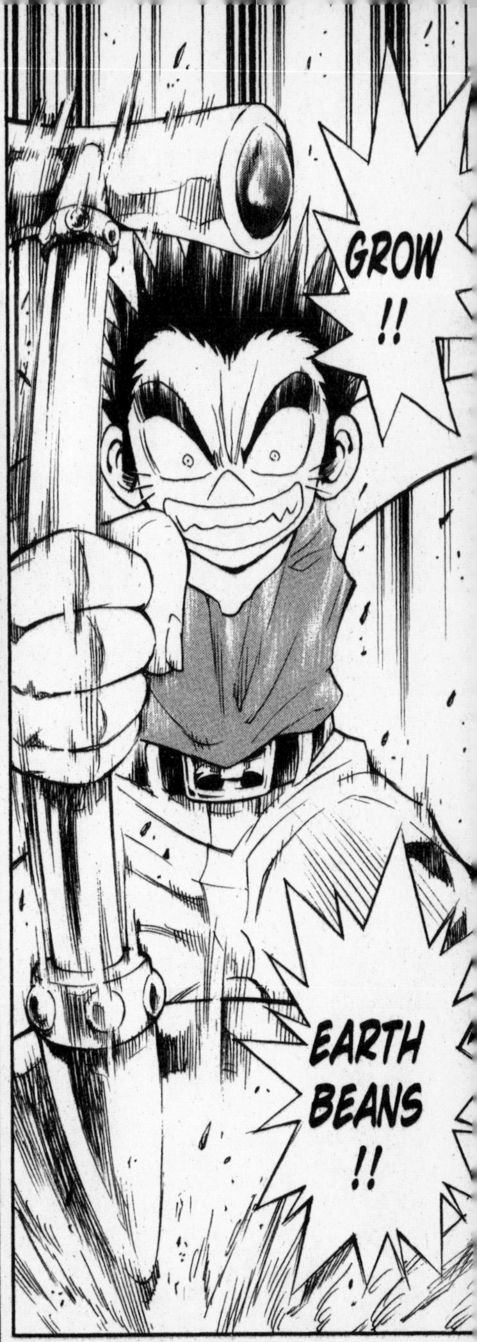
GROW
!!
EARTH
BEANS
!!
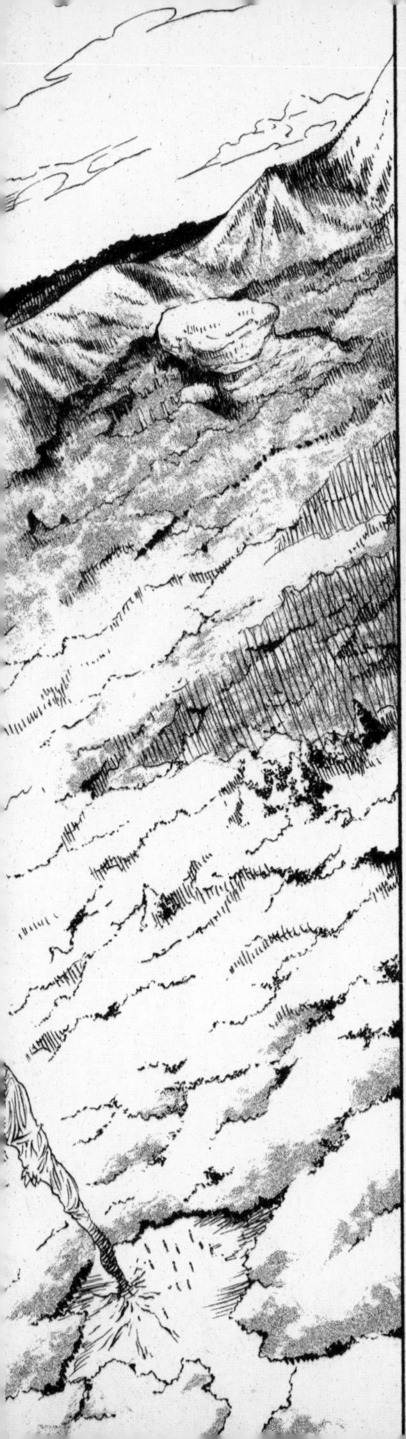

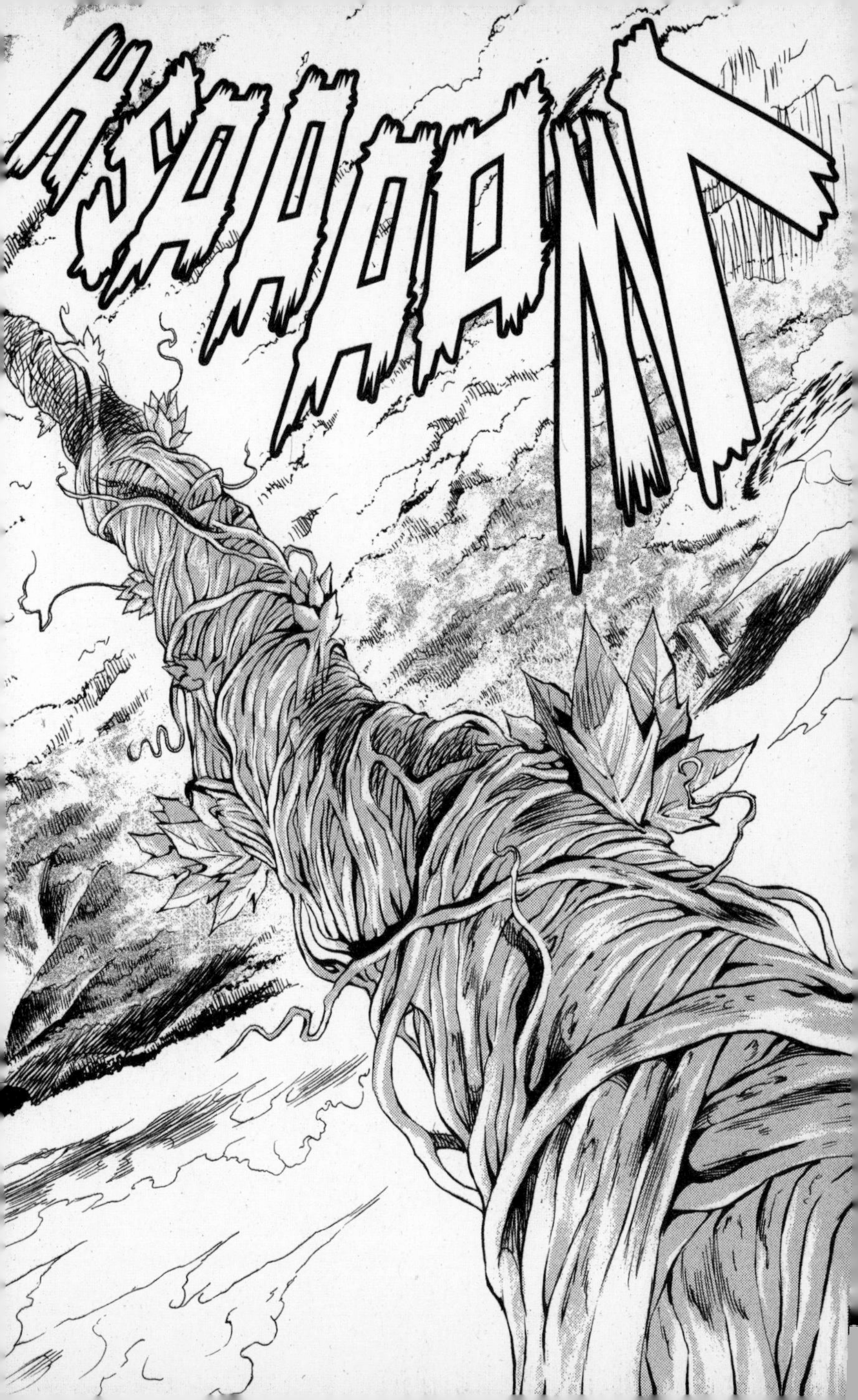

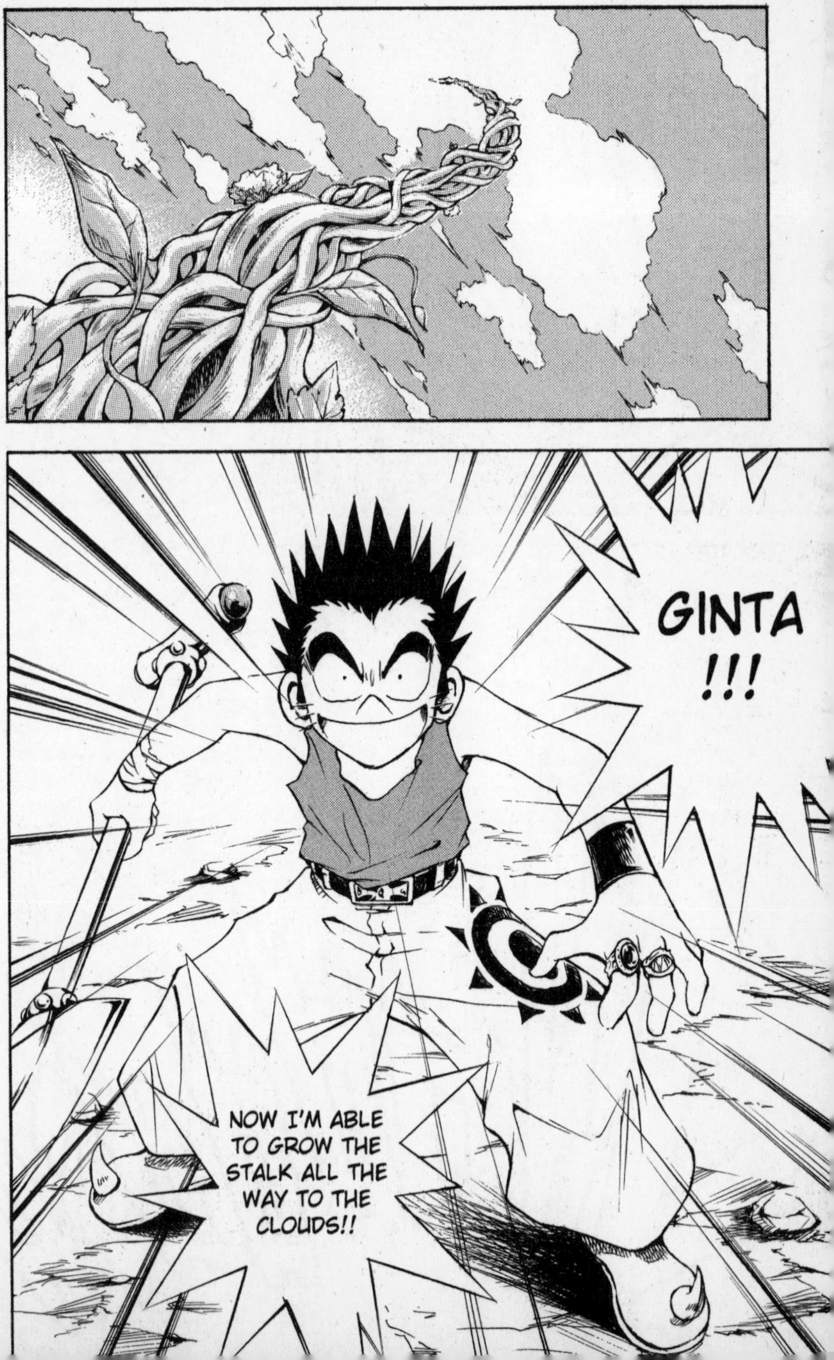
GINTA !!!
NOW I'M ABLE TO GROW THE STALK ALL THE WAY TO THE CLOUDS!!

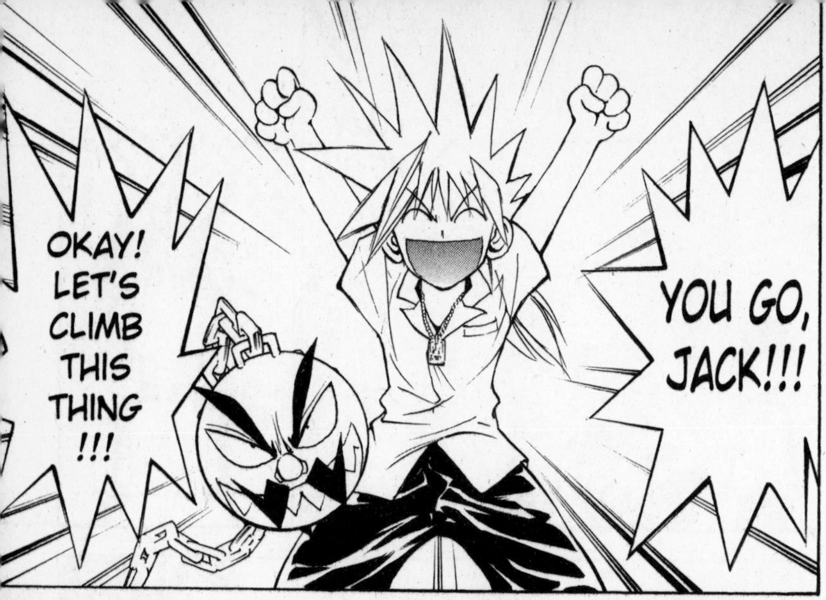
YOU GO, JACK!!!
OKAY! LET'S CLIMB THIS THING!!!

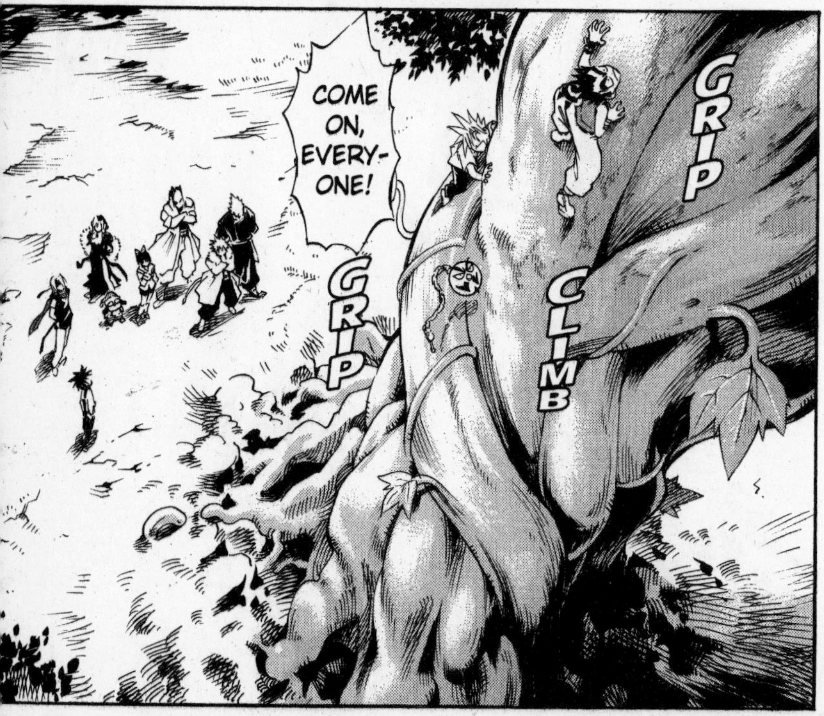
GRIP
CLIMB
COME ON, EVERY-ONE!
GRIP

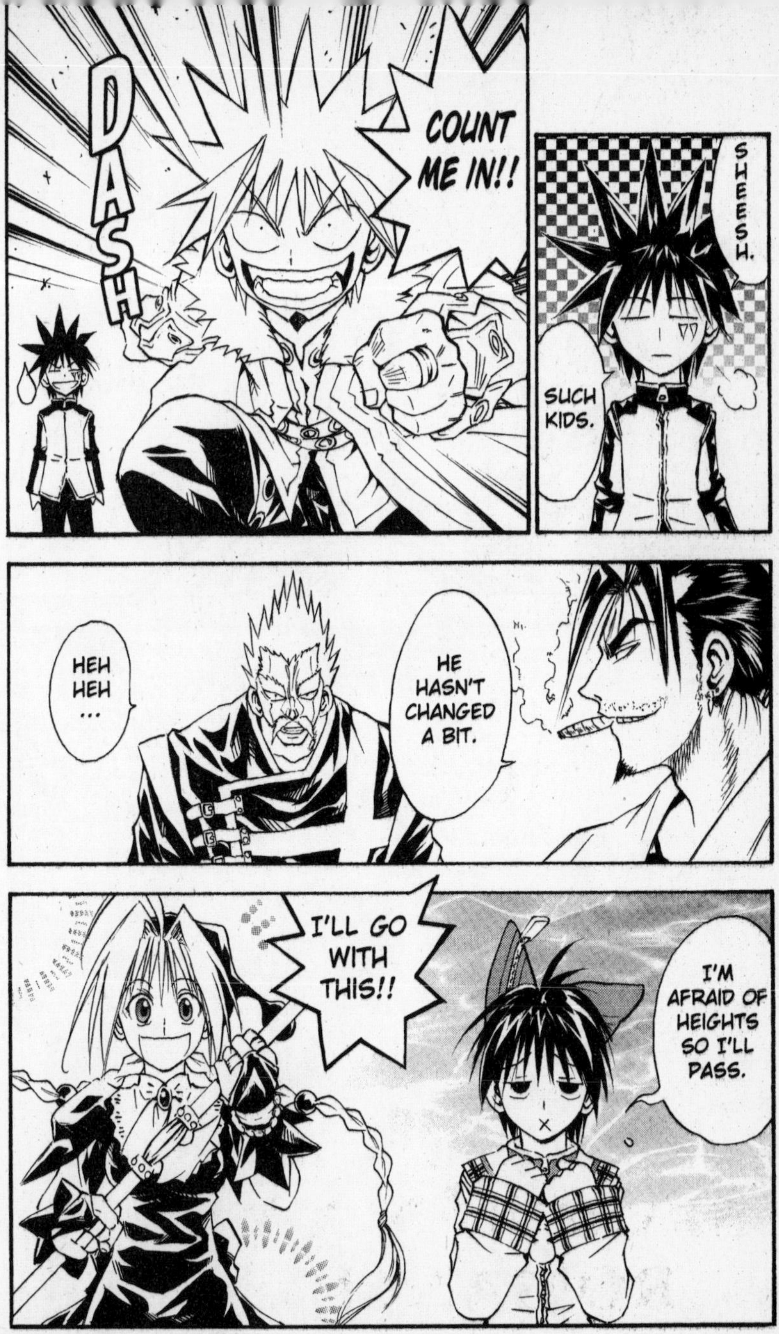
SHEESH.
SUCH KIDS.
COUNT ME IN!!
DASH
HE HASN'T CHANGED A BIT.
HEH HEH ...
I'M AFRAID OF HEIGHTS SO I'LL PASS.
I'LL GO WITH THIS!!

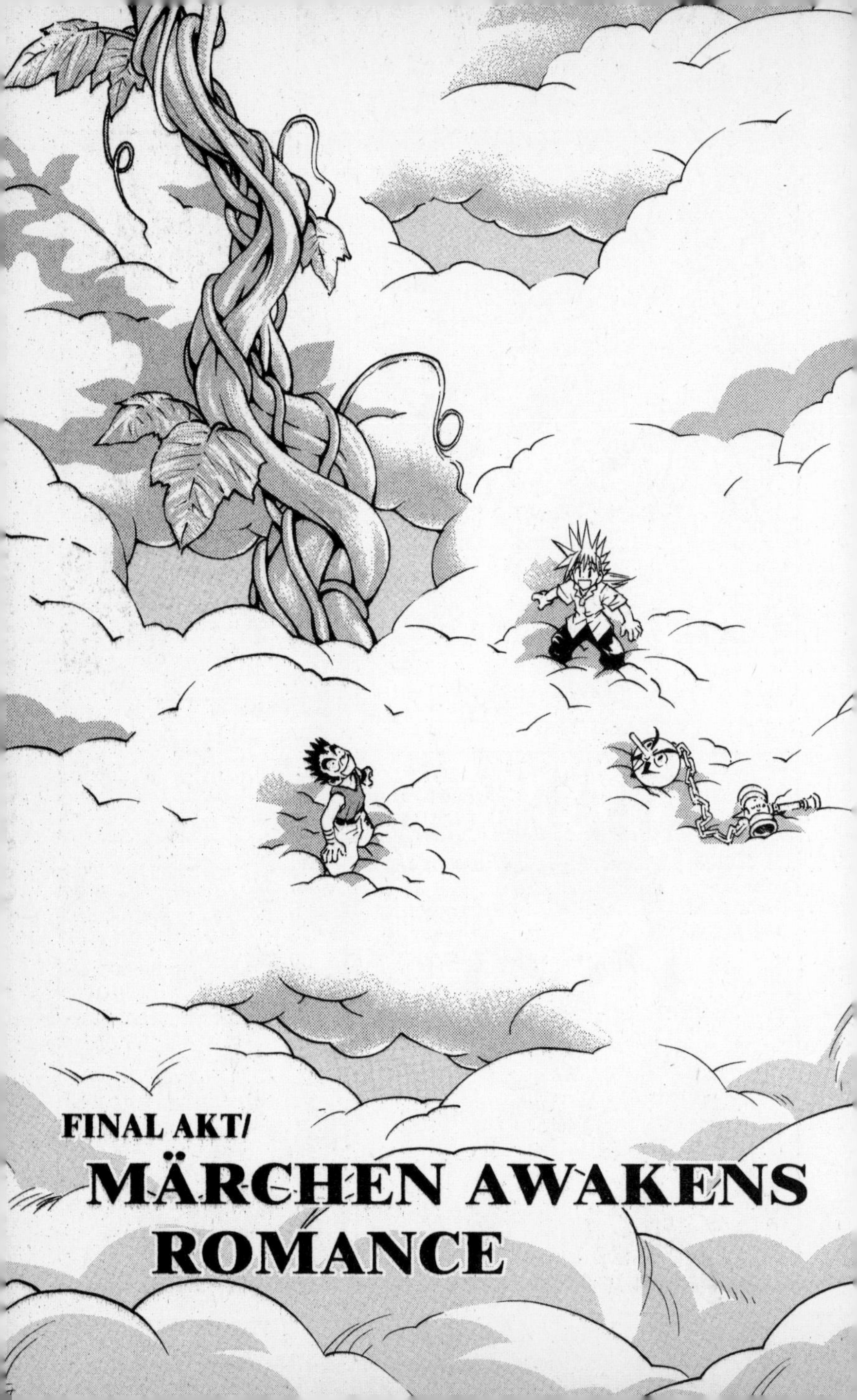
FINAL AKT/
MÄRCHEN AWAKENS
ROMANCE

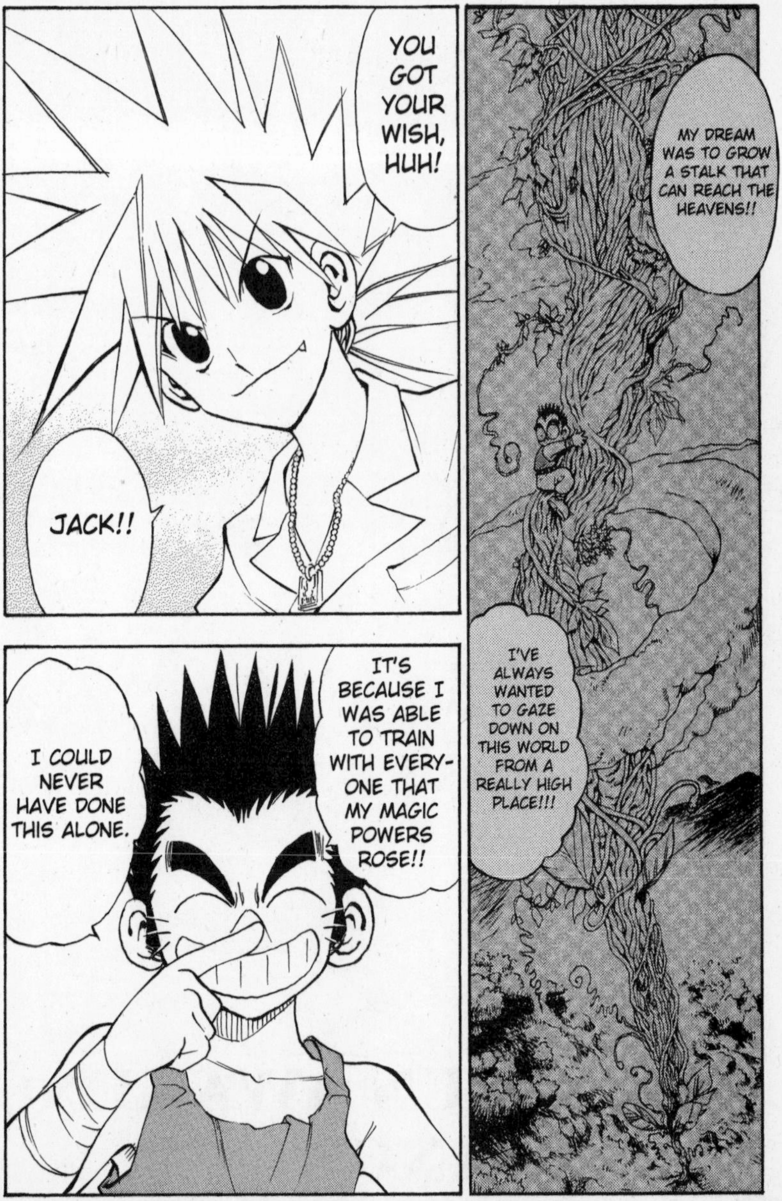
MY DREAM WAS TO GROW A STALK THAT CAN REACH THE HEAVENS!!
I'VE ALWAYS WANTED TO GAZE DOWN ON THIS WORLD FROM A REALLY HIGH PLACE!!!
YOU GOT YOUR WISH, HUH!
JACK!!
IT'S BECAUSE I WAS ABLE TO TRAIN WITH EVERY-ONE THAT MY MAGIC POWERS ROSE!!
I COULD NEVER HAVE DONE THIS ALONE.

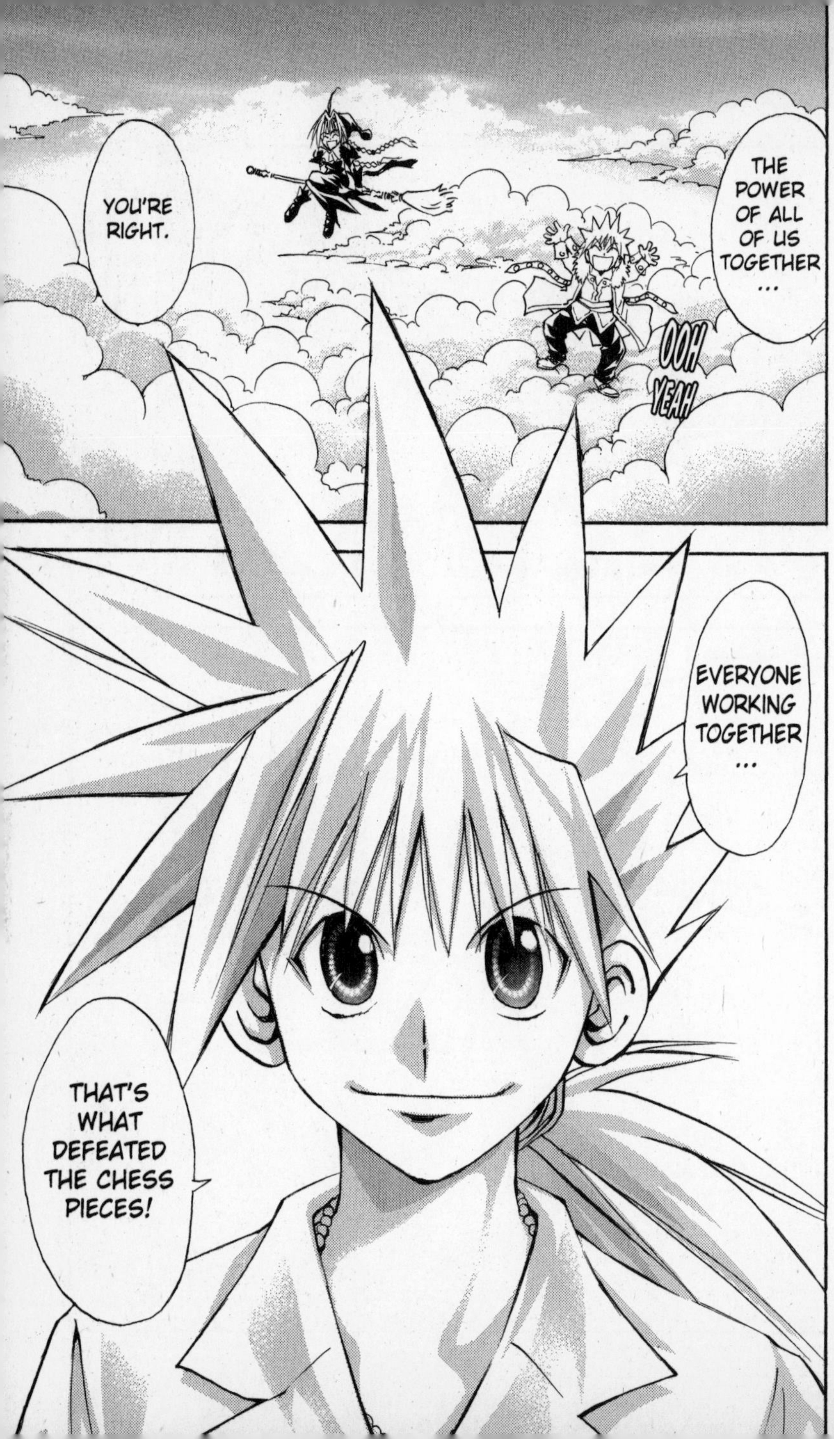
THE POWER OF ALL OF US TOGETHER ...
OOH YEAH
YOU'RE RIGHT.
EVERYONE WORKING TOGETHER ...
THAT'S WHAT DEFEATED THE CHESS PIECES!

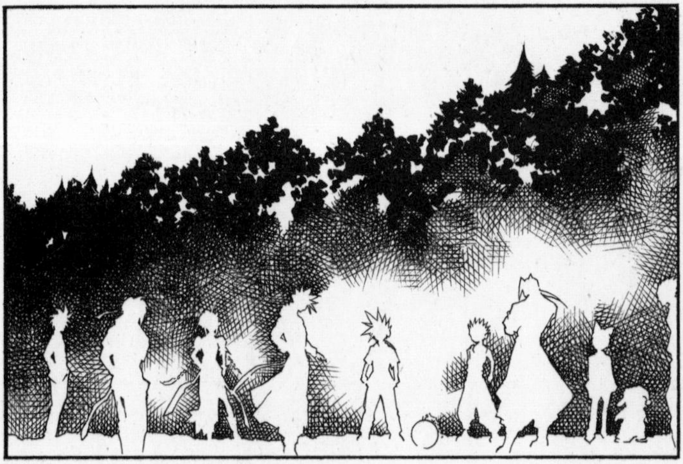

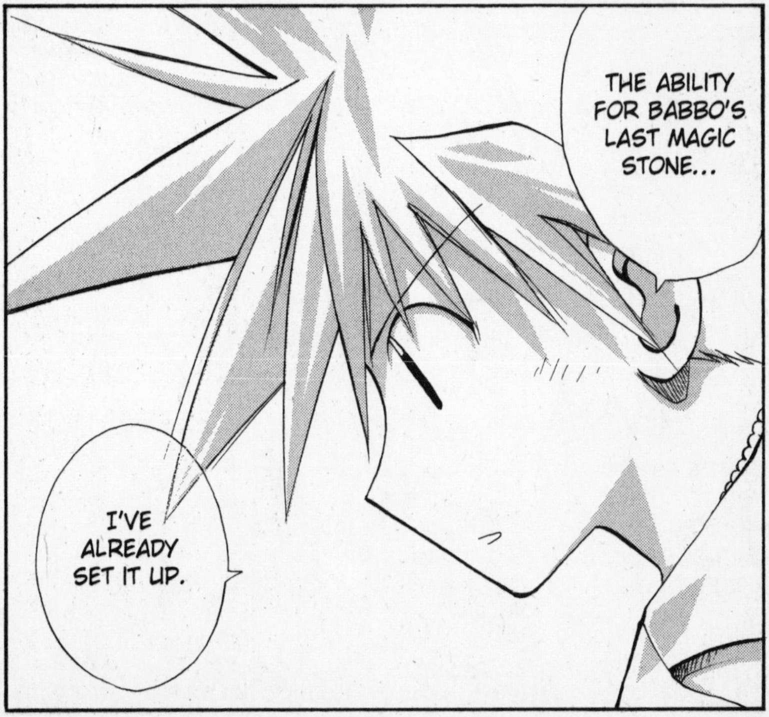
THE ABILITY FOR BABBO'S LAST MAGIC STONE...
I'VE ALREADY SET IT UP.

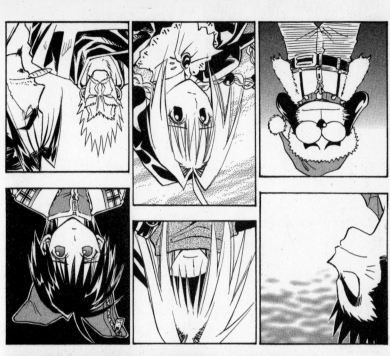

REVERSE GATEKEEPER CLOWN...?

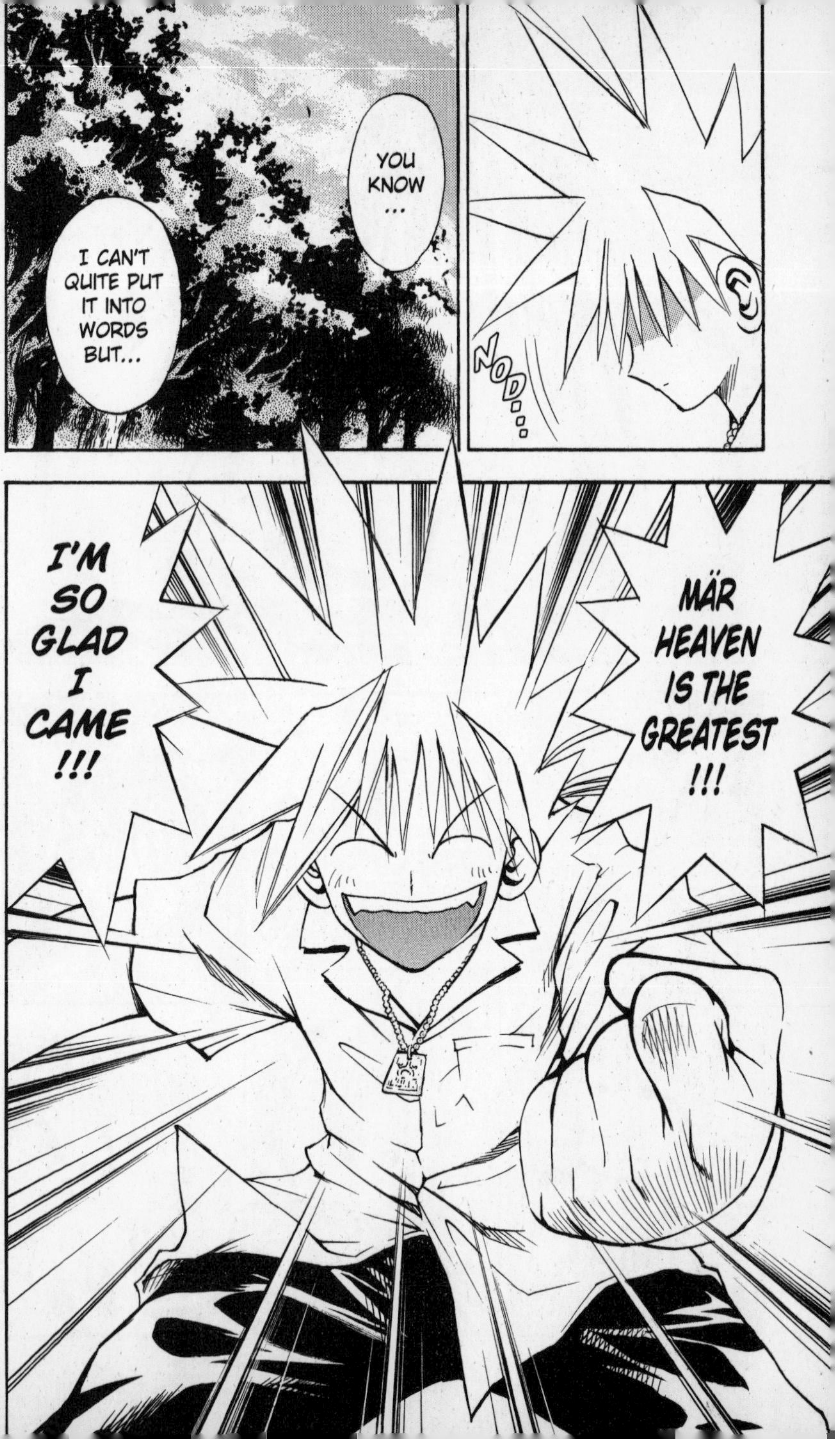
NOD...
YOU KNOW...
I CAN'T QUITE PUT IT INTO WORDS BUT...
MÄR HEAVEN IS THE GREATEST!!!
I'M SO GLAD I CAME!!!

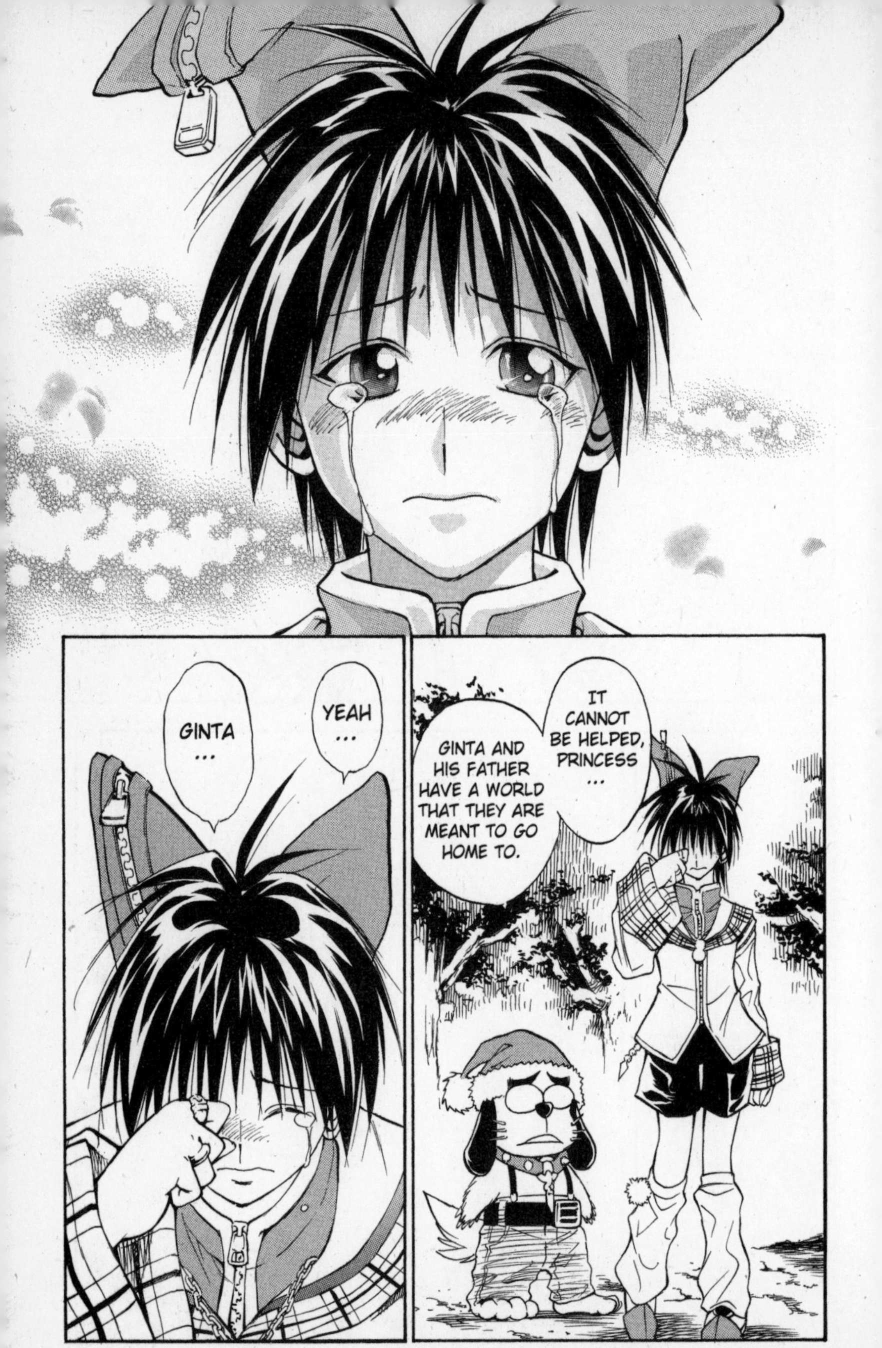
IT CANNOT BE HELPED, PRINCESS ...
GINTA AND HIS FATHER HAVE A WORLD THAT THEY ARE MEANT TO GO HOME TO.
YEAH ...
GINTA ...

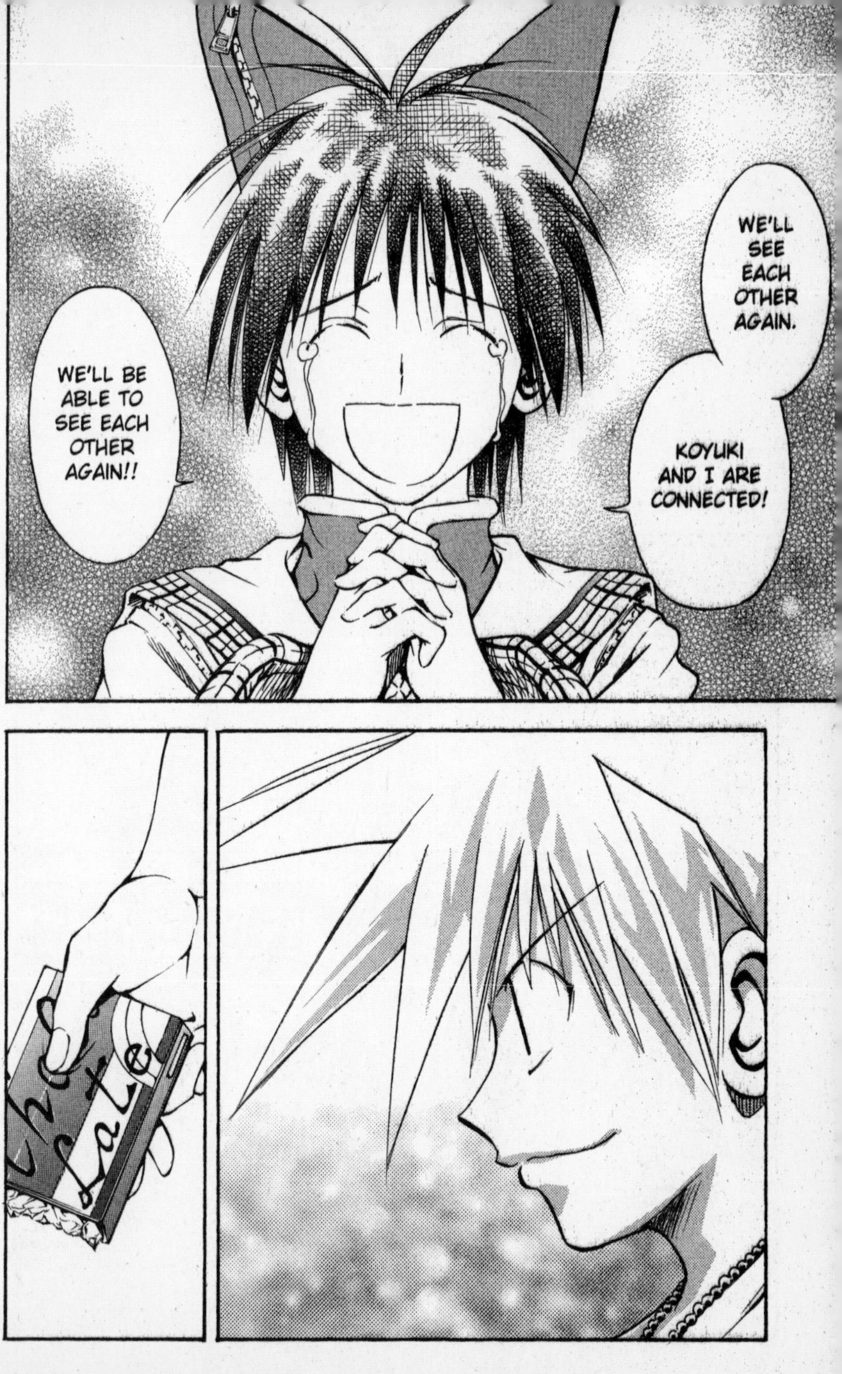
WE'LL SEE EACH OTHER AGAIN.
KOYUKI AND I ARE CONNECTED!
WE'LL BE ABLE TO SEE EACH OTHER AGAIN!!

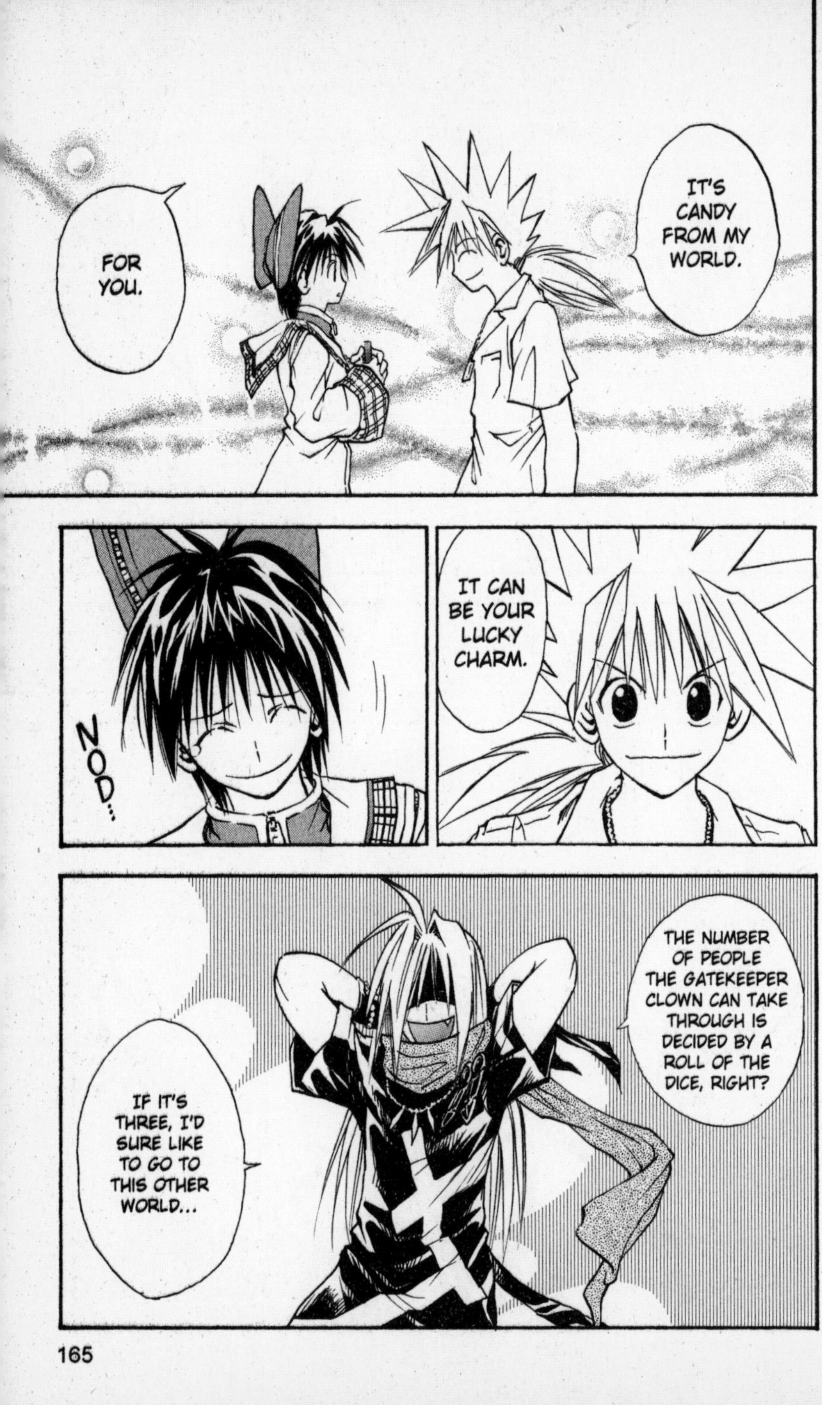
IT'S CANDY FROM MY WORLD.
FOR YOU.
IT CAN BE YOUR LUCKY CHARM.
NOD...
THE NUMBER OF PEOPLE THE GATEKEEPER CLOWN CAN TAKE THROUGH IS DECIDED BY A ROLL OF THE DICE, RIGHT?
IF IT'S THREE, I'D SURE LIKE TO GO TO THIS OTHER WORLD...

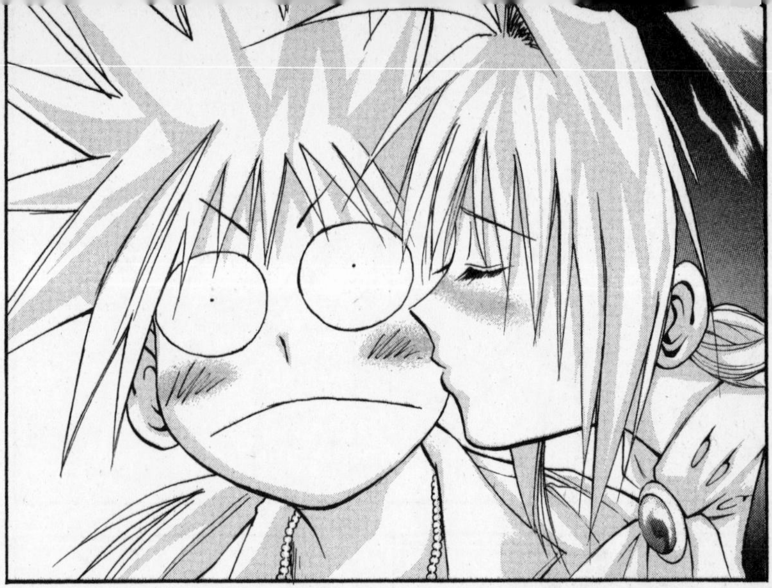

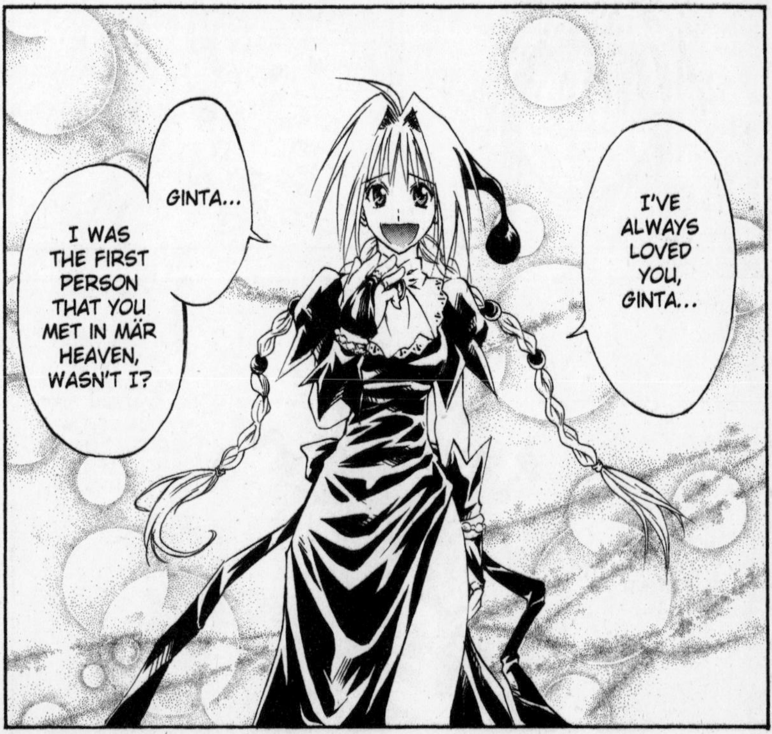
I'VE ALWAYS LOVED YOU, GINTA...
GINTA...
I WAS THE FIRST PERSON THAT YOU MET IN MÄR HEAVEN, WASN'T I?

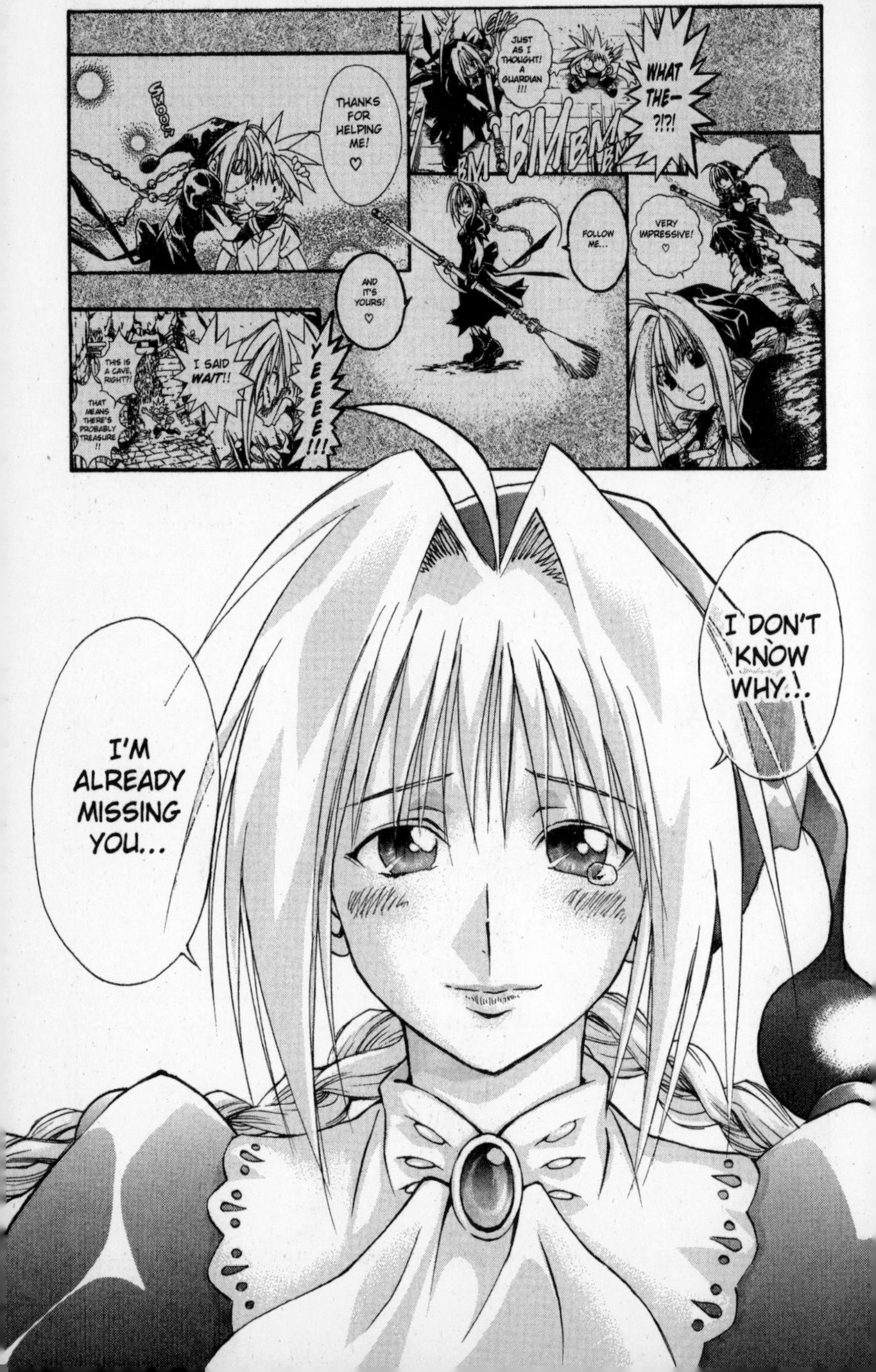
WHAT THE—?!?!
JUST AS I THOUGHT! A GUARDIAN!!!
BMBMBM
THANKS FOR HELPING ME! ♡
SWOOP
VERY IMPRESSIVE! ♡
FOLLOW ME...
AND IT'S YOURS! ♡
YEEEEE!!!
I SAID WAIT!!
THIS IS A CAVE, RIGHT?!
THAT MEANS THERE'S PROBABLY TREASURE!!
I DON'T KNOW WHY...
I'M ALREADY MISSING YOU...

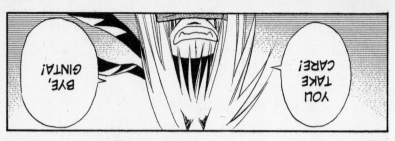

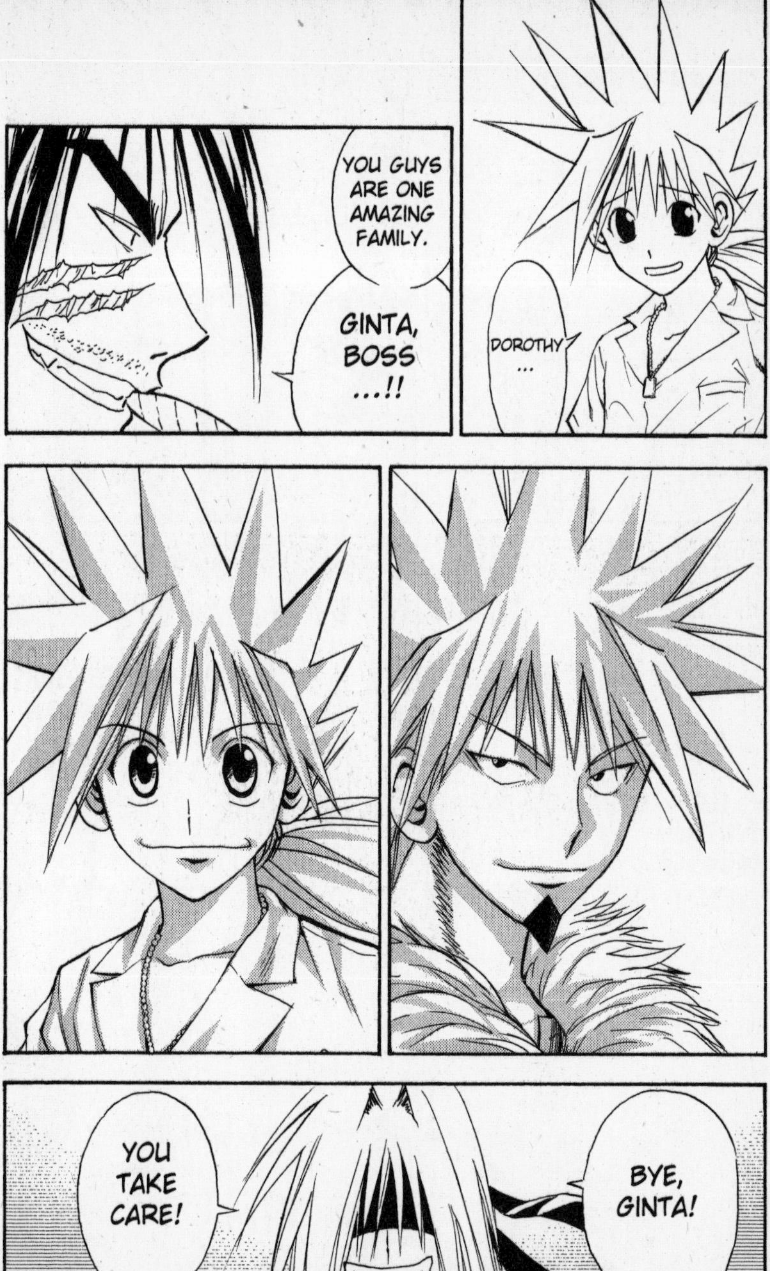
DOROTHY ...
YOU GUYS ARE ONE AMAZING FAMILY.
GINTA, BOSS ...!!
BYE, GINTA!
YOU TAKE CARE!

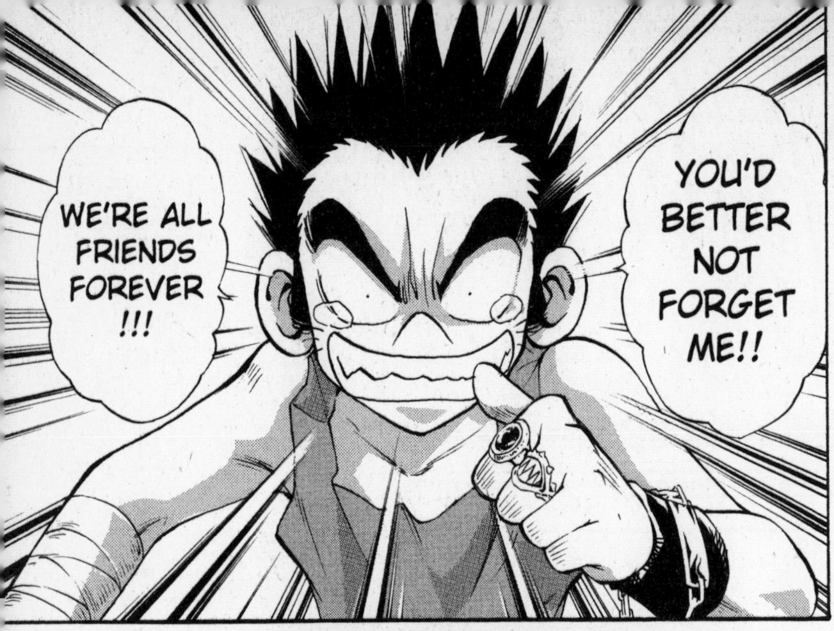
YOU'D BETTER NOT FORGET ME!!
WE'RE ALL FRIENDS FOREVER !!!

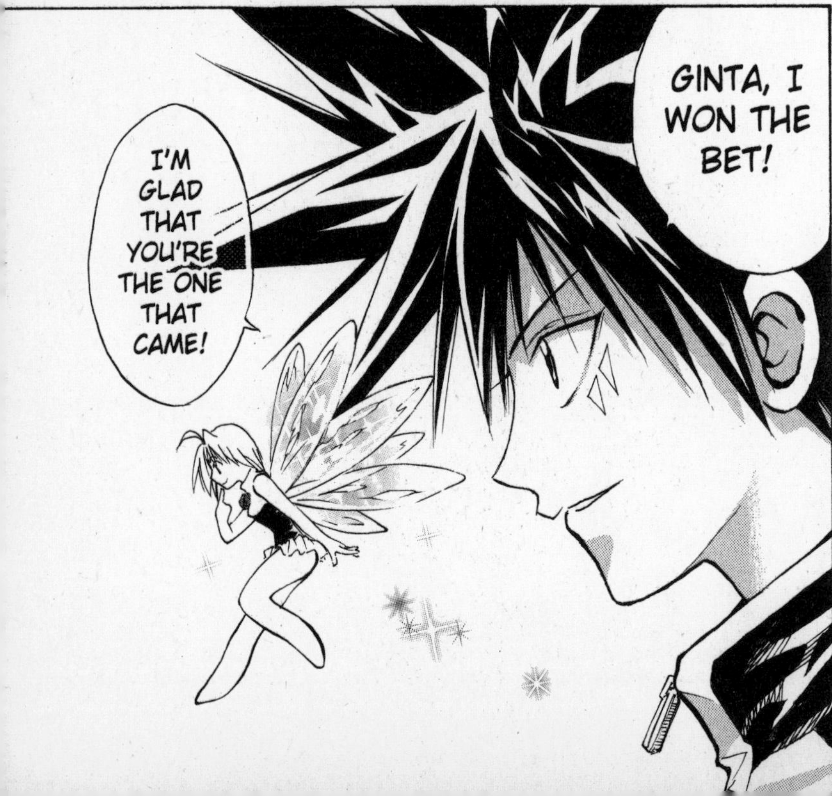
GINTA, I WON THE BET!
I'M GLAD THAT YOU'RE THE ONE THAT CAME!

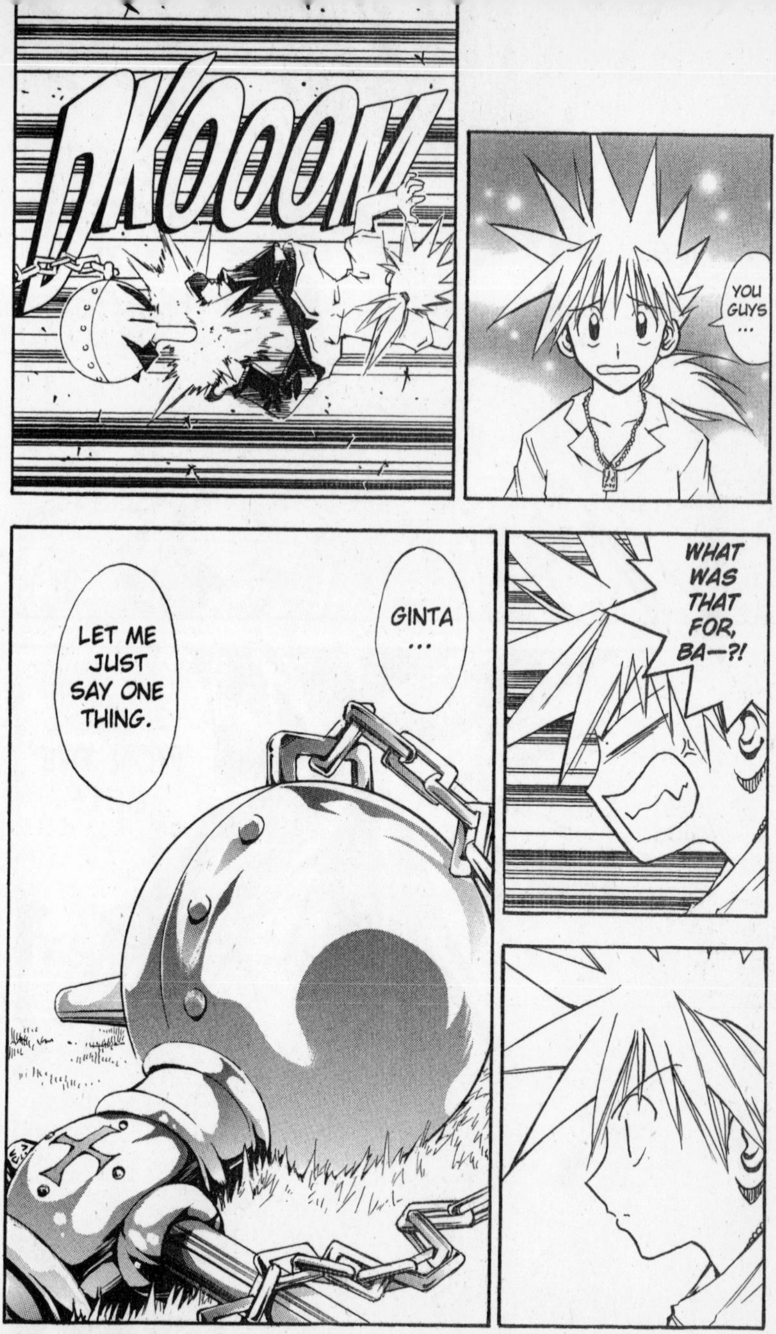
YOU GUYS ...
DKOOOM
WHAT WAS THAT FOR, BA—?!
GINTA ...
LET ME JUST SAY ONE THING.

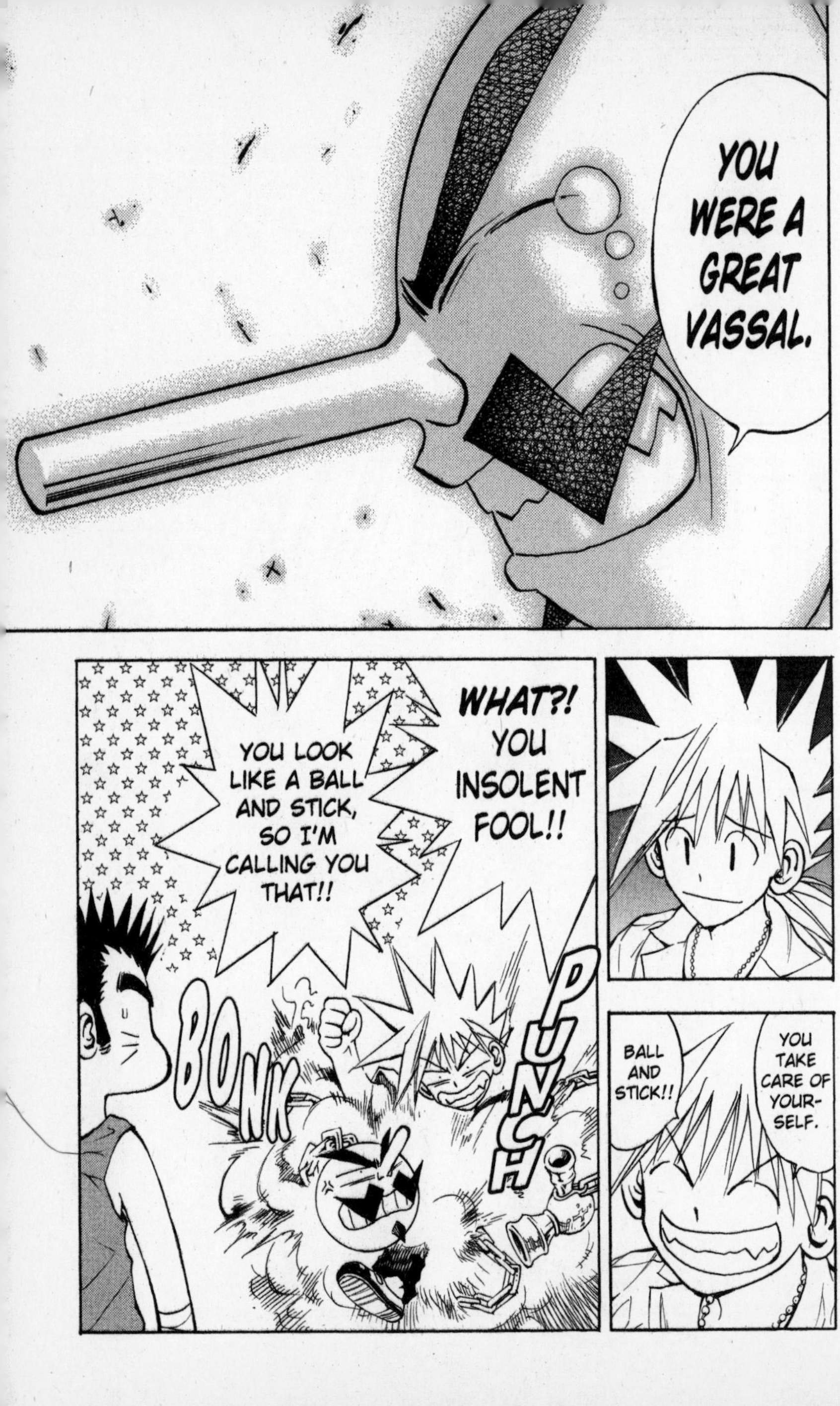
YOU WERE A GREAT VASSAL.
YOU TAKE CARE OF YOUR-SELF.
BALL AND STICK!!
YOU LOOK LIKE A BALL AND STICK, SO I'M CALLING YOU THAT!!
WHAT?! YOU INSOLENT FOOL!!
BONK
PUNCH

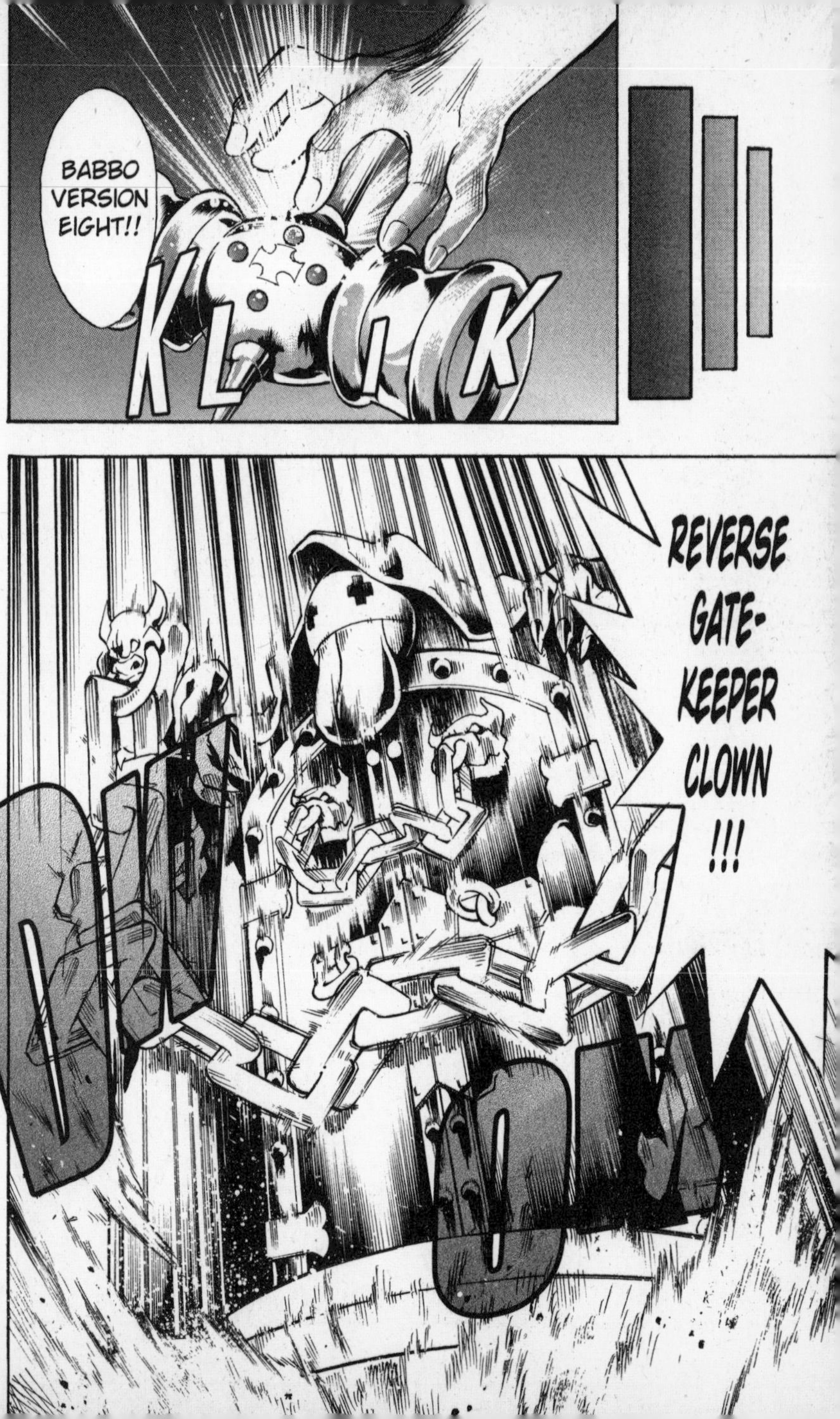
BABBO VERSION EIGHT!!
KLIK
REVERSE GATE-KEEPER CLOWN !!!

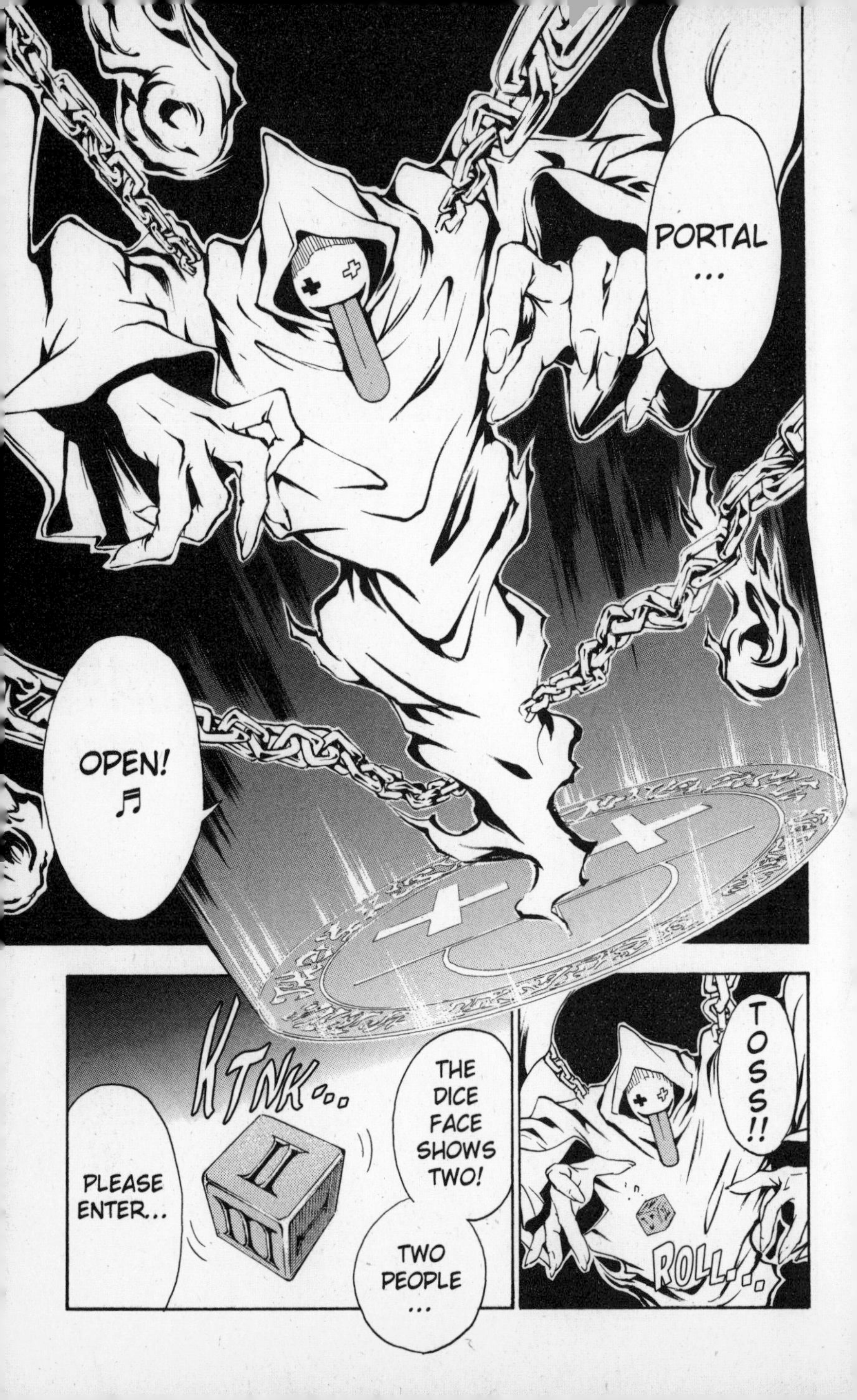
PORTAL ...
OPEN! ♬
TOSS!!
ROLL..
THE DICE FACE SHOWS TWO!
TWO PEOPLE ...
KTNK...
PLEASE ENTER...

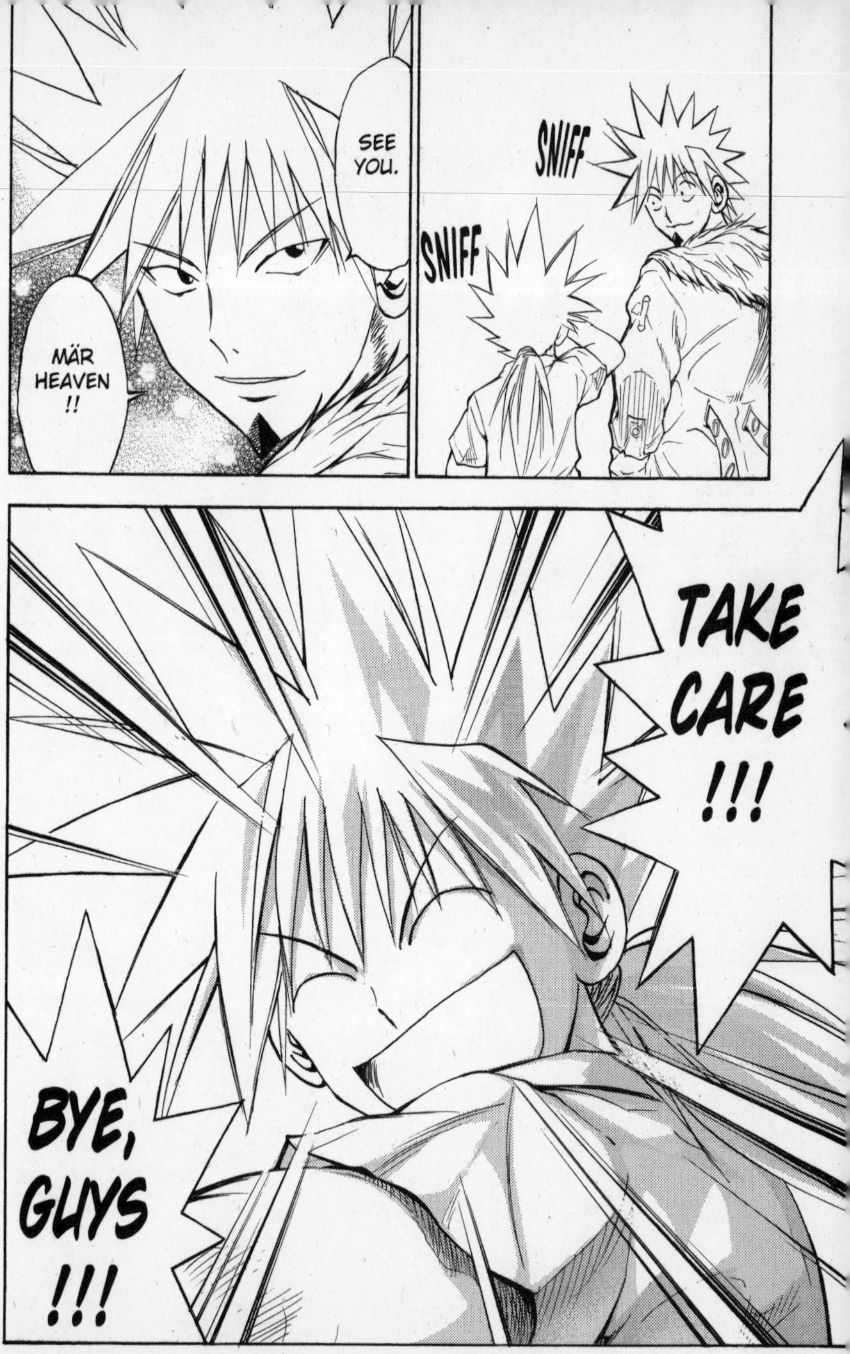
SNIFF
SNIFF
SEE YOU.
MÄR HEAVEN !!
TAKE CARE !!!
BYE, GUYS !!!

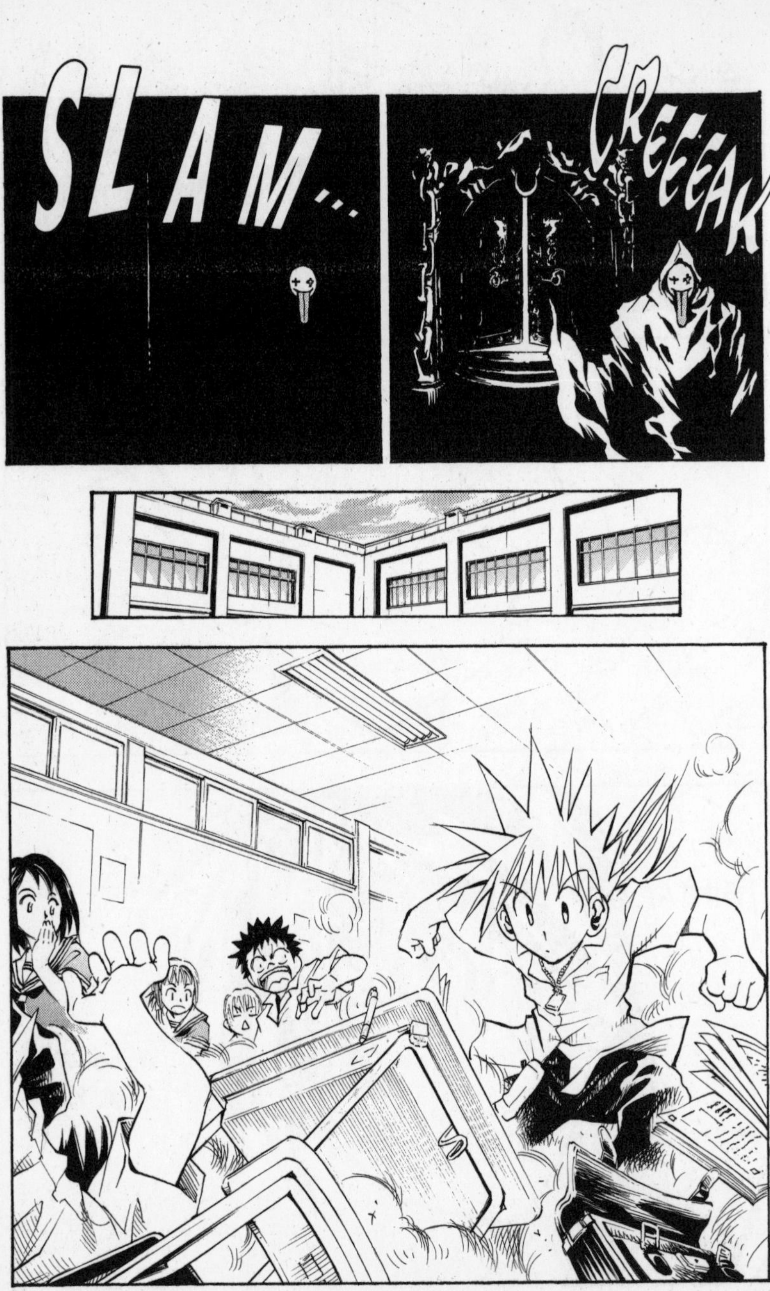
CREEEAK
SLAM...

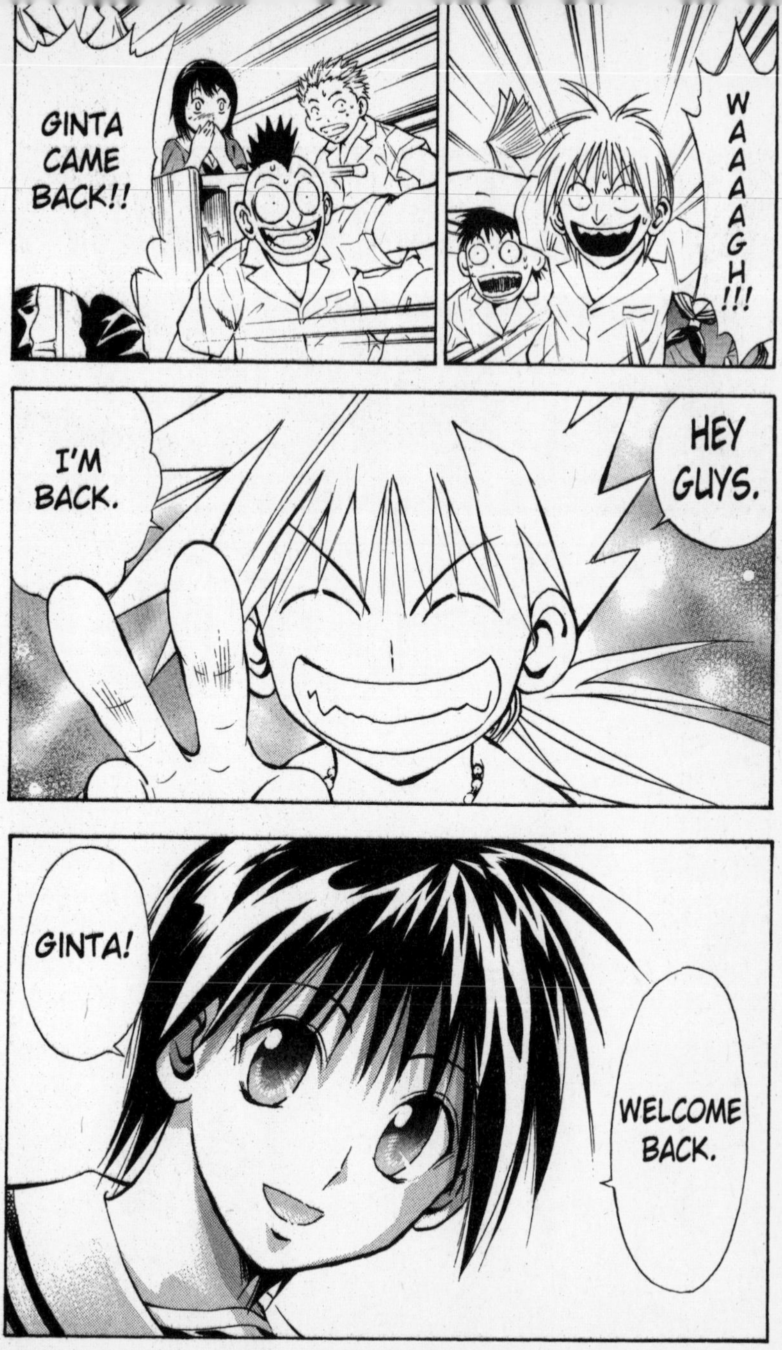
WAAAAAGH!!!
GINTA CAME BACK!!
HEY GUYS.
I'M BACK.
GINTA!
WELCOME BACK.

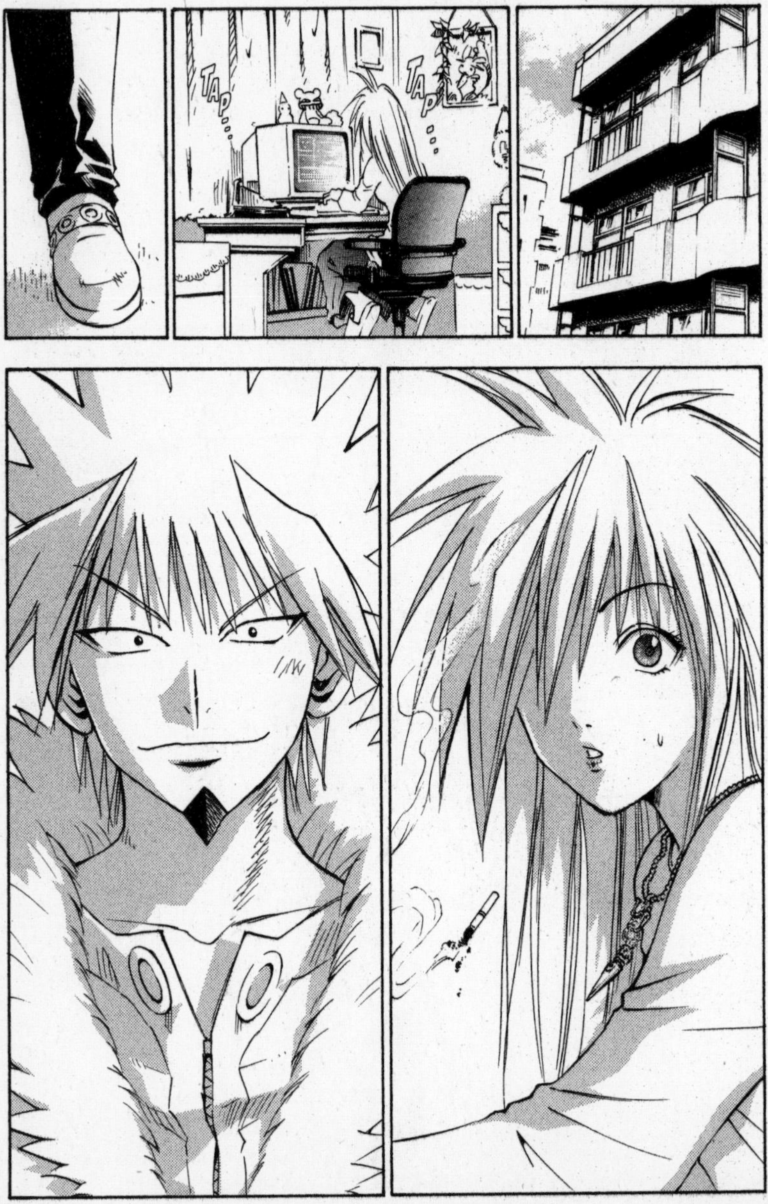
TAP...
TAP...

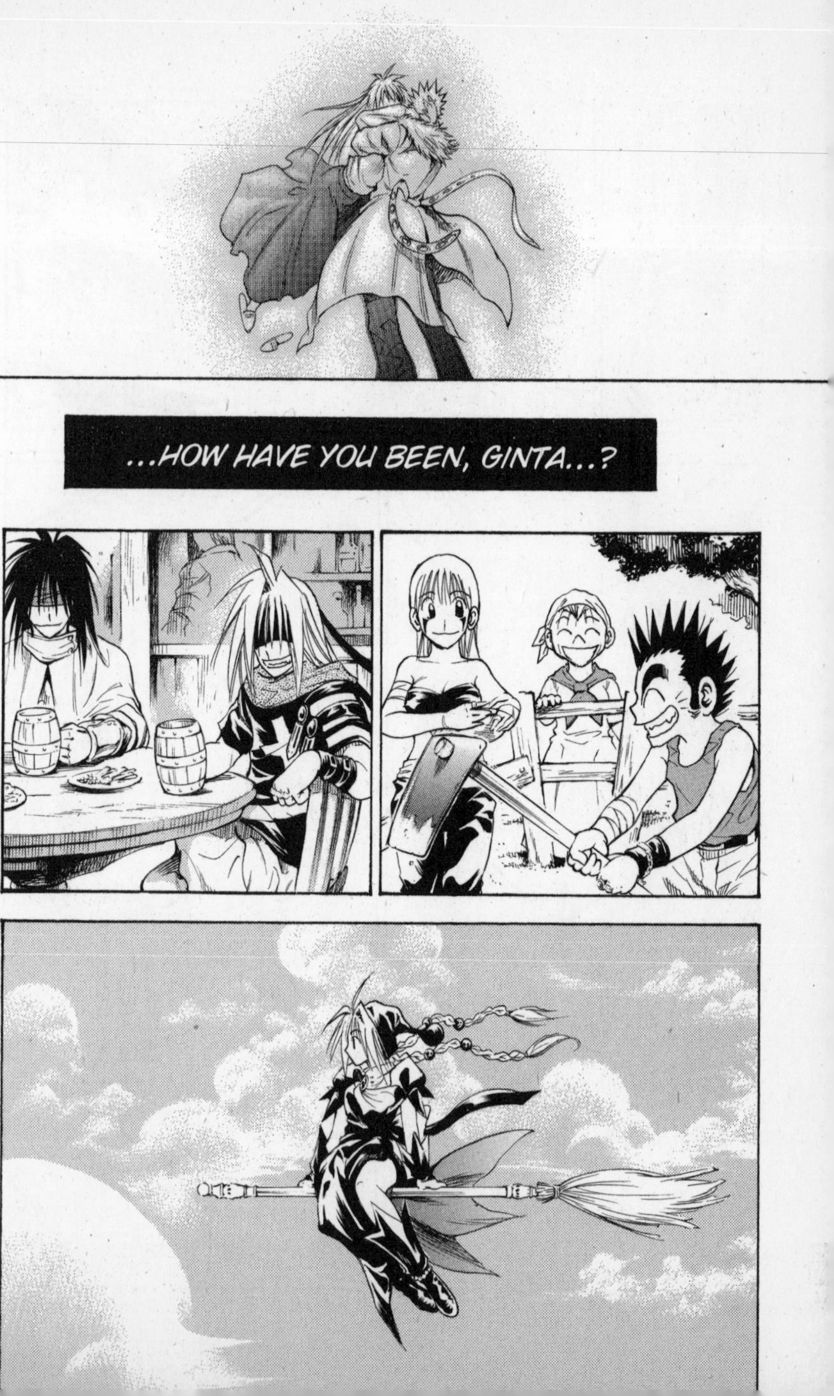
...HOW HAVE YOU BEEN, GINTA...?

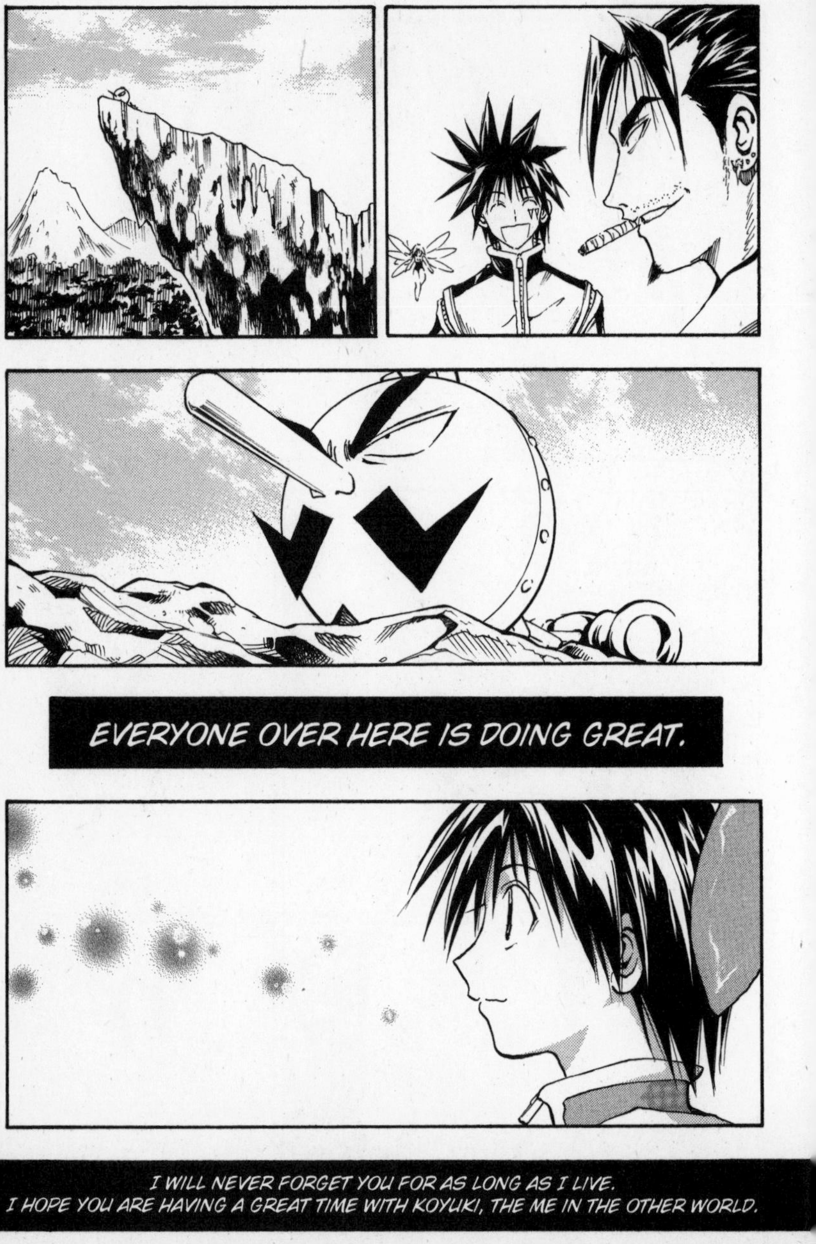
EVERYONE OVER HERE IS DOING GREAT.
I WILL NEVER FORGET YOU FOR AS LONG AS I LIVE.
I HOPE YOU ARE HAVING A GREAT TIME WITH KOYUKI, THE ME IN THE OTHER WORLD.

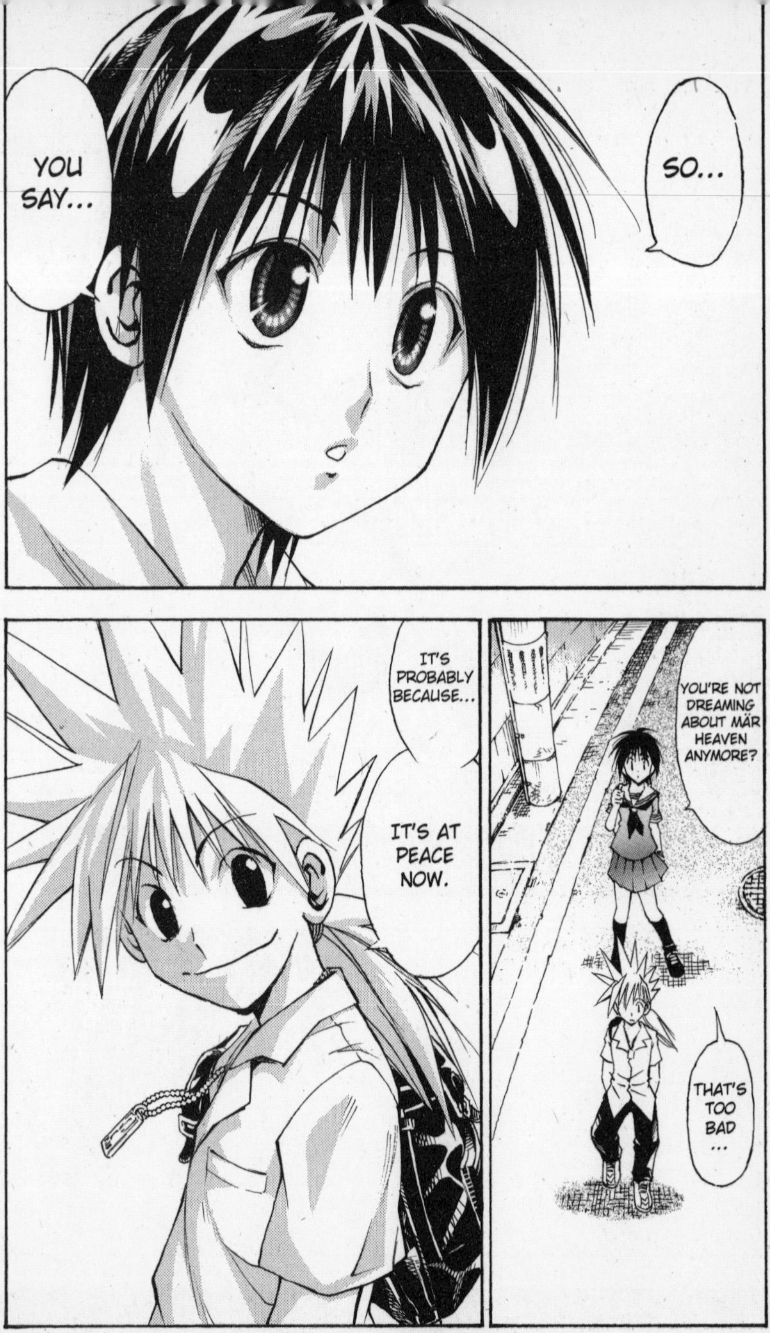
SO...
YOU SAY...
YOU'RE NOT DREAMING ABOUT MÄR HEAVEN ANYMORE?
THAT'S TOO BAD...
IT'S PROBABLY BECAUSE...
IT'S AT PEACE NOW.

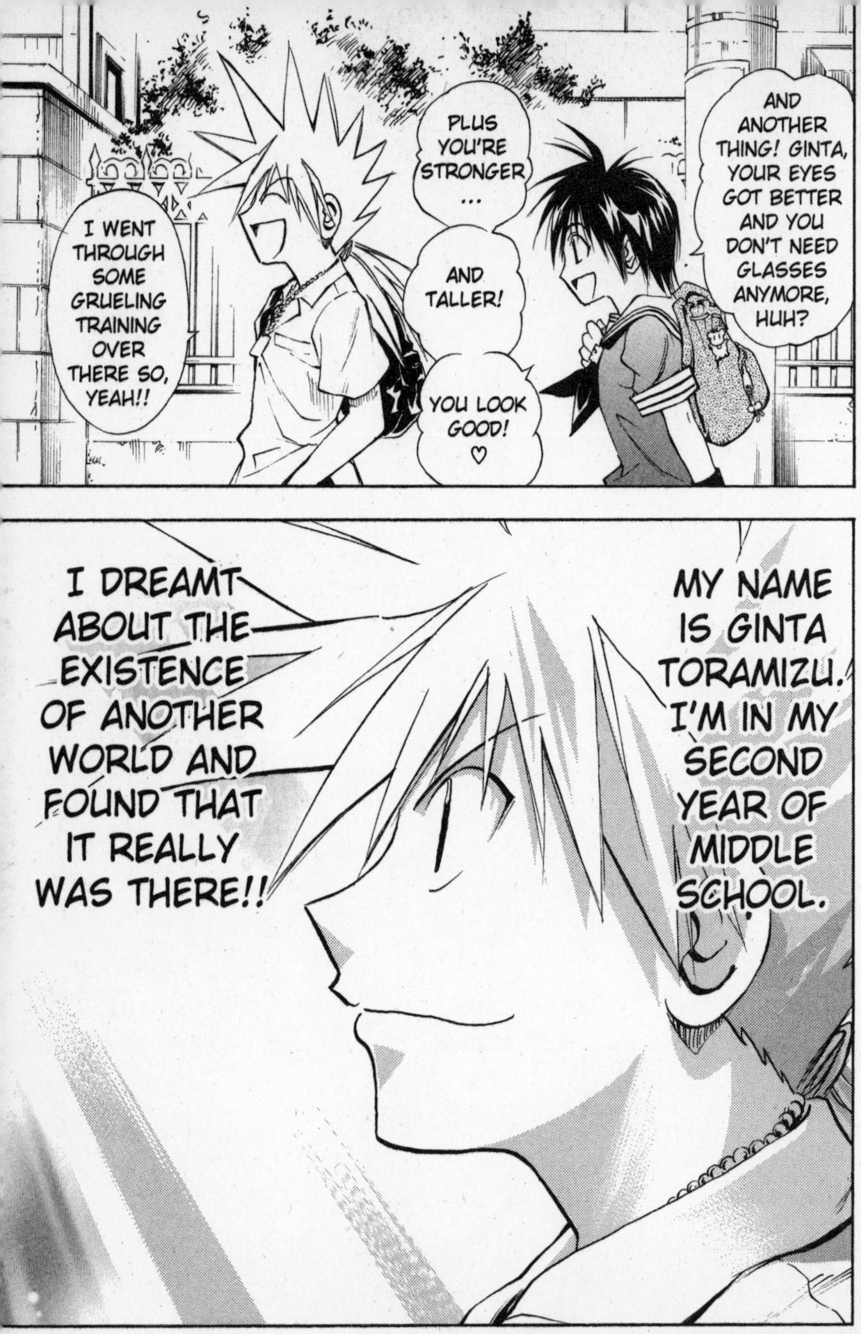
AND ANOTHER THING! GINTA, YOUR EYES GOT BETTER AND YOU DON'T NEED GLASSES ANYMORE, HUH?
PLUS YOU'RE STRONGER...
AND TALLER!
YOU LOOK GOOD! ♡
I WENT THROUGH SOME GRUELING TRAINING OVER THERE SO, YEAH!!
MY NAME IS GINTA TORAMIZU. I'M IN MY SECOND YEAR OF MIDDLE SCHOOL.
I DREAMT ABOUT THE EXISTENCE OF ANOTHER WORLD AND FOUND THAT IT REALLY WAS THERE!!

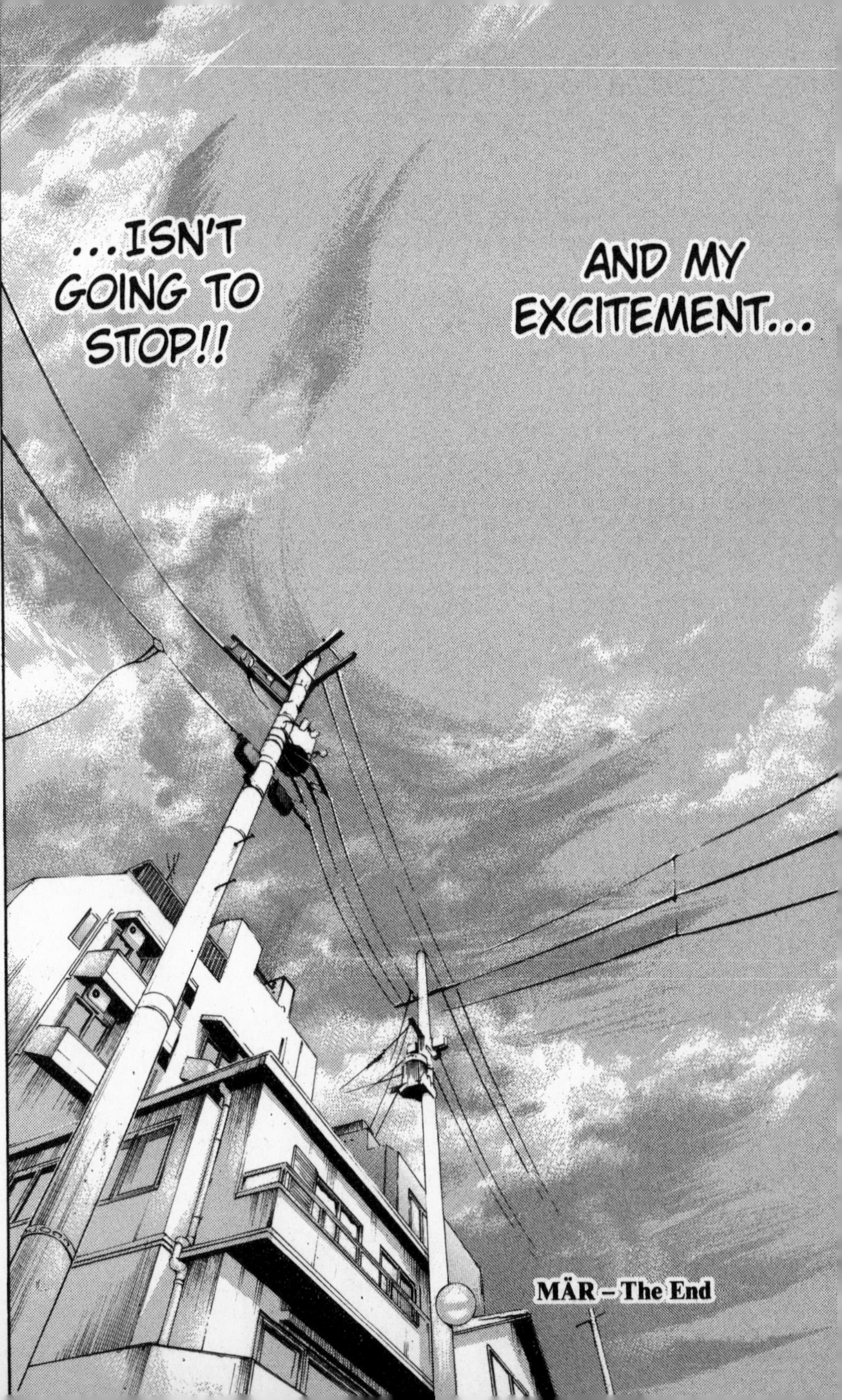
AND MY EXCITEMENT...
...ISN'T GOING TO STOP!!
MÄR – The End

MÄR

MÄRCHEN AWAKENS ROMANCE

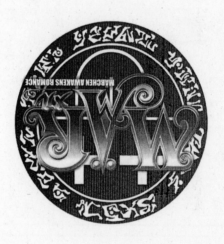

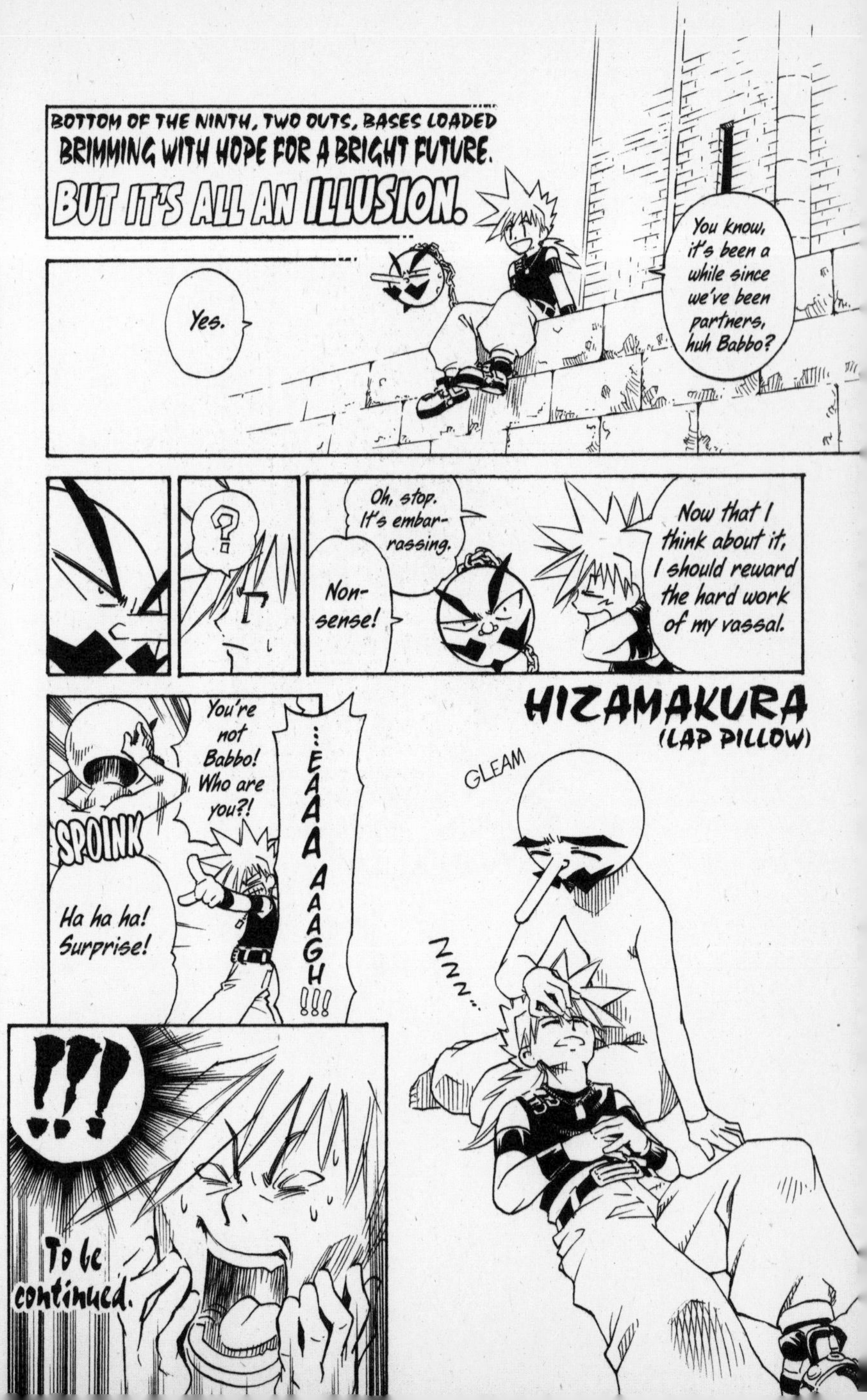
BOTTOM OF THE NINTH, TWO OUTS, BASES LOADED
BRIMMING WITH HOPE FOR A BRIGHT FUTURE.
BUT IT'S ALL AN ILLUSION.
You know, it's been a while since we've been partners, huh Babbo?
Yes.
Now that I think about it, I should reward the hard work of my vassal.
Oh, stop. It's embar-rassing.
Non-sense!
?
HIZAMAKURA
(LAP PILLOW)
GLEAM
NNN...
...EAAAAAAGH!!!
You're not Babbo! Who are you?!
SPOINK
Ha ha ha! Surprise!
!!!
To be continued.

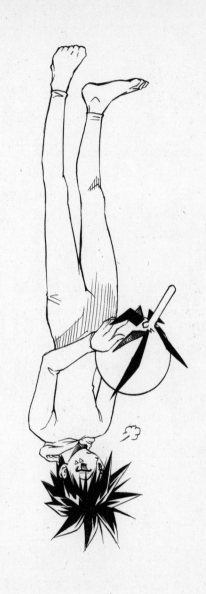

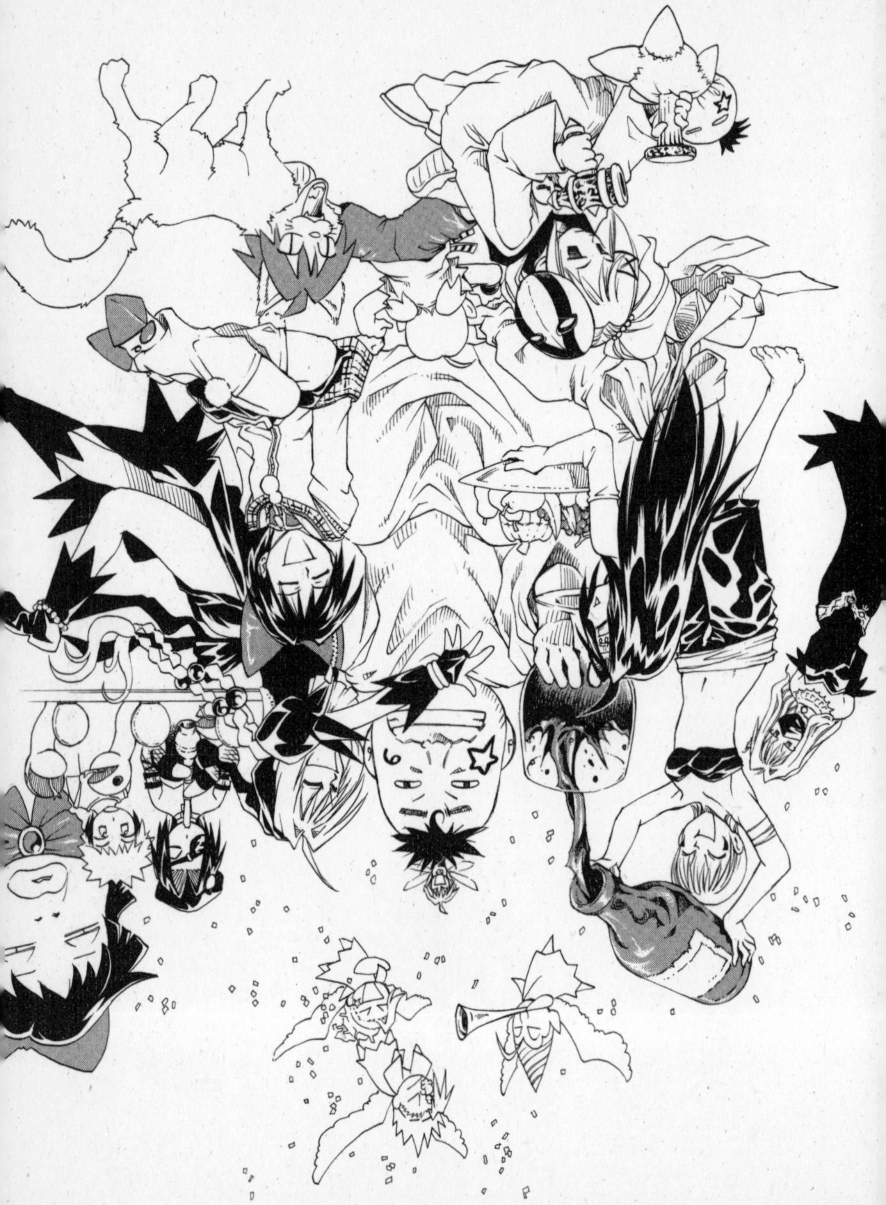

ACID VOMIT

Title lettering: Anzai

Story: GB

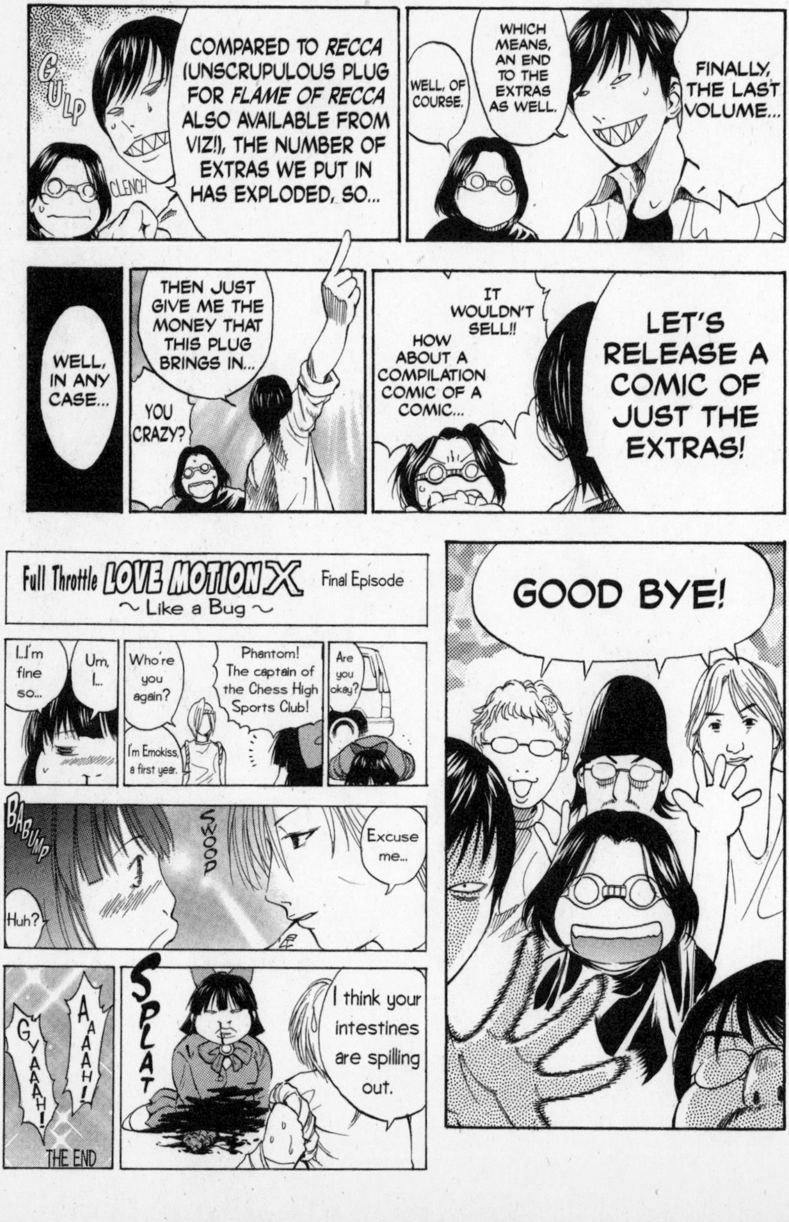
FINALLY, THE LAST VOLUME...
WHICH MEANS, AN END TO THE EXTRAS AS WELL.
WELL, OF COURSE.
COMPARED TO *RECCA* (UNSCRUPULOUS PLUG FOR *FLAME OF RECCA* ALSO AVAILABLE FROM VIZ!), THE NUMBER OF EXTRAS WE PUT IN HAS EXPLODED, SO...
GULP
CLENCH
LET'S RELEASE A COMIC OF JUST THE EXTRAS!
IT WOULDN'T SELL!!
HOW ABOUT A COMPILATION COMIC OF A COMIC...
THEN JUST GIVE ME THE MONEY THAT THIS PLUG BRINGS IN...
YOU CRAZY?
WELL, IN ANY CASE...
GOOD BYE!
Full Throttle LOVE MOTION X Final Episode
~ Like a Bug ~
Are you okay?
Phantom! The captain of the Chess High Sports Club!
Who're you again?
I'm Emokiss, a first year.
Um, I...
I...I'm fine so...
Excuse me...
SWOOP
Huh?
BABUMP
I think your intestines are spilling out.
SPLAT
AAAAH!
GYAAAH!
THE END

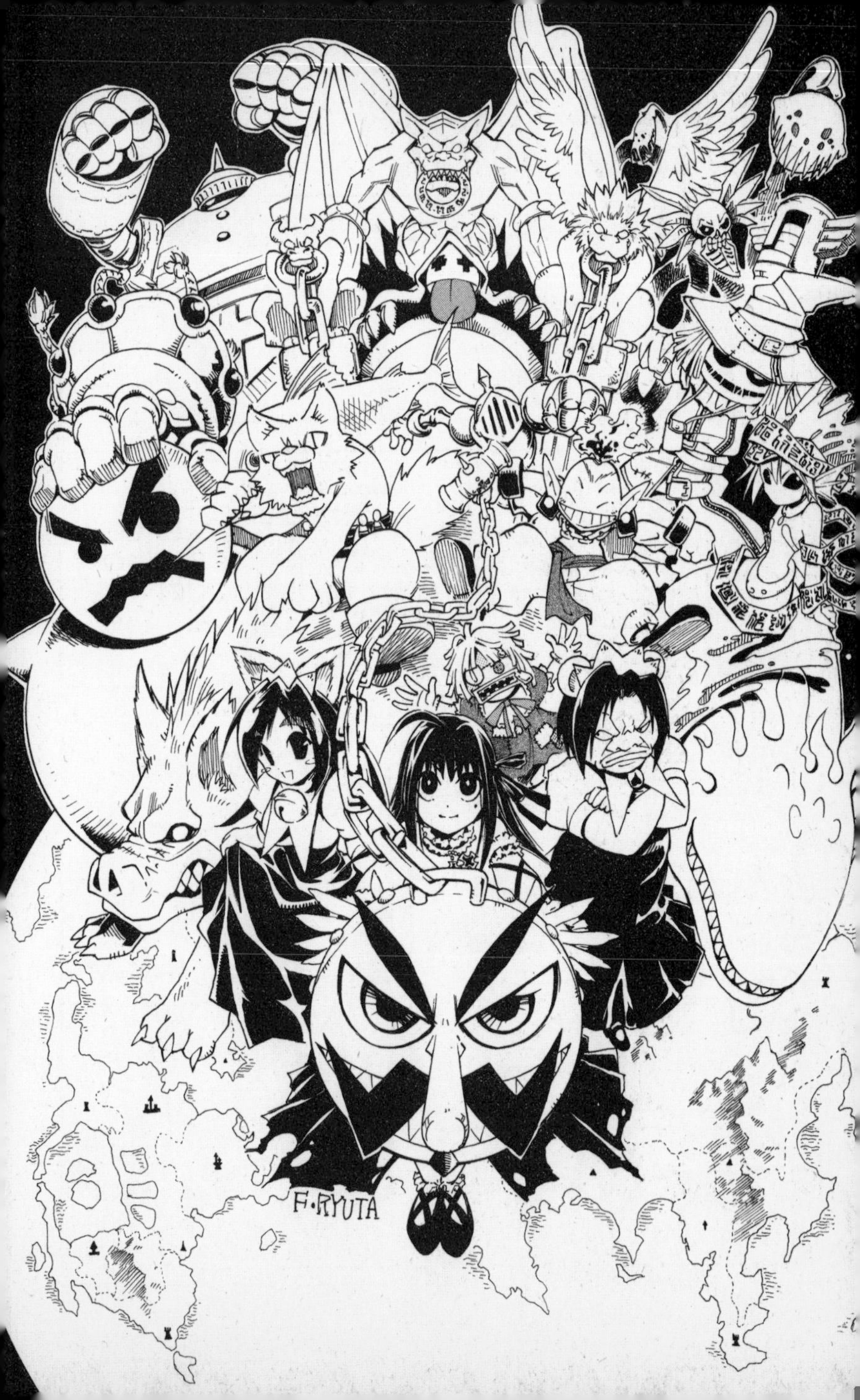
F・RYUTA

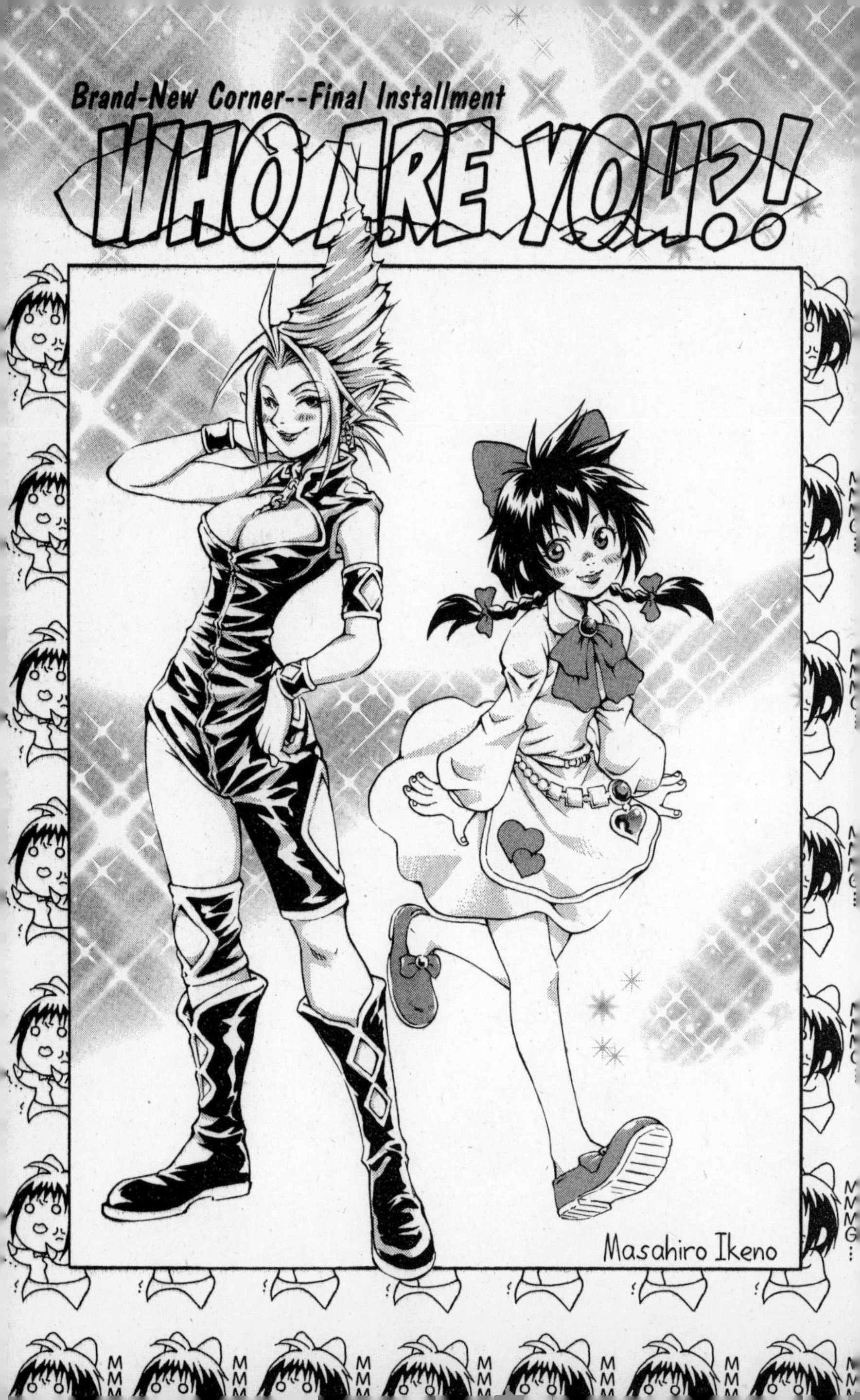
Brand-New Corner--Final Installment
WHO ARE YOU?!
Masahiro Ikeno
MMNG...

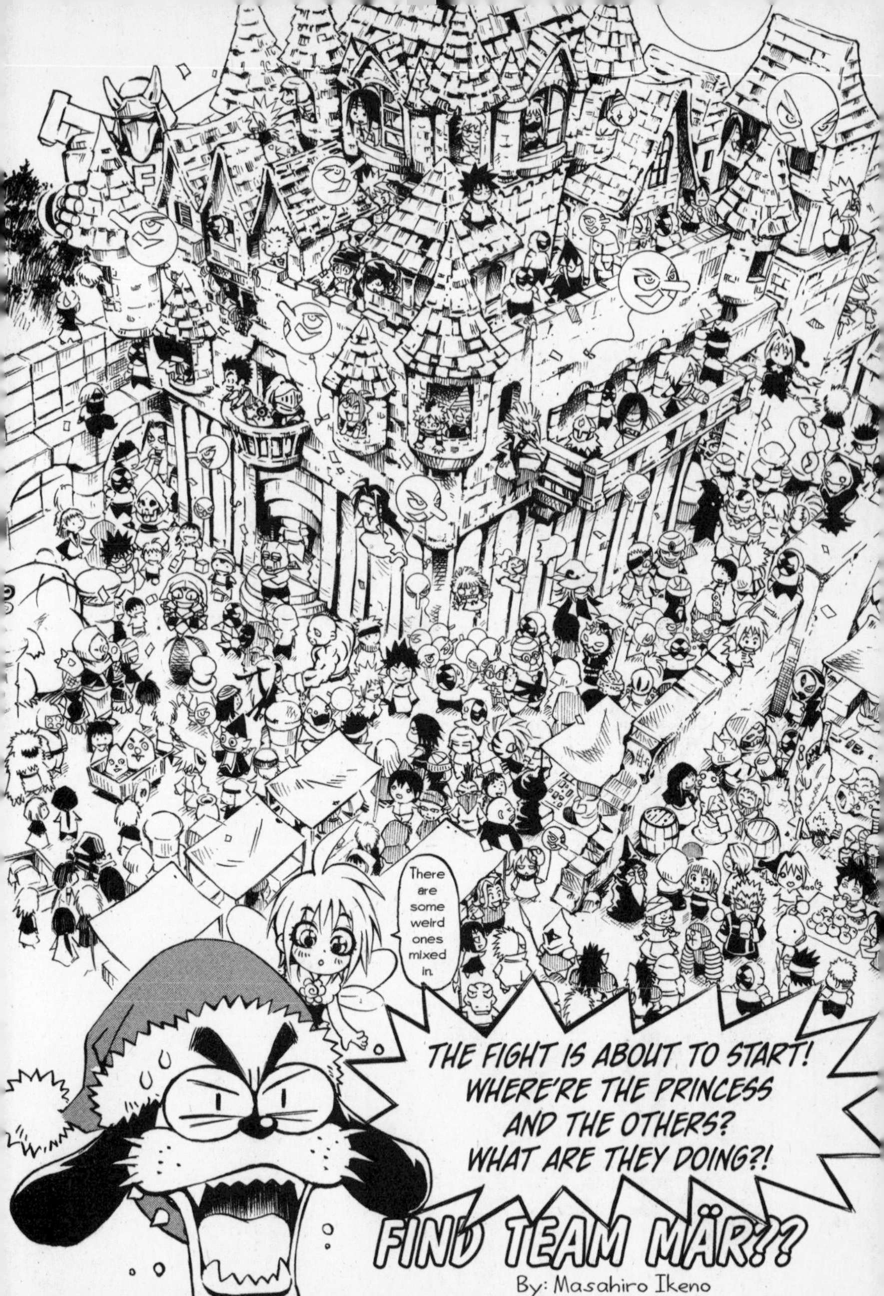
There are some weird ones mixed in.
THE FIGHT IS ABOUT TO START! WHERE'RE THE PRINCESS AND THE OTHERS? WHAT ARE THEY DOING?!
FIND TEAM MÄR?!?
By: Masahiro Ikeno

MR. NANASHI

HIROSHI MATSUNOBU

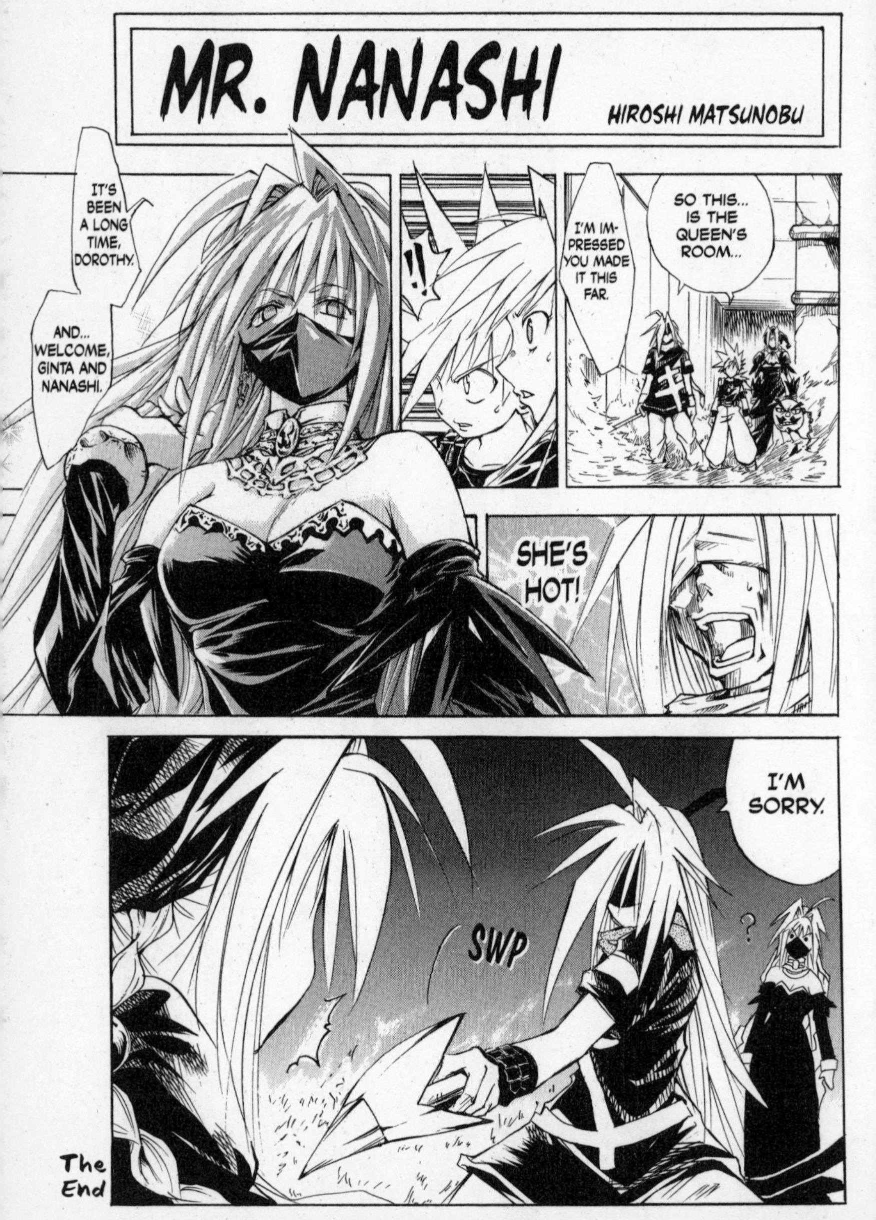
SO THIS... IS THE QUEEN'S ROOM...
I'M IMPRESSED YOU MADE IT THIS FAR.
!!
IT'S BEEN A LONG TIME, DOROTHY.
AND... WELCOME, GINTA AND NANASHI.
SHE'S HOT!
I'M SORRY.
?
SWP
The End

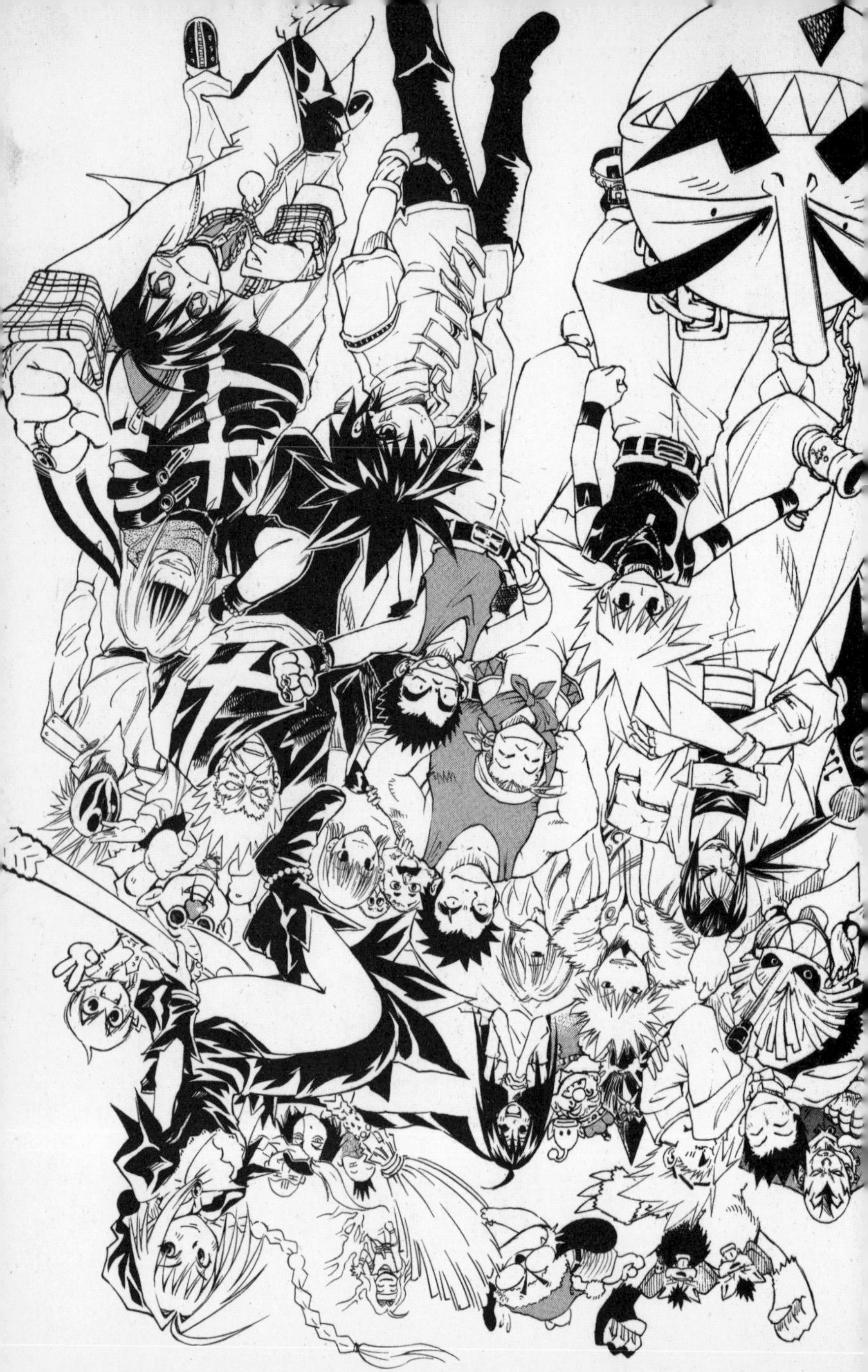

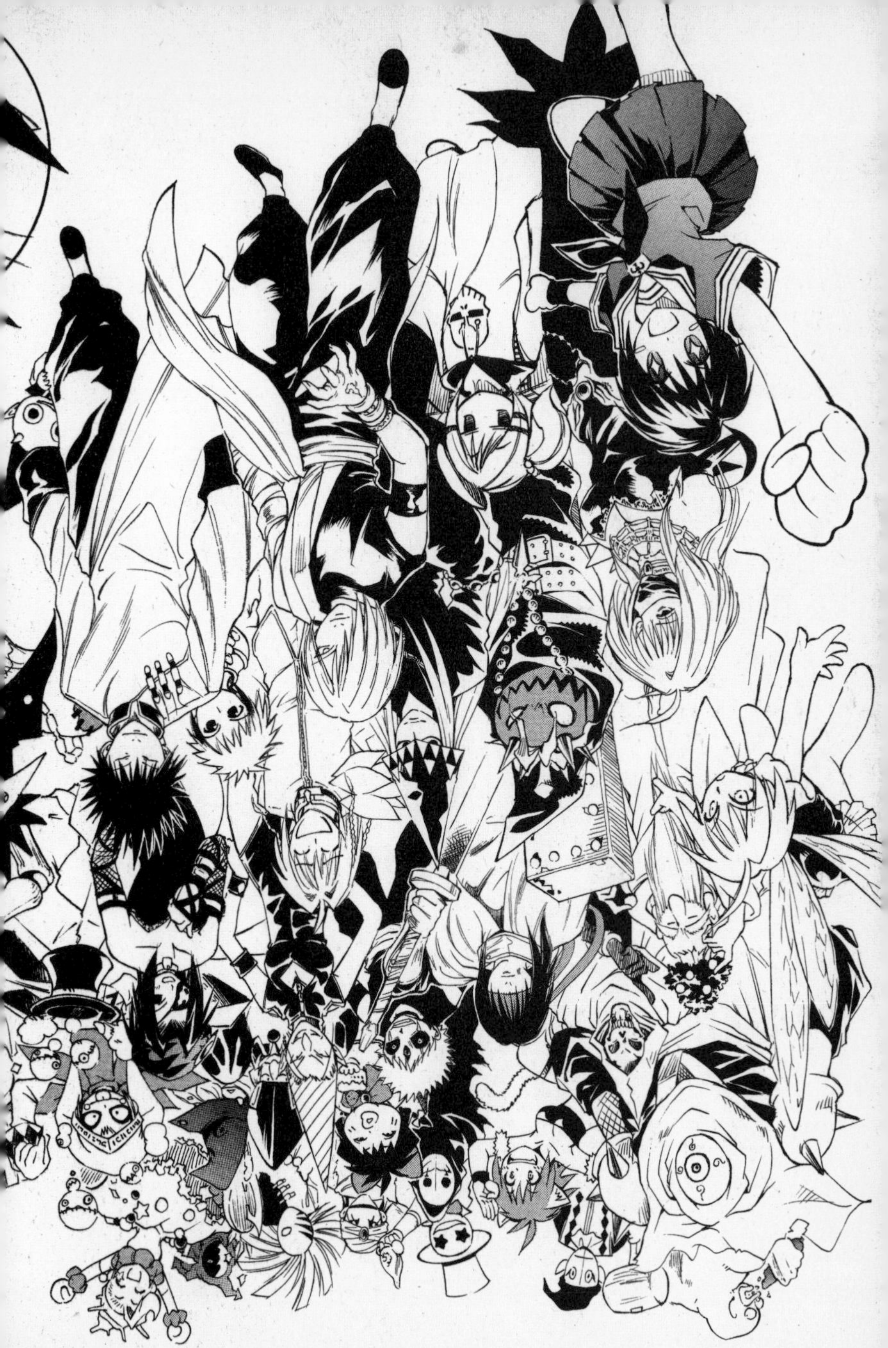

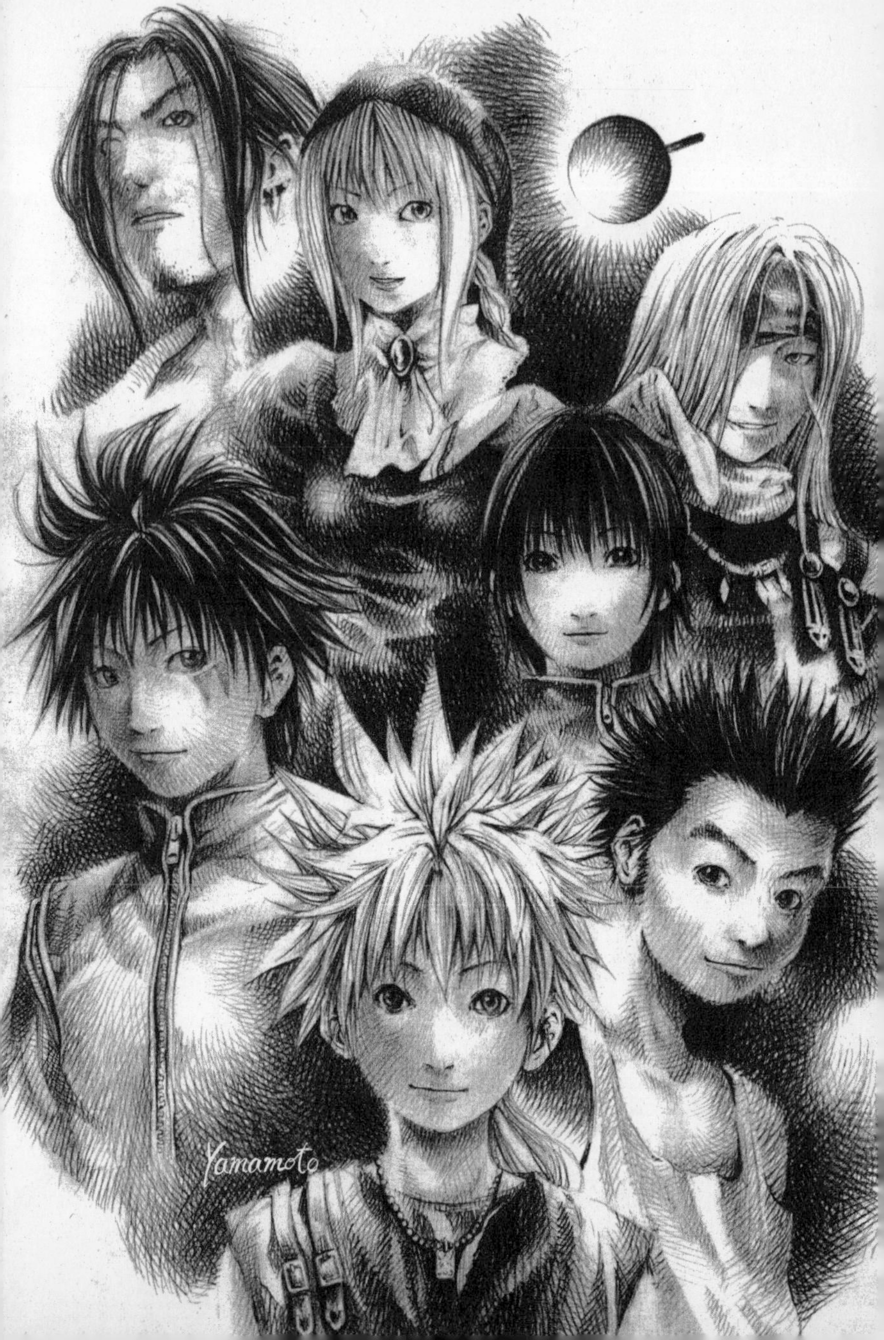
Yamamoto

BONUS POP FINAL

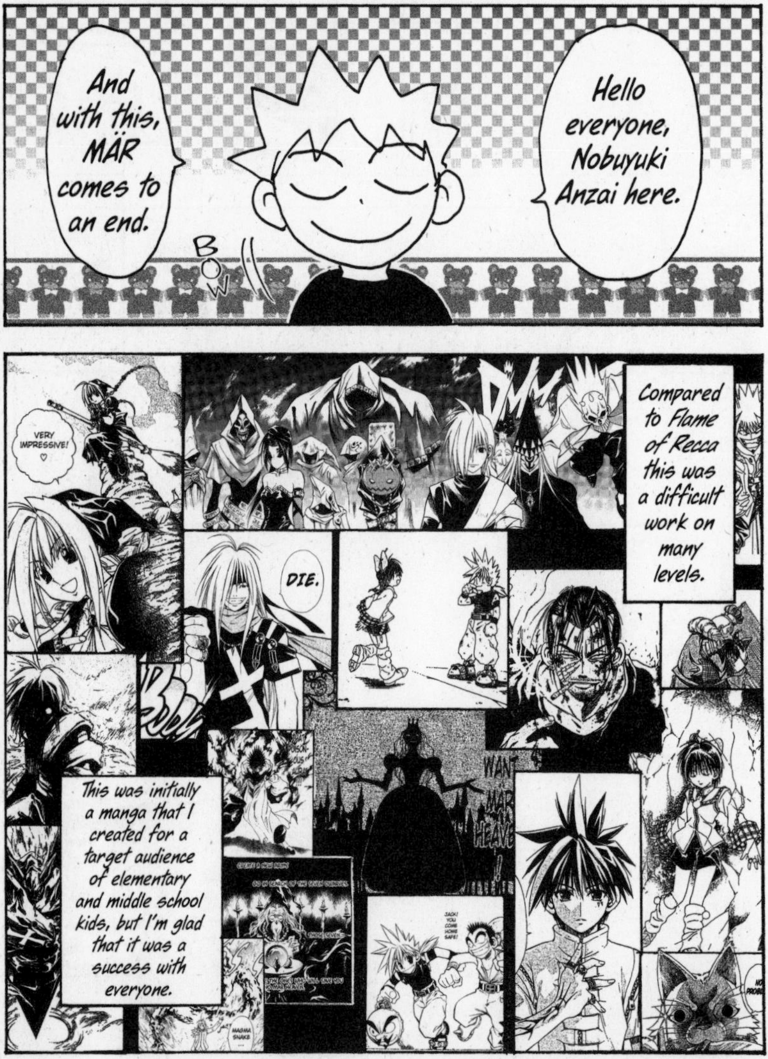

Hello everyone, Nobuyuki Anzai here.
And with this, MÄR comes to an end.
BOW
Compared to Flame of Recca this was a difficult work on many levels.
VERY IMPRESSIVE! ♡
DIE.
This was initially a manga that I created for a target audience of elementary and middle school kids, but I'm glad that it was a success with everyone.
JACK! YOU CAME HOME SAFE!
MAGMA SNAKE ...

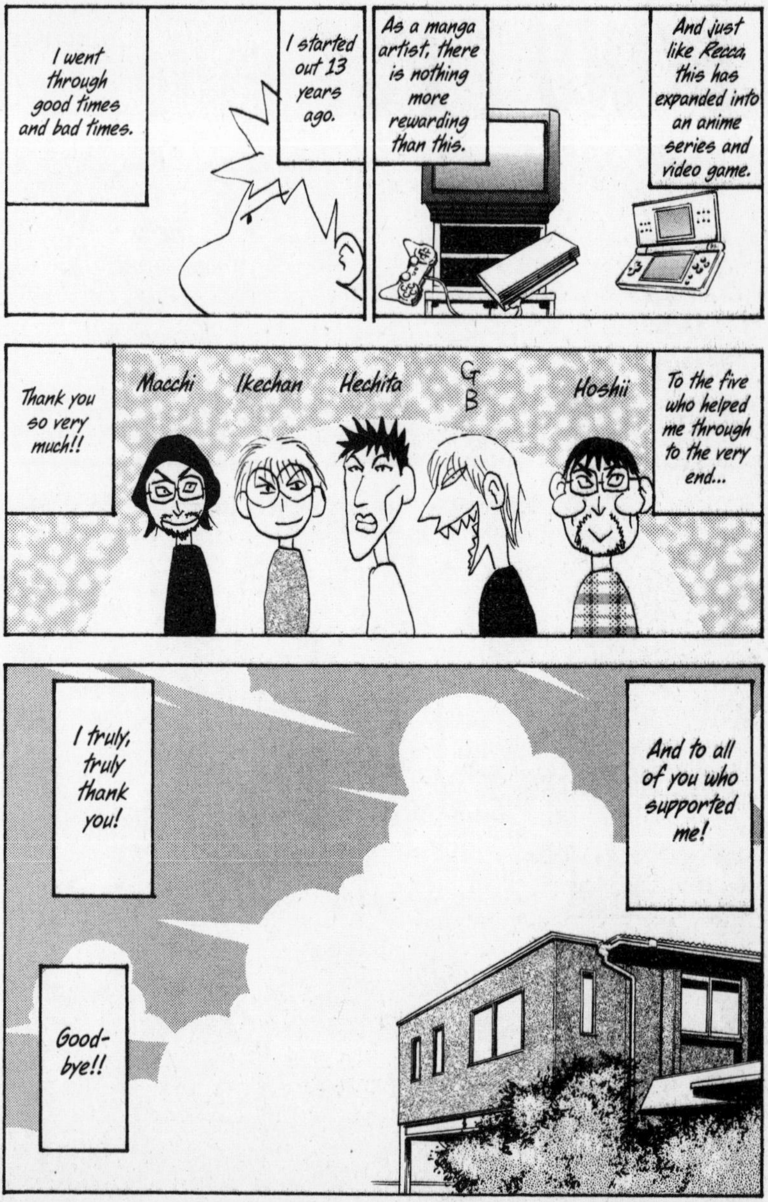
And just like Recca, this has expanded into an anime series and video game.
As a manga artist, there is nothing more rewarding than this.
I started out 13 years ago.
I went through good times and bad times.
To the five who helped me through to the very end...
Hoshii
GB
Hechita
Ikechan
Macchi
Thank you so very much!!
And to all of you who supported me!
I truly, truly thank you!
Good-bye!!

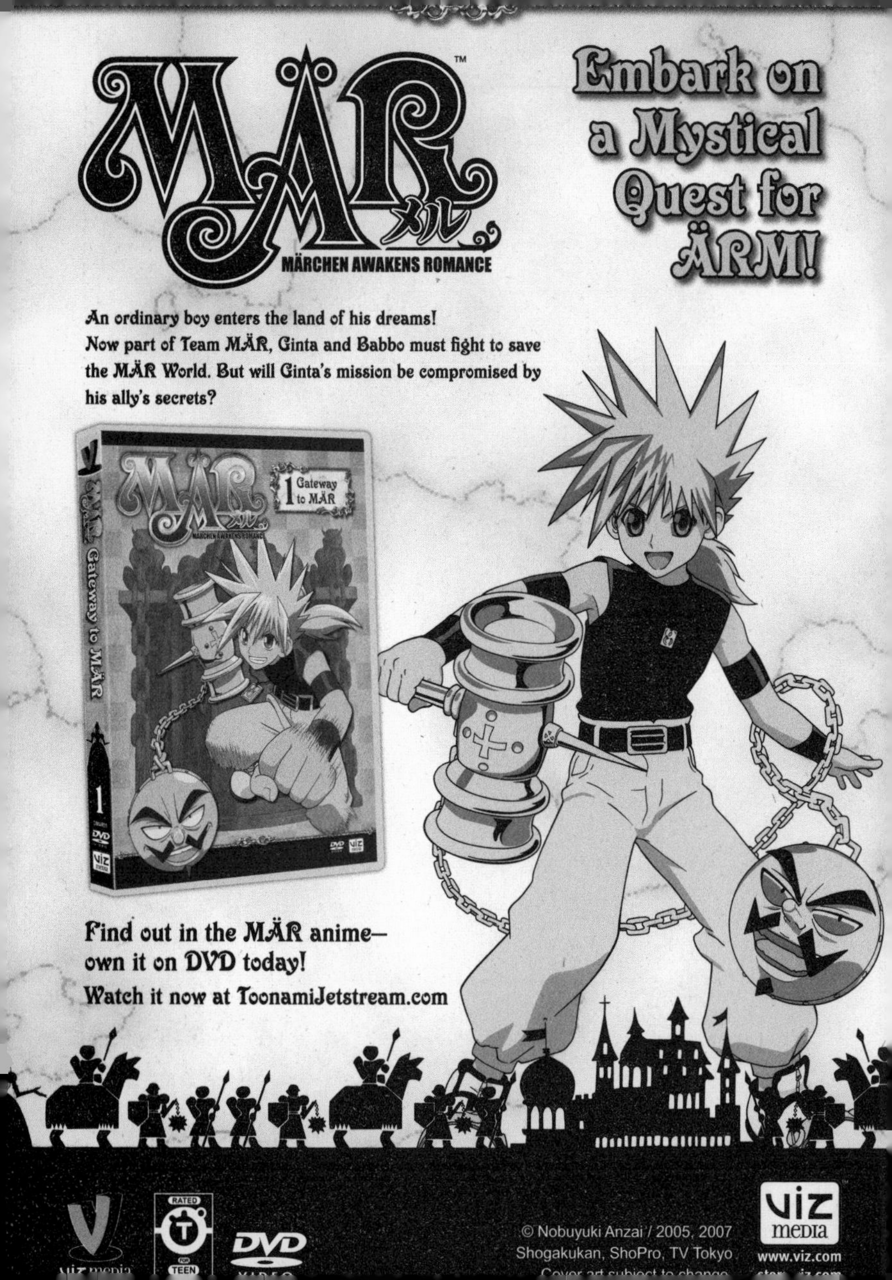
MÄR™
MÄRCHEN AWAKENS ROMANCE
Embark on a Mystical Quest for ÄRM!
An ordinary boy enters the land of his dreams!
Now part of Team MÄR, Ginta and Babbo must fight to save the MÄR World. But will Ginta's mission be compromised by his ally's secrets?
1 Gateway to MÄR
Find out in the MÄR anime—own it on DVD today!
Watch it now at ToonamiJetstream.com
RATED T FOR TEEN
DVD
© Nobuyuki Anzai / 2005, 2007 Shogakukan, ShoPro, TV Tokyo
VIZ MEDIA
www.viz.com

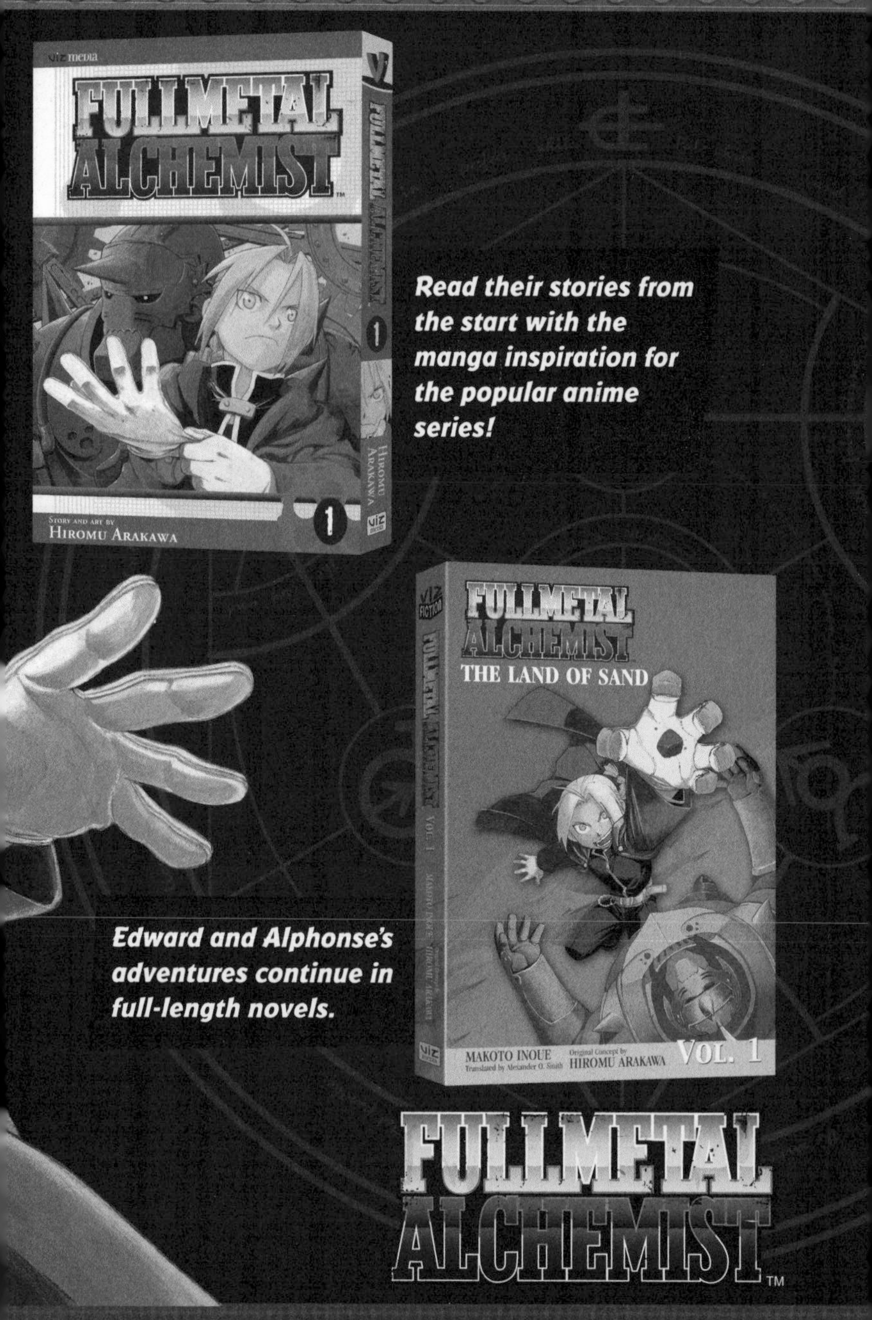
viz media
FULLMETAL ALCHEMIST™
1
Story and art by
Hiromu Arakawa
Read their stories from the start with the manga inspiration for the popular anime series!
VIZ FICTION
FULLMETAL ALCHEMIST
THE LAND OF SAND
MAKOTO INOUE
Translated by Alexander O. Smith
Original Concept by
HIROMU ARAKAWA
VOL. 1
Edward and Alphonse's adventures continue in full-length novels.
FULLMETAL ALCHEMIST™

LOVE MANGA?
LET US KNOW WHAT YOU THINK!